MICKEY MANTLE'S GREATEST HITS

BY

DAVID S. NUTTALL

S.P.i.
BOOKS

For further information, contact:

S.P.I. Books
136 West 22nd Street
New York, NY 10011
Tel: 212/633-2023
FAX: 212/633-2123

Library of Congress Cataloging-in-Publication Data available.

ISBN: 1-56171-974-9

Photographs, and their copyright information, provided by The Baseball Hall of Fame,
Cooperstown, New York.

DEDICATION

To Sheri, my understanding wife and life partner who from the beginning with love, belief, and support, made everything possible with each step on a long journey

ACKNOWLEDGMENTS

At SPI Books, Inc., I have my publisher, Mr. Ian Shapolsky, and the SPI staff services of Isaac Mozeson and Robin Souza to thank for their editorial expertise.

I would also like to thank the Baseball Hall of Fame of Cooperstown, New York in general, and Ms. Darci Harrington, Senior Photo Researcher, quite specifically, for her valuable assistance in helping select the photographic portfolio on Mickey Mantle presented in this book.

I would also like to extend my thanks to the Lane Public Library of Hamilton, Ohio, as well as the collective and individual assistance and encouragement accorded me by Hamilton City School District Librarians Linda Less, Michaela Ward, and Joan Fields-Cox.

I would also be remiss if I withheld praise for the King Library of Miami University in Oxford, Ohio who shared with me its vast wealth of resources and its able, professional and courteous assistance in the Microfilm Department.

I would also like to personally thank Professor John Hughes, Geology Department (Chair), Miami University, and one of the truest fans of the national pastime, whose objective eye and constant encouragement was a beacon during some very long nights.

And lastly, I have more thanks and unwavering gratitude in my heart for the love of my life, my precious Sheri, who made everything possible by her constancy, her respect, and her patience and understanding of the work I did and continue to do. No one deserves the confidence and assurance she has given me. I will always be humble and thankful for so pure a gift as her trust.

TABLE OF CONTENTS

INTRODUCTION

When he approached the plate to take his cuts in the Fifties and Sixties, every eye in the stands of the grand old ballyard, every player on the field, and especially every hurler on the mound focused intensely on this slim-waisted, bulky-shouldered, bulging-muscled physical specimen in pinstripes. The slugging center fielder played for the New York Yankees and struck fear into American League pitchers for almost two decades. He was lightning in a bottle. Each time he stepped into the batter's box, the young, blond-haired ballplayer would await the pitch—coiled and poised—to unleash a mighty swing from either side of the plate. His Louisville-made bludgeon would sweep mightily through the strike zone with rippling ferocity.

When the young ballplayer's powerful swing connected with the hurler's pitch, the ball would suddenly be launched like a flashing bolt to carry to great, unprecedented distances. Just as quickly, with awesome authority and Herculean bat command, the ball would be jettisoned into elegantly soaring, towering arches, the young ballplayer's power generating gargantuan shots that lept to the furthest outreaches of Yankee Stadium and opposing ballyards alike. No park could contain the young slugger's power. The youthful ballplayer managed to launch colossal home runs with such frequency and incredible consistency that it harkened back to the bygone days of the left-handed slugging of "Babe" Ruth and Lou Gehrig and the right-handed clubbing of Jimmie Foxx and Josh Gibson.

Just as unbelievably, early in this young man's career, before the march of time and disabling injuries overtook him, he ran faster and covered more ground more quickly than anyone on the Yankees' roster, anyone on the same field of play, or, for that matter, anyone anywhere in the big leagues. Batting left-handed, the young outfielder with the speed of a deer could get down the line on a drag bunt in 3.1 seconds. This same young ballplayer—born, raised, and groomed to play the National Game—was also a switch-hitter of the first magnitude, hitting from both sides of the plate and representing an enormous, constant long-ball danger to Yankee opponents. From either side of the plate, the young crew-cutted kid from an Oklahoma mining town could power a baseball unbelievable distances—more than 500 feet from either side of the plate. As his manager, Casey Stengel, said, "This boy hits the ball over buildings." The unassuming man-child would become the cornerstone of the New York Yankee dynasty in the third phase of a near half-century run of team excellence and supremacy in baseball.

And through it all, he persevered during most of his eighteen-year tenure, utilizing tremendous personal courage to overcome great physical travail and a long list of crippling injuries. This he did in order to perform on the baseball diamond while leading the Bronx Bombers to the highest echelons of baseball preeminence. The young, unassuming ballplayer, so shy and modest, yet blessed with the God-given combination of speed and power, was the Golden Boy in the Golden Age of Baseball. His name was Mickey Charles Mantle.

This brings us to the focus of this book: the courageous and clutch play of Mickey Mantle. As Babe Ruth and Joe DiMaggio came to embody the great pin-striped teams of their times, so Mickey Mantle earned the same kind of niche for the Yankee teams of his day. The supremacy of the New York Yankees began in 1920 with the "Babe Ruth Era." It came with the arrival of the "Great Bambino" from beantown to the Big Apple, the development of Murderer's Row, and the ever-productive presence of Lou Gehrig. As a result, Babe Ruth's Yankees would capture ten pennants. One year after the Babe's departure from the game, Yankee excellence would be maintained, in 1936, with the first year of the "Joe DiMaggio Era," the initial appearance of the "Yankee Clipper," and the cultivation of the Bronx Bombers. With particularly strong contributions made by Bill Dickey, Charlie Keller, and Tommy Henrich, the record of Joe DiMaggio's pinstripers would account for ten more pennants.

And so it is, with Ruth and DiMaggio demarcating two legs of the greatest run of team excellence in baseball history, 1920 to 1951, that the final leg of Yankee greatness would begin its finishing phase of half-century domination of major league baseball, with the "Mickey Mantle Era." With the introduction of the young and powerful switch-hitter to the Yankee lineup, the "Last Great Yankee"—and a considerable supporting cast of teammates such as Yogi Berra, Hank Bauer,

Moose Skowron, Elston Howard, and Roger Maris—would give the Bronx Bombers of the Fifties and Sixties an additional twelve American League pennants. Though Mickey Mantle's career would extend four years past the final October glories of the Yankee franchise, it does not diminish the impact that this great Hall-of-Fame career had on this, the greatest of all major league baseball franchises. From 1951 to 1964, the Yankee teams of the Mantle Era would produce twelve pennants. In Mantle's final four years as a Yankee, the Bombers would falter, but not before Mickey, the "Magnificent Yankee," had already secured his place in the hallowed halls of Cooperstown.

As a lifelong fan of the greatest game ever invented, I feel that I am qualified by virtue of the great respect and appreciation I hold for the history of the game to advance one particular notion. In my humble opinion, the following declaration represents one of the sport's greatest truths. George Herman ("Babe") Ruth is the greatest left-handed hitter who ever lived. It is also true, in my belief, that, in the history of major league baseball, Henry "Hammerin' Hank" Aaron is the greatest right-handed hitter who ever played the game. And finally, throughout the annals of baseball excellence, Mickey Mantle was the greatest switch-hitter who ever graced the field. Period.

Of course, baseball fans and purists alike reserve the right to name their own all-time hitters from both sides of the plate. For left-handed batters, a formidable number of advocates most assuredly believe that Ted Williams was the best left-handed hitter ever to swing a bat. Of course, these declarations do not go unchallenged. Others believe that the best left-handed hitter must be Stan Musial. Or even Ty Cobb. As to right-handed hitters, other, just as exhilarated baseball devotees clamor to name their best right-handed hitters. Some believe in the claim that Rogers Hornsby was the best right-handed hitter ever. Other devoted fans have advanced the proposition that it must be Josh Gibson. But...still other fans, enthusiasts, and historians resist that particular notion, protesting instead that their candidate, the "Yankee Clipper," Joe DiMaggio himself, has gone unjustly ignored. To this group of purists, DiMaggio is not only the best right-handed hitter ever, but, most assuredly to them, the best hitter ever. There will always be arguments like these among baseball fans. However, when you talk about switch-hitters, there is no debate. Mickey Mantle was the best. As yet, he has not been seriously challenged. Not by future Hall-of-Famer Pete Rose. Not by future Hall-of-Famer Eddie Murray. Not even by entrenched Hall-of-Famer Frankie Frisch.

No one switch-hitter in baseball history did more for his team than did Mickey Mantle for the New York Yankees. Number Seven inspired fears in the heart of his opponents such as few other ballplayers ever did in baseball history. For eighteen years, Mickey Mantle pounded out home runs in fifteen American League ballparks, connecting for phenomenal results with a furious frequency. One in five home runs of all of the 554 round-trippers Mantle hit in regulation and World Series play accounted for the winning run in the game for the Yankees. This mind-boggling statistic in clutch power only takes into consideration those games decided by Mickey's longballs, not the winning runs he batted in with singles, doubles, or triples—only home runs.

No switch-hitter represented such devastation in offensive production as did Mantle with the Bronx Bombers. Unlike the cases of Ruth and DiMaggio, however, there has been no other Yankee like Mickey Mantle before or since.

Chapter One

THE EARLY YEARS

In Spavinaw, Oklahoma, Mickey Charles Mantle was born on October 20, 1931, at a time when criminals Bonnie and Clyde roamed that part of the country, robbing and killing. The Era of Prohibition reigned, as the Depression gripped the nation. In particular, the "Dust Bowl" states, such as Oklahoma, were especially hard-hit.

Elven Mantle, Mickey's dad, failed in farming and became quickly disillusioned with grading roads. Eventually, Elven "Mutt" Mantle, the hard-working tenant farmer, would move his family to Commerce, OK, where he would pursue a living as a zinc and lead miner. Mutt, and his wife, Lovell, would watch as their flock of children grew to maturity.

By decade's end, the Mantles would, beginning with Mickey, welcome the arrival of four more offspring, and raise their five children with scant resources. Mickey would, along with the rest of the family, make do on $50 a month in the tiny town of Spavinaw and the mining reserve of Commerce. A reflective Mickey would look back on his youth and recall the days when he was six-years-old, watching by the side of the road as long and endless caravans of beat-up jalopies and road-weary pickup trucks, convoying whole families of financially depressed "Okies," headed to points West.

With little money available to the hard-working clan, the Mantles would spend their days passing time together, having as much fun as their extremely limited resources could buy. For Mickey, it was playing ball. Not only was baseball a release for Mickey and his siblings to escape their dreary existence, if only for nine innings at a time, but it was a dream for the young boy that was nourished by his family, encouraged by his father, and intensely pursued by the young and muscular athlete.

With respect to the family, there was an ever-present, insidious specter with which the family had to deal, a dark cloud that seemed to hover over the Mantle abode. It was the curse of Hodgkin's disease, which would befall the clan, striking all the males of the Mantle lineage in one way or another. Mutt himself would die of this pernicious ailment. Indeed, every male in the Mantle clan, including Mickey's Grampa Charlie, uncles Tunney and Emmett, and later, perhaps even more tragically, Mickey's own son, Billy, would also be touched by this disease before they reached their respective forty-first birthdays.

Commerce, Oklahoma, from which the young Yankee clouter-to-be hailed, boasted a population of only 2,422 hard-working citizens. The tiny hamlet was comprised of a Main Street that stretched a mere seven blocks and housed miners and their poor, but proud, families. Even the houses themselves had no numbers for their addresses. One of those modest families was headed by Mutt Mantle, who provided for his wife and family of five children by descending each day into the dusty, gaseous bowels of the earth. He wanted better for his kids, especially for his firstborn, a son he named after his favorite baseball player, catcher Mickey Cochrane of the Philadelphia Athletics.

Baseball made the young boy's heart beat. His father made sure of that. Mutt Mantle would play with his young firstborn every day when he came home from work. He also educated his son the best he could in the finer points of playing the game. This included, at age six, learning how to switch-hit. Mutt had become a firm believer that there would come a time in the future when baseball managers would platoon players based solely on what side of the plate they hit the ball. Hoping to avoid this pratfall for his boy, he taught Mickey how to hit from that side of the plate opposite from the side that the hurler pitched. It would be the first of many momentous decisions that Mutt Mantle made on behalf of his boy. To train the youngster, Mutt, a right-handed thrower and semi-pro infielder himself, would make Mickey hit from the left side. For batting right-handed, Mutt would, after work, get his father, Mickey's granddad, a lefty, to throw to him. "The Great Switcher," who would thrive in the American League in this century's Fifties and Sixties, was developed in the late Thirties in the Oklahoma sandlots near Commerce, in the northeastern corner of the state.

Mickey Mantle grew up listening to the daily lullabies sung to him over the radio airwaves by Harry Caray, in the Forties. Caray covered the games played by the St. Louis Cardinals. The beauty of baseball for kids playing the game is that it can be played anywhere on make-believe fields at any time during the daylight hours. For Mickey, it was a large nearby quarry where the neighborhood kids would gather to play, skipping meals and running around their makeshift basepaths from sunup to sundown. No one played longer at the game in that tiny community or played better than did Mickey. Graced with the body, speed, great reflexes, and the power and strength that God gives only to few athletes, Mickey translated those gifts into playing football, basketball, and baseball. But it was baseball that was in his blood.

Late in his high school sports career, however, while playing football, Mickey received a painful blow to his shin that would develop into osteomylitis. Osteomylitis is a serious bone disease that causes a deterioration of the effected bone area. A worried mother raced her son to the local hospital where a doctor recommended amputation. Angrily, Mrs. Mantle rejected this advice out of hand and took Mickey to a different hospital and a different physician, who dealt with the young boy's injured leg without cutting it off. It was a turning point in Mickey's life, but a chapter that would never close for the permanently hampered gazelle. It marked the onset of constant pain in Mickey Mantle's life and in the irrepressible pursuit of his baseball career. It also marked the beginning of one of the most courageous, clutch-filled major league careers ever generated by one man on a baseball diamond in the annals of baseball greatness.

His career started professionally when, on June 13, 1949, Mickey Charles Mantle signed a minor league contract offered by Yankee scout Tom Greenwade calling for payment to the raw, green country kid of $1,100 in bonus money and $400 for his first year. Upon seeing Mickey still in his early stages of development, and reflecting on his good luck as a scout, Greenwade, who, later in this book shares many of his innermost impressions, would add revealingly, "I thought to myself, 'This is how Paul Krichell must have felt, the first time he saw Lou Gehrig.'"

MINOR LEAGUE EXPERIENCE
1949-1950

Year	Team	G	AB	R	H	2B	3B	HR	RBI	BA
1949	Independence (D)	89	323	54	101	15	7	7	63	313

One of the young ballplayer's more glaring problems was his penchant for making errors from his infield position of shortstop. He committed 47 during his first professional campaign.

Year	Team	G	AB	R	H	2B	3B	HR	RBI	BA
1950	Joplin (C)	137	519	141	199	30	12	26	136	.383

Mantle's tallies in runs scored, base hits, and batting average led the Western Association. So would his number of errors, 55, through which he and his team would suffer. The young Mick's statistics reflect the eye-popping performance that would lead to the 1951 pronouncement by Yankee Manager Casey Stengel that the young Oklahoman slugger was the Yankees' premier rookie prospect. Catapulting over the four higher minor league classifications while jumping straight to the big leagues is the first such quantum leap in thirty years for the Yankees. Mickey Mantle would be nineteen-years-old and going to the intimidating "Big Apple" to play ball for the defending world champions of baseball known as the Bronx Bombers, the winningest behemoths of big league baseball, the New York Yankees.

Later, with author Mickey Herskowitz, Mantle would recall, "I was a classic country bumpkin, who came to the big city carrying a cardboard suitcase [containing his meager] wardrobe of two pairs of slacks and a pastel-colored sports coat."

Casey Stengel, the wise and rumpled old manager of the champion Yankees, would go so far as to make a request of the press to take it easy on the young rookie. "The kid has never seen concrete," the "Old Perfesser" would counsel.

Five years later, Arthur Daley of *The New York Times* would later reflect on the image of the young kid coming to the big city, confessing his impression that the young Mantle had been "lionized" with "extravagant raves." Glowing accolades from Casey and other Yankee officials dotted the press coverage of the spring training of the defending world champions. The veteran Yankee observer for the *Times* would describe the feeling that the young kid from the remotest of rural mining towns must have experienced. As Daley noted, the courting of Mickey's excessive talent must be "a bewildering, head-spinning process, particularly to a fundamentally shy introvert like Mantle."

At the end of the young ballplayer's 1950 season with the Joplin Miners, the Yankees brought Mickey up to their ball club where he would sit on the bench for the remainder of the year. It was understood that he would not bust into the lineup or even get into one contest. But, on September 17, 1950, while warming up in Sportsman's Park in St. Louis for the first time in a Yankee uniform, the young athlete would receive the thrill of his life. After watching the diminutive Phil Rizzuto, "the human vacuum cleaner," workout at shortstop. The 160-pound Mantle took some warm-up grounders at shortstop himself. It would be as close to the action as he would get. It would not matter. The young, giddy boy was beside himself with delight. Next year he would be given a shot in spring training to make the parent club.

At Ebbets Field, on that April day in 1951 which marked Mickey Mantle's playing debut in New York City, two Yankee sluggers, the venerated Joe DiMaggio and the prized rookie prospect Mickey Mantle, pose for posterity. It is the Yankee Changing of the Guard.

Chapter Two

ALL ROLLED INTO ONE

—1951—

In the Nation and the World: As the "Kid" from Oklahoma prepared to play his first year in the majors, in 1951, America enjoyed a simple state of mind, uncomplicated and secure amid a postwar period of booming growth, across-the-board prosperity, and mind-boggling affluence. The nation possessed an innocence underscored by the glowing confidence of a generation mindful of its significant role in the global Allied victory of World War II.

A new kind of warfare, however, the Cold War—fighting the menace of Communism—had started immediately after World War II, as the United States became the most powerful country in the world. This new kind of warfare pitted democratic institutions around the world against the monolithic Communist enemy, freedom against tyranny, and individual liberty against a Moscow-centered dictatorship. We weren't fighting the Soviet Union's troops or armies, except for the ideological combat that was being played out over both sides of the 38th Parallel cutting through

Korea. The Korean Conflict was being fought by a UN peacekeeping force comprised mostly of U.S. Armed Forces against aggressive Chinese Communist troops.

It was also a time of the H-bomb. For American society, nevertheless, it was a time of white picket fences, two-car garages, peacetime technological advances for suburban-minded millions who sought peace, harmony, and domestic tranquility. It was also a time when city-dwellers would retreat from crime-ridden urban centers to put up stakes in new domestic havens just outside city limits: the suburbs.

This mindset translated itself into a higher, newer appreciation in the United States for the pursuit of happiness. A deeper fondness by Americans was given to leisure time, family entertainment, sports, and a new, mass produced invention called television. This innocent age in America would lead to giving birth to and raising the largest U.S. generation ever recorded in this nation's glorious history, the Baby Boom Generation. It was also "prime time" for the National Pastime.

The growth of television had made it easier for current issues, and exciting and tragic events alike, to be transmitted to the multitudes. Television would perform this function for millions of Americans for anything they seemed to desire—including the growing number of telecasts of baseball games and other sporting events. The movie-house newsreels of sports were now being brought into the everyday American's living room for their enjoyment.

Innovations and First Appearances: A wave of peacetime technology would provide Americans with sugarless gum, Dacron suits, commercial electronic computers, power steering in automobiles and "Dennis the Menace" in comic strips.

Movies: In theaters across the land in 1951, Americans swarmed by the millions into cinema houses to catch the latest wave of movies exploding across wider-angled screens. A sampling of films in circulation for the year includes *The African Queen*, *An American in Paris, A Place in the Sun, Captain Horatio Hornblower, A Streetcar Named Desire, Jim Thorpe: All American, The Red Badge of Courage, The Desert Fox,* Walt Disney's *Alice in Wonderland*, Danny Kaye's *On the Riviera*, and Alfred Hitchcock's *Stranger On a Train*.

Television: Meanwhile, in America's living rooms, family members gathered around television sets to be chilled, thrilled or amused by such episodes on the "boob tube" as: Arthur Godfrey's *Talent Scouts*, *Beat the Clock*, *I Love Lucy*, *The Lone Ranger, Captain Video*, and *Amos and Andy*.

The Juke Box: Americans young and old tapped their feet and snapped their fingers to tunes on records, in juke boxes, and on the radio, such as: "Tennessee Waltz" by Patti Page; "Mule Train" by Frankie Laine; "Too Young" by Nat King Cole; "Be My Love" by Mario Lanza; "On Top of Old Smoky" by the Weavers and Gordon Jenkins; "If" by Perry Como; and "Mockin' Bird Hill" by Patti Page.

Deaths: A prominent, brilliant musician of his day, a genius at the piano, Eddy Duchin, would die this year.

Sports: In professional basketball, the Rochester Royals would beat the New York Knicks, four games to three, for the NBA championship. In pro football, the Los Angeles Rams would clobber the Cleveland Browns, 24–17. In college hoops, Kentucky would win the NCAA Basketball championship. And in pro golf, Ben Hogan would win the U.S. Open.

Baseball Transitions: In 1951, key personnel changes in baseball took place as Mickey Mantle was introduced to the American League. On the White Sox, Minnie Minoso would join the ranks of the Pale Hose; but the Sox would lose Chico Carrasquel. Slugger Gus Zernial would join the Philadelphia A's; and on the Yankees, Tommy Henrich would not be returning to play for the Bombers. Outfielder Cliff Mapes would also leave the Yanks, traded elsewhere to make room for the rookie outfielder from Oklahoma, and lefthander Tommy Byrne would not return to the fold. "Whitey" Ford would enlist in the U.S. armed forces. And finally, the ultimate closer for the Yanks, Joe Page, would simply vanish from the baseball scene.

THE 1951 SPRING TRAINING

On March 2, 1951, Mickey's idol, Joe DiMaggio, would hold a brief press conference with the spring training corps of sportswriters covering the Yankees. Standing before the press, "the Clipper" would tell the media hounds that his plans were to retire after this season. Joe D would say, "I want to have one good year and then hang 'em up for good. And it will have to be this year." Shortly thereafter, James P. Dawson of *The New York Times* would write, "Mickey Mantle, rookie from Commerce, Oklahoma, will be the subject of an extensive experiment in the Yankee training campaign. No less an authority than Manager Casey Stengel revealed this information today, one of those rare days when rain dampened activities in the Valley of the Sun [Phoenix, Arizona]. Stengel said he would work the 19-year-old Mantle in center field, and immediately speculation arose over whether the Yanks regarded the rookie as the eventual successor of the great Joe DiMaggio."

Spring training would be very eventful for the Oklahoma ballplayer as the young slugger proved his mettle with the big club. Already, by March 19th, Ol' Casey had been singing the young slugger's praises, as he would face the best that the AAA Pacific Coast League could offer. Referring to the rookie "phenom," to the gathered journalists, the Yankee chief would call Mickey "the best switch-hitter I've ever seen." Casey told the media, "There's never been anyone like this kid which we got from Joplin. He has more speed than any slugger and more slug than any speedster— and nobody has ever had more of both them together."

In 1951's grapefruit league, the Yankees were spending the majority of their spring dates in California playing such teams as the Pacific Coast League's Oakland and Hollywood Stars. The shy, blond athlete was already being referred to as "the most spectacular rookie in a Bomber camp since Joe DiMaggio came up in 1936." His exploits were becoming legion as the crusty Casey decided what to do with the young athlete, so uniformly gifted for an aspiring rookie. Mantle was one of three rookies—infielder Gil McDougald and right-handed hurler Tom Morgan being the other two—that Stengel was leaning towards retaining for the Yankees. These three brilliant freshmen shone brightly in these early spring days. As part of his education, Mantle was shuffled off to Yankee rightfielder Tommy Henrich to receive instructions in the art of outfielding and in the science of hitting. Henrich had run his course as a ballplayer, suffering through a string of major leg injuries. He was directed to teach the corn-fed "Okie" kid how to patrol the right-field environs of major league play, how to use sunglasses, how to throw from the outfield, and how to use his speed to run down long and difficult fly balls.

The nineteen-year-old athlete was proving to be truely phenomenal. He had equally distributed power for driving the ball tremendous distances from both sides of the plate as well as the blazing speed of a deer on the basepaths. In one of these early contests, Mickey had attempted to drag a bunt, which he would smack back to the pitcher. Knowing the fleet athlete was a sure out, the pitcher risked no unnecessary movements, fielded the ball quickly, and fired it to first base. Still, the best he could do was barely nip the young base burner by a half-step. Glowingly, *The New York Times* contributing sportswriter James P. Dawson would write that Mantle "demonstrated [that] he can do everything a ball player should do, and do it well." Describing his speed of foot, the wizened "Ol' Perfesser" himself, Casey Stengel, was heard to say, that he ran so fast that he didn't so much as "bend the grass when he stepped on it."

Through Casey Stengel, who was daily huddling with the press, the declaration was made that Mantle was the coming of the next great Yankee. Casey confided to baseball journalists like Roger Kahn that having Mickey Mantle was like having "Babe Ruth, Lou Gehrig, and Joe DiMaggio, all rolled into one." In terms of speed, Stengel was quoted further to say, "My God, the boy runs faster than Cobb!"

The real story, however, is the young husky slugger's power. Already, at Seals Stadium in San Francisco, Mantle powered home runs from both sides of the plate in the same game to the opposite field. His first home run, batting from the right-hand side of the plate, would be a line drive that would go where Gil McDougald had never seen a left-handed batter go. In fact, there had been only ten or twelve home runs hit over that fence in the history of the park. McDougald would recall that he had never seen a ball hit "so fast that you wouldn't believe it." The white pill simply vanished with supersonic speed, having been rifled over 400 feet and over Guerrero Street, aligning the distant right-field barrier.

But now, let's *be* there and review Mickey Mantle's entire slugging career.

March 26, 1951: The Yankees were playing in an exhibition game against the University of Southern California Trojans at USC when the 165-pound Mantle unloads off a USC pitcher. His hit not only carries the entire playing field in right-center field—over the 400-foot marker—but also traverses another great expanse on the fly, the adjoining width of a practice football field at an angle, which adds an additional 180 feet to the flight of the ball before it comes to rest at the campus boulevard aligning the practice football field. It is a monstrous shot, the likes of which no one in attendance has ever seen. This game, with this strong college ball club, turns into a laugher early on, as the Yankees whip the Trojans, 15–1. The youthful Mantle has homered twice, tripled, and driven home seven of his teammates.

The Yankees' game this day with the University of Southern California represents the concluding phase of the California leg of their exhibition games with college teams and Pacific Coast League rosters.

Now the Yankees resume their final leg of their spring training by revisiting their home base in Phoenix, Arizona. After the game, Mickey will later remember, the students and other fans in the stands who saw this Goliath-like poke made it "absolute bedlam" for him after the game, screeching for his autograph, tearing at his clothes, giving him scraps of paper to sign. Other observers, including his teammates, believe that this may have been the longest home run hit by anyone anywhere...ever.

Mantle has knocked everyone, including cynical veterans and one crusty curmudgeon, Casey Stengel, off their feet this spring with the size of his potential. During one session with reporters, as the "Ol' Perfessor" watches the young kid take batting practice in the cage before a game, the manager says, "Now I know how McGraw felt the first time he saw Ott."

Because of all the media attention that the young slugger was receiving, the military once again, got interested in taking another close look at the young athlete to measure his prospects for military service.

April 5, 1951: Mantle's draft board calls for another physical examination after receiving numerous letters from parents who wonder how such a prized athlete can be overlooked for military duty when their own sons are filling up various military barracks across the land. On April 11th, Mickey Mantle is directed to report to his draft board, in Miami, Oklahoma. It is Mantle's second appearance before the board, where, once again, he undergoes another thorough physical. Six months before, Mantle had taken his first physical for the Army, where he was deemed unfit for military service because of his osteomylitis. Once again, because of the ever-present nature of the disease in his leg, Mickey is classified 4-F and is shuttled back to the Yankees to rejoin the club and to undertake his big league career.

April 15, 1951: In Brooklyn, the old, bow-legged man and the young slugger take up positions below the 19-foot concave concrete wall and the 19-foot screen atop the right-field billboard-covered masonry. The two men, a raw rookie and a former player, a green kid and his managerial mentor, are talking baseball. Casey Stengel is briefly discussing the idiosyncratic nature of the Ebbets Field right-field wall. Based on his days as a Giant's outfielder as well as a Dodger right fielder, Casey is instructing the young man how to play the many intricacies of the quirky barrier. Suddenly, Casey stops talking, squints his eyes, and looks at the strong-jawed youth who is gazing at his manager with a quizzical look. Mickey naïvely remarks, with more than a touch of wonder, "You mean, you played here?" Astonished at the depths of the naïveté of this nineteen-year-old kid with Bunyanesque power, Stengel can only shake his head. After a pause, Casey finally responds, stating, "Yeah, whaddya think, I was born sixty years old?"

In the exhibition game itself with the hated Dodgers, Mickey Mantle belts the first home run of his professional career in New York City before 12,789 fanatical Flatbush fans. This first round-tripper in the Big Apple comes off Dodger righthander Jim Romano in the ninth inning, as the ball rockets over the right-center field scoreboard and out of the band box that is Brooklyn's fabled Ebbets Field. As the young, crewcutted bruiser crosses the plate, Mantle collects on his home run—his ninth roundtripper of the spring, and his fourth hit in this contest. As he crosses the plate, Mickey shakes hands with the batboy as well as teammate Cliff Mapes. On the back of Mantle's uniform is No. 6. Mantle smiles at Mapes, who greets the young slugger with a congratulatory smile of his own. On Mapes's back is No. 7. Destiny will intercede with these two teammates in terms of their respective uniform numbers. Upon his return from the minor leagues later this same year, Mantle will be issued a new uniform number. Cliff Mapes will no longer be with the team, having been traded to the St. Louis Browns on July 31st, and Mantle will be given Mapes's old number: Number 7. The Dodgers take the game, 7–6.

After the game, the Yankees catch the train and head south for Washington, D.C., for their Opening Day game against the Washington Senators. It is on this train that Mickey Charles Mantle signs his first major league contract with the New York Yankees. It is on the advice and support of Casey Stengel himself that the young "phenom" be signed and retained for the pending big league season and that the amount be $1,500 above the major league minimum.

THE 1951 REGULAR SEASON
13 HOME RUNS

April 16, 1951: It is Opening Day at Griffith Stadium, with President Harry S. Truman scheduled to throw out the first pitch before an expected crowd of 33,000 Washingtonians. Mother Nature, however, steps in not only to rain the game out, but also to delay for one game the major league debut of Mickey Mantle. Other outstanding newcomers who have been welcomed to the Yankee fold include right-handed pitcher Tom Morgan, utility infielder Gil McDougald, and outfielder Bob Cerv. On this day, after the game is canceled, the Yankees pack their things for their immediate transport back to New York for the next day's home opener against the visiting Boston Red Sox.

April 17, 1951: At Yankee Stadium, before the Stadium's Opening Day crowd of nearly 45,000 cheering rooters—more than 18 times greater than the population of his hometown—Mantle appears for the first time as a rookie in the major leagues, wearing Number Six on his back, his assigned number on the Yankee roster. The first major league pitcher that Mickey faces in his career is Red Sox lefthander Bill Wight. The nervous 19-year-old grounds out to the second baseman. The young rookie is not as concerned with Wight as he is about the great Red Sox leftfielder Ted Williams and how to play him on defense. Mickey's worries over Williams are miscast. Williams would single to center field, fly out to left, and walk. In the field, Mickey's first putout will come when Walt Dropo lifts a routine fly ball to right field that the young flychaser catches for the out. In Mickey's second plate appearance, he pops out. Then, in the sixth, with Jackie Jensen on third with a leadoff double and Phil Rizzuto on first having bunted for a hit, Mickey comes up to face Wight.

Batting right-handed, Mantle singles through the hole between shortstop and third for a clean single and an RBI when Jensen scores. At the plate, for the game, nineteen-year-old Mickey goes 1-for-4 and drives in a teammate as the Yanks beat the Boston Red Sox, 5–0, behind the six-hit pitching of strong-armed Vic Raschi.

From here on, readers will be provided a handy summary and chronology of Mickey Mantle's home run achievements. Included, will be: the number of each homer represented, the date of the homer, the opposing team, the pitcher, the site, the score, and the attendance.

H.R.#	DATE	OPPONENT	PITCHER	SITE	SCORE	ATTEND.
1.	May 1	Chicago	Randy Gumpert	Chicago	8–3, NY	14,776

At Old Comiskey Park in Chicago, rookie Mickey Mantle of the New York Yankees has broken into the Yankee lineup. Due to troublesome neck spasms experienced by the great but fading Joe DiMaggio, Mantle is playing right field. Because of the Clipper's aches and pains, rightfielder Jackie Jensen moves to center field and Mantle takes up his position in right field. In the sixth inning of this day's game, switch-hitting Mantle produces his first home run as a Yankee, coming as it does from the left side of the plate. On this day, the sensational rookie belts the ball long, while batting from the left side off White Sox righthander Randy Gumpert. Mickey connects, driving the ball 450 feet away to the left corner of the center field grandstand for a two-run shot. The Yankees win the contest, 8–3. It is 31 years to the day that Babe Ruth hit his first home run as a member of the New York Yankees.

May 3, 1951: At Sportsman's Park, rookie infielder Gil McDougald of the New York Yankees, en route to the AL Rookie of the Year Award, drives in six runs in the ninth inning, which leads the Yanks to a 17–3 clubbing of the St. Louis Browns. This ties a modern-era major league record responsible for RBIs in one inning.

2.	May 4	St. Louis	Duane Pillette	St. Louis(n)	8–1, NY	4,545

Mantle smacks a sixth-inning, 450-foot, two-run home run over the rightfield pavilion roof of Sportsman's Park.

3.	May 13	Philadelphia	Alex Kellner (LH)	Philadelphia (first game)	8–1, NY	19,780
4.	May 16	Cleveland	Dick Rozek (LH)	Stadium	11–3, NY	20,705

It is the first home run that Mickey Mantle ever hits in pinstripes, as the Bombers do battle with the Indians at Yankee Stadium. Mickey blasts a 420-foot shot that sails deep into the lower left field grandstand bleachers at Yankee Stadium. It is the first of 266 home runs at the storied stadium that Mantle will hit, and more than any ballplayer ever to play in the Bronx since the 1923 construction of the "House That Ruth Built." Mickey goes 2-for-4, scores three runs, and bats in four Yankee runs in the 11–3 triumph.

May 24, 1951: On this overcast and drizzly day at Yankee Stadium, before a dampened crowd of 11,193 excited Bronx rooters, Mickey goes 0-for-5 but reaches base twice when he strikes out on a wild pitch. The second time this occurs, in the sixth, Mantle bolts from the batter's box and before Detroit catcher Joe Ginsberg can retrieve the ball, the speedy "Comet from Commerce," also dubbed "Boy Wonder" by some reporters, winds up at second base. After striking out, the young speed merchant has blazed from home plate to second base in the bat of an eyelash. The next batter, Joe DiMaggio, then belts out a towering home run very long and deep to left field. The ball barely misses the remote upper deck of the left field grandstand. The Yankees crush the Tigers in the process, 11–1.

May 26, 1951: Demonstrating his great strength, his "lightning in a bottle" power, the left-handed-hitting Mantle connects off Dick Fowler of the Philadelphia Athletics with the bases loaded deep to the "Death Valley" center field expanse of Yankee Stadium. Before a large crowd of ecstatic Bronx spectators in the great ballyard, the ball soars off the young slugger's bat in a towering arc to center field, coming down on the railing of the bleachers, more than 450 feet away. There it caroms wildly, giving the young Mickey a bases-clearing triple. The Yankees triumph 8–5 over the Philadelphia A's.

May 30, 1951: In a doubleheader at Fenway Park, the Yankees are playing the Boston Red Sox when lefthander Chuck Stobbs, on the mound for the hometown Sox, strikes out Mickey in his last three at-bats in the first contest. Then, in the second tilt, Mantle strikes out in his first two at-bats against Willard Nixon. The young man explodes as he returns to the bench after his fifth strikeout in a row, savagely kicking at the concrete steps of the dugout. After finding a seat on the pine, the nineteen-year-old begins to cry. The pressures of failing are starting to get to the "Kid," who is growing more and more inconsolable. American League pitching is getting older and wiser with respect to the rookie phenom. After returning to the outfield for the home half of the inning, old Casey tells himself, "Pretty tough on a young feller when you ask him to go out and do a man's job." In this series with Boston, clearly the writing is on the wall. The young Mantle is striking out a lot. American pitching has caught up with the budding star and the word is out. In the middle innings of the second game, Casey pulls the kid from the game, summons Cliff Mapes off the bench, telling him, "Get in there for Mantle. We need someone who can hit the ball."

But the truth is that cunning opponents of the young slugger have noted a kink in the young but terrifying knight's armor. The immature, inexperienced ballplayer is over-eager to achieve. This is his chance and he is failing. One weakness appears to be emerging: a fast ball high and inside. The young batter thus worked with high and tight fast balls—the notion speeding over AL pitching grapevines—are too tempting for the young slugger to ignore. As a result, the green rookie is looking for the pitch, ready to destroy the pitch, and even more intensely preparing for that eventuality. Mantle soon finds himself, however, behind in the count, pressuring himself more and more and generating disastrous results in offensive production. While hitting now, Mantle has been reduced with regularity to over-swinging, a little more mightily, and soon enough with scant relish for discrimination, swinging wildly at pitches in the dirt, flailing at anything humming in towards the plate.

At this point in time, although Mantle's raw power is universally accepted, recognized, hailed and feared, it remains undisciplined. Casey has no choice. He must either sit the boy down, in the heat of yet another hot American League pennant race where, while sitting on the bench, he could never shake out of his slump. Or Casey must decide to send him down to the Triple-A minors in Kansas City for some immediate seasoning. This latter option will be exercised with the assignment being given to Kansas City manager George Selkirk. The former Yankee outfielder is to provide the watchful eye and individual attention required by the young, frustrated ballplayer. Casey decides that the answer lies in his old hometown, Kansas City, for Mickey.

June 8, 1951: In the largest attended night game ever watched at old Comiskey Park, before 53,940 excited South Siders, the Chicago White Sox play host to the touring New York Yankees. Casey has thought of benching the kid from Oklahoma, but decides to play the young stalwart. The shy powerhouse rifles a single to right field that scores the game-tying run. On defense, he throws out Chisox keystoner Nellie Fox, who tries the young outfielder's arm. Tagging up at third on a fly to right by Minnie Minoso, Fox finds himself dead at the plate. Yankee pitching ace, righthander Vic Raschi, beats the Pale Hose, 4–2. At this point, the young rookie leads all Yankees with 33 RBIs.

| 5. | June 19 (first game) | Chicago | Lou Kretlow | Stadium | 11–9, NY | 61,596 (60,441 pd.) |

The young Mantle belts a three-run home run into the right-center field bleachers.

| 6. | June 19 (second game) | Chicago | Joe Dobson | Stadium | 5–4, Chi | 61,596 (60,441 pd.) |
| 7. | July 7 | Boston | Ellis Kinder | Boston | 10–4, NY | 33,161 |

July 12, 1951: At Municipal Stadium, there is a featured pitching confrontation between staff aces Bob Feller of the Cleveland Indians and Allie Reynolds of the New York Yankees. The Yanks toil in a 1–0 masterpiece spun by Reynolds who no-hits the hometown Indians. The Yankees' one run comes as the result of a home run to right field by Gene Woodling in the seventh inning. This dramatic face-off is the opening game of a twin bill to be played this day. The closest thing to a hit that is genuinely close occurs when Sam Chapman belts a long fly to right which normally would have carried over the right field fence but for the weather. As the ball carries deep to right, the wind is powerful enough to actually blow it back to rightfielder Hank Bauer, situated at the low, field-level railing, where he makes the catch and the putout. Later, with two outs in the ninth inning and Bobby Avila up to bat, Reynolds signals Gil McDougald, who appears to "Superchief" to be too close to the batter at third base. Reynolds will then work Avila to a 2–1 count. The gritty righthander then puts a little something extra on his fast ball, and inexplicably falls down.

Embarrassed, Reynolds regains his composure, moves forward in his motion, starts his wind-up, pushes off the rubber, and fires strike three past Avila. In the second game, Vic Raschi clinches the sweep with a pitching victory. The "Yankee Clipper" will also contribute when he launches a three-run home run off Chuck Stobbs that seals the triumph.

As the Yankees reach Detroit to open a series with the Tigers on July 16th, Mickey Mantle is notified by Casey Stengel to report to him in the visitor's clubhouse office for a brief word. Casey has allowed Mickey to dress and to go out for batting practice. Then, with everyone out on the field, Casey asks one of his coaches to go out and send Mantle in to see him. The fretting youngster enters Casey's office, where the old man sits the rookie down. Casey tells the distraught kid that he has to send him down. Words are of no use to Casey. Before too long, Mickey Mantle is in tears, as is Stengel himself. Casey promises the young ballplayer that he will be recalled soon enough after getting more seasoning.

After the touching, tearful scene between the "Perfesser" and the kid, Casey tells reporters of the demotion, stating, "Get this, too: We wouldn't be in second place right now if it wasn't for this kid. Look at his record. A two-sixty average, seven homers, five triples, more than anybody on the club, and forty-five runs batted in—which nobody on the team has more. Of course, he also got fifty-two strikeouts, which is more than anybody, too. But the kid can field, he can throw, and he can run as well as hit. There ain't nobody better than him when he gets on base. Only he's got to learn to cut down on his strikeouts. He's got to learn to bunt better. He's got to get on base more. That's all. And then he'll be back, and I'll bet you that when he does he won't go down anymore."

Mickey is to be sent down to the Class AAA Kansas City Blues. The ostensible reason for the personnel change is a roster move to get rookie lefthander Art Schallock on the team. This, in turn, gives the young slugger some seasoning at Triple AAA ball. Better to hit and play everyday with Kansas City than to sit on the Yankee bench in the majors. From the hotel in Detroit, the young Mantle will head for Minneapolis, where Kansas City, the team he is to join, is slated to play. In his first at-bat, back in the bushes, Mickey drags a bunt for a base hit.

The next thing that the young and gifted, albeit slumping, slugger will hear from his new manager, George Selkirk, is that he has not been sent down to the bushes to bunt. Armed with this inspirational message, from this point in time onward, the frustrated young rookie will then go 0-for-22. Mantle calls his father to tell Mutt he is probably all washed up and that he wants to quit. A dejected young slugger says to his father, "I don't think I can play baseball anymore." Mutt Mantle then asks where his son is staying in Kansas City, to which his son replies "La Salle Hotel," where he and his team are lodging. Mickey's father then tells his son to stay where he is and that he will be there right away.

Mutt Mantle gets in the old family car and drives 150 miles, some five hours on the road, to Kansas City. Finally, the disturbed father arrives at the La Salle. When his father knocks on the door to his room, Mickey cracks the portal to let him in. The elder Mantle bursts into the room, grabs Mickey's cardboard suitcase, throws it on the bed, and starts putting the young ballplayer's clothes into it. Mickey asks his dad what he is doing. Irritated beyond belief, Mutt tells his son that he is disappointed in him, that he thought he had raised a man, that his son is nothing but a coward. As for packing his bag, Mutt tells the youngster that he is taking him home to work in the zinc mines, like him, for the rest of his life.

This is not the reaction Mickey expected. Instead of an encouraging pep talk, the young ballplayer gets dressed down in doom and groomed for gloom by his stern, no-nonsense father. If he wants to quit, his father says, then, "Let's go now and quit wasting everybody's time." The young Mantle then listens to his father intently. Before too long, the young ballplayer's confidence has been newly restored and his attitude rightly adjusted. The father-son discussion has soon reduced Mickey to pleading with his father to give him another chance to pursue his professional baseball career. The young ballplayer, newly chastened, will resume that career by proceeding to go on a hitting tear with Kansas City.

Almost immediately, Mantle goes on a batting binge. It is, in Mickey Mantle's opinion, the turning point in his career, the watershed moment of his life in baseball. In 40 games with Kansas City, including his inauspicious 1-for-23 beginning, the young slugger will break out of his slump with a vengeance, pelting the ball at a .414 clip. The reborn Mantle will end up hitting .361, powering 11 home runs, and batting in 50 tallies. As he has hoped for and promised, old Casey Stengel sees to it that Mickey is recalled August 20th and reinserted into the lineup by August 24th. Upon seeing him back from Kansas City and in the Yankee clubhouse again, the old manager, weathered and wizened, greets the youngster with, "I told you you'd be back." Indeed, Mickey Mantle is back, never again to leave the New York Yankees—for 17 more years.

FINAL MINOR LEAGUE EXPERIENCE

Year	Team	G	AB	R	H	2B	3B	HR	RBI	BA
1951	K. C. (Class AAA)	40	166	32	60	9	3	11	50	.361
	Minor League Tot.	266	1008	227	360			43	249	.357

Immediately prior to his recall, the young prospect is yet again ordered, at the personal direction of the Selective Service Director, General Lewis B. Hershey, to report for another Army induction physical. At Fort Sill, in Oklahoma, besides the Army physicians assigned to examine the young athlete, there are three civilian bone specialists in attendance as well. After finding nothing that will change their original 4-F classification after three days of intensive medical scrutiny, the military allows the aspiring big leaguer to return to the Yankees with no further interruption to the young man's blossoming career. Mickey Mantle is recalled to the Yankees from Kansas City on August 20, 1951.

After rejoining the Yankees on August 23rd, it becomes evident that some of the dynamics on the team have changed. Outfielder Cliff Mapes, Number Seven since the beginning of the year, has been traded away to the Browns in St. Louis. Now, the young Mantle, who had earlier been assigned Number Six, is reassigned this newly available number. Beginning this day and for the rest of his playing career, Mickey Mantle will wear Number 7 for the New York Yankees. After him, no one will.

8.	Aug. 25	Cleveland	Mike Garcia		Cleveland	7–3, NY	66,110

After being reinserted back into the Yankee lineup, Mickey makes the most of the opportunity afforded him by Stengel. Sporting his new Yankee uniform number, Number 7, Mickey lifts a high fly ball towards left-center field at Municipal Stadium. The opposite-field, two-run shot comes off hard-throwing Mike Garcia, who is en route to a 20–13 record this year. It has become clear now that the "Kid" belongs in the big leagues.

| 9. | Aug. 29 | St. Louis | Satchel Paige | St. Louis | 15–2, NY | 5,554 |

The young slugger connects off the black pitching legend. The powerful Mantle poles a three-run home run off the black hurler in the ninth inning of the Browns' contest at old Sportsman's Park. Mickey's four RBI output unfolds before the entire Mantle clan of Miami, Oklahoma, who make the trip to St. Louis. In the Forties, Mutt, Mickey, and his three brothers had made the trip before, to watch the Cardinals play on weekends—once even to see the World Series. Now the family has made the trip to Sportsman's Park to watch the family's firstborn play for the New York Yankees.

| 10. | Sept. 8 | Wash. | Sid Hudson | Wash.,D.C. | 4–0, NY | 35,314 |

The young Mantle with the crinkled bill of his Yankee ballcap sitting pertly atop his crewcut head and without benefit of a protective batting helmet, connects mightily for a three-run, game-winning, 450-foot home run deep into the right-center field bleachers at Yankee Stadium.

| 11. | Sep. 9 (first game) | Wash. | Dick Starr | Wash.,D.C. | 7–5, NY | 37,711 |
| 12. | Sep. 13 | Detroit | Virgil Trucks | Stadium | 9–2, Det. | 12,150 |

Batting leadoff, Mantle connects on the first pitch of the game, belting the ball into the upper deck of the right field grandstand at Yankee Stadium. For the "Kid," it is another of his powerful wallops, and soars high into the third deck. Behind the plate is umpire Bill McKinley, who can only gawk at the shot. Watching the ball almost sail out of Yankee Stadium, McKinley will later call this particular shot "the most amazing thing I ever saw." Recalling further, the disbelieving home plate umpire gapes as he watches the ball slam against "the bottom of the flag-holder on the top of the right field stands." After Mickey circles the bases, Detroit catcher Bob Swift looks at McKinley, sheepishly stating, "I must have called the wrong pitch."

September 16, 1951: Before 70,040 restless fans packed into Yankee Stadium, Mickey faces Indian fireballing ace Bob Feller batting leadoff. Meanwhile, Manager Casey Stengel has slipped Joe DiMaggio from his normal cleanup slot down to fifth, behind "Yogi" Berra. With the score pitted at 3–1 in favor of the Yankees, Mickey leads off the bottom of the fifth frame when he decides to try a drag bunt. After laying down Feller's offering, Mantle turns on the after-burners and races over the bag for a base hit. The next batter, Joe Collins, sacrifices Mantle to second. Gil McDougald then drives the ball deep to left—which Sam Chapman, the Indian leftfielder, flags down for a fine catch. Berra is then purposefully passed to get to "Joe D," the fading star of yesteryear. The Clipper makes Feller's decision regrettable as he pounds the ball deep into the left-center field section of the stadium's "Death Valley." The ball falls safely in the expansive gap, scoreing both Berra and Mantle. DiMaggio pulls up with the long triple that concludes the scoring in the game. The New York Yankees have now taken over first place for good, having just edged Cleveland out of the top spot by a scant margin of .003 percentage points. The Yankees have beaten Bob Feller and the visiting Tribesmen, 5–1, as Allie Reynolds mops up the Indians the rest of the way.

September 17, 1951: Ed Lopat wins his 20th pitching victory of the year and the New York Yankees beat Bob Lemon and the Cleveland Indians, 2–1. The key instrument is a perfect squeeze play at home, executed by Phil Rizzuto, scoring Joe DiMaggio standing up with the winning run, and giving the Bombers a full, one-game lead in the standings.

| 13. | Sep. 19 | Chicago | Lou Kretlow | Stadium | 5–3, NY | 12,127 |

The young rookie pounds out a three-run, game-winning home run for the pinstripes which sails over the right field railing situated to the right of the Yankee bullpen.

September 28, 1951: On the last day of the season at Yankee Stadium, the Yankees are poised to take the title. The Yankee starting hurler will need very little as he forcefully shuts down Boston with a clutch pitching performance. The masterful pinstriped righthander, Allie Reynolds, has moved through the game mowing down the Red Sox. After craftily mixing his pitches and working the batters with expert skill and control, Reynolds is one putout away from pitching a no-hitter when the dangerous Red Sox's Ted Williams comes to the plate.

To this point, Reynolds has allowed nothing remotely close to a safety. But then, as "Teddy Ballgame" unlooses his majestic swing, he lifts a high pop-up in foul territory under which Yankee catcher Yogi Berra is camped for the descent of the ball. At the last second, the ball swerves towards the earth, hitting Berra's glove before falling to the ground for an error. This gives Ted Williams a second chance to spoil Reynolds' no-hitter. On the next pitch, Williams lifts another foul pop-up. This time when the ball falls earthward, Berra makes the catch that seals the Reynolds no-hitter.

As a result of Berra's final putout, "Superchief" Reynolds has tossed his second no-hitter of the year. The pitching gem ties a major league record. Reynolds not only beats the Boston Red Sox, wins the 8–0 game, but has set up the nightcap for the clinching of the American League pennant. Indeed, the Yankees are not to be denied, as Vic Raschi seals the win by holding the Sox to three runs in an 11–3, pennant-clinching victory for the Yanks. In a historic footnote of the game, "Joltin' Joe" DiMaggio belts out the final home run of his fabled career. As for the young Mantle, the heir apparent to the great "Yankee Clipper," the young rookie knocks in three runs, having banged out two doubles while scoring two others.

THE 1951 NEW YORK YANKEES

First Place: With a 98–56 Record Under Manager Casey Stengel.

Yankee Stadium Attendance: 1,950,107

MICKEY MANTLE'S 1951 HITTING RECORD

G	AB	R	H	2B	3B	HR	HR%	RBI	SA	BB	SO	SB	AVE.
96	341	61	91	11	5	13	3.8	65	.443	43	74	8	.267

In the 96 games that Mickey Mantle appeared in during 1951, he played in the outfield 86 times, while appearing in 10 games as a pinchhitter. In his rookie campaign, Mickey Mantle hit .267, while the major leagues averaged .261 with both teams scoring an average of 9.10 runs per game and both teams hitting 1.5 home runs per contest.

Mickey's 1951 Salary: $7,500

World Series Winning Share: $6,445

Injuries or Operations: Four years earlier, Mickey had been diagnosed with osteomyelitis. His left leg had almost been amputated on doctor's advice, which was rejected by his mother. Mrs. Mantle had adamantly denied permission. It turned out that 60 penicillin injections would work to save Mickey's left leg and probably his life. As a result, however, the young Mantle's leg was permanently deformed, lacking some of the bone and leaving a gap between his ankle and his knee. During this off-season, Mantle undergoes a cartilage operation on his right knee, which had been so severely injured during the second game of the World Series.

Number of Games in Which Mantle Homered: 13

Winning Record When Mickey Mantle Homered: 11–2, a winning percentage of .846

THE 1951 WORLD SERIES

October 4, 1951: At Yankee Stadium, where the Series opens this day, the Giants win the game behind the strong seven-hit pitching of Dave Koslo. The impressive heart of the Yankee lineup: Mantle, DiMaggio, Berra, and Bauer go 1-for-15 collectively, as Koslo snubs the Bombers with pitching efficiency and breaking balls. The Yankees bow, 5–1, to the Giants, to the crafty Koslo, and to the cunningly impatient Monte Irvin, who is enjoying, perhaps, the best World Series debut ever in Series history. Monte Irvin collects four hits in his first game of World Series competition. In fact, Irvin ties a Series record in his first seven minutes of play. Irvin spontaneously combusts, when he generates a first-inning steal of home plate off Allie "Superchief" Reynolds. It is the eleventh time in Series history that a man has stolen home in the World Series. In the interim, Mickey is held hitless. Still the nervous nineteen-year-old walks twice.

October 5, 1951: Leading off for the Yankees in Game Two of the World Series, played this afternoon at Yankee Stadium, Mickey drags a bunt for a single. After Hank Bauer flies out, Phil Rizzuto singles, as does Gil McDougald, who knocks in the young Mantle with the Yankees' first run in the game. In the third frame, Mantle strikes out against Giant hurler Larry Jansen. Then, in the fifth inning, Mickey Mantle is racing after a fly ball hit into the right-center field alley by Willie Mays. The towering gapper is drifting to an area between the swift young rookie and the venerable DiMaggio. But as the fly ball descends, it is closer to Joltin' Joe. Both pinstriped defenders converge on the high fly. The fleet-footed Mantle is about to overtake the ball and make the catch when he hears DiMaggio's voice say, "I've got it."

Changing gears, Mantle is about to make his adjustments when, suddenly, the young deer-like phantom goes down like he's been shot with a rifle. Bomber shortstop Phil Rizzuto recalls hearing from his position in the infield the crack of the young athlete's leg bone. At high speed, Mantle is pulling up to let DiMaggio make the catch, when he goes down in a heap. By so doing, the young rookie had caught his cleats on an exposed water sprinkler, tripped badly at full speed and broken his kneecap, which the young horrified outfielder and others had heard audibly pop. The Clipper himself will get the ball back into the infield and then immediately bend over the fallen athlete. "You okay, kid?" Paralyzed by the fear that his career is over, Mickey lies motionless on the turf, his right hand covering his face. The mercury-like, power-hitting "Commerce Comet" will miss the rest of this World Series.

The young ballplayer is carried off the field by stretcher. The next morning, Mickey and his father will take a cab to Lenox Hill Hospital. The worried young man and his emaciated-looking father are getting out of the cab when the crippled ballplayer leans on his father, normally a solidly built, granite-like man. The young

Mantle and his weakened father both collapse to the street. It is the first time the younger Mantle realizes that something is seriously wrong, something horribly different from his father's normally robust demeanor.

Dr. Sid Gaynor, renowned orthopedist and club physician for the New York Yankees, has accompanied the Mantles to the hospital. He will later tell the press that the young right fielder's right knee had taken "a terrific jolt. Why, with an older man, the cartilage would have torn right out of there. He's out for the Series, of course. It's a bad sprain. I'll X-ray it tomorrow morning and he'll be all right." Consequently, Mantle will undergo the first of six knee operations that he will have to endure in his injury-laced career. The injury will take five months to mend.

Later, upon reflection with the baseball sage Roger Kahn, Mickey will provide the details that explain his long and painful passage through a most significant regimen of critical injuries. Mantle will tell Kahn, "In '51, my rookie year, I was in right. DiMaggio called me off a fly ball late. I tore up my right knee. After that, I started straining muscles; the bad knee was affecting the whole leg. In '52, I was running to first and a hamstring tore in my right leg and I went down with all my weight on my left knee. After that I had *two* bad knees. A matching pair. Next year, I broke a foot and couldn't play at all for a spell. After that, some bit of bone came off my right shoulder and worked into the muscle. So I have a sore arm all the time."

Now, as he lays in disrepair, he learns for the first time that his father has been admitted to the same hospital and is now ensconced in the same room as himself.

Mutt Mantle is a deathly ill man whose time is nearing. Tragically, it will be determined quickly that the rookie's father is suffering from a fatal disease. Unbeknownst to either father or son, the young and the proud but weakened father, will watch the rest of the Series from their hospital beds. It is shortly afterwards that Mickey is informed that Mutt, in the next bed, is dying of Hodgkin's Disease. No Mantle male has lived past his forties. Tragically, the ill-fated Mutt will not be an exception.

Back at the stadium, in Game Two, Eddie Lopat will scatter five hits, three of which Monte Irvin will collect. Irvin's performance ties another World Series record. The Negro star has banged out seven hits in two consecutive Series contests. But Irvin is the only highlight among the many Giants' lowlights, struggling against Lopat's masterful off-speed deliveries. The Yankees produce their first victory in the series, 3–1. The Yanks later take the series from the Giants, four games to two. Mickey's initial performance in World Series play provides no clue as to what is to come. The young Mantle has singled once in five official at-bats, scored once, walked twice, and fanned once.

Whitey Ford, Mickey, and Billy Martin, the trio of teammates, celebrating another battle in the baseball wars of 1953. Celebrating would take on an old familiarity between the three friends which would oftentimes lead to after hours hijinx and disciplinary complications with their manager, Casey Stengel.

Chapter Three

NIGHT RIDERS IN PINSTRIPES

—1952 & 1953—

In the Nation and the World: In 1952, the Cold War was in full swing, as successful H-Bomb testing began. Dwight D. Eisenhower was elected U.S. President when he defeated Adlai Stevenson at the polls, while the U.S., as a World War II victor, ended its postwar occupation of Japan. In the President's Cabinet, the office of a new governmental agency called Health, Education, and Welfare was created. Meanwhile, overseas, truce negotiations began at Panmunjon to end the conflict in Korea. Both sides negotiated the release of an exchange of their captured wounded and prisoners-of-war. And in Sing Sing Prison in New York, the Rosenbergs were executed for their suspected roles in giving the secret of the A-bomb to the Russians.

Fads and Movies: In the hijinx-filled days of 1952, bored but thrill-seeking male college students would conduct panty raids among sorority houses on college campuses all over America. Among the baby brothers of these college hounds, "beanies" with propellor tops would multiply everywhere. Other new pastimes would be launched nationwide such as stamp collecting and autograph hoarding by millions of memorabilia-mad hobbyists. And by the following year, the advent of 3-D movies would mark the wearing of specially prepared cardboard glasses with tinted lenses inside movie houses all over America.

Innovations and First Appearances: In 1952, the postage-stamp-sized lots of grassy yards on new suburban sites of American homes everywhere became inundated with new contraptions called gas lawn mowers, which gave young people an easier way to mow their lawns. The home movie phenomenon would receive a tremendous boost with the invention of 16mm home movie projectors that allowed for the parents of Baby Boomers to record the fascinating comings and goings of their daily increasing flock.

Bowling alley automatic pin-boy machines began to mark the bowling craze sweeping the nation. Automatic food vending machines offering candy bars, cigarettes, and prepackaged foods began to show up in subways, on street corners, and on sidewalks everywhere. Cinerama widened and curved the movie screen producing a 3-D effect without the funny 3-D "glasses."

"MAD" comic books highlighting Albert E. Newman, a new cartoon caricature who would become popular with the growing numbers of the burgeoning Baby Boomers. Cigarette filter tips would make their appearance. Holiday Inns would begin to dot the American landscape. And SONY pocket transistor radios would be sold by the millions to bee-boppin' teenagers who were rustling their feet to snappy new tunes heard on the pocket-size devices. And within a year, DC-7 propeller planes would start making commercial flights everywhere in the country.

Playboy Magazine hit magazine racks in stores all over the nation. *TV Guide* made its way into American homes. And the revolutionary release by General Motors of the first wave of Chevrolet Corvettes provided the car-crazed millions of sports-minded Americans with something beautiful and thrillingfor a Sunday drive.

Movies: In 1952, *High Noon, The Greatest Show on Earth, Moulin Rouge, Viva Zapata, Singing in the Rain, The Quiet Man,* and *Viva Zapata* vied with one another as Americans poured through movie lobbies everywhere to be thrilled by the movie fare of the day. The following year, 1953, would mark the cinematic debuts of the following flicks: *Roman Holiday, From Here to Eternity, The Robe, Kiss Me Kate, Calamity Jane, Stalag 17, Gentlemen Prefer Blondes, Shane,* and Walt Disney's *Peter Pan.*

Television: By 1952, television was well on its way to replacing radio as the chief vehicle of entertainment for the everyday American. Titillating the millions of television viewers were the many choices given by three and sometimes four network channels. TV offers *You Bet Your Life* with Groucho Marx, Sid Caeser's *Your Show of Shows, Our Miss Brooks, Adventures of Ozzie and Harriet*, and *The Dinah Shore Show*. Within a year, new programs would begin to be propagated into small-screen images transmitting such comedic vehicles as *Studio One, George Burns and Gracie Allen Show, The Red Skelton Show*, Buick's *Milton Berle Show, My Little Margie, This Is Your Life*, and *Life of Riley*. These telecasts were broadcast to increasing numbers, reaching the hundreds of thousands of television sets that were becoming more and more bountiful in this newest of entertainment industries. The television event of the year was when Lucille Ball and Desi Arnaz celebrate the real-life birth of little Ricky on *I Love Lucy*, their popular TV show. In fact, the special program was aired on the same day that Lucy actually gave birth.

The Juke Box: In 1952, love ballads and finger-snapping tunes entertained millions as the nickels and dimes of the parents of the Baby Boom generation were dropped into the coin slots of jukes all over the country. Resounding, melodic hits cropped up everywhere, including "Cry" by Johnny Ray, Percy Faith's "Delicado," "Tell Me Why" by the Four Aces, and "Here in My Heart" by Al Martino. By the next year, more pop standards were given a coast-to-coast hearing by music-loving millions, who hummed to the 1953 renderings of "Song From the Moulin Rouge" by Percy Faith, "Vaya Con Dios" by Les Paul and Mary Ford, "Doggie In the Window" by Patti Page, "Why Don't You Believe Me?" by Joni James, "Pretend" by Nat King Cole.

Deaths: Crossing the bar in 1952 were Admiral John Dewey, actor John Garfield, actress Hattie McDaniel, educator Maria Montessori, and linguist George Santayana. Within a year's time, Americans would be saddened by the passing of playwright Eugene O'Neill and Senator Robert Taft. In the U.S.S.R., Soviet Security Chief Laurenti Beria was eliminated in the latest row of yet another high-level purge during what would be the last year of the Stalin rein of terror in Mother Russia. In 1953, the Soviet state itself was rocked to its roots by the news that its "savior," and modern-day merchant for the mass murder of his own people, Joseph Stalin, had died of heart failure.

Sports: In the summer months of 1952, the Olympic Games in Melbourne, Australia, were celebrated. American middleweight Floyd Patterson would win the Olympic gold medal when he knocked out his opponent in the first round. Bob Richards took gold in the pole vault. And Bob Mathias won the decathlon for the United States. In professional football, Bert Rechichar of the Baltimore Colts would kick a record 56-yard field goal in a regular season game; the Detroit Lions would beat the Cleveland Browns, 17–16, in the NFL championship game. Ben Hogan would win the trifecta of Golf's Grand Slam: winning the Masters, the U.S. Open, and the British Open. In Basketball, the Minneapolis Lakers would beat the New York Knicks for the NBA championship. And one year later, the world of pro basketball welcomed a new champion as the Minneapolis Lakers defeated the New York Knicks, four games to one. And in pro boxing, Rocky Marciano knocked out "Jersey Joe" Walcott in the 13th round to become the new heavyweight champion of the world, a title he would never relinquish inside the ring.

Baseball Transitions: In 1952, 15,000,000 Americans paid admission to get into big league ballyards around the country to watch major league baseball. The sport, because of television and its higher revenues, was beginning to cultivate a new relationship with its fans, bringing more and more millions of dollars to the game. This phenomenon heralded, via the mass acceptance and consequent production of television sets across the country, the Golden Age of Baseball. Elsewhere, with resentment and bitterness over a second war-time tour of duty, Ted Williams left baseball a second time by belting out a home run before the Fenway faithful. After the game, "Teddy Ballgame" would once again be fated to fly combat missions for the Marine reserves during the Korean War effort.

Meanwhile, the 1952 New York Yankees and other American League teams sported a new, brightly colored 50th Year Anniversary patch on their uniforms as the Bombers attempted to win their fifth straight world championship. The Yankees had already braced themselves for playing without the Hall-of-Fame services of Joe DiMaggio, who announced to the press on December 11, 1951, that his playing days were over. The "Yankee Clipper" admitted that he was not the same player anymore, that he was no longer the Joe DiMaggio the baseball world had come to expect and appreciate. The brilliant, but flickering flame of greatness had gone out. The Yankees also lost Jerry Coleman to the U.S. mobilization effort generated by the Korean Conflict. Coleman was replaced by utility infielder Billy Martin, who rejoined the Yanks. The Yankees also lost Jackie Jensen via a trade, but picked up Irv Noren in the process.

The change on the face of Yankee personnel began to crystallize the next year. The Bombers lost Spec Shea. But the Yanks also picked up the pitching services of Johnny Sain. One year later, in 1953, Whitey Ford returned to the Yankees after finishing his obligation to military service. In the AL ballyards, Cleveland lost Steve Gromek, while the Philadelphia A's lost Elmer Valo. The Washington Senators picked up the six-year veteran, former Red Sox left-handed hurler Chuck Stobbs, and within a year Boston and big league baseball were both relieved and delighted, as Ted Williams returns to the game to resume his career in Beantown. Appearing before the flocking Fenway hordes for the first time since his return from the Korean War, the "Splendid Splinter" returned to baseball as he had left it—with a home run.

After answering the reservists' call to duty, Williams had come home to do what he does best. Meanwhile, the Red Sox bade farewell to Dom DiMaggio to retirement and Walt Dropo via a trade with Detroit. For their part, the Tigers would make room for Dropo by getting rid of Vic Wertz, who went to the St. Louis Browns.

On a personal note: the young Mickey Mantle himself, and his beautiful young wife, Merlyn, increased their family number. The child-bearing years of the proud parents would yield four sons. Supplementing his Yankee salary, the "Kid from Oklahoma" would also make $18,000 this year as a highly paid endorser of various commercial products. Some of Mickey's endorsements included Wheaties breakfast cereal, Camel cigarettes, Beech-nut gum, Esquire socks, Van Heusen shirts, Haggar slacks, and Louisville sluggers. On the diamond, Mickey would move through these two years attempting to reach his unbelievable potential. It is during this period that Mickey Mantle will confirm the suspicion that the young slugger belongs among the highest-rated of major league prospects who ever lived.

Not only does the young ballplayer belong in the big leagues, he will come to be looked upon as one of its dominating forces. For the Yankees, Mickey Mantle will begin his long reign as the centerpiece of the vaunted Bomber offensive attack.

THE 1952 REGULAR SEASON

23 HOME RUNS

H.R.#	DATE	OPPONENT	PITCHER	SITE	SCORE	ATTND.
14.	Apr. 21	Philadelphia	Bobby Shantz (LH)	Stadium	5–1, NY	8,294

Mantle launches a towering drive that carries into the lower left-field grandstand at Yankee Stadium. The blow is pounded off the small Gold Glove southpaw who is en route to a 24–7 record this year and the AL Most Valuable Player Award.

H.R.#	DATE	OPPONENT	PITCHER	SITE	SCORE	ATTND.
15.	Apr. 30 (first game)	St. Louis	Bob Cain (LH)	Stadium	9–4, St. L.	18,509

The young slugger connects for a 420-foot drive to left field at Yankee Stadium.

Beginning May 6, 1952: Mantle misses five games when he learns of the death of his father in a Denver hospital. Mutt Mantle has died of Hodgkin's Disease, at thirty nine. Mantle leaves New York to return to Oklahoma to attend the funeral. Eight years before, when he was thirteen-years-old, Mickey had attended his grandfather's funeral, who had also died prematurely—of Hodgkin's Disease. Knowing the virulence of this particular disease and its genetic bond, Mickey himself has always expected to die at an early age, believing that the Hodgkin's curse would claim him between the ages of forty and forty-five. After surviving his forties and fifties, and despite a long addiction to alcohol, Mickey will quote his friend Bobby Layne, pro football Hall of Fame quarterback and a well-known hell-raiser, saying, "If I knew that I would live this long, I would have taken better care of myself."

May 20, 1952: At Comiskey Park, before 33,294 avid Sox rooters, Mickey Mantle begins his first game as the starting centerfielder for the New York Yankees and collects four base hits, all singles, in a game against the hometown Pale Hose. The speedy youngster scores once and knocks in another as the Yankees win the game, 4–3.

| 16. | May 30
(first game) | Philadelphia | Bobby Shantz (LH) | Stadium | 2–1, Phil | 30,005 |

Mickey connects on one of the lefthander's offerings for a towering, 420-foot drive that lands on the ledge atop the auxiliary scoreboard in left field next to the visitors' bullpen.

June 3, 1952: At Yankee Stadium, 32,125 bustling Bronx boosters crowd into the magnificent ballyard where they take note of a personnel change at the centerfield position. After sitting down on the bench for a brief time, and being moved by Stengel back to right field for a few games, Mickey Mantle, Number Seven, returns to center field, this time to stay. Once again, Mickey collects four hits, all off fireballer Billy Pierce of the Chicago White Sox, and scores twice against the touring nine from the Windy City. The Bombers beat the visiting Sox, 4–3.

| 17. | June 15
(first game) | Cleveland | Bob Lemon | Cleveland | 8–2, NY | 69,468 |

Mantle hits his first home run of the year from the left-hand side of the plate, a three-run home run at Municipal Stadium off future Hall-of-Famer Bob Lemon. The Cleveland righthander is en route to a 22–11 pitching record this year. The day is somewhat of a turning point in the mind of the wizened Casey Stengel and in the career of the young slugger from Oklahoma. As of this day, Mantle becomes the Yankees' regular centerfielder. The blond, crewcut youngster, Mickey Mantle of Commerce, Oklahoma, has replaced the elegant rovings in center field of the Bronx Bomber, Joe DiMaggio, who retired in 1951.

| 18. | June 17 | Detroit | Billy Hoeft (LH) | Detroit | 7–6, Det.
(in 11) | 47,544 |

Mantle's 400-foot home run ties the game at Briggs Stadium, though the Bombers will still absorb the pain of an eventual extra-inning defeat.

| 19. | June 22
(second game) | Chicago | Marv Grissom | Chicago | 2–1, Chi | 47,970 |
| 20. | June 27 | Philadelphia | Bob Hooper | Stadium(n) | 10–0, NY | 26,749 |

Mickey connects for the first run of the game which proves to be the game-winner.

21.   July 5   Philadelphia   Alex Kellner (LH)   Philadelphia 3–1, NY   9,111

Philadelphia catcher Joe Tipton slyly watches as the young "Mick" comes up to take his swings from the right side of the plate. Tipton, who admires Mantle's "tape-measure" home runs, asks the young slugger if there is one pitch he would like to see. The Oklahoman says sure, he'd like to see a change-up. The mischievous Tipton assures him that it will be the next pitch. On the next pitch, Kellner throws a change-up and Mantle unloads on it. The result is a towering drive into the upper left field grandstand at Connie Mack Stadium. When Mantle reaches home plate, Tipton takes off his mask and winks at Mickey over their little secret.

22.   July 6   Philadelphia   Bobby Shantz (LH)   Philadelphia 5–2, NY   31,935
      (first game)

THE 1952 ALL-STAR GAME

SHIBE PARK IN PHILADELPHIA, PENNSYLVANIA

July 8, 1952: In a rain-abbreviated midsummer classic, Hank Sauer of the Chicago Cubs leads the Nationals to a 3–2 victory. Mickey has not been voted onto the team, but had been selected as a reserve by Manager Casey Stengel, as is his perogative. Since starting centerfielder Dom DiMaggio of the Boston Red Sox plays the entire game, the young Mantle does not get into it. He is, however, awed by all of the great stars in the game amassed in one place in the summer celebration of baseball.

23.   July 13   Detroit   Marlin Stuart   Stadium   11–1, NY   30,775
      (first game)

Mickey's home run comes in support of Vic Raschi's masterful one-hitter, which he spins against the Tigers. Only Tiger backstop Joe Ginsberg can manage a safety against the hard-throwing Yankee righthander when he homers just into the seats down the right field line.

24.   July 13   Detroit   Hal Newhouser (LH)   Stadium   12–2, NY   30,775
      (second game)

Mantle's home run against the future Hall of Fame southpaw goes to the opposite field, sailing far into right-center field and the remote, scoreboard-adorned bleachers.

July 14, 1952: Playing the Yankees at the stadium before 6,611 stout and hearty New Yorkers, Walt Dropo of the visiting Detroit Tigers goes 5-for-5 with two RBIs. As a result of Dropo's timely hitting, the Tigers beat the Bronx Bombers, 8–2.

| 25. | July 15 | Cleveland | Early Wynn | Stadium(n) | 7–3, NY | 43,673 |

In this night game, Mantle's home run comes off the hard-throwing righthander, who is at the peak of his skills and also working this year on a 23-12 pitching record.

| 26. | July 17 (first game) | Cleveland | Steve Gromek | Stadium(tn) | 11–6, Cle. | 51,114 |
| 27. | July 25 | Detroit | Art Houtteman | Detroit | 2–1, Det | 41,538 |

Mickey connects for a long, towering shot into the upper right field tier at Briggs Stadium. The young kid also collects two singles for this evening's efforts.

| 28. | July 26 | Detroit | Ted Gray (LH) | Detroit | 10–6, Det. (in 11) | 13,060 |

Mantle blasts his first career grand-slam home run, which lands in the upper left field tier of Briggs Stadium.

| 29. | July 29 | Chicago | Chuck Stobbs (LH) | Chicago | 10–7, Chi | 38,967 |

Mantle connects for his second career grand-slam home run—a game-winner—coming at Comiskey Park in the ninth inning, three days after walloping his first career grand slam. The Yankees, as a result, retain their three-game lead over the Indians.

| 30. | Aug. 11 | Boston | Sid Hudson | Stadium(n) | 7–0, NY | 51,005 |
| 31. | Aug. 11 | Boston | Ralph Brickner | Stadium(n) | 7–0, NY | 51,005 |

Mantle's shot carries deep into the Yankee bullpen in right-center field at the Stadium. In this series with the Red Sox, Mantle has been lethal, collecting six hits in 10 at-bats, walking three times, and basically knocking out Boston single-handedly from contention. After the last game in this crucial series, Boston Manager Lou Boudreau talks to some of the sportswriters, saying, "Without him, the Yankees would be just another team this year. He's the reason they stay up there in first place."

From this point onward in the season, though the young slugger will finish the year batting .311, Mickey will hit .362 down the stretch and will be doing this while in great pain. As his leg bulges from the fluid that keeps building up in his injured right knee, it has to be regularly drained. This condition was growing more and more frequent.

Mantle arranges for corrective surgery in the off-season. Years later, Dr. Austin Schlecher, a friend of Roger Kahn, baseball scribe supreme, would see a 1952 X-ray of Mantle's right knee and claim, "With that osteo and cartilage damage in his right knee, there is no question of his coming into the Army. He couldn't make it through basic training. My question is, How can he play ball? He must have a high tolerance for pain."

For now, however, Mickey must play through the pain to contribute to the cause: another Yankee pennant.

August 25, 1952: At Yankee Stadium, hurler Virgil Trucks of the visiting Detroit Tigers pitches a 1–0 no-hitter against the New York Yankees. It is Trucks's second 1–0 no-hitter this season, the first one coming May 15th against the Senators. In this phenomenal year with the cellar-dwelling Tigers, Trucks will also pitch another 1–0 masterpiece, a complete game, one-hit victory against the Washington Senators. In that game, Trucks gives up a single on the first pitch of the game to Washington leadoff hitter Eddie Yost. It is the last hit the Senators will get in the game. This overpowering moundsmanship proves all the more astounding in light of the fact that Trucks's record with Detroit this year will be 5-19. Still, for this day, Trucks ties a major league record by hurling a second no hitter in the same season and it comes against the Mickey Mantle–led New York Yankees.

There is one close call. In the third inning, Phil Rizzuto grounds a routine skipper to shortstop Johnny Pesky, who makes the play but gets the ball stuck in his glove while throwing to first. This miscue allows the diminutive "Scooter" to reach first base on the late throw. The official scorer will first rule that the play is an error, then change it to a hit, and then back to an error. On the Yankee bench, meanwhile, Casey Stengel will erupt in anger, insisting that the play should have been ruled a hit. Stengel does not want the Yankees to be no-hit by the lowly Tigers—not before the home folks. And yet Stengel rails in vain. In the ninth, Mantle steps to the plate to face the tireless Trucks. In short order, Trucks fans the young Mantle, gets Collins to fly out to right-center, and gets Bauer on a one-hop ground out to Tiger second baseman Al Federoff.

As Trucks leaves the mound with his no-hitter in the books, the polite, admiring, but measly turnout gives the hard-throwing hurler a nice round of applause. In four months' time, the flame-throwing Trucks will be traded to the equally lowly St. Louis Browns. Virgil Trucks is one of only two pitchers in Mickey Mantle's career who will pitch a no-hitter against the New York Yankees.

| 32. | Aug. 30 | Wash. | Randy Gumpert | Stadium | 6–4, NY | 41,558 |

On Old Timers Day, Mickey lines one into the right field seats.

| 33. | Sept. 14 | Cleveland | Lou Brissie (LH) | Cleveland | 7–1, NY | 73,609 |

The Yankees are amid their last Western road trip of the year. After first playing in Chicago for 2 games, the Bombers now arrive on this day to play a single in Cleveland. Before a typically gigantic Cleveland crowd, the largest crowd ever in his career to see Mickey Mantle homer, the Yankees produce a 7–1 triumph over the hometown Tribe. The clean-shaven kid from Oklahoma singles and doubles off Mike Garcia before connecting for his home run to left field off southpaw reliever Lou Brissie in the fifth. The key hit is a bases-loaded, bases-clearing double by Yogi Berra in the third inning. The Yankees leave town floating in happy delirium with a 1½-game lead in the American League.

| 34. | Sept. 17 | Detroit | Bill Wight(LH) | Detroit | 12-3, NY | 6,879 |

Mantle pounds out a gigantic, 450-foot home run that, along with his two doubles, helps the Yankees win this lopsided contest.

| 35. | Sept. 24 | Boston | Mel Parnell(LH) | Boston | 8-6, NY | 17,651 |
| | (second game) | | | | | |

In this key, late-season doubleheader, the Yankees are attempting to extend their lead over the trailing Cleveland Indians. In the third inning of the first game, Mickey doubles in the first Yankee run of the game. The game ends in regulation, tied at 2–2. In the meantime, the Fenway scoreboard reports that the Cleveland nine have beaten their opponent by a huge margin. Now in the tenth inning, Mickey comes to the plate with two outs and Phil Rizzuto on first after having singled. On a 1-and-1 pitch, Mantle powers the ball like a stroke of lightning over the head of Dom DiMaggio in center field. Rizzuto's tally proves to be the game-winner.

In the nightcap of the twin bill, Mickey once again singles in the Yankees' first run. Later in the fourth, the young slugger clobbers a three-run home run that gives the Yankees a considerable lead and retires Parnell for the afternoon. With the Yankees leading, 7–0, the Red Sox make a come back, however, reducing the margin to one run in the eighth when Boston scores two off Bob Kuzava, who cannot hold the Sox. In the Yankee ninth, with Phil Rizzuto on first, Mickey attempts to get on first base with a bunt that does not work. On the next offering, Mantle slams the ball deep to right, scoring Rizzuto. Of the Yankees' eight runs in the game, he has dominated the diamond, responsible for six of them. The Bronx Bombers are now two games ahead of the pack with only one week left in the season.

| 36. | Sept. 26 | Philadelphia | Harry Byrd | Phil.(n) | 5-2, NY | 21,633 |
| | | | | (in 11) | | |

The Yankees clinch the American League pennant with this evening's victory at Shibe Park. It is also during this particular game that pitcher Harry Byrd strikes out Mantle for the 106th time this year. Mantle will strike out five more times this year, which will give him a total of 111 strikeouts. This figure will lead the league and establish a new Yankee club record for strikeouts in a year. The New York Yankees have played a 154-game schedule. Mantle has played in 142 games, missing five of the contests because of his father's death. He missed the other seven because of problems from his ailing right knee.

Referring to the role that Mickey Mantle had in the pennant stretch of the 1952 season, Casey Stengel will tell reporters, "That youngster Mantle, not twenty-one years old, and still wet behind the ears, was the reason. He picked up this team when we were down and nearly out, and his speed and his big bat brought us back to win. Just like Joe DiMaggio did the last couple of years."

THE 1952 NEW YORK YANKEES

First Place: in the American League with a 95-59 record under Manager Casey Stengel.

Yankee Stadium Attendance: 1,629,665

1952 Awards: Mickey Mantle is voted onto the major league All-Star Team as an outfielder.

Mickey Mantle's League-Leading Categories: Mantle, with 111 strikeouts (also sets new Yankee club record), also finishes second in the league in doubles with 37 to Ferris Fain's 43. Mantle takes second as well, with a .530 slugging average to Larry Doby's .541 slugging average. The young Mantle leads all American League outfielders in double plays, but he has also made 14 errors.

MICKEY MANTLE'S 1952 HITTING RECORD

G	AB	R	H	2B	3B	HR	HR%	RBI	SA	BB	SO	SB	AVE.
142	549	94	171	37	7	23	4.2	87	.530	75	111	4	.311

In 1952, Mickey Mantle hits .311 while the major leagues average .253 with both teams scoring an average 8.35 runs per game and both teams hitting 1.37 home runs per contest. For the 142 games that Mickey Mantle appears in during 1952, he plays in the outfield 141 times. He also plays one game at third base, while appearing in no games as a pinch-hitter.

Mickey's 1952 Salary: $10,000

World Series Winning Share: $6,026

Number of Games in Which Mantle Homered: 22

Winning Record When Mickey Mantle Homers: 14–8, a winning percentage of .636

THE 1952 WORLD SERIES

October 1, 1952: Before rushing out onto Ebbets Field to start the Opening Game of the 1952 World Series, Casey Stengel gives the Yankees a pep talk that only the "Ol' Perfesser" can deliver. Casey tells his team, "Don't go kiddin' yourselves about these here Dodgers. Look who they got. Robinson, who can hit and run those bases like a jackrabbit. Then 'Duke' Snider, and Hodges. Why that Hodges is so strong, when he hits the ball it just vanishes. And Campanella and Furillo, they're pretty good, and they got great pitching, and they run like greyhounds at the track. Now, you all got to keep your thinking caps on all the time against this team." Thus inspired, the Yankees go out and lose the game, 4–2, against the Bums, as Duke Snider poles a two-run home run, pacing the Dodgers to their Opening Game victory. Mickey collects two singles in the contest.

October 2, 1952: In Game Two of the Series, played this day at Ebbets Field, the Yanks are down a game after losing the opener, 4–2, having been powered to victory by Duke Snider's home run over the right-center field scoreboard clock and Joe Black's clutch pitching. On this day, however, Yankee stopper Vic Raschi will even matters when he scatters three hits.

In the eighth inning of the contest, the young Yankee centerfielder undertakes a chance proposition. After Jackie Robinson singles up the middle, the risk-taking Mantle decides on making a dangerous bluff. With the nerve of a burglar and the daring of his youth, Mickey will attempt to draw the ever-aggressive Robinson into an over-commitment. Mickey makes his move by feigning a hard throw to first base to catch the veteran Robbie, taking a wide turn. At this instant, 33,792 Ebbets Field patrons hold their breath. For his part, Jackie, believing that the ball is going to be rifled to first base, bolts for second base. Mantle then checks his throw with a convincing charade, corrects himself and fires the ball on a clothesline from his position in center field to second sacker Billy Martin. The volatile Martin will catch the ball some twenty feet before Jackie's arrival and make a hard tag on the befuddled Robinson, who has taken Mantle's bait. After getting up and dusting himself off, Robinson looks out at center field before heading back to the dugout. Jackie then takes time to tip his cap to the "Kid from Commerce."

The Yankees win the contest, 7–1, knotting up the Series at one game apiece. Yankee spark plug Billy Martin's three-run home run to left field is the key blow in the Bomber victory at Brooklyn's old ballyard. Mickey collects two singles and a double.

October 3, 1952: The Dodgers move to the Bronx to play the New York Yankees in Game Three of the Series. Yogi Berra will connect early in the game off Dodger starter "Preacher" Roe. Berra's round-tripper is his third (lifetime) in World Series competition. But the fates will turn on their former hero when it counts most. In the bottom of the ninth inning, because of Berra's passed ball on a pitch thrown by Yankee fireman Tom Morgan, two Dodger runs scamper home, which in turn provide the winning margin in the contest. In the home half of the inning, Yankee Johnny Mize comes to the plate to pinch-hit against the southpaw "Preacher." Mize propels a home run off the spit-balling Roe, but it is not enough. The Dodgers still win, 5–3, as Roe edges out Eddie Lopat, who has never lost a World Series match before now. The Dodgers take a 2–1 edge in the Series.

October 4, 1952: In the teeming ballyard before 71,787 excited fans in the Bronx, Allie "Superchief" Reynolds strikes out ten Dodger batters, including Jackie Robinson three times, and Roy Campanella twice. Reynolds will scatter four hits as the Bombers eke out a 2–0 triumph to even the Series. Johnny Mize poles a home run off Joe Black in the fourth inning which provides the Yankees with the only run that the Bombers will need for the victory. Soon after, however, at a key juncture in the game, Dodger Manager Charlie Dressen will put on a suicide squeeze play with Andy Pafko on third base and Joe Black at bat. Billy Martin, however, has picked up the sign from his position at second base. (In the minors, Martin had played for Dressen and will realize what the Dodger manager is planning.) Martin knew that a slight touch at Dressen's throat was the sign for the suicide,.Now armed with this new covert knowlege, Martin flashes the sign to Yogi, who, in turn, called for a pitch out from "Superchief." Reynolds will pinpoint his pitch, low and outside so that Black, the batter, cannot reach the ball. Subsiquently, when the play unfolds, sure enough, Pafko breaks for home and the play is on. Reynolds throws the ball wide and low, paralyzing batter Joe Black, who cannot put his bat on the ball. Berra receives the ball with Pafko twenty feet from home plate. The frustrated Dodger runner is caught alone and abandoned and "out" at the plate. In the eighth, Mickey Mantle triples and scores on a relay error committed by "Pee Wee" Reese during the play that gives the Yankees an insurance run. The two runs scored by the Yankees in the game are all Allie Reynolds will need as the Bomber righthander beats rookie pitching sensation Joe Black, 2–0. The Yankees and Dodgers own two games apiece in the Series win column.

October 5, 1952: In Game Five, played at Yankee Stadium, 70,536 excited New Yorkers and members of the hopeful Flock from Flatbush have converged in the Bronx to root on their Big Apple big leaguers. In the fifth inning, Duke Snider poles a two-run home run into the right field grandstand. In response, Johnny Mize blasts a three-run home run off Carl Erskine in the bottom of the fifth inning. It is the third consecutive World Series contest in which Johnny Mize has homered—an unprecedented achievement in World Series competition. (This impressive feat will ultimately be shared by Hank Bauer of the 1958 New York Yankees and Reggie Jackson of the 1977 New York Yankees.) Still, in the fifth frame with the Yankees in the lead, 5–4, there is an immediate meeting on the mound between Dressen and Erskine. Erskine is frantic, thinking, "In the fifth inning my control slips. A walk. Some hits, Mize rips one. I'm behind 5–4. And here comes Dressen. I'm thinking, 'Oh, no. I got good stuff.' My curve was sharp. It was October fifth. My fifth wedding anniversary. The fifth inning [of the fifth game]. I've given the Yankees five runs. Five must be my unlucky number."...The fives had done me in. Suddenly, Dressen says, "Isn't this your anniversary? Are you gonna take Betty out and celebrate tonight?" Erskine is dumfounded, and thinks, "I can't believe it. There's seventy thousand people watching, more than live in my hometown, Anderson, Indiana, and he's asking me what I'm doing that night. I tell him, yes, I was planning to take Betty someplace quiet. 'Well,' Dressen says, 'then see if you can get this game over before it gets dark.' I get the next nineteen in a row."

After this brief exchange, Dressen departs and Erskine, the lean fastballer from the land of Hoosiers proceeds to settle down very nicely. For the next four innings, the righthander holds the Bronx Bombers to a measley hit. The proud hurler from the Heartland has not been short of help. The gazelle-like Duke Snider has made a sensational leaping catch of a long drive by Johnny Mize in deep right-center field, climbing the wall near the scoreboard to do it. Andy Pafko contributes a mighty effort as well, leaving his feet to make a leaping catch to rob the Yankees of another home run. And Carl Furillo, nicknamed the "Reading Rifle" because of the cannon strength of his throwing arm in rifling out aggressive runners, also leaps up gamely at the low fence railing, which serves once more to steal yet another Bomber, Gene Woodling, of another Yankee round-tripper.

Erskine has been masterful in his toil, but is showing signs of cracking. His teammates and one umpire pick up the slack. One of Erskine's 19 consecutive "outs" later proves to be tainted. Leading off the 10th frame, pitcher Johnny Sain dribbles a grounder to Jackie Robinson at second base. Jackie makes the stop but has difficulty getting it out of his glove. He throws hurriedly to Gil Hodges at first base, but the ball arrives after Sain has already stepped on the bag, apparently beating the throw. This is not to be, however, as first base umpire Art Passarella calls Sain out. (The next day, an Associated Press photograph will be printed in the tabloids showing Sain's foot on the bag with the ball still in flight a few feet from Hodges' glove.) Afterwards, the next batter, Phil Rizzuto, bangs a hot shot down the third-base line. The wizard-like third baseman Billy Cox makes an awe-inspiring backhanded stop of the feisty "Scooter's" sharply hit grasscutter down the line. Erskine and his resourceful teammates have fashioned near-perfection, retiring the last 19 Yankee batters the Dodger hurler has faced. Throughout the game, in a Series record footnote, Jackie Robinson works Yankee pitching for four walks. Buoyed by this rash of good fortune on defense, the Dodgers move to the forefront on offense during the next inning.

The scrappy Dodgers produce the winning run on a Duke Snider safety in the 11th. As a result, after the dust settles on the on the mound, at the end of the game, Erskine emerges unscathed having gone the distance in this 11-inning Series classic. The winning hit, fashioned when "Duke" Snider doubles off the right-field wall over Hank Bauer's head. Snider's timely blow drives in the go-ahead and eventual winning run, assuring victory for the Dodgers, 6–5. Snider has driven in four of the Dodger tallies. With the breaks finally going for him and his sharp curve ball working its magic, Carl Erskine has finally tasted the fruits of the first World Series pitching victory of his career and gives the Bums a 3–2 edge in games played.

October 6, 1952: Before 30,037 screaming Ebbets Field paying patrons in Brooklyn, gathered together for Game Six, the potential contest which could eliminate the Yankees. Snider gives the Dodgers and starter Billy Loes a 1–0 lead in the sixth inning. He powers a ball out of the ballpark, a booming home run that sails over the 38-foot-high screen in right field, bounding over Bedford Avenue and bouncing into the service area of a gas station situated across the street—some 450 feet away. The Dodgers lead the game, 1–0. In the seventh, however, Yankee catcher Yogi Berra ties the game with a clutch home run of his own. Later in the inning, Gene Woodling singles and is balked to second base by Loes. Pitcher-hitter Vic Raschi then bounces a ball back to Loes, who cannot see the sharply hit, high-hopping ball coming directly at him until it strikes him on the knee, caroming wildly in the direction of first baseman Gil Hodges.

Through the open, sun-drenched turnstiles of the Ebbets grandstands behind the plate, the rays of the afternoon sun have shone brightly through the separated columns that splashed across Loes's field of vision. The Dodger righthander becomes one of the few ballplayers in baseball history to actually lose a ground ball in the sun.

One inning later, 20-year-old Mickey Mantle becomes the youngest major league ballplayer ever to hit a home run in a post-season game, a record that will stand for 44 years. The lightning-like, 400-foot drive is as magnificent as it is soaring, carrying high over the STADLER sign of the extreme left-center outfield panel, the left field/center field juncture of the center field barrier. Shortly thereafter, in the home half of the same frame, Duke Snider's second home run off reliable righthander Vic Raschi brings the Dodgers back to within one run. The Duke's second round-tripper in the same game represents the eleventh time in Series' history that such a thing has occurred. As a result, therefore, the timely swat by the "Kid from Oklahoma" will lead the Yankees to the top, 3–2. Mickey's insurance home run becomes the winning run. Once again the Series is tied, which—at three games apiece—sets up the crucial, all-deciding seventh game.

October 7, 1952: In the dramatic finale of the '52 World Series, played this day at Ebbets Field, the Brooklyn Dodgers play host to the mighty Bronx Bombers for the final face-off of the year in the baseball season. Early in this decisive contest of yet another "Subway Series" classic, a cat-and-mouse confrontation between the contenders' two pitching staffs unfolds. Every play is vital, since the slightest mistake may lead to either team's demise.

In the sixth inning, the Yankees snap the 2–2 tie and move ahead to stay when the clean-shaven Mantle belts a long home run off the Dodgers' rangy righthander, Joe Black. The ball is propelled mightily over the slanted right field wall, the 38-foot-high right-center field screen, just to the right of the SCHAEFER BEER scoreboard's BULOVA clock. The ball carries high and far over Bedford Avenue until it lands beyond a sea of scrambling Brooklyn teenagers running after the clout, now bounding into the parking lot of the service station across the street. The Yankees now enjoy a tenuous lead when Casey Stengel decides to bring in Bob "Sarge" Kuzava, his left-handed ace reliever. Starting in the seventh and proceeding for the rest of the game, journeyman reliever Kuzava retires the last eight batters in order. The situation that the lefthander has inherited is fraught with danger, however. In the seventh inning with the bases loaded, the first Dodger he sees is Duke Snider, who has already pounded out a record-tying four World Series home runs. Then, on a full count, after working the left-handed slugger cagily, Kuzava gets the "Duke of Flatbush" to pop up. The second batter he will face, however, is the clutch-hitting Jackie Robinson.

As "Sarge" works the battling Robinson, from the Yankee bench an aged, raspy voice is heard, as Ol' Casey barks at Jackie, yelling, "Duck-ass! Duck-ass!" Practicing psychological warfare, Stengel is attempting to get Jackie's goat by making fun of the waddle-like, pigeon-toed run of the flashy Dodger performer. Then, on a 3–2 pitch, Kuzava lets go with a slow, snappy curve on the outside corner. Fooled slightly by the pitch, Robinson pops up feebly between the mound and first base. Kuzava looks at first baseman Joe Collins while Collins looks at him. Both remain stationary, however. With Dodger runners circling the bases in case the short pop falls, Yankee second baseman Billy Martin sizes up the scene and knows that neither of his indecisive teammates can make the catch. Martin springs into action, charges forward, simultaneously avoiding the Dodger runner who is scooting towards second from first. Kuzava, still not moving to make the catch, starts calling out, "Joe, Joe." Collins begins to awaken from his temporary slumber. Now, beginning to move, but dangerously late, it becomes clear in this split-second that Collins will not be able to make the catch; it is up to the fireplug Martin, who, after dodging one Dodger runner, sprints into the grassy infield area, dashes towards an area just to the right of the mound and towards home plate. Just as the ball descends close to the earth, Billy Martin spears the ball desperately with his glove and makes the catch knee-high at the last instant, saving the game, and preserving the tentative Yankee lead.

Once again, the Dodgers will fall to the Yankees. The game will end with Mantle's long-range blow proving to be the key marker. Duke Snider, a National League veteran of five years, has established several World Series records on offense in this seven-game set. The powerful, clutch centerfielder has set new standards in the October Classic, collecting 15 total extra bases, while accumulating 24 total bases. The "Duke" has also tied four other records: four home runs in the Series, six long hits, eight RBIs, and two home runs in one game. Because of Snider's Series heroics and his long-ball glories in the National League, the "Duke of Flatbush," along with Mickey and Willie Mays of the New York Giants, will become one of the Big Apple's most scintillating sources of animated dialogue in the hot-stove league of the off-season. The newest, most facinating topic of discussion among Big Apple fans, principally, in the Bronx, Brooklyn, and over at Coogan's Bluff, and other baseball devotees everywhere, focuses on the question as to who is the best centerfielder in baseball. This fascinating debate will carry forward for the next half-decade. Mickey, Willie, and the "Duke" will each become legends of their day. It will only be evident after 1957 and the move to the West Coast by both the Dodger and Giant franchises that the Big Apple will belong to Mickey Mantle alone.

For now, however, the Yankees are the world champions of baseball. After the game, Jackie Robinson, having suffered through the deciding game's dismal results, moves into the Yankee dressing room to congratulate the hated Yankees. One of the Bombers that he seeks out is Mickey Mantle. Jackie Robinson tells the twenty-year-old sensation, "You're going to be a hell of a player." The opinion of the black pioneer athlete is, as he has been on many occasions, wholly correct and the young Mickey Mantle will never forget this moment of grace and courtesy. Mickey will always remember Jackie Robinson's gesture as in the wake of his team's defeat as showing "a lot of class," while giving credit to the other team.

1953 SPRING TRAINING

By the time of spring training the next year, Mickey Mantle has had off-season knee surgery. He has also happily awaited the arrival of his firstborn, as Merlyn, in Oklahoma, prepares for the arrival of the new Mantle addition, Mickey takes off for spring training and another year of major league baseball.

April 9, 1953: In still another sensational spring season, the Yankee traveling road show has arrived at Forbes Field to play the Pittsburgh Pirates. Actually, everyone has arrived with the exception of Whitey Ford, Billy Martin, and Mickey. Having missed the Yankee plane from Cincinnati, where the team had played the day before, the three night riders in travel grays realize only too late that their transportation to Steeltown has already departed. After screwing up the Yankee logistics the night before, the three delinquent ballplayers, out on the town in the Queen City, scurry to the airport in an attempt to catch a later flight. Once at the airport, however, they come to learn that a rainstorm has cancelled all future flights that evening. Whitey then comes up with the idea that the three ballplayers hire a taxi to take them to the city of the Three Rivers. And so it is, after a whole night of driving, that the three caballeros arrive in Pittsburgh just in time to suit up for the game.

In the game itself, the young Mantle provides everyone in the ballyard with a moment that no one will ever forget. In the seventh inning, the young slugger leads off while batting cleanup in an exhibition game against the local Bucs. Mickey is facing rookie hurler Bill MacDonald when the righthander grooves a fast ball to the powerful, if tardy, basher. Springing forward and unloosing his powerful swing, Mantle steps into the pitch and connects, propelling the ball in a monstrously deep and towering drive which soars to a tremendous height, spanning the course of the Pirate playing field towards straightaway right field.

Lofted powerfully in a high trajectory, the ball is jettisoned at tremendous speeds until it actually leaves the field of play at the juncture 360 feet away from home plate. The abused ball is still climbing when, soon, the clout becomes one of young Mantle's trademark "tape-measure" blasts, carrying over the 100-foot-high grandstand roof in right field and out of the massive ballyard. At this point in time, only Babe Ruth and Ted Beard had ever belted a ball over the right field roof at Forbes Field. For "The Babe", it was his final home run of his storied career. For Mickey, it is his final home run, his fourth, of the 1953 spring season. The Yankees lose the contest, 10–5, but 9,506 Buccaneer boosters sitting in awe of the titanic blast they just observed take note of the young switch-hitter's great power and will recall it seven years later when a more mature Mantle shows up to play their Pirates in a uniquely unforgettable World Series.

April 12, 1953: In the final game of the traditional subway exhibition series which concludes the Yankee spring training, the young Oklahoman "strong-boy" approaches the plate on this damp and rainy day to face Dodger lefthander Johnny Podres. While 6,000 drenched Brooklynites sit and watch the ball game unfold in the increasing drizzle, they begin listening to the following announcement, which airs out over the Ebbets Field loudspeaker system. The Dodger broadcaster makes a surprising statement, relishing his words, while reporting to the Flatbush faithful, "Now hitting, Number Seven, Mickey Mantle….Mickey doesn't know it yet, but he has just become the father of an eight-pound, twelve-ounce baby boy." Almost simultaneous with his firstborn's birth in Oklahoma, this declaration is made, and the young Mantle learns he has become the father of a red-haired newborn who is named Mickey Elvin, after Mickey's late father and his late grandfather. The game is not completed when, in the third inning, the rains come and wash it away. Now with a new family, the young Yankee centerfielder approaches the season with a new and exciting resolve.

THE 1953 REGULAR SEASON
21 HOME RUNS

H.R.#	DATE	OPPONENT	PITCHER	SITE	SCORE	ATTND.
37.	Apr. 17	Wash.	Chuck Stobbs(LH)	Wash., D.C.	7–3, NY	4,206

Griffith Stadium is a very tough home run park. It is in 1945, for example, that for the entire season, not one Washington Senator hitter cleared a fence for a home run in their own home ballpark. On this day, Mickey Mantle begins a legendary string of "tape-measure" blasts which will frequently dot the map of his illustrious American League travels. The Mantlesque "tape-measure" home run is born this day when Mickey launches a uniquely prodigious home run at Griffith. Borrowing a bat from Loren Babe, the young switch-hitting powerhouse is batting right-handed against the Washington southpaw in the fifth inning, with Yogi Berra on first base with a walk. The talented Mantle slams a Chuck Stobbs fast ball 565 feet to left-center which zooms out of the stadium, high and far, ticking the huge scoreboard.

The colorful Ballantine scoreboard itself is situated 60 feet higher than the last of the thirty-two rows of the distant grandstand bleachers in left-center field. The ball then caroms slightly off the scoreboard structure before bounding out of the ballyard, which itself is measured at a 515 feet. After "ticking" the scoreboard, the velocity and force of the blow makes the ball carom slightly off the high, protruding score board of the stadium. As the ball continues to fly, it sails past the turnstiles of the left-center field bleachers, carries over the street, and comes to rest finally, some 565 feet away from home plate. The ball lands in the backyard of Mr. Perry L. Cool at 434 Oakdale Street, a block away from Griffith Stadium. The horsrhide nugget of this historic blast is soon held by ten-year-old Donald Dunaway, who saw the ball clear the ancient stadium. The "tape-measure" shot is unprecedented in kind, and "measured" by paces made by Yankee publicity director "Red" Patterson. The Yankee frontman in promotions will proudly boast how he marched it off. The monster shot not only celebrates the arrival of his firstborn with this, his first homerun of the year, but it also proves to be the game-winner.

38.	Apr. 23	Boston	Ellis Kinder	Stadium	6–3, NY	10,045

With two outs and two on, Mantle propels a ninth-inning, game-winning, three-run, 400-foot home run into the right-center field bleachers. It is one of the few times this year that Kinder will lose in relief as he establishes a major league record for "saves" in a single season with twenty-seven.

39.	Apr. 28	St. Louis	Bob Cain(LH)	St. Louis(n)	7–6, NY	13,463
				(in 10)		

Facing Bob Cain of the Browns, Mickey Mantle is poised for the offering from the St. Louis southpaw. Out of Cain's whipping left-handed arm delivery, making a blur of the Browns' '53 arm patch called "Brownie"—the caricature invention of Brown owner Bill Veeck—the ball comes whistling towards the plate. Uncoiling from his right-handed batting stance, Mickey Mantle connects on the fast ball, launching a monstrously high and long, 484-foot, three-run shot that sails out of storied Sportsman's Park. Fifty feet behind the 350-foot-long left field foul line stands the grand and magnificent, the structurally dominant Budweiser scoreboard which sits atop the left field bleachers. Above the newly revamped scoreboard and the newly painted, red-bordered, grandly displayed letters spelling out "BUDWEISER," the ball sails past the left field light standard. The abused ball proceeds to fly over the left field grandstand, and beyond the new mechanical Budweiser "Eagle," logo of the Anheuser-Busch Brewery. The handsome bird had been selected by the new owner of Sportsman's Park and the new President of the St. Louis Cardinals, August Busch, Jr. During home run celebrations for the home team, the Eagle's wings flap in admiration to the home team blow. Now as the ball flies past the motionless sentinel, the mechanical bald eagle appears to watch in awe itself as the Mantle-propelled, white-rocket missile speeds past its remote perch of solemn monitor over major league baseball goings-on in St. Louis.

Yankee teammate Gene Woodling, who saw both the Griffith Stadium shot and this one this evening, declares later that this particular skybolt was "even better [than the Griffith shot], but they publicized the one in Washington so much that they had to lay quiet on that one." The handful of St. Louis witnesses experiencing the bullet-like flight of the towering drive, sit in a dazed stupor as they witness the sheer power of the blow. This particular long-range belt carries over the distant scoreboard in left field off lefty Bob Cain of the St. Louis Browns. Expert onlookers gape in awe, before estimating the distance at somewhere between 485 and 530 feet.

The long ball has cleared everything so quickly that it could only be estimated to have traveled as long as 530 feet. Bill Veeck will later recall that, the next night, Satchel Paige will be pitching when Mantle comes to the plate again, but this time to bat left-handed against the Negro League pitching legend. Paige will throw a pitch that Mickey tattoos, producing what Veeck calls "a screaming line drive to the centerfielder." Paige walks into the dugout and shares his impressions of the Yankees with Veeck. "Ol' Satch" Paige, remembering the powerful, muscular young blond kid who hammered the ball from the right side of the plate in the game the night before, now experiences this young powerfully built blond kid hitting left-handed against him. The great "Satchel" states curiously, "Jeez, them Yankees sure get them great kids. Last night a kid busts up the game and tonight this other kid hits one like that off the old man. Where they come up with two kids like that?"

Meanwhile, in this evening's game, the contest moves into the 10th inning, which is highlighted by a brawl between the players, beer bottles thrown from the stands, and extra-inning dramatics. Brown catcher Clint Courtney, the first catcher ever to wear glasses, is bowled over at home plate by Gil McDougald when the Yankee infielder attempts to score from second base on an infield hit. McDougald's go-ahead run is challenged in the home half of the inning when Courtney slams a long drive to right field. After the ball bounds back from off the wall, the outfield relay is on target at second base, where Courtney is trying to stretch the hit into a double. With Rizzuto covering the bag, Courtney comes in with spikes high. In the process, Rizzuto gets cut badly from Courtney's bruising slide. The fireworks begin at this point as both benches clear, featuring a classic face-off between Billy Martin and the irascible Courtney. Umpire John Stevens emerges from the fray with a separated shoulder. The largest fine in baseball history for a players' brawl, $850, is levied against six of the players participating in the hostilities. Courtney, the culprit who provoked the violence, pays $250. This particular victory helps the Yankees move into first place.

| 40. | Apr. 30 | Chicago | Gene Bearden(LH) | Chicago | 6–1, NY | 7,656 |

The young "Switch of Swat" belts out a towering 400-foot home run which descends near the railing of the left-center wall of Comiskey Park. It was described as a shot with which a fan interfered before it had a chance to clear the wall. The blast would not quite make the fence and should have been ruled a ground-rule double because of fans' interference. But the man with the last word, the umpire, will not see it that way and will rule the wallop a homer.

| 41. | May 9 | Boston | Willie Werle(LH) | Boston | 6–4, NY | 26,065 |

Besides the home run, Mantle also unloads on another pitch during the contest which carries all the way to the front of the right-center field Red Sox bullpen, where the fiery-tempered Boston outfielder, Jimmy Piersall, makes a sensational, home-run-robbing catch of Mantle's drive. In Jimmy Piersall's first full year back from being treated for emotional problems, the quirky but fearless rightfielder robs the Yankees' Mickey Mantle of the drive—which would have carried into the Red Sox bullpen in right-center field. The 21-year-old Mantle, meanwhile, is having a banner year in his third season, where he is destined to garner a .295 batting average, 21 home runs, and 92 RBIs.

May 16, 1953: At Yankee Stadium, before a crowd of 22,966 disappointed fans, the game between the Chicago White Sox and the New York Yankees is on the line in the ninth inning with the bases loaded and heavy-hitting Vern Stephens, a current, leading American League slugger, scheduled to come to the plate. "Buster" Stephens is the proud possessor of ten career grand slams. Chisox Manager Paul Richards sends up left-handed pitcher Tommy Byrne to pinch-hit for Stephens. Byrne is not your run-of-the-mill pitcher-hitter. Byrne has clubbed six career home runs as a hitter. Now, with the bases loaded, and facing Ewell "the Whip" Blackwell, whose skills are fading, Byrne pounds out a long, high fly that carries deep into the right field grandstand for a pinch-hit grand-slam home run. The Chisox win the contest, 5–3, as a result. As for young Mantle, the young flyhawk goes 1-for-4 and will thus sustain an 11-game hitting streak.

| 42. | May 25 | Boston | Mickey McDermott(LH) | Stadium | 14–10, Bos. | 28,371 |

Mickey connects for a 400-foot opposite-field blast into the right field grandstand at Yankee Stadium in this marathon game that lasts three hours and 52 minutes.

The Yankees win the last four games that they play in May and are en route to winning the first 14 games of June. At a May game played at Yankee Stadium, the Duke of Windsor will ask to meet Mickey Mantle. During the introductions, the former King of England tells the young slugger, "I've heard about you." Mickey's unaffected, wide-eyed response: "I've heard about you, too."

| 43. | June 4 | Chicago | Billy Pierce(LH) | Chicago | 9–5, Chi | 10,011 |
| | | | | | (in 10) | |

Mickey launches a 435-foot home run into the visitors' bullpen in Comiskey Park, while adding two other hits as well.

| 44. | June 5 | St. Louis | "Bobo" Holloman | St. Louis | 5–0, NY | 9,361 |

Mickey unleashes a 405-foot home run to right-center field at Sportsman's Park. Bobo Holloman's major-league debut on May 6th had resulted in the only debut no-hitter ever pitched in major league history by a rookie pitcher. Holloman had blanked the Philadelphia Athletics on no hits in his first big league start. The no-hit master-piece would be Holloman's only complete game in his major league career. Despite the heroics by the Browns' pitcher, Holloman's career will take a sharp downturn will lead to a hasty exit from the big league scene. Mickey's long ball will help hasten Bobo's exit.

| 45. | June 11 | Detroit | Art Houtteman | Detroit | 6–3, NY | 5,366 |

The switch-hitting Mantle of the New York Yankees unleashes a titanic blast at Briggs Stadium, powering a fast ball delivery from Art Houtteman which helps lead the Yankees to a 6–3 victory over the Tigers. The ball is slammed onto the right field roof of the old park by the left-handed slugger. With two outs in the seventh inning, an additional "tape-measure" blast comes off the bat of first baseman Joe Collins, who pounds out a long home run which will also land on the roof of the 98-foot-high press box over the 370-foot sign. The Collins blow off Houttemann is as prodigious as it is timely. Still, Mickey's shot is the game-winner.

The Yankees win, 6–3.

| 46. | June 18 (first game) | St. Louis | Bob Cain(LH) | Stadium | 5–0, NY | 15,953 |

Mantle pounds out a towering home run into the lower left field seats, adding insurance to the Bomber win.

| 47. | June 21 (first game) | Detroit | Hal Newhouser(LH) | Stadium | 6–3, NY | 26,387 |

In the first inning of the first game of a doubleheader, Mantle pounds out an opposite-field clout which lands 425 feet away into the rear of the Yankee bullpen in right-center field. This particular smash will awaken Mickey's bat, which had been silent for ten games. In the twin bill, Mantle will collect four other hits, including a double and a triple. In short order, however, Mantle will pull a muscle in his left thigh, which will cause him to miss six games. In the six games of his absence, the Yankees will drop four.

| 48. | June 23 | Chicago | Virgil Trucks | Stadium(n) | 11–3, Chi | 46,756 |

Mantle's round-tripper comes off Trucks, who is enjoying a 20-10 pitching year for the White Sox. On this particular pitch, Trucks jams the left-handed-hitting slugger. Many of the multitudinous gawkers who are observing Mantle and his reaction to the pitch (more than the fly ball itself) find themselves confused as the angry young battler slams his bat down in disgust as the very high arch of the ball appears to forebode failure. The ball, however, as teammate Hank Bauer will later note, "kept carrying" until it "went into the bleachers." Sometimes even when the young slugger misses, the result is the same, such is his strength.

| 49. | July 6 (first game) | Philadelphia | Frank Fanovich(LH) | Phil.(tn) | 10–5, NY | 22,297 |

In the sixth inning of the first game of a doubleheader, Mickey is coiled at the plate awaiting the first pitch from the A's lefthander. He has missed six games due to a sore thigh. Now he is appearing as a pinch-hitter in the sixth inning with the bases loaded.

Unleashing his mighty swing, the young belter pounds out a booming, 530-foot drive, another of his patented "tape-measure" blows. The ball soars over the left-center field, double-deck bleachers, and out of the venerable Connie Mack Stadium. It is the only pinch-hit grand-slam home run that the "Mick" will hit in his career.

THE 1953 ALL-STAR GAME
CROSLEY FIELD IN CINCINNATI, OHIO
JULY 14

At Crosley Field in Cincinnati, before 30,846 fans of the All-Star Classic, the National League emerges victorious, 5–1, as Cardinal outfielder Enos "Country" Slaughter has an "all-star" day getting two hits, scoring two runs, stealing a base, and making a sliding catch in the outfield for a clutch, stylish putout. Ted Williams, who is en route to rejoining the Boston Red Sox from his military tour of duty in the Korea returns to baseball, throwing out the first ball in the midsummer classic. It is the "Splendid Splinter's" first public appearance. It is also the only time that the legendary "Satchel" Paige will make an All-Star Game appearance.

Paige enters the game to relieve in the eighth inning, trailing, 3–0, to the Nationals. The 5–1 tilt, in favor of the National League, had been touted as a slugfest. After all, 18 future Hall-of-Famers are gracing the cozy confines of Crosley Field. However, there will be only one extra-base hit, a double by Brooklyn's "Pee Wee" Reese. Though nursing a "charlie horse," Mickey Mantle plays in his first All-Star Game, going 0-for-2 through seven innings before he is subbed for by Billy Hunter of the St. Louis Browns.

50.	July 26 (first game)	Detroit	Al Aber(LH)	Detroit	5–3, Det.	49,717
51.	July 26 (second game)	Detroit	Steve Gromek	Detroit	14–4, Det.	49,717

Mickey clouts a prodigious, soaring drive that lands on the right field roof at Briggs Stadium. The defeat, however, is marred further by a brawl between Billy Martin and Tiger catcher Matt Batts.

August 4, 1953: Before, 21,031 excited Bronx boosters under the copper-green roof of Yankee Stadium, the hometown pinstriped hurler Vic Raschi of the New York Yankees establishes an American League hitting record for pitchers. Raschi drives in seven runs in a single game. In the second inning, the versatile hitter knocks in two runs with a single. And in the inning that follows, the veteran righthander doubles to left, clearing the bases and collecting three more RBIs. In the next frame, Raschi collects another single, which again drives in two runs. As for his own contributions, though the young centerfielder will make an error in the contest, Mickey does go 2-for-5 with a double and two runs scored. The Yanks win the tilt, 15–0. Yankee hurler Vic Raschi has just established an American League hitting record for pitchers with his seven runs batted in against the Detroit Tigers.

| 52. | Aug 7 | Chicago | Connie Johnson | Stadium | 6–1, NY | 27,063 |

The Chicago White Sox visit Yankee Stadium, trailing the Yankees by five games. The pinstripers win the opening game of this crucial set with the Chisox, 6–1. The mercuric Mantle's round-tripper is of the inside-the-park variety which drives in three runs and complements home runs by Yogi Berra and Billy Martin. It is the game-winner, since after Mantle's blow no other runs are required for the Yankee victory.

August 8, 1953: The Yankees are hosting the Chisox in a doublebill. The Yankees win both games, the first contest with Whitey Ford's five-hit, 1–0 victory and, in the second tilt, Bob Kuzava's one-hit, 3–0 shutout. The Chisox season of high expectations ends this day, giving the Yankees smooth sailing to their fifth straight pennant. Mickey does not play in the game, nursing a slightly injured right knee.

Mantle returns to the lineup after being on the shelf from August 8th to 18th. For the year, Mantle will miss 14 games due to injury. Mickey has a sprained left knee, but because he has favored it, it has affected his "healthy leg" by tearing ligaments in his right knee. Mantle will play rather than sit. He will also wear a heavy brace for the remainder of the season.

| 53. | Sept 1 | Chicago | Virgil Trucks | Chicago(n) | 3–2, NY | 45,003 |

Mickey Mantle's poke off the right-handed fireballer proves to be a seventh-inning, game winning home run at Comiskey Park.

| 54. | Sept 7 | Boston | Mel Parnell(LH) | Boston | 7–4, Bos. | 33,123 |

Mickey launches a long drive high and long over the left-center portion of the inviting "Green Monster" against Mel Parnell, the southpaw ace of the Sox pitching staff, now en route to a 21-8 winning record. This home run was particularly significant since a few days before, Mickey had received a death threat from a Boston fan who claimed that he would shoot Mickey from the stands in Fenway Park if he should play in the series there. The FBI advise Mantle to skip the series since any sniper could easily mark him as a target from a thousand different unseen spots in the ballpark. After belting the home run, Mantle will recall later that he never ran around the bases faster than he did this day in Beantown.

| 55. | Sept 9 | Chicago | Billy Pierce(LH) | Stadium(n) | 9–3, NY | 34,691 |

Mantle swats a drive into the left field grandstand seats of Yankee Stadium.

| 56. | Sept 12 | Detroit | Billy Hoeft(LH) | Stadium | 13–4, NY | 11,543 |

On a 3–2 count, the young "Mick" connects for a high, rising prodigious shot into the left field upper deck. The majestic clout is still climbing when it impacts 425 feet away, some 80 feet above the playing field and into the upper tier seats at Yankee Stadium. The young Mantle becomes the 16th batter ever to reach this remote, high-altitude location in the massive ballyard, the left field upper deck. An Arizona professor cites that the king-size blast had probably been traveling at 155 miles per hour—which would have generated enough force to span a distance of 620 feet had the ball enjoyed uninterrupted free flight instead of crashing into the high grandstand. The three-run shot slams into the rows of bleachers a half-dozen seats beyond the upper deck's railing, crashing into the seats "with such force [that] it rebounded all the way [back] onto the playing field." (Only Zeb Eaton, Walt Dropo, and Jimmie Foxx have ever generated the power to reach this remote section of the park.) Yankee teammate Gil McDougald compares this drive favorably to the 565-foot Griffith Stadium home run, the first of the original "tape-measure" homers. McDougald believes this shot off Hoeft to have been hit harder than the historic April shot earlier in the year. The prodigious right-handed shot spurs a Yankee eight-run explosion. In the third inning, Mantle unleashes another towering shot which would carry some 420 feet to the left center expanse before it would finally be caught for an out.

September 14, 1953: The New York Yankees clinch the pennant at Yankee Stadium for their 20th American League pennant. The Yankees beat the Cleveland Indians, 8–5, when Yogi Berra blasts a two-run home run. Billy Martin also drives in four runs. The Indians will finish second in the American League race 8½ games behind the rampaging New York Yankees.

| 57. | Sept 20 | Boston | Mickey McDermott(LH) | Boston | 10–8, NY | 29,188 |

THE 1953 NEW YORK YANKEES

First Place: with a 99-52 Record under Manager Casey Stengel.

Yankee Stadium Attendance: 1,538,007

MICKEY MANTLE'S 1953 HITTING RECORD

G	AB	R	H	2B	3B	HR	HR%	RBI	SA	BB	SO	SB	AVE.
127	461	105	136	24	3	21	4.6	92	.497	79	90	8	.295

In 1953, Mickey Mantle hit .295 while the major leagues averaged .264 with both teams scoring an average 9.21 runs per game and both teams hitting 1.67 home runs per contest. During the 127 games that Mantle appeared in 1953, he played in the outfield 121 times as well as one game at shortstop. He also appeared in five games as a pinchhitter. Mantle missed 24 games as a result of complications arising from the off-season operation on his right knee.

Mickey's 1953 Salary: $12,500

World Series Winning Share: $8,280.68

Number of Games in Which Mantle Homered: 21

Winning Record When Mickey Mantle Homered: 15-6, a winning percentage of .714

THE 1953 WORLD SERIES

October 1, 1953: It is Game Two of the World Series at Yankee Stadium and the Yankees are up one game over the Dodgers. Billy Martin clubs a home run off Dodger lefthander "Preacher" Roe, which ties the game in the seventh, 1–1. The change-of-pace, off-speed artist Yankee lefty Eddie Lopat has locked horns with the Brooklyn spit-baller, both of them pitted against respectively powerful lineups. In fact, the Dodgers at this point in time have beaten 18 straight southpaws, such is the vaunted right-handed power of the Brooklyn Dodgers' lineup. Later, the Bums from Flatbush are in the field in the bottom half of the eighth inning when the young, dangerous, and sober-faced Mickey Mantle approaches the plate hitting right-handed against the "Preacher," the crafty portsider. With two outs, the score tied, and Hank Bauer on first base, Mickey Mantle belts a game-winning, two-run home run off the Dodger lefty. Though the young ballplayer, having started his swing, is set off-balance with one of the "Preacher's" off-speed deliveries, a change-up, Mickey more than makes up for it, making the necessary adjustments, while slamming the ball hard toward the left field foul pole. Dodger leftfielder Jackie Robinson reacts nary a bit, simply keeping his hands on his knees, rightfully certain that the ball is gone. Robinson is correct for the screaming line drive rockets out of the yard. Mickey's drive is pulled deep into the lower left field grandstand. The blow wins the game, 4–2, for the hometown Bronx Bombers. As the Series moves to Ebbets Field, the Yankees luxuriate in a two-game-to-nothing advantage.

October 2, 1953: In Game Three of the Series, played this day at Ebbets Field, Dodger righthander Carl Erskine outduels Vic Raschi, one quarter of the Yankees' "Big Four." The Dodger hurler from tiny Anderson, Indiana, summons up a sterling performance, doling out a pesky six hits while striking out 14 frustrated Yankees. Two of the Bombers fall mercilessly to Erskine's pinpoint control and ungodly overhand curve ball. Not only does Mantle strike out four times in the contest, but so does Joe Collins. Mickey calls it "probably the worst day I ever had at the plate."

Meanwhile, Bomber backstop Yogi Berra ties a Series record by getting hit by a pitch twice in the same game. With the contest still undecided in the bottom of the eighth, Roy Campanella, as a one-time National League Most Valuable Player and destined to win the award again this year, comes to the plate. Knowing the peril that

"Campy's" bat represents, Yankee manager Stengel goes out to the mound to talk with Raschi. Stengel advises, "Don't throw him a high fast ball." When the bow-legged manager gets back to the top step of the dugout, he turns around and shouts at Raschi, "Don't throw him a high fast ball." Years later, talking with author Dom Forker, Raschi ask the writer, "What do you think I threw him?" The veteran righthander confesses that he threw Campanella "a high fast ball" and the Dodger backstop belted it for a game-winning home run.

With the strikeout record in hand, already in the book, Carl Erskine is facing Joe Collins, who has already struck out four times during the game and now stands on the brink of World Series infamy—fanning five times in one game, an experience suffered by one ballplayer only once before in Series history. But such an inglorious end to a miserable afternoon is escaped when the flummoxed Collins taps meekly back to Erskine for the final out in the game. Erskine still breaks the record for most strikeouts in a game. The Brooks win Game Three, 3–2. Campanella's solo shot not only wins the game for the Dodgers, but heralds an impending national television appearance that will take place later in the evening. Campanella will appear on a national TV hookup in the inaugural telecast of a "live" television experiment produced and presented by broadcasting legend Edward R. Murrow. It is a new format for television viewing. The show is called "Person to Person" and showcases Campanella at home with his family, beaming proudly over his 1951 National League Most Valuable Player trophy, his proud wife, and his happy children.

October 3, 1953: In Game Four of the World Series, Mickey Mantle strikes out in his first at-bat which gives him five Series strikeouts in succession and ties a World Series record shared by three others. Still, in the first inning, the brave Dodgers will thrash Whitey Ford harshly, rudely greeting their crafty opponent with three runs scored against and an early shower. In the contest, Duke Snider collects three hits, including two doubles and a solo home run. Junior Gilliam also enjoys a field day, slashing three doubles off the besieged Yankee staff. For his part, Dodger righthander Billy Loes chokes off the Yankees in the ninth inning, setting them down and certifying Brooklyn's 7–3 victory.

October 4, 1953: In Game Five of the Series, the New York Yankees face off with the Dodgers, resulting in a classic Ebbets Field slugfest. The tone of the game is set when the first batter in the game, Yankee outfielder Gene Woodling, plasters a Johnny Podres pitch over the wall for a leadoff home run. Then, in the third inning after a key error by Gil Hodges, the bases are loaded for Mickey Mantle.

After having struck out five consecutive times in the previous two games—only the fourth such kind of letdown in Series history—the young slugger comes to the plate to face one of the veteran Dodger relief pitchers. Though he is destined to strike out eight times in this Series, the Yankee switch-hitter faces righthander Russell "Mad Monk" Meyer of the Brooklyn Dodgers, hoping to make amends. Batting left-handed against Meyer with the bases jammed, Mickey assumes his stance in the box preparing to bat against Meyer's multi-faceted repertoire of pitches. With one swing of the bat, Mantle's five K's are forgotten as he powers one of the "Mad Monk's" sharp-breaking curves into a soaring home run towards the opposite-field sector. The blurring spheroid disappears high over the flag-bedecked wall in left-center field and into the second deck of the grandstand at Ebbets Field. Leftfielder Jackie Robinson moves slowly to his left following the long flight of the ball, but knows that it is hopeless as he watches the rocket shot land in the stands high over the TYDOL billboard in left-center field.

Mantle begins to round the bases as the ball disappears into the second deck of the grandstand. Mantle's upper-deck home run comes with the bases loaded for a grand-slam home run and sparks the Yankees to an astonishing Series victory over the shell-shocked Bums, who cannot keep up with the Yankee juggernaut. Mickey Mantle becomes the fourth player in Series history to hit a grand-slam home run. The mighty Mantlesque blow provides the difference in the game, as the Yanks prevail, 11–7. The timely blast complements the Yankee attack, which includes the aforementioned round-tripper by Gene Woodling, who became the fifth player in Series history to hit a home run when leading off the game. In addition, Billy Martin and Gil McDougald also shared long-ball honors for the visiting Bombers. On the Dodger side of the scorecard, Billy Cox and Junior Gilliam will attempt to offset the great Bomber offensive with home runs of their own. But it is not to be, as the Dodgers fail to respond effectively to the Yankee onslaught.

After the game, Meyer is asked about the Mantle shot and replies, "When you throw your best pitch and a guy hits it like that Mantle did, there's just nothing you can do about it. The pitch was a curve ball, on the outside corner and just above Mickey's knees. Carl Erskine had told me that Mantle had been pulling away from almost every pitch. But on this one it was as if somebody had told him where the pitch was going to be. He stepped into it almost before I let the ball go." Expanding on his answer years later, Meyer added, "I believe it was the longest and hardest ball ever hit off me."

October 5, 1953: In Game Six of the World Series, played this day at Yankee Stadium, the hard-fought, one-run contest is transformed in the ninth inning when Carl Furillo homers off Allie Reynolds on a 2-2 pitch that knots the score at threes. In the bottom half of the ninth inning, however, Billy Martin's clutch single up the middle drives in Hank Bauer with the winning run of the Series. The game is decided on the last pitch in the Series when the scrappy second sacker Billy Martin caps his October laurels by driving in the winning run of the last game with a ninth-inning bingo up the middle. In addition, the battling infielder becomes the first and only player ever to collect 12 hits in a six-game Series. This unprecedented feat paces his team to the world championship in six games. It is the fifth year in a row that the Yankees prove victorious in the World Series, a record that stands unparalleled in the half-century history of World Series play.

In the final analysis, Mickey had struck out eight times in the Series, but still managed to sock out two home runs, as many as anyone in the Series. The power-house Dodgers would not have to hang their heads in shame, however. As a team, the Dodgers hit .300, the highest ever to date for a losing team in World Series competition.

THE OFF-SEASON

Playing in a basketball game in a recreational league, Mickey turns his bad knee the wrong way on a fast break. The injury requires corrective surgery in which the physician removes a piece of torn cartilage. Beginning in the 1954 spring training session, Mickey will favor his knee, which will lead, for the rest of his career, to a host of other pulls and strains. Later, while writing with Herb Gluck, one of his biographers, Mickey will describe the physical consequences of this accident in the book titled *The Mick*. Mantle explained his injury as follows: "As a result, I began favoring that leg, which eventually weakened the other knee and led to pulls and strains elsewhere. The arms, the shoulders, the back—they dogged me season after season. Nobody to blame but myself."

After pressure from Yankee doctors, Mickey consents to a knee operation in November which will hopefully stop the steady deterioration of his right knee. At this point in time, however, there will be a permanent five-per-cent loss of efficiency in the knee, ten percent at the most. It will never be recovered. The loose cartilage must be removed or the knee will simply get worse.

Mickey's long-ball power and growing dominance in the American League is in evidence in this game against the Detroit Tigers.

Chapter Four

COMING OF AGE

—1954 & 1955—

In the Nation and the World: Outside baseball in 1954, prosperity in the mid-Fifties was balanced by the disturbing ever-present ramifications of the Cold War and the first real advances of a growing civil rights movement in the United States. President Eisenhower authorized a slight modification in the Nation's "Pledge of Allegiance," altering the text from "one nation indivisible" to read: "one nation, under God, indivisible..." Across the land, gas prices rose from the 1954 rates of 21 cents per gallon to a hefty 29 cents per gallon. Meanwhile, the U.S. Air Force had developed the F-100 "Supersabre," the first supersonic combat jet for air-to-air combat. It was also in this year the Supreme Court ruling in Brown vs. the Board of Education ended the practices of "separate, but equal" facilities, guaranteeing instead equal opportunities for all races and creeds in U.S. education.

In addition, there was a small war in Vietnam that pitted the Vietnamese people against their French colonial powers (who themselves would be defeated this year at Dienbienphu). Vietnam would then be divided into North and South Vietnam at the 37th Parallel. Meanwhile, Senator Joe McCarthy of the Republican Party was on a reckless rampage, trampling the civil liberties of various individuals. The megalomaniacal senator charged the Democratic Party with "20 years of treason." In another social note of import, the retired "Yankee Clipper," Joe DiMaggio would wed Marilyn Monroe, only to separate and divorce nine months later.

In the following year, 1955, President Eisenhower suffered a heart attack that caused the stock market to lose $14 billion. On the Cold War front, Nikita Khrushchev became the new Soviet Premier. The United States began to funnel $216 million in aid to Indochina. The first color television was marketed to the American public by RCA for $1,000. The presidential press conference was televised for the first time. The minimum wage went up from 75 cents an hour to a dollar-an-hour. And the Baby Boom, the fantastic postwar surge in birth rates, had created a shortage of 120,000 school teachers and 300,000 school rooms. Furthermore, in public safety, for the first time ever, smog became a public concern.

Fads: Fads in 1954 reflected the innocence of the period, as "mooning," that is, the baring of one's backside, served to convey the ultimate insult. Raccoon coats flourished, as did felt skirts with poodle appliqués. Americans were introduced to a new dance craze called the Mambo, which was sweeping the country; and other forms for being entertained would include raffles, bingo, and roller skating marathons. Pizza overtook hamburgers as the most popular snack. Hairstyle fads—flat tops, crew-cuts, and teenage "duck-tails"—were becoming commonplace among the populace. And "cruising" reflected the widescale practice of youthful drivers, roaming American streets in their hot rods with their radios blaring and girlfriends cooing. Liberace, his obvious musical artistry, his outlandish style in fashion, his candelabra, and his ever-present smile took the country by storm.

Innovations and First Appearances: 1954 introduced some revolutionary expressions to the American way of life. Swanson came out with America's first menu of TV dinners. The cha-cha, still another form of dance, was popular. Street newspaper vending machines appeared everywhere on street corners across America. TRIX breakfast cereal began to appear on breakfast tables. LEVI's faded blue denims became the fashion craze. In November, Veterans Day was celebrated, replacing Armistice Day. Colonel Sanders' Kentucky Fried Chicken was sold over the counter for the first time. Electronic computers began to proliferate in businesses all over the nation.

In the following year, Davy Crockett coonskin caps became the rage with young Boomers. Disneyland opens in Anaheim, California. And Jacqueline Cochrane became the first woman to fly faster than the speed of sound. The first automobile safety belt laws were developed. And electric stoves for home use began to multiply in American kitchens everywhere. Nieman-Marcus opened its doors. Two-seated Ford Thunderbirds would dazzle the American driver on U.S. highways across the land. And the Long Island Expressway was built. The Ann Landers advice column became syndicated. Chase Manhattan Bank, Sperry-Rand Corporation, and the Dreyfus Fund conducted business for the first time. Roll-on deodorants and Revlon's "no-smear" lipstick were developed. And only half of American adults went to church on Sundays. The construction of suburbia continued to grow as new housing units proliferated and shopping centers multiplied everywhere in the U.S.

Movies: In 1954, motion pictures released included *The Caine Mutiny*, *On the Waterfront*, *Seven Brides for Seven Brothers*, *The Glenn Miller Story*, *The Country Girl*, *20,000 Leagues Under the Sea*, *The Caine Mutiny*, *White Christmas*, *Sabrina*, *Rear Window*, *The Creature from the Black Lagoon*, and *There's No Business Like Show Business*. In the following year, Americans flooded movie lobbies to be chilled and thrilled by Hollywood efforts such as *East of Eden*, *Mister Roberts*, *Guys and Dolls*, *Blood Alley*, *Love Is a Many Splendored Thing*, *Daddy Long Legs*, *The Bridges at Toko-Ri*, *Marty*, *To Catch a Thief*, *Oklahoma*, *The Seven Year Itch*, and Walt Disney's *Lady and the Tramp* and *Davy Crockett, King of the Wild Frontier*.

Television: In 1954, television viewing took an upswing as more and more American households purchased the "boob tube." Thirty-minute escapes were reflected in various episodes stemming from programs like *Father Knows Best*, *G.E. Theater with Ronald Reagan*, *Your Hit Parade*, *Dragnet*, *The U.S. Steel Hour*, and *Disneyland*. The following year *The Adventures of Rin Tin Tin*, *Make Room For Daddy*, *The Ed Sullivan Show*, *The Adventures of Robin Hood*, and *The $64,000 Question* splashed across the tiny screens which were multiplying by millions in America.

The Juke Box: Pop music offered the first notes of rock-n-roll heard for the first time nationwide. Some of 1954's more popular standards included "Young at Heart" by Frank Sinatra, "Hey, There" by Rosemary Clooney, "Oh! My Pa-Pa" by Eddie Fisher, "Hernando's Hideaway," "Cara Mia," and "Shake, Rattle, and Roll." The next year, 1955, made way for Dean Martin's "Memories Are Made of This," Tennessee Ernie Ford's "Sixteen Tons," "Mr. Sandman" by the Chordettes, Fess Parker's "Ballad of Davy Crockett," "Cherry Pink and Apple Blossom White," by Perez Prado and his Orchestra, Julie London's "Cry Me a River," Georgia Gibbs's "Dance With Me Henry," "Young at Heart" and "Love and Marriage" by Frank Sinatra, "Secret Love" by Doris Day, Chuck Berry's "Maybelline," "Moments to Remember" by the

Four Lads, "Only You" by the Platters, "Rock Around the Clock" by Bill Haley, Mitch Miller's "Yellow Rose of Texas," "Three Coins in the Fountain" by the Four Aces, "Sincerely" by the McGuire Sisters, Bing Crosby's "White Christmas," "Something's Gotta Give" and "That Old Black Magic" by Sammy Davis, Jr., and Gale Storm's "I Hear You Knocking."

Deaths: America was saddened in 1954 at the passing of popular personalities of a bygone era, including actors Sidney Greenstreet and Cedric Hardwicke. Grantland Rice and Glenn "Pop" Warner, a sportswriting icon and a coaching legend, would die. And artist Henri Matisse was gone. The following year, James Dean was killed in a one-car accident. Aging actor Lionel Barrymore perished and Hollywood lost one of its earliest stars as silent screen legend Theda Bara died. Atomic theorist Albert Einstein, perhaps one of mankind's greatest thinkers, died in his bed. And Cordell Hull and actress Carmen Miranda were buried. In baseball, the old-timers mourned the passing of Honus Wagner, Cy Young, and Clark Griffith. In addition, Dr. Charles Kinsey passed from the scene.

Sports: In 1954, runner Roger Bannister broke the four-minute mile. The Cleveland Browns took the Detroit Lions, 56–10, for the NFL Championship. And the Minneapolis Lakers beat the Syracuse Nationals, four games to three, for the professional basketball championship. The next year, 1955, would see the Syracuse Nationals beat the Fort Wayne Pistons, four games to three, for the NBA championship. And on the pro gridiron, the Cleveland Browns knocked off the Los Angeles Rams, 38–14, for the NFL championship.

Baseball Transitions: Meanwhile, in this third phase of the Mantle Era in Yankee history, baseball began to shed its traditional cloaks as it bent its rules, adapting to more modern practices. The tradition between innings of the diamond's defensemen tossing their gloves at locations still on the field and near their fielding positions was now disallowed. Henceforth, fielders on both teams would be directed to take their gloves with them back to the bench after completing their innings in the field. In addition, baseball re-adopted the "sacrifice fly" rule, which remains, to date, on the books. The re-application of an old rule declared that a fly ball to the outfield that scored a runner who had tagged up would result in the batter being accorded credit for a run batted in without being charged with an official at-bat.

In the meantime, certain personnel changes for the year also made themselves manifest for 1954. The St. Louis Browns moved to Baltimore, where they opened their schedule as the Baltimore Orioles in their new digs at Memorial Stadium. The New York Yankees, meanwhile, lost Billy Martin to military service in early April. The Yankees also lost Johnny Mize, who retired, but they recovered the talents of Jerry Coleman, who returned from Korea. Significant additions to the Yankee destiny were welcomed when rookie slugger "Moose" Skowron and Andy Carey joined the club. From the Yankee instructional school in Phoenix, pitcher Bob Grim was promoted to the parent club, where he was fated to become a mainstay of the staff. Though the considerable talents of the young Grim were a gain, the veteran services of Bob Kuzava were lost. Meanwhile, the Cleveland Indians lost Luke Easter and traded Ray Boone to Detroit. Boston lost Dick Gernert and Mickey McDermott, but picked up the hard-throwing rookie Frank Sullivan. The Senators lost Jackie Jensen, who jumped to the Red Sox, but picked up the slugging talents of Roy Sievers and the pitching skills of Camilo Pascual and Dean Stone. The Philadelphia A's picked up Arnie Portocarrero, but lost Bobby Shantz. And, the Detroit Tigers celebrated the welcome arrival of a heralded rookie prospect named Al Kaline.

The following year, 1955, batting helmets became optional for batters at the major league level. And there were other changes in one of the front offices in the league, as the ownership of the Philadelphia A's passed from the Connie Mack family for $3.5 million to Arnold Johnson who immediately moved the franchise to Kansas City. It was also to be noted that 1955 would welcome the return to the Yankees of Tommy Byrne, while heralding the coming of rookies Johnny Kucks and Elston Howard. In addition and more significantly, in a trade with the Orioles, the Yankees made room on their pitching staff for Don Larsen and Bob Turley. As a result, the Yanks would make room on their roster, yielding up Jerry Coleman, Bobby Brown, Allie Reynolds and Johnny Sain. Simultaneous with these personnel alterations among the Yankees, other American League changes took place with some of their opponents. For example, 1955 would see Detroit lose Walt Dropo, who went to Chicago. For their part, the White Sox picked up Dick Donovan and Dixie Howell. The Indians lose fireballer Bob Feller, but pick up flame-thrower Herb Score. The Red Sox lost Mel Parnell, but added Ike Delock. And Detroit picked up Frank Lary, a future "Yankee Killer." Finally, much to Mickey Mantle's joy, Washington acquired Pedro Ramos.

THE 1954 REGULAR SEASON

27 HOME RUNS

H.R.#	DATE	OPPONENT	PITCHER	SITE	SCORE	ATTND.
58.	Apr. 19 (second game)	Boston	Mel Parnell(LH)	Boston	5–0, NY	27,762

At Fenway Park, Mantle's home run helps the Yankees sweep the Red Sox on the strength of pitcher Jim McDonald's one-hitter in the first game. Boston's only safety is a bloop single by Harry Agganis in the second inning. Mickey's home run helps the traveling Bombers beat the Beantown nine in the second tilt.

| 59. | Apr. 21 | Boston | Leo Kiely(LH) | Stadium | 5–1, NY | 26,356 |

Mantle pastes a four-master in back-to-back fashion with Yogi Berra as the "Kid's" drive sails into the distant right-center field bleachers.

May 2, 1954: Before 24,416 chilled denizens of the Bronx, Billy Hoeft of the Detroit Tigers twirls a one-hitter against the New York Yankees, stingily holding the Bombers to a fifth-inning double. The game is shortened, however, when the rains come, relegating the game to the books as an abbreviated yet official five-inning contest. The Tigers shoot down the Bombers, 4–0.

| 60. | May 7 | Philadelphia | Morrie Martin(LH) | Stadium | 2–0, NY | 5,805 |

The "Oklahoma Kid" slugs a game-winning home run which lands six rows beyond the left field, upper deck railing. The towering shot clears the railing and travels 425-feet, producing the game-winning margin. The ball impacts beyond the double row of boxes situated two decks above the 402-foot marker at the playing field level. Mickey's blow was the first in a tandem back-to-back sequence with Berra.

| 61. | May 21 | Boston | Frank Sullivan | Stadium(n) | 6–3, Bos | 30,119 |

Batting against rookie righthander Frank Sullivan, who is making his first major league start, Mantle bombs one of the hurler's pitches into the right-center field bleachers beyond the auxiliary scoreboard at Yankee Stadium. Mantle's blow comes after having struck out three times prior to his final at-bat in this night's game. The rookie Red Sox hurler learns a valuable lesson. Although Sullivan fans Mantle three times, he discovers that the potential danger of pitching to the young switch-hitter is ever present. One pitching mistake can cost you and your team.

| 62. | May 22 | Boston | "Tex" Clevenger | Stadium | 7–0, NY | 27,734 |

Combined with Mickey's long homer into the right-center field bleachers are two singles, a long triple, and four RBIs.

| 63. | May 23 | Boston | Bill Henry(LH) | Stadium | 10–9, Bos | 38,524 |

Mantle's long home run into the left field seats ties the game in the third inning.

| 64. | May 25 | Wash. | Sonny Dixon | Wash., D.C.(n) | 9–3, NY | 12,664 |
| 65. | May 29 | Boston | Sid Hudson | Boston | 10–2, NY | 21,992 |

Mickey wallops a towering home run to the opposite field and over the "Green Monster" at the 379-foot marker.

| 66. | May 30 | Boston | Willard Nixon | Boston | 3–1, Bos | 27,407 |

Mickey's home run ties game in the sixth.

June 2, 1954: At Yankee Stadium, the New York Yankees tag Indian starter Early Wynn in the first inning for seven runs. The burly righthander fails to get one out for his efforts. In comes Cleveland southpaw Don Mossi, who adds to Cleveland's woes with some faulty fielding. Starting in the second inning, however, Mossi will set down the Yankees in a short but superb stint of relief. Mossi will then be followed to the mound by a collective roster of relievers: in the third inning, Ray Narleski; in the fourth and fifth frames, Bob Hooper; Mike Garcia in the sixth and seventh innings; and Hal Newhouser from the eighth inning through the 10th. The four firemen will collectively hold the Bronx Bombers hitless the rest of the way.

Throughout the game, the Tribe chips away at the first-inning-generated 7–0 Yankee lead until the Cleveland Indians tie the game in regulation before overtaking the cruising Yanks in the tenth inning. In the course of the night game, Mickey had collected a single in the seven-run, first-inning outburst, he scored one run and drove in another. But like the rest of his teammates, he will be hitless the rest of the way. He will also be rudely awakened to the difficult prospect of overcoming the great expanse of Yankee Stadium's great "Death Valley." At one point, Mickey connects for a clout which will span the same distance of Larry Doby's home run of some 440 feet into the right-center field bleachers. Mantle's 440-foot smash, however, is caught for the putout by the galloping Doby, who corrals the ball near the left-center field wall. Cleveland wins, 8–7.

| 67. | June 6 (second game) | Baltimore | Don Larsen | Stadium | 5–2, NY | 26,768 |

Mickey poles a home run into the remote right-center field bleachers.

| 68. | June 10 | Detroit | Ralph Branca | Stadium | 9–5, NY | 7,058 |

Mantle and Bobby Brown belt out back-to-back home runs.

69.	June 20 (first game)	Chicago	Mike Fornieles	Chi.	16–6, NY	37,075
70.	June 26	Cleveland	Bob Hooper	Cleveland(n)	11–9, NY	46,192
71.	June 30	Boston	Willard Nixon	Boston	6–1, Bos	9,399

Mantle powers a long, fifth-inning fly to the opposite field for a home run. The ball sails over the netting above the "Green Monster." It is the only run for the Bombers in a 6–1 loss. Pitcher Tom Morgan of the New York Yankees is pitching the third inning of the Yankee game when he hits three batters in the same inning that ties a major league record. Morgan had started the inning giving up a double to Grady Hatton.

The unfortunate Red Sox batters to feel the sting of Morgan's wildness are Billy Goodman on the hand, Milt Bolling in the back, and Ted Lepcio on the hand. At this point in the season, the young Mantle is tied with Yogi Berra for the team leadership in RBIs.

| 72. | July 1 | Boston | Frank Sullivan | Bos. | 8–7, NY | 8,118 |
| 73. | July 3 | Wash. | Bob Porterfield | Stadium(n) | 3–2, NY | 20,011 |

In a Stadium night game, Mantle launches an opposite-field, three-run, game-winning home run 400 feet into the left field seats off the Washington righthander,.The talented Porterfield generated a 22-10 pitching record the year before.

| 74. | July 5 | Philadelphia | Arnie Portocarrero | Philadelphia | 7–4, NY | 19,661 |
| | (first game) | | | | | |

Mantle's shot comes back-to-back with Joe Collins and proves to be a game-winner.

| 75. | July 7 | Boston | Tom Brewer | Stadium | 17–9, NY | 12,910 |

Mickey's shot lands in a towering arc into the right field upper deck at Yankee Stadium. Mantle adds two other hits during the slugfest.

THE 1954 ALL-STAR GAME

MUNICIPAL STADIUM IN CLEVELAND, OHIO
JULY 13

At Cleveland's Municipal Stadium, the American League All-Stars pound out an 11–9 victory over their National League counterparts in what proves to be the highest-scoring game in the history of the midsummer classic. Hometown slugger Al Rosen, playing with an injured index finger, goes 3-for-4, including a home run off Phillies ace Robin Roberts. Rosen will add a second home run to his performance, knocking in five RBIs during the contest. In the eighth inning, in what will have been the go-ahead run, Cardinal sparkplug "Red" Schoendienst is caught as he attempts to steal home off Washington Senator lefthander Dean Stone. The Senator lefty is given credit for the win of the All-Star Game without having retired even one batter.

Meanwhile, appearing for the first time in the midsummer classic is the sensational Willie Mays, who will, from this point on, play in the midseason All-Star Game each year for the remainder of his 22-year career: 24 All-Star Games with 17 National League victories. On the other hand, on this day Duke Snider goes 3-for-4 with 2 RBIs. As for Mickey, the last of the "Big Apple" All-Star centerfielders, the Yankee slugger strikes out once but still goes 2-for-5 with one run scored. When he crosses the plate, the Mantle tally proves to be the tie-breaker. As for Casey Stengel, Manager of the American League All-Stars for the first time out of four tries, leads the American League to their ultimate victory.

| 76. | July 19 | Detroit | Ted Gray(LH) | Stadium | 8–0, NY | 7,463 |

Mantle poles a home run deep into the left field grandstand bleachers at Yankee Stadium.

77.	July 22	Chicago	Don Johnson	Stadium	4–3, NY	36,732
	(first game)				(in 10)	

With two outs in the 10th inning, Mickey rips into the pitch, dispatching the ball forthwith for a 10th-inning, game-winning home run that sails beyond the stadium's playing field.

78.	July 28	Chicago	Jack Harshman(LH)	Chicago	7–5, NY	38,056

Mantle unleashes a ninth-inning, three-run game-winner at Yankee Stadium.

79.	Aug. 5	Cleveland	Early Wynn	Cleveland	5–2, NY	49,483
					Ladies' Day	(32,144 pd.)

Mantle has come to accept the burly righthander as the most generous "cousin" that he will develop during his career, connecting for 13 home runs—more than any other pitcher in his career. Wynn, a future Hall-of Famer, is at the top of his skills en route this year to a 23-11 pitching record.

80.	Aug. 5	Cleveland	Ray Narleski	Cleveland	5–2, NY	49,483
					Ladies' Day	(32,144 pd.)

Before a Ladies' Day crowd of 49,483 excited Cleveland Indian boosters, Joe Collins has really connected as the ball arches high and very deep into the upper deck of the right-center field bleachers. The ball lands short of the Chesterfeld King sign that hangs on the rafters of the right-center field grandstand. After circling the bases, Collins passes Mickey in the on-deck circle, and snidely quips, "Go chase that, kid!" On the next pitch, Mantle, himself, connects off Narleski, which makes Collins' legitimately long home run ball pale in comparison. Mantle's ball soars over Collins' landing area and some 75 feet past the distant Chesterfeld King cigarette sign in the right-center grandstand. After circling the bases, his head characteristically down, Mantle crosses the plate and walks over to the dugout bench. Sitting next to Collins on the pine, without looking at his teammate, the young blond crew cutted slugger asks the hefty first baseman, "What did you say, Joe?" An ungracious loser, Collins snarls, saying bitterly, "Go shit in your hat." The young Mantle laughs. Then both men laugh. The Cleveland fans, however, are not amused. The back-to-back numbers sink the Tribe.

81.	Aug. 8	Detroit	Billy Hoeft(LH)	Detroit	10–8, Det	24,431
					(in 10)	

Besides belting one ball that makes the seats, Mickey pounds another ball which sails out of Briggs Stadium down the right field line, over the 100-foot-high roof, and out of the ballpark. The ball clears Briggs but soars out of the stadium in foul territory, missing the pole by six feet. With two men aboard, the three-run shot would have won the game and probably would have been the longest opposite-field home run ever hit by anyone anywhere.

82.	Aug. 12	Philadelphia	Arnie Portocarrero	Stadium	5–4, NY	13,890
	(first game)					

Mickey's late-inning, game-winning blast is a solo shot which provides the winning margin.

83.	Aug. 15	Boston	Hal "Skinny" Brown	Stadium	14–9, NY	23,822
84.	Sept. 2	Cleveland	Bob Lemon	Stadium	3–2, NY	39,494

Mickey belts a towering drive that carries halfway up the right field upper deck at Yankee Stadium, 100 feet above the 340-foot sign. Mantle's round-tripper comes off Lemon during one of the future Hall of Fame hurler's banner years, in the midst of forging a 23–7 record.

September 12, 1954: At Municipal Stadium in Cleveland, the Indians play host to the New York Yankees before 84,587 paying customers, the largest-ever attendance for baseball observances in American League history. The Yankees are in town to play a double-header with the league-leading Indians. Before this all-time capacity crowd for a twinight twin bill in Cleveland, however, the New York Yankees are desperately attempting to seize their sixth pennant in a row. The Indians quash the Yankees' hopes by sweeping the doubleheader with 4–1 and 3–2 victories.

The youthful ballplayer is playing before the largest crowd to date in his life and strikes out three times. But he is not that nervous: The twenty-one-year-old slugger does get one hit, connecting for a double and scoring the lone Yankee run in the 4–1 loss. In the second game, Mantle fans again three more times and the Bombers lose, 3–2, having dropped two. The two losses place the Yankees 8½ games back and effectively eliminate the pin-striped Bombers from the race. The Yankees are out of the running and will never challenge the mighty Tribe again.

September 19, 1954: At Shibe Park, two days after the Cleveland Indians have clinched the American League pennant, the Philadelphia Athletics play their final American League game in the "City of Brotherly Love." The A's nine are scheduled next year to transfer their franchise operations to Kansas City. In the game itself, before a paltry gathering of 1,715 diehard fans, the touring Yankees beat the exiting Athletics, 4–2. It is the Yankees' 100th victory this year and a feat not accomplished by any of Casey Stengel's pennant-winning rosters ever. Despite hitting the century mark, the Yankees still finish in second place. For his part, Mickey goes 0-for-4.

September 26, 1954: With the AL pennant already clinched by Cleveland, Yankee manager Casey Stengel seeks to establish a record-setting number of wins for a second-place finisher. Pursuing this end, Stengel stacks the infield with power hitters, starting with Eddie Robinson at first base, Bill "Moose" Skowron at second base, Mickey Mantle at shortstop, and Yogi Berra at third base. The strategy backfires, however, as the Yankees still manage a loss against the Philadelphia A's, 8–6. For the year, Mantle has missed eight games because of continuing problems with his right knee.

THE 1954 NEW YORK YANKEES

Second Place: with a 103–51 record under Manager Casey Stengel

Yankee Stadium Attendance: 1,475,171

Mickey Mantle's League-leading Categories: Mickey Mantle with 129 runs scored (led majors) and with 107 strikeouts (led majors). On defense, Mickey would lead all American League outfielders with 25 assists.

MICKEY MANTLE'S 1954 HITTING RECORD

G	AB	R	H	2B	3B	HR	HR%	RBI	SA	BB	SO	SB	AVE.
146	543	129	163	17	12	27	5.0	102	.525	102	107	5	.300

In 1954, Mickey Mantle hit .300 while the major leagues averaged .261, with both teams scoring an average 8.76 runs per game and both teams hitting 1.57 home runs per contest. During the 146 games that Mickey Mantle appeared in 1954, he played in the outfield 144 times as well as playing shortstop in four games and one game at second base.

Mickey's 1954 Salary: $17,000

Injuries or Operations: cyst removed

Number Of Games in Which Mantle Homered: 26

Winning Record When Mickey Mantle Homered: 21–5, a winning percentage of .846

THE 1955 REGULAR SEASON
LEAGUE-LEADING 37 HOME RUNS

H.R.#	DATE	OPPONENT	PITCHER	SITE	SCORE	ATTND.
85.	Apr. 13	Wash.	Ted Abernathy	Stadium	19–1, NY	11,251

Mantle's belt soars high and far until it reaches the right-center field bleachers.

April 14, 1955: The New York Yankees become the fifth team in the American League to break the color line by integrating their ranks with catcher Elston Howard.

On this day, Howard gets his first major league hit versus the Boston Red Sox. In the last three years, the Yankees have been able to count on rookie crops that have contributed producers to the Yankee rosters, already strong, and now getting stronger. Since 1952, when Mickey became a starter as a sophomore, rookie regulars in pinstripes have included Andy Carey, Bill Skowron, Bob Grim, Johnny Kucks, Bobby Richardson, and Tom Sturdivant.

| 86. | Apr. 18 | Baltimore | Harry Byrd | Baltimore(n) | 6–0, NY | 35,372 |

Mantle poles a blast into the right field bleachers at Memorial Stadium.

| 87. | Apr. 28 | Kansas City | Charlie Bishop | K.C.(n) | 11–4, NY | 32,559 |

The shot off Bishop pushes the fifth run across the plate that is the game-winner.

April 29, 1955: Playing before the largest attendance figure in the brief major league history of Municipal Stadium in Kansas City—33,471 frenzied KC rooters—the Athletics play host to the visiting Yankees. The cheering throngs are ecstatic over the A's 6–0 whitewash of the dreaded Bombers. The bats of the powerful Yankees go down meekly in the face of the southpaw mastery of tiny Bobby Shantz who surrenders a mere three hits. Mickey goes 0-for-2.

| 88. | May 3 | Cleveland | Mike Garcia | Cleveland(n) | 7–4, Cle | 24,813 |

Throughout the Fifties, the hardthrowing Garcia had put together the best year, last year, for giving up the fewest home runs in a single season—six. In his career, Mantle would pole four home runs off Garcia. As for this particular contest, a night game, Mantle's shot will come to no avail.

| 89. | May 6 | Boston | Frank Sullivan | Boston | 6–0, NY | 7,033 |

The first runs in the game belong to those runs batted in by Mickey Mantle's swat.

| 90. | May 7 | Boston | Ike Delock | Boston | 9–6, NY | 29,925 |

The ball lands 420 feet away over the 17-foot-high center field wall and into the bleachers at Fenway Park which breaks the tie in the eighth inning.

| 91. | May 11 | Cleveland | Early Wynn | Stadium | 4–3, Cle | 16,012 |

Mickey goes 2-for-4 with one run scored coming off his solo home run. Mantle adds another RBI against his tough-as-nails rival, but all in vain as the Indians edge the Yankees, 4–3.

| 92. | May 13 | Detroit | Steve Gromek | Stadium | 5–2, NY | 7,177 |

Mickey begins the day by socking a mammoth home run that is lined into the remote right-center field bleachers. Mantle's prodigious blast is belted to a point between the Yankee bullpen in right field and the 407-foot marker in right-center field. Hitting left-handed, Mickey's first-inning, long-range belt is the first of three home runs on this day, the most he will ever hit in a single game. As a result of his longball production, Mickey will drive in all of the Yankees' five runs in a game.

| 93. | May 13 | Detroit | Steve Gromek | Stadium | 5–2, NY | 7,177 |

Mantle's second titanic home run this day carries 430 feet into the distant upper reaches of the right-center field grandstand bleachers at Yankee Stadium for the second time in the game. Again, the "Mick" has connected left-handed off Gromek, borrowing once again the discarded bat of Enos Slaughter, who has recently been traded to Kansas City.

| 94. | May 13 | Detroit | Bob Miller(LH) | Stadium | 5–2, NY | 7,177 |

It has been a day of sevens. Performing before 7,177 cheering spectators, Mickey Mantle, Number Seven, who started the game with seven home runs for the year, is seven days removed from his last game-winning home run. He has added three longballs to his total on this day, which gives him a tie for the major league lead. Mickey had knocked in all of the Yankees' five runs in a seven-run game. Mantle joins an elite club of sluggers, seven Yankees in all, who have accomplished this rare feat: Joe DiMaggio and Lou Gehrig, who accomplished it three times in their careers; Tony Lazzeri, who did it twice, and "Babe" Ruth, Bill Dickey, Charlie Keller, and Johnny Mize, who each did it once as Yankees. Mantle's third monumental shot was rocketed to a distant point some seven rows below the great massive scoreboard atop the right-center field bleachers. Mickey's first two blows had been connected off righthander Steve Gromek, who recorded his second loss in seven decisions. Mickey's good friend Whitey Ford also got in on the "sevens," winning the game but retiring in the seventh. Even the Tigers played a bit part, not scoring a run until the seventh. Mickey's third home run is the most prodigious of the three, traveling farther, with more speed and arc than the previous two long-range clouts. The Yankees win the game, 5–2, as a result of Mantle's three colossal shots. The three wallops would measure together for a combined 1,300 feet. Choosing not to use his own bat on this day, while batting right-handed, Mantle had used "Moose" Skowron's bat to face the left-handed Miller. Belting home runs from both sides of the plate in the same game had never been done in the American League before this day. It is the first of ten times in his career that "The Mick" will connect from both sides of the plate in the same game—a major league record that will stand for 39 years until Eddie Murray breaks the mark with 11 such career occurrences.

On this record-setting day, there is also a character to Mantle's home runs that is unique to his longball prowess. All three of Mantle's four-baggers have been crashed over the great right-center field sector of the vast center field bleachers, spanning the great "Death Valley" three times in the same game, an unprecedented, unparalleled achievement. The final shot off Miller once again courses through the air in a towering trajectory and over the right-center field wall some 407 feet away and over the auxiliary score board just to the left of the Yankee bullpen in deep right-center field. This clout had been wallopped even deeper and once again towards the farthest reaches of the playing field—some 455 feet away. Mantle adds a single, going 4-for-4. Since before he was born, no batter at the plate in Yankee Stadium had ever reached the distant right-center field block of bleachers twice in the same game. On this day, Mickey does it three times in one game and from both sides of the plate.

May 15, 1955: In a double-header against the Kansas City A's, Mickey Mantle collects four hits in nine at-bats during the twin bill. In the last four games, Mickey has collected ten hits in 17 at-bats and is now batting a solid .311 for the year.

| 95. | May 18 | Chicago | Mike Fornieles | Stadium(n) | 11–6, NY | 10,600 |

In the play before Mickey's plate appearance, the bases are loaded with Hank Bauer on first, when there is a ground ball to opposing second baseman Nellie Fox. To prevent the double play, Bauer collides with Fox, whose relay throw after tagging out Bauer arrives late. A stormy controversy had ensued after Gil McDougald scores from third. The Sox claim that Bauer has interfered with Fox's attempt at a double play, which should be awarded, ending the inning. As the heated argument continues between Sox Manager Marty Marion and the umpires, Mickey and opposing catcher Clint Courtney look on. Finally, the ruling from the umpires is handed down. It is affirmed that Bauer had run into Fox before he fielded the ground ball. Bauer's interference therefore results in a dead ball. The umpires then wave the runners, Gil McDougald and Billy Hunters back to third and second. In the meantime, as the umpires and the Sox sort things out, Mickey turns to Courtney and says, "I don't know what all the fuss is about. I'm going to hit one out of here." Now, with the bases loaded, Mantle sets himself. On Fornieles' second pitch—BOOM!—Mickey belts a 400-foot grand-slam home run which ices a runaway thrashing of the visiting Sox.

| 96. | June 3 | Chicago | Jack Harshman(LH) | Chicago(n) | 3–2, NY | 40,020 |

Mantle pounds out a moon shot in this night contest when he slams the ball against the left-center facing of the second deck at Comiskey Park.

| 97. | June 5 | Chicago | Billy Pierce(LH) | Chicago | 3–2, NY | 37,561 |
| | (second game) | | | | (in 10) | |

Facing southpaw Billy Pierce before 37,561 White Sox rooters huddled in Old Comiskey Park, the visiting New York Yankees are led by the slugging Mickey Mantle in a double-header against the White Sox. In the fourth inning of the second game, Mantle propels a monstrous, right-handed, 500-foot shot off Chicago southpaw Billy Pierce that lands atop the left-center field grandstand roof of the ancient ballyard.

| 98. | June 6 | Detroit | Bob Miller(LH) | | Detroit | 7–5, NY | 9,538 |

Having returned to the welcome nestle of Briggs Stadium, Mantle unleashes a prodigious, ninth-inning, 450-foot shot that courses past the large and deepest expanse of the Briggs Stadium center fielf and over the center field background screen in dead-center field. While hitting in front of the 9,538 paying customers inside Briggs, Mantle has blasted a pitch from lefty Bob Miller of the Detroit Tigers which sparks four of his teammates to launch homers of their own in the 7–5 Yankee triumph.

| 99. | June 17 | Chicago | Dick Donovan | | Stadium(n) | 2–1, Chi | 33,744 |

The Yankee flyhawk propels the ball to a point ten rows up in the top tier of the tripled-decked right field grandstand at Yankee Stadium.

| 100. | June 19 | Chicago | Sandy Consuegra | | Stadium | 5–2, NY | 44,060 |
| | (second game) | | | | | | |

Mantle's prodigious home run ball lands 20 rows up into the right-field upper deck at Yankee Stadium.

| 101. | June 21 | Kansas City | Alex Kellner(LH) | | Stadium(n) | 6–2, NY | 14,932 |

Mantle muscles a first-inning change-of-speed pitch from southpaw Alex Kellner for a 486-foot home run to dead-center field at Yankee Stadium. The ball sails over the 30-foot, two-inch-high "visibility screen." Mickey becomes the only ballplayer ever to hit a ball over the 461-foot sign at the remotest section of "Death Valley" in Yankee Stadium. Kellner's let up pitch shot over the playing field scaled the center field wall, bulleted over the blacked-out hitter's background, and landed nine rows behind the railing, some 25 feet deep into the remote bleachers. Swinging at the ball right-handed against the left-handed Kellner with a borrowed bat from Hank Bauer, Mantle has connected viciously, smashing the change-up delivery of the portsider, and, by so doing, provided the force necessary to power the ball the enormous length of the monster drive. With this prodigious blast, Mickey scorched the ball some 486 feet. The ball is caught by spectator Oscar Alonso, age 38. It is the first time in the 32-year history of the green-copper-roofed stadium that any batter has cleared the distant center-field fence of the greatest of ballyards, the storied home of legends. The rising, laser-like line drive, as A's southpaw Bobby Shantz recalls, "rocketed" past Kellner's left ear and disappeared into the center field bleachers. "For sheer force and velocity, I never saw anything like it. It actually sounded like an explosion." A's manager Lou Boudreau and future Hall-of-Famer, declares that this drive is the hardest hit ball that he has ever seen in his 21 years of on-field service in major league baseball.

| 102. | June 22 | Kansas City | Art Ditmar | | Stadium | 6–1, NY | 13,953 |

Mickey belts out a long, 415-foot, game-winning blast into the right-center field bleachers at Yankee Stadium.

| 103. | July 10 | Wash. | Dean Stone(LH) | Wash., D.C. | 6–4, Wash | 15,243 |
| | (first game) | | | | | |

Mantle powers a 425-foot shot into the remote left field bleachers at Griffith Stadium.

| 104. | July 10 | Wash. | Dean Stone(LH) | Wash., D.C. | 6–4, Wash | 15,243 |
| | (first game) | | | | | |

Teammate "Whitey" Ford is working on a no-hitter that is eventually spoiled by Carlos Paula who homers in the fifth inning into the right-center field bullpen to spoil Whitey's bid at the "no-no." Paula would later double to help the Nats win it. In vain support, Mantle will launch a long, towering blow that will sail 15 rows high into the left-center field bleachers at Griffith Stadium. The "Mick's" ball had soared 450 feet into the intimidatingly remote left field grandstand.

| 105. | July 10 | Wash. | Ted Abernathy | Wash., D.C. | 8–3, NY |
| | (second game) | | | | |

In the top of the eighth, Mantle belts an opposite-field home run which sails into the imposingly distant left-center field bleachers, from the left-hand side of the plate— an opposite-field "tape" which seals the victory for the Yankees with this game-winning blow over the Senators.

THE 1955 ALL-STAR GAME

COUNTY STADIUM IN MILWAUKEE, WISCONSIN
JULY 12

In a classic All-Star Game finish at County Stadium before 45,314 short-sleeved patrons in Milwaukee, Stan "The Man" Musial of the St. Louis Cardinals poles a long, curving, high line drive off the first delivery of Boston Red Sox righthander Frank Sullivan in the 12th inning. The ball sails deep into the right field grandstands for a clutch, game-ending game-winning home run. The Musial shot will seal the contest for the Nationals, a 6–5 triumph over the American League, who has wasted an early 5–0 lead. At the top of the inning, the AL Stars had had their chance to strike back against a local hometown boy, tall and lanky Milwaukee hurler Gene Conley. But Conley will strike out Al Kaline, Mickey Vernon, and Al Rosen in succession. In the first inning of the contest, Mickey Mantle of the New York Yankees had ignited the Americans with a three-run home run off Robin Roberts of the Philadelphia Phillies. Mantle's flashing bat will account for another hit as well giving Mickey a 2-for-6 batting performance for the game. Only five All-Stars in the game will play the entire 12 innings: Ted Kluszweski and Red Schoendienst for the National League; Mickey Vernon, Al Kaline, and Mickey Mantle for the Americans.

106.	July 28	Chicago	Connie Johnson	Stadium 3–2, Chi		14,062

Mantle picks up Connie Johnson's pitch and slams the ball, propelling a ninth-inning long-range clout against the right-field facing of the upper deck at Yankee Stadium.

107.	July 31 (first game)	Kansas City	Alex Kellner(LH)	Stadium	5–2, NY	21,550

After Hank Bauer belts out a lead-off home run in the initial stanza, Mantle homers back-to-back with Yogi Berra later the same frame. Mickey's blast alights into the right-center field bleachers.

108.	Aug. 4	Cleveland	Ray Narleski	Stadium	6–3, NY	19,643

The ninth-inning shot lands deep into the upper deck of the right field grandstand.

109.	Aug. 7 (second game)	Detroit	Frank Lary	Stadium	3–2, NY (in 10)	39,145
110.	Aug. 7 (second game)	Detroit	"Babe" Birrer	Stadium	3–2, NY (in 10)	39,145

Mickey poles a towering, 10th-inning, game-winning, game-ending home run at Yankee Stadium.

August 11, 1955: Before 34,289 delighted Bronx boosters, Ted Williams of the Boston Red Sox collects the 2,000th hit of his career, a bloop single in the first inning over the infield to left-center field, falling meekly between the scampering figures of Mickey, shortstop Phil Rizzuto, and left fielder Elston Howard. The milestone safety comes as it does against fireballer Bob Turley of the New York Yankees. "Teddy Ballgame" refers to the lame hit after the game, calling it the "cheapest of the year." Then the future Hall of Fame slugger says, "What the hell, I'll take it." For his part, Mickey goes 0-for-4. The Yankees win, 3–2.

111.	Aug. 14 (first game)	Baltimore	Ed Lopat(LH)	Baltimore	7–2, NY	19,216

Mantle's shot to left field brings home the game-winning run for the Yankee win.

112.	Aug. 15 (second game)	Baltimore	Ray Moore	Baltimore	12–6, NY	13,152
113.	Aug. 15 (second game)	Baltimore	Art Schallock(LH)	Baltimore	12–6, NY	13,152

Mantle belts home runs from both sides of the plate in the same game for the second time in his career. The right-handed blow also provides the game-winning margin.

114.	Aug. 16	Boston	Frank Sullivan	Boston(n)	13–6, NY	34,152
115.	Aug. 19	Baltimore	Jim Wilson	Stadium(n)	8–0, NY	14,602
116.	Aug. 21	Baltimore	Ed Lopat(LH)	Stadium	6–1, NY	13,924
117.	Aug. 24	Detroit	Steve Gromek	Detroit	3–2, NY	17,598

Fashioning a back-to-back sequence of home runs with Yogi Berra, Mantle's tail ending homer proves to be the ninth-inning, game-ending game-winner. The ball lands in the upper deck of the right field grandstand.

| 118. | Aug. 28 | Chicago | Connie Johnson | Chicago | 6–1, NY | 50,990 |
| | (first game) | | | | | |

Mantle's blow is the game-winner for the Bombers.

| 119. | Aug. 31 | Kansas City | Arnie Portocarrero | K.C.(n) | 11–6, NY | 32,690 |
| 120. | Sept. 2 | Wash. | Bob Porterfield | Stadium | 4–2, NY | 14,594 |

Mickey unleashes a three-run, game-winning home run which sails deep into the lower right field grandstand at Yankee Stadium. Meanwhile, Edward "Whitey" Ford is twirling a one-hitter against the visiting Nats. Carlos Paula spoils Whitey's potential brush with immortality when he bangs out a clean single. It is at this point in time when Billy Martin returns to the Yankees, having fulfilled his obligation to serve his country in the military. The Mantle-Ford-Martin drinking triumvirate is whole again—the pin-striped night riders are reunited.

| 121. | Sept. 4 | Wash. | Pedro Ramos | Stadium | 8–3, NY | 22,327 |

Mickey's clout sails into the right-center field bleachers at Yankee Stadium.

September 7, 1955: The pin-striped southpaw Edward "Whitey" Ford pitches his second consecutive one-hitter in his last two pitching appearances for the New York Yankees. The crafty southpaw beats the Kansas City Athletics. Not only has Ford fashioned a brilliant one-hitter, but his opponent, A's righthander Arnie Portocarrero, had started the game stringing together a hitless streak himself, retiring the first 13 Yankee batters he would face. "Whitey" takes his no-hitter into the seventh inning. Then, with two outs, the crafty lefthander would will a low-breaking curve ball on the outside corner. Athletics infielder Jim Finigan will slice a drive towards the right field foul line. The ball would land fair before bouncing and curving into the stands for a ground-rule double. Portocarrero's eventual six-hitter will not match Ford's brilliance, which wins for the Bombers, 2–1. Among his own at-bats, Mantle loops a single over the infield for his only hit of the game.

September 16, 1955: In a stadium night game with the Red Sox, Mantle suffers a severe muscle tear in the back of his right thigh while attempting to beat out a drag bunt. The young slugger is shelved for the last eight playing days of the season. Mantle will appear two more times during the year in pinch-hitting assignments. His poor, injury-ridden status will also prove to forecast a poor World Series showing as a result of his deteriorated state of fitness.

September 23, 1955: After losing to the Boston Red Sox, 8–4, in the initial contest of today's twin bill, the New York Yankees clinch the pennant when they beat the Sox, 3–2. Mickey will not play in the game. With the American League flag on the line, Don Larsen with the help of "Whitey" Ford, who mops up the Red Sox, secures the 3–2 triumph. Protecting a 4–1 lead, and with one out and two on, Ford will come into the game in the eighth inning to nail things down. "Whitey" will face the heart of the hot-hitting Red Sox lineup that includes Billy Goodman, Ted Williams, and Jackie Jensen. The Yankees have come back to face Ellis Kinder, who has pitched to protect a one-run lead with two outs in the ninth inning. And then in the form of Hank Bauer and Yogi Berra, the pin-striped lightning will strike. Bauer's homer ties it. Then, "Yogi's" home run wins it. For the fifth time in six years, the AL flag belongs to the Bombers. Of course, for the game, Mickey will not play, still nursing his wounds and resting for the Series.

THE 1955 NEW YORK YANKEES

First Place: with a 96-58 record under Manager Casey Stengel.

Yankee Stadium Attendance: 1,490,138

Mickey Mantle's League-leading Categories: Mickey Mantle with 37 home runs, 113 walks (led majors), 11 triples, which ties teammate Andy Carey for the league lead, and with a .611 slugging average. Mantle was second in the league in total bases, with 316 to Al Kaline's 321. Mantle was also second with 121 runs scored to Al Smith's 123. In addition, Mantle was second in the league in home run percentage, with 7.2 to Gus Zernial's 7.3

MICKEY MANTLE'S 1955 HITTING RECORD

G	AB	R	H	2B	3B	HR	HR%	RBI	SA	BB	SO	SB	AVE.
147	517	121	158	25	11	37	7.2	99	.611	113	97	8	.306

In 1955, Mickey Mantle hit .306 while the major leagues averaged .258 with both teams scoring an average of 8.96 runs per game and both teams hitting 1.8 home runs per contest. During the 147 games that Mickey Mantle appeared in during

1955, he played in the outfield 145 times, while appearing in two games at short-stop.

Mickey's 1955 Salary: $32,500

World Series Losing Share: $5,598

Number of Games in Which Mantle Homered: 32

Winning Record When Mickey Mantle Homered: 27–5, a winning percentage of .844

THE 1955 WORLD SERIES

September 30, 1955: In Game Three of the Series, before 34,209 screaming Brooklyn fans at the old ballyard in Flatbush, the Dodgers are down two games to none. Now they play host to the Bronx Bombers at the flag-bedecked Ebbets Field. The game features Johnny Podres of the Dodgers pitted against "Bullet Bob" Turley of the New York Yankees. In the Dodger home half of the first inning, with "Pee Wee" Reese hugging first base, Roy Campanella drives a long, two-out, rocket-like home run to left-center field. The clout sails under the red, white, and blue bunting of the decorative upper deck. The Brooks take the lead, 2–0. It is a sign of things to come. The day belongs to the Bums. The Dodgers will bang out 11 hits.

Leading off the top half of the second inning, a gimpy Mickey Mantle approaches the plate, limping on his right leg. The young ballplayer has missed the first two games because of the late-season injury to his right thigh. Mickey's movements have been reduced from a burning flash to a turtle's crawl. Now facing Podres, he pounds out a home run off the young southpaw, who is 23 years old this very day. Podres had tried one of his patented change-ups, low and away. When Podres' delivery arrives plateward, Mantle detonates the offering. As he starts his canter towards first base, Mickey will watch the ball disappear over the remotest section of the left-center field corner of the playing field some 410 feet away. A pattern is emerging with the young Mantle. Even when the kid is in pain, he keeps his home run punch. Stengel cannot afford to keep him out of the lineup for too long. Though the young slugger is painfully hampered, he still manages to produce. Though he homers, Mickey is pretty much through for the Series. Team physician Dr. Sid Gaynor will later tell reporters, "If Mickey says he hurts, believe me he hurts. His pain threshold is remarkable, ten times higher than DiMaggio's."

Still in the second, and a long way to go in the game, Bill Skowron leads off second base after doubling. Then, Phil Rizzuto comes to the plate. After a conference on the mound with Manager Walter Alston, Podres gets back to work. Serving up one of his off-speed pitches, "Scooter" lines the ball to left for a single. Charging the ball, leftfielder Sandy Amoros takes the ball on one hop, fumbles it slightly, then let flies to home plate as Skowron rounds third and heads for home. The throw by Amoros is on line and precedes "Moose" to the plate by some 20 feet. Roy Campanella is standing at home with the ball when the former Purdue football player rocks into "Campy" in a mighty collision at home. Campy has manfully stood his ground for the play there and will tag the 197-pound Skowron high during the collision. In so doing, however, the ball is jarred loose as the powerful Skowron tumbles across the plate for the tally and a 2–2 deadlock.

With the score knotted at 2–2 in the third frame, Jackie Robinson singles. Typically, as Jackie takes his lead at first base, he proves distracting to Yankee pitcher Bob Turley, darting back and forth, stopping, starting, jiggling and juggling, feigning and menacing. Turley's concentration falters as he fires the ball into the ribs of the next batter, Sandy Amoros. The following batter, Johnny Podres, comes to the plate. Now Jackie, who had thrilled the Flock of Flatbush in Game One with a steal of home off "Whitey" Ford, starts once more with his constant bluffing, threatening, menacing, distracting. Podres lays down a bunt that evades the Yankee fireballer coming off the mound. Not only is the play not made by Turley, but as Podres churns down the first base line with all the speed he can muster, he actually makes it to first safely. Now the bases are loaded, with "Junior" Gilliam coming to the plate. Again, Robinson does his bit, faking a charge, disturbing the discombobulated Turley. Jackie's daring along the third base line—jockeying back and forth, dancing and darting—becomes too much for Turley. Some of the taunting Robinson's more ambitious drives down the third base line actually cover at least half the distance to the plate before he teasingly returns to third safely. Not only does "Bullet Bob" show a consummate lack of poise, but underscores it when he walks Gilliam on four pitches. Jackie trots home with the tie-breaking run.

Jackie's run breaks the tie. Robinson, with his vaunted aggressiveness and intimidating tactics, has manufactured a run entirely by himself, the exception being his own single that started it all; there have been no hits. The Dodgers are now up, 3–2. Reliever Tom Morgan comes in to spell the defeated Turley. Promptly, Morgan walks Pee Wee Reese, the Dodger captain, on four pitches. Now, the Brooks take a two-run lead. Campanella later adds a double and a single, which gives the All-Star backstop three runs batted in during this intra-city fray in the Big Apple. The Dodgers capture the contest, 8–3.

October 1, 1955: At Ebbets Field for Game Four, before 36,242 frenzied members of the Flatbush faithful, Mickey Mantle contribute nothing to the fortunes of the gray-flanneled Bombers, striking out twice, singling inconsequentially to right, and meekly tapping back to Clem Labine twice. On the strength of home runs by Duke Snider, Roy Campanella, and Gil Hodges and a clutch relief performance by Labine, the Dodgers beat the Yankees, 8–5.

October 2, 1955: In Game Five of the New York–based World Series, before 36,796 exultant Brooklyn rooters the Dodgers break into the scoring column first when Sandy Amoros homers to right field with Gil Hodges aboard. The Dodgers are up, 2–0. In the next inning, Duke Snider poles a home run deep over the high, right-field barrier which gives the Dodgers a 3–0 lead. The Yankees finally get on the board, when Billy Martin singled in Yogi. Berra had singled off the base of the right-center field scoreboard and advanced to second when Eddie Robinson fumbled the ball. In the fifth frame, the "Duke of Flatbush" once again would smash a home run over the 38-foot high right-field screen and the Dodgers are up, 4–1. "Duke" Snider has now propelled his second home run in the same Series game. It is the 13th time in Series history that a participant has accomplished this feat. This accomplishment ties the only two players who have ever belted two home runs in the same game twice, Lou Gehrig and "Babe" Ruth. The "Duke" has had a sensational World Series against the New York Yankees for the second time in his career. During the Decade of the Fifties, "Duke" Snider will lead all of the major leagues with 326 home runs and 1,031 RBIs, and all National League ballplayers with 970 runs scored.

Meanwhile, through six innings, rookie hurler Roger Craig has held the Yankees to one run on three hits. Then, tiring in the seventh, Craig would yield a pinch-hit home run to Bob Cerv that would soar into the left field grandstand. Elston Howard would then walk and that would be all for Roger Craig. In would come Clem Labine, to set the Yankees down. But, in the top of the next frame, the eighth, Yogi Berra would blast a home run off Labine and the score would be 4–3. The "Bums" do add another run, however, and Clem Labine shines the rest of the way. The Dodgers win, 5–3. For the first time in World Series history, a team has come back from being down two games to none to win three games in a row. The Yankees will come back in the next game, 5–1 at Yankee Stadium without an appearance from Mantle. In Game Seven, the Yankees drop the finale, 2–0, to Johnny Podres' masterful off-speed pitching. Mickey had pinch-hit for Bob Grim in the seventh only to pop out to "Pee Wee" Reese. After Elston Howard grounded out to the Dodger captain for the last out of the game, the Dodgers would win the game, 2–0. For the first time in their long history, the colorful Brooklyn Dodgers would win the world championship of baseball and Mickey would return to Oklahoma, an off-season of rest for his weary legs, and a welcome respite with his growing family.

Mantle demonstrates his long-ball prowess that would lead to one of baseball's most historic individual seasons: the 1956 Triple Crown title.

Chapter Five

BREAKOUT
—1956—

In the Nation and the World: In 1956, it was the pinnacle season in the career of Mickey Mantle and the United States was beginning to experience the pains and prosperity that came with growing into its role as a super power and leader of the Free World. President Eisenhower was re-elected with a landslide victory over Adlai E. Stevenson at the election booths. In civil rights, the war against segregation was manifested in Alabama with the Montgomery Bus Boycott, led by Dr. Martin Luther King, Jr. This nonviolent protest promoted a citywide Negro boycott of buses, which, in turn, led to the cessation of bus segregation. America was shocked at the Cold War convulsions taking place in Eastern Europe, as epitomized by the Hungarian Revolution. Ngo Nhu Diem was elected President of South Vietnam. Egypt and Israel clashed in the Middle East, requiring the dispatching of U.S. emergency forces to the Sinai Peninsula. Actress Grace Kelly married Prince Rainier of Monaco.

Fads: In 1956, lovesick teens began to wear their "steady's" ring around their neck. Captain Midnight decoders were making the rounds among the burgeoning Baby Boomers. And anything with Elvis on it was selling like hotcakes. Pop is dead! Long live the King! And the newest of family diversions—drive-in theaters—were flourishing, approaching 7,000 nationwide.

Innovations and First Appearances: 1956 was also a year when the Salk Vaccine was made available to long lines of children and their parents, who took advantage of this miracle polio preventative. RAID began its battle with bugs in American households. SALEM menthol cigarettes were sold by the millions for the first time in the U.S. All-steel convertible tops began to appear on the nation's highways. Proctor and Gamble began mass manufacturing PAMPERS, disposable diapers—an indispensable device for the increasing millions of Baby Boomers appearing at unprecedented rates.

Movies: Meanwhile, in 1956, cinematic epics had burst onto the American scene to dazzle the millions of U.S. moviegoers. Classics like *Giant, The King and I, Around the World in Eighty Days, Moby Dick,* and *The Bridge on the River Kwai* were making the rounds. And there was other big-screen fare in both light entertainment and heavy, drama-dripping sagas: *Carousel, The Court Jester, The Ten Commandments, The Teahouse of August Moon, High Society, Love Me Tender, The Prince and the Showgirl,* and *Paths of Glory.*

Television: 1956 is also a year when TV sets were blaring across the nation with their own flare for both drama and wit. Shows like *Alfred Hitchcock Presents, December Bride, The Life and Legend of Wyatt Earp, The Steve Allen Show, The Phil Silvers Show,* and *The Millionaire* were working their small-screen magic on millions of Americans who were staying up late to take in their living-room viewing options.

The Juke Box: Radios and juke boxes were adapting more and more to the younger generation's musical wishes as the times appeared to be evolving towards more and more youthful and finger-snapping beats. New standards appeared on the scene as bobby-soxers were proliferating in all sectors of the country. Such flourishing 45 hits include "Be-Bop-A-Lula" by Gene Vincent and his Blue Caps, Fats Domino's "Blueberry Hill," "Eddie My Love" by the Chordettes, Pat Boone's "Friendly Persuasion," "Great Pretender" by the Platters, "Walk the Line," by Johnny Cash, "Jamaica Farewell" by Harry Belafonte, "Long Tall Sally" by Little Richard, Vic Damone's "On the Street Where You Live," "Church Bells May Ring" by the Diamonds, Little Richard's

"Tutti Frutti," Doris Day's "Whatever Will Be, Will Be (Que Sera, Sera)," and Elvis Presley released 15 major record hits that landed on the charts, including "Heartbreak Hotel," "Blue Suede Shoes," and "Hound Dog."

Deaths: 1956 marked the passing of the most famous of movie vampires, actor Bela Lugosi. Also Big Band leader Tommy Dorsey had gone to his musical reward. And perhaps the greatest of all American women athletes, Babe Didrikson Zaharias, had come to a tragically premature end from cancer. In baseball, fans of another era were saddened by the knowledge that Hall-of-Famers Al Simmons and Connie Mack had passed on.

Sports: In 1956, the Olympics showcased shining performances in Melbourne, Australia, where some of the more noteworthy highlights would include a gold medal for the American basketball team led by center Bill Russell. American sprinter Bobby Morrow won three gold medals in the 100-meter dash, the 200-meter sprint, and 400-meter relay. And Bob Richards won the gold for the pole vault. Muscleman Parry O'Brien would win the gold by setting a new Olympic record with a heave of 60 feet, 11-inches of the shot put. On the pro gridiron, the New York Giants routed the Chicago Bears, 47–7, for the NFL championship, and, in professional basketball, the Philadelphia 76er's trounced the Fort Wayne Pistons, four games to one, to dominate the NBA scene.

Baseball Transitions: The face of American League baseball, as always, was changing. Some of the main vanguards were moving on as Cleveland lost Larry Doby, Ralph Kiner, Art Houtteman, and Ray Narleski. The Tribe did pick up the slack somewhat as they landed the slugging services of Rocky Colavito. The Chicago White Sox lost Chico Carrasquel, but land Luis Aparicio, a sensational rookie shortstop. The Sox also lost pitcher Virgil Trucks but signed up Bob Keegan and Gerry Staley. Boston looked forward to improving on its record from the year before when the club picked up the hitting wonder Mickey Vernon. Still the Sox forfeited pitchers George Susce, Jr., and Leo Kiely, while adding Dave Sisler and Bob Porterfield to the Fenway roster. Detroit bid farewell to pitcher Ned Garver but picked up righthander Paul Foytack. And the Yankees promoted Tom Sturdivant, having lost the once formidable services of the now-fading Eddie Lopat.

THE 1956 SPRING TRAINING

March 11, 1956: In what will become a showcase year for the switch-hitting behemoth, Mickey Mantle provides a glimpse of the coming of greatness. In a spring game against the St. Louis Cardinals, while playing at St. Petersburg, Mantle will connect for a long home run off Larry Jackson. The powerful blow will be jettisoned over the head of the all-time Cardinal great, Stan "The Man" Musial. The Redbird legend will later recall this blast, describing to Roger Kahn how the ball "…cleared my head [in right field] by more than any homer I remember. The ball traveled more than 500 feet."

This spring, Stan "The Man" has noticed, as have others, that there is something new, something different this season with the pin-striped, ripening long-ball legend. Musial will add his observations, confiding to Kahn, "He's looking better. People think that a hard swinger strikes out, just because he swings hard, but that's only part of it. It's not only the swing, it's the pitches that you decide to swing at. Mickey used to get impatient, make up his mind early and swing at some curve balls in the dirt. And he'd chase the high fast ball. Well, you don't want to do that in the major leagues, or else you'll see a lot of high fast balls out of the strike zone." Musial, the National League hitting legend, tells his trusted press friend, "This spring the kid is letting bad pitches go. If he beeps it up, and he bats .350, I can't say I'll be surprised."

March 20, 1956: At Al Lang Stadium in St. Petersburg, the young slugger, coming into his own, belts out a mammoth home run. The gifted switch-hitter is batting left-handed against Bob Mave when he launches a towering, soaring home run to dead-left, the opposite field, that missiles over the fence. The ball keeps carrying long and far, spanning a long lawn, and landing in the water, displacing a flock of angry pelicans fishing for lunch in Tampa Bay.

March 24, 1956: As the Yankees begin to think about moving north for the anticipated season opener, Mantle connects again, the fifth home run that he has belted in a little over ten games. On this day, at Miami Stadium, Mantle shows no favorites as he once again connects for another 500-foot belt that soars this time, against the defending World Champions, the Brooklyn Dodgers. Brimming with a justified confidence and a ripening maturity, Mickey Mantle is ready, able, healthy, and eager for the coming 1956 season.

THE 1956 REGULAR SEASON

TRIPLE CROWN-WINNING 52 HOME RUNS

H.R.#	DATE	OPPONENT	PITCHER	SITE	SCORE	ATTND.
122.	Apr. 17	Wash.	Camilo Pascual	Wash., D.C.	10–4, NY	27,837

In what will develop into the "breakout" year of his career—and with President Dwight D. Eisenhower in attendance to throw out the first ball of the baseball season—Mickey Mantle approaches the plate on this gray, overcast day in the nation's capitol. In his first at-bat of the 1956 baseball season and the imminent Triple Crown year, the maturing Mantle connects for a long home run over the 438-foot marker in center field. This is the deepest section of the playing field at Griffith Stadium, just to the right of straight-away center field. The ball climbs high and long until it soars over the 31-foot-high wall, crosses Fifth Street, and crashes on the roof of a building situated at 2014 Fifth. It is a deep, towering, and breathtaking wallop, a 525-foot blast by the beltin' Bronx Bomber. The rapidly vanishing blurry white object that had been the Pascual pitch disappears over the high right field barrier, leaving the slack-jawed, eyes-agape assembly gathered together in the nation's capital in stunned awe.

123.	Apr. 17	Wash.	Camilo Pascual	Wash., D.C.	10–4, NY	27,837

As if to celebrate the presence of the popular President seated in the first base presidential box, "The Mick" will launch yet another Opening Day longball. Crushing another home run in the sixth inning, Mantle's power produces a three-run special in front of the joyous Ike. Mantle's prodigious shot, another monstrous 500-foot home run, sails over the playing field like a rocket. The abused ball also clears the 31-foot-high wall over the 408-foot marker in center field to the left of the center field flagpole and flies into the clump of large trees 20 feet beyond the grand old ballyard. Only Babe Ruth has ever reached this clump of trees and cleared the 31-foot structure in center field. And only Mickey, Babe Ruth, and Clint Johnson ever cleared the 31-foot barrier in that part of the park. The Cleveland Indians' Larry Doby hits a ball just as far, but it does not scale the 31-foot-high right field wall.

The Mantlesque blast will later be considered the longest ball ever hit in that section of the spacious ballpark. Casey Stengel will later comment, "They tell me the other feller which hit that tree was Ruth. When his ball landed, it shook some kids outta that tree. The tree's got bigger in 25 years, and so's the kids "The Babe" shook outta it."

Following the game, the young slugger is asked to talk with the President. During the brief conversation, Ike will tell the young slugger, "Mickey, that was powerful slugging you did out there this afternoon. I don't think I've ever seen anyone hit a ball farther. You know, I do know something about the game. I played some ball at West Point." All that Mickey can bring himself to say is, "Thanks." Returning to the dugout, the young man confides in his teammates, saying, "Can you imagine the President of the United States shaking my hand? And me a former miner from Commerce. I sure wish Dad could have seen that today." Then, after a pause, he adds, "Maybe, I guess he did after all."

124.	Apr. 20	Boston	Ike Delock	Stadium	7–1, NY	17,543

In front of New York City Mayor Robert Wagner, attending the stadium opener, Mantle pounds out a three-run, seventh-inning home run into the right field bleachers.

125.	Apr. 21	Boston	George Susce	Stadium	14–10, NY	26,644

At Yankee Stadium, the pin-striped Bronx Bombers beat the Red Sox in what Mickey Mantle will call "one of those typical Yankee-Red Sox slugfests." After talking Yankee Manager Casey Stengel out of "sitting" him because of a thigh injury, Mantle, gets three hits, including a "tape-measure" shot, high and deep, into the upper right field grandstands. This particular 435-foot, two-run home run is especially elegant with its powered arc that threatens to scale the stadium's heights. And as it carries hard it finally slams 20 rows deep into the right field upper deck at Yankee Stadium. Red Sox legend Ted Williams, watching the blast soar high over his head, marveling at the sheer prodigiousness of the belt, will later claim that it was "the hardest ball I've ever seen hit off a Red Sox pitcher." Sitting in the visitors' bullpen in left-center field, another Red Sox pitcher, righthander Tom Brewer, who from his vantage point experienced the right-to-left panoramic profile of the "tape-measure" flight, described the shot, relating that "if the seat hadn't stopped that one, the ball woulda gone out of the stadium and maybe outta the Bronx!" The Yankee juggernaut also accounts for six other dingers that pace the Bombers to the 14–10 slugfest victory.

April 27, 1956: In the first game of the series with the Red Sox in Boston, Mantle powers a home run into the fourth row of the center field bleachers, thirty-five feet above the playing field. The ball is bulleted to its distant landing point before crashing backwards, out of the bleachers and down onto the field. Red Sox centerfielder Jimmy Piersall plays the ball as if it had bounced off the center field wall. The umpires can not determine that the ball has disappeared into the grandstand and rule that the ball is in play. Mantle, meanwhile, has raced to third base, having missed the flight of the ball, hustling on the basepaths. Mantle, though homering to center field, only gets credit for a triple. Yankee manager Casey Stengel argues loudly that the ball is a home run. The "Ol' Perfesser" protests in vain, and gets ejected. The Yanks lose the game, 6–4.

In addition, Mantle pulls the lateral ligament behind his right knee trying to beat out a drag bunt in his last at-bat during this game. Casey Stengel wants Mantle to sit out the next day. Mantle plays.

126.	May 1	Detroit	Steve Gromek	Stadium	9–2, NY	6,771
127.	May 2	Detroit	Frank Lary	Stadium	8–1, Det.	5,318

Mantle's ninth-inning home run is only one of three hits given up by Lary, who is en route to a 21–13 season. The Tiger righthander is in the process of earning the reputation and nickname of "Yankee Killer."

| 128. | May 3 | Kansas City | Art Ceccarelli(LH) | Stadium | 8–7, K.C. | 4,308 |

Mantle pounds out a tremendous drive: a fourth-inning, 440-foot home run into the left field grandstand bleachers.

| 129. | May 5 | Kansas City | Lou Kretlow | Stadium | 5–2, NY | 15,830 |
| | | | | | | Ladies' Day |

The pin-striped slugger pounds out a two-run home run off a change-up that sails up into the right field upper deck some six rows beyond the decks railing. Sports reporters take note of the fact that the young Mantle is 13 games ahead of Babe Ruth's 1927 pace.

| 130. | May 5 | Kansas City | Moe Burtschy | Stadium | 5–2, NY | 15,830 |

Number Seven slams a second titanic home run that crashes into the third-tier facade in right field, before ricocheting into the bullpen gate in right-center field another 100 feet away. A's field chief Lou Boudreau, long the witness to many of Mantle's "tape-measure" bombs, describes the 510-foot drive as "a line drive. I thought it was going out of the park." The blow comes in sequence to Yogi Berra's clout for back-to-back roundtrippers for the pinstripes. As if to underscore his versatility, after connecting twice for roundtrippers, Mantle lays down a perfect drag bunt down the third base line for another run batted in.

Yankee Manager Casey Stengel, as is his rule, asks Mickey to sit down in order to rest his body, currently riddled with physical ailments. On this day, Mantle has a knot in his thigh. He also has a sore foot from slamming a foul ball off his instep during batting practice. Insisting to Stengel that he can play with pain, Mantle refuses to ride the bench while he is enjoying this smooth groove in his hitting stroke. Stengel accedes to his slugger's desires.

| 131. | May 8 | Cleveland | Early Wynn | Stadium | 4–3, NY | 8,784 |

Continuing his dominance over one of the AL's premier hurlers, Mantle lines a home run into the right field seats against the bullnecked thrower, who once again is enjoying a 20-game-winning season. Wynn will compile a 20-9 pitching record this year, his fourth such season in the last six years. Mantle's seventh-inning blast gives the Bombers their 4–3 victory over the Indians.

| 132. | May 10 | Cleveland | Bob Lemon | Stadium | 7–2, Cle | 10,382 |

Mantle pounds a change-up into the right-center field bleachers at Yankee Stadium off Lemon who wins the game, one of the 20 games he will win in 32 decisions. Mickey will finish the Cleveland series, batting .446 for the year.

| 133. | May 14 | Cleveland | Bob Lemon | Cleveland(n) | 3–2, Cle | 18,950 |

In this night game, Mantle homers back-to-back with Gil McDougald. Jerry Coleman, current teammate and veteran Mantle observer, will add his impression of the bulky basher, stating that this year, beginning with his impressive Opening Day performance at the nation's capital there has been a significant difference in Mickey's batting approach. Coleman will relate to the *Times'*s Arthur Daley, "...it gave him confidence. I've noticed since that he's giving into the pitchers. If they pitch him outside, he'll slice to the opposite field. Last year he'd have tried to overpower them by pulling the ball anyway. The boy has come of age." As for this day, the Yankees, as a result of this loss, lose ground to the Indians, who take over first place by mere percentage points.

134.	May 16	Cleveland	Bud Daley(LH)	Cleveland	4–1, NY	6,263

In the seventh inning, Mickey connects off Bud Daley on this cold day for a 485-foot blast that carries over the center field fence at Municipal Stadium and into the center field bleachers. Only two players have ever reached this most remote center-field grandstands, Mantle's one of them.

It is also at this point in time when the personal side of Mickey's baseball world is dramatically affected as Casey Stengel opts to sit Billy Martin, Mickey's only on-the-road roommate and Mickey's alter-ego the past five years as a Yankee. Martin is Mickey's adopted brother, chief running buddy, and easily the best friend he ever had. Now, with a little helpful nudge from Yankee General Manager George Weiss—who dislikes the feisty, hot-tempered second sacker—Stengel has reasoned that it is time to give a young infielder named Bobby Richardson an opportunity to break the Yankee lineup. As it turns out, the days of Billy Martin as the regular Yankee second baseman are numbered.

135.	May 18	Chicago	Billy Pierce(LH)	Chicago(n)	8–7, NY (in 10)	36,192

Before a huge, awe-struck gathering of Toddlin' Town nighthawks, Mickey comes to the plate to take his cuts. With one aboard, Mantle homers in a steep, towering drive. His drive ties the game. The ball is rocketed in a highward arc that lands some 15 rows up in the upper left field deck at Comiskey Park. The prodigious blow comes off Billy Pierce, another of Mickey's "cousins"—who, this year will earn a 20–9 pitching record in the American League.

136.	May 18	Chicago	"Dixie" Howell	Chicago(n)	8–7, NY	36,192

Still in the same game, but now facing "Dixie" Howell, Mantle bats left-handed and belts a screaming liner to right field that carries high over the right field wall. The mighty, eighth-inning wallop lands in the upper tier of the right field grandstand at Comiskey Park and ties the game. Mickey, who is having a banner year, is, as a result of this evening's performance, hitting .409 and has 15 home runs for the year. For the third time in his career, Mantle has hit home runs from both sides of the plate in the same game. His accomplishments include two other hits, four runs scored, and three teammates knocked in during this skirmish.

137.   May 21   Kansas City   Moe Burtschy   Kansas City   8–5, NY   13,799

In the fifth inning against the Kansas City A's, Mickey Mantle of the New York Yankees propels another of his "tape-measure" specials, blasting the ball 450 feet to right field as the ball carries over the right field fence and the second more distant right field barrier separating the ballpark from the street adjacent to the ballyard. The clout comes off Edward "Moe" Burtschy, the Kansas City Athletics right hander. The Yankees win, 8–4. Only Larry Doby and Harry "Suitcase" Simpson have accomplished this particular long-range, "tape-measure" feat.

138.   May 24   Detroit   "Duke" Maas   Detroit   11–4, NY   8,305

Mickey goes 5-for-5 as well as homering back-to-back with Joe Collins at Briggs Stadium.

139.   May 29   Boston   Willard Nixon   Stadium   7–3, Bos.   12,287

Nixon is pitching a no-hitter against the Yankees with two outs in the eighth, when Billy Martin breaks up Nixon's bid for immortality with a triple. Being the on-deck batter, Mantle follows with a blast that carries deep into the lower right field bleachers.

140.   May 30   Wash.   Pedro Ramos   Stadium   4–3, NY   29,825
      (first game)

No one has ever hit a fair ball out of Yankee Stadium. On a 2–2 count in the fifth inning, with two Yankee runners aboard, Mantle launches the ball that, with the crack of his bat, is rocketed high in a soaring, towering fly ball that keeps climbing and climbing as it heads for the highest, uppermost reaches of the filigree atop the third tier of the grandstand structure. Finally, the king-sized clout peaks and begins its inevitable descent. The ball, now on the way down, hits the filigree within 18 inches of clearing the copper-green roof of Yankee Stadium. Mantle calls this shot off Ramos "the best ball I ever hit left-handed." Mantle also becomes the first slugger ever to hit the uppermost facade. Engineering experts estimate that this mighty clout, had it been unimpeded, would have traveled between 550 and 600 feet from home plate. First base coach Bill Dickey, a Yankee veteran who harkens back to the days of Ruth, Gehrig, and DiMaggio, and an opposing eyewitness to the longball exploits of the likes of Hank Greenberg and Jimmie Foxx, declares, "Mantle has more power than any man I've ever seen."

141.   May 30   Wash.   Camilo Pascual   Stadium   12–5, NY   29,825
      (second game)

Mantle launches another fifth-inning shot that sails over the right-center field bleachers until it lands at the base of the gigantic Yankee scoreboard. This 465-foot wallop is another milestone home run for Mickey Mantle. It establishes a new major league home run standard for the season through the month of May with 20.

No major league hitter in history has hit 16 home runs in the month of May before now. Nor has any switch-hitter in big league history ever hit more home runs in any month. For the day, besides his "tape-measure" home runs, Mantle has also doubled and singled twice. One of his singles was a drag bunt he beat out for a hit and his 12th of the year thus far.

At this point in the season, Mickey is hitting .425, having scored 45 runs, on 65 hits, 135 total bases, 20 home runs, and 50 RBIs.

142.	June 5	Kansas City	Lou Kretlow	Stadium(n)	7–4, KC	15,053

Playing against the Athletics, Mantle must cope with one of enemy Manager Lou Boudreau's famous shifts, such as the one he had designed against the formidable Ted Williams in the Forties. Now, Boudreau has moved five of his players to the extreme right-hand side of second base.

The leftfielder has moved in to play a very deep third base as the third baseman will be positioned at a point up the middle in very shallow center field. Seeking to beat the "shift," Mantle, the speediest ballplayer in the big leagues from home plate to first base, attempts unsuccessfully to drag bunt himself aboard. As a result of this distraction, Mantle will fan twice against Kretlow. Later on, however, with a man aboard and the "shift" off, "The Mick" will connect for a home run later in the night game.

June 11, 1956: There is a continuing discussion that seems to have captivated the baseball-loving populace in the United States, embracing the notion that the cork-center ball is "livelier" this year than in times past. As of this date, 192 major league ballplayers have belted 745 home runs, that shrinks to a disproportionate few the 140 ballplayers in the big leagues who had hammered out 320 roundtrippers in the same amount of time in the 1927 season.

143.	June 14	Chicago	Jim Wilson	Stadium	5–1, NY	9,315

Mantle slashes a two-out, ninth-inning home run that ties the game while simultaneously sailing 20 rows deep into the upper, right field grandstand at Yankee Stadium. The normally stoic veteran White Sox great—and currently the Chisox Manager—future Hall-of-Famer Marty Marion, is awed by the spectacle of the shot, stating later, "It went way up there," pointing high into the upper right-field grandstand. Narrating further, Marion said, "Way up there. He swung just as easy, and whup! It was gone. Way up there. I never saw anything like it." Marion thought a lot of Mantle, adding, "I'd say that Mantle is the greatest player in either league." Asked what he believed Mantle's weaknesses to be, Marion said, "Let's see—uh, yes. There's one thing he can't do very well. He can't throw left-handed."

| 144. | June 15 | Cleveland | Mike Garcia | Cleveland(n) | 6–2, NY | 34,025 |
| 145. | June 16 | Cleveland | Herb Score(LH) | Cleveland(n) | 3–1, NY | 40,964 |

In this night contest, Mantle launches a two-run game-winner off the rookie lefthander, who will knock out a 20-9 pitching record this year.

| 146. | June 18 | Detroit | Paul Foytack | Detroit | 7–4, NY | 12,072 |

Against substantial gusts of wind blowing 18 miles an hour straight in from right field, Mantle launches a prodigious, eighth-inning, three-run, 525-foot home run that cuts through the gale, spans the field, and lands on the roof of Briggs Stadium, itself 110 feet above the playing field, and just to the right of the 370-foot marker in right-center field. Outside the historic ballpark, driving on Trumbull Avenue, a man is listening to Mel Ott call the ballgame over the radio when he actually sees the ball come flying onto Trumbull Avenue after bouncing on top of the massive right field roof and down into the street. The driver stops his car, scampers after the bouncing ball, and retrieves it. The next day, will take the ball to Mickey, who will sign the "tape-measure" souvenir.

During his career, Mantle will hit four balls out of Briggs Stadium, more than any player in the long history of the historic structure variously named Navin Field/Briggs Stadium/Tiger Stadium. The monstrous, game-winning, three-run longball leads the visiting Yankees to a 7–4 victory over the Tigers.

Sportswriters are starting to catch fire themselves in heaping praises on a maturing Mickey Mantle. Sports columnist Clif Keane this very day inscribes a comparison between the young Mantle and the aging but legendary hitter, "The Thumper" in Beantown. Writing about Ted Williams and Mickey in the same breath, Keane writes: "When the ballplayers start to talk about another player like the Sox were talking about Mantle tonight, you know he's great. They're talking about him the way they used to talk about Williams years ago."

| 147. | June 20 | Detroit | Billy Hoeft(LH) | Detroit(n) | 4–1, NY | 47,756 |

The Mick's mighty clout is pounded into the upper tier of the straightaway center field grandstand above the 440-foot marker and the 14-foot-high center field fence, where it lands at a point four rows from the top of the center field bleachers. The mighty wallop off the crafty lefthander, who will put together a 20-14 pitching record for this year, reaches a titanic measurement of 525 feet.

| 148. | June 20 | Detroit | Billy Hoeft(LH) | Detroit(n) | 4–1, NY | 47,756 |

Mantle powers a second mammoth-sized crash that slams into the seats of the right-of-center center field bleachers in the second tier above the 370-foot sign at Briggs

Stadium. Hoeft will later relate that both drives had come off off-speed pitches that caused both balls to be propelled as far as they went, generated solely by Mickey's own power and strength. Mantle is now 18 games ahead of Ruth's 1927 pace for 60 home runs. Later during the contest, fans who have reveled at the mighty power of the young centerfielder jump down on to the field and rush the young slugger to shake his hand and clap him on the back. The game is held up briefly until the mesmerized devoted clutch of opposing fans can be cleared from the playing field. In fact, the fans cannot be dispersed until the homegrown Detroit grounds keepers turn on the water sprinklers. In this game alone, Mantle has hit two balls over 1,000 feet off the bedraggled Hoeft. In three days, the three home runs during this amazing run of king-sized production have been calculated to exceed an astonishing 1,500 feet.

June 29, 1956: Playing against the lowly Washington Senators at Yankee Stadium, Mickey walks four times in the game, facing both Pedro Ramos and Bud Byerly. This most versatile, most-feared, phantom-like centerfielder does score twice, however, without officially getting credited with having made an official at-bat. Meanwhile, the Yanks win the contest, 3–1. Bomber righthander Bob Grim unfurls an overpowering two-hitter against the Senators as the 20,528 raving rooters make their way to their respective Big Apple abodes, delighted with their home team in the Bronx.

| 149. | July 1 (second game) | Wash. | Dean Stone(LH) | Stadium | 8–6, NY | 25,702 |

Mickey connects for another tremendous 525-foot wallop that lands in the upper deck of the left field grandstand and ties the game.

| 150. | July 1 (second game) | Wash. | Bud Byerly | Stadium | 8–6, NY | 25,702 |

Mickey slams the late-inning offering for the game-winning, two-run home run that lands deep into the second half of the Yankee bullpen in right-center field. It is also the fourth career occasion that Mantle has belted home runs from both sides of the plate in the same game.

On July 4th, Mantle attempts to put some extra snap on a throw to the plate from center field in a game against the Boston Red Sox. After fielding a hit by Jimmy Piersall and throwing the ball, Mickey had felt a twinge in his right knee. He has strained the lateral ligaments of his right knee. He will miss four games as a result. He will also receive treatment this year for a neck injury.

THE 1956 ALL-STAR GAME

GRIFFITH STADIUM IN WASHINGTON, D.C.
JULY 10

After watching Mickey Mantle dress for the All-Star Game, Cleveland's Early Wynn tells reporters, "I watched him dress. I watched him bandage that knee—that whole leg—and I saw what he had to go through every day to play. And now I'll never be able to praise him enough. Seeing those legs, his power becomes unbelievable."

In the game itself, played this year at Griffith Stadium in the nation's capital, before 28,843 excited American League fans, the National League outpaces the American League, 7–3. The winning NL effort is paced by home runs by Stan Musial and Willie Mays, the Giant slugger's coming in the fourth in a pinch-hitting role off Yankee southpaw Whitey Ford. The ball is walloped 450 feet halfway up the high and deep left-center field bleachers. In addition, there are three fielding gems made by Cardinals third baseman Ken Boyer, who will also contribute three hits. The Nationals win the game despite back-to-back, sixth-inning, All-Star home runs off Warren Spahn by Ted Williams and Mickey Mantle, a line-drive shot over the left field barrier.

Mantle also ties the All-Star record for strikeouts in a single game as a batter by fanning three times in this, the 23rd midsummer classic in history. In respective appearances against some of the most stellar National League hurlers, Mickey can not solve Bob Friend of the Pittsburgh Pirates, or Warren Spahn of the Milwaukee Braves, or Johnny Antonelli of the San Francisco Giants. The National League wins, 7–3.

151.	July 14	Cleveland	Herb Score(LH)	Stadium	5-4, NY	27,358
					(in 10)	

Mantle wallops the ball, a solo shot that lands 20 feet behind the 402-foot marker adjacent to the visitors' bullpen.

152.	July 18	Detroit	Paul Foytack	Stadium	8-4,Det	23,169
	(first game)					

Mantle connects for a drive into the right-center field bleachers.

153.	July 22	Kansas City	Art Ditmar	Stadium	7-4, K.C.	26,923
	(first game)					

In the at-bat prior to this one, Kansas City Manager Lou Boudreau had decided to employ the "Mantle shift" by moving a third infielder to the second base side of the infield. Mantle had then dragged a bunt down the third-base line for a bunt single.

In Mantle's next at-bat, in the seventh inning, the shift will not be on when Mantle connects for a two-run shot. The ball is propelled to a distant point in the right-center field bleachers beyond the right field auxiliary scoreboard.

| 154. | July 30 | Cleveland | Bob Lemon | Cleveland(n) | 13-6, NY | 22,659 |

In the second inning, Mantle connects for a grand slam home run into the right field bleachers at Municiple Stadium. Mantle's six RBIs, and particularly the grand slam, accounts for the go-ahead and game-winning tallies.

| 155. | July 30 | Cleveland | Bob Feller | Cleveland | 13-6, NY | 22,659 |

Belting out his second home run of the game, Mantle leads the Yankees past the aspiring Tribe with six runs batted in, establishing a 10-game lead at the top of the American League pack.

| 156. | Aug. 4 | Detroit | Virgil Trucks | Detroit | 5-4, Det | 24,908 |
| 157. | Aug. 4 | Detroit | Virgil Trucks | Detroit | 5-4, Det | 24,908 |

Mantle's two home runs are trumped by Tiger great Al Kaline's pair of roundtrippers that drive in all of the Tigers' five runs.

| 158. | Aug. 5 | Detroit | Jim Bunning | Detroit | 8-5, Det | 30,310 |

Mickey propels the ball, high and far until it crashes against the facade of the upper-most right field grandstand facade at Briggs Stadium.

August 7, 1956: At Fenway Park, before 36,350 excited Beantown spectators, the largest crowd since World War II, the Yankees are in town to take on the wilting Red Sox. It is the largest Fenway Park crowd ever to watch a day game. Playing against the New York Yankees, Red Sox slugging outfielder Ted Williams drops a routine fly ball to left field, hit by Mickey Mantle. Later in the same inning, after making a difficult catch in left-center field of a long drive by Yogi Berra, Williams returns to the bench. While trotting in from left field, the angry outfielder—who is receiving a cascade of abuse from the fans, first spits towards the right field comple-ment of Bosox fans and then turns towards the left field flock of boo-birds and spits in their direction as well. Ted's own fit of anger is not completed. After Williams reaches the dugout, he steps back onto the field and spits again, blatantly register-ing his open and symbolic disgust for the abusive, front-running fans who applaud his exploits one minute only to denigrate him the next after a miscue. And then, of course, he spits towards the press box. Ill feelings aside, the Red Sox still manage to eke out the victory when Tommy Byrne walks Williams with the bases loaded in the bottom of the 11th. Ted's temper outburst will cost him $5,000 when owner Tom Yawkey hears of the incident.

| 159. | Aug. 8 | Wash. | Camilo Pascual | Wash., D.C.(n) | 12-2, NY | 17,874 |

Mickey slices a long drive for an opposite field shot to left field.

| 160. | Aug. 9 | Wash. | Hal Griggs | Wash., D.C. | 15-7, NY | 6,948 |

Mickey connects for a powerful, two-run, opposite-field shot into the remote left-center field bleachers at Griffith Stadium from the left side of the plate.

| 161. | Aug. 11 | Baltimore | Hal "Skinny" Brown | Stadium | 10-5, Bal | 15,000 |
| | | | | | | (plus 5,000 Yankee juniors) |

Mantle launches a seventh-inning, three-run home run that is powered into the upper deck of the right field grandstand at Yankee Stadium.

Now hitting .371, Mantle's 40th home run of the year marks the first time— since Joe DiMaggio did it in 1937—that a Yankee has hit 40 home runs, the only year in his career that he would. "The Mick" is also 11 games ahead of Babe Ruth in his pursuit of 60 home runs and the Yankees are 8½ games ahead of the American League pack.

162.	Aug. 12	Baltimore	Don Ferrarese(LH)	Stadium	6-2, NY	27,178
	(first game)					
163.	Aug. 14	Boston	Mel Parnell(LH)	Stadium(n)	12-2, NY	52,409

With President Eisenhower in attendance at this night game, Mantle clubs a two-run home run deep into the lower left field stands at Yankee Stadium.

At this point in time, just after the series with Boston, Ted Williams is batting .393 for the season with 41 games to play, while Mickey trails with a .380 mark. In the three-game set with the Red Sox, Mantle hits .444 in the series with Ted hitting .625. Now, however, Mickey slips into a horrendous slump, collecting only three hits in 33 at-bats, his batting average dipping 18 points to .358.

| 164. | Aug. 23 | Chicago | Paul LaPalme(LH) | Stadium | 6-4, Chi | 22,971 |
| | (second game) | | | | | |

Mickey unloads once more with still another "tape-measure" shot. It lands 20 rows in the left field upper deck, some 550 feet away.

The ball's majestic trajectory misses clearing the left field roof of Yankee Stadium by a mere 20 feet. The Chisox lefthander will later relate, "It was the longest ball I ever saw. It was hit so hard and fast that no one knew where it was. The noise was so loud on impact that it sounded like an explosion. It looked like a golf ball disappearing." LaPalme believes that this magnificent poke would have carried out of the stadium if Mickey had hit it in the direction of the left field bullpen. LaPalme's battery mate, White Sox catcher Les Moss, calls this latest of prodigious Mantle bombs the longest ball he had ever seen. Mantle adds a booming triple, that spans the "Death Valley" sector of the stadium's center field area. The ball slams against the center field wall 460 feet away from home plate.

In a side note, in the opposing batting order, Nellie Fox would give Mickey Mantle a permanent memory on this same night. Mickey will later recall it as "one of the greatest exhibitions in hitting I have ever seen...line drives all over the place." In the twin bill, Fox will collect seven base hits.

165.   Aug. 25   Chicago   Dick Donovan   Stadium   4–2, Chi   60,683

On the same day of the Yankee's annual Old Timers' Day, Mantle connects for a two-run blow that slices into the left field bleachers for an opposite field poke. The young slugger goes 3-for-4, scores one run, and accounts for two runs batted in. Sadly, this game marks the day when Phil "Scooter" Rizzuto, the regular Yankee shortstop for the bulk of the postwar period, and whose brilliance and clutch performances cut a swath through six superb World Series performances, is cut from the roster to make room for Enos "Country" Slaughter. During the pre-game festivities, Mickey gets to see a lot of Old Timers arriving at Yankee Stadium to participate in the celebration. Mantle appreciates seeing Ty Cobb and Charlie Gehringer. Older Yankees have also shown up. Such pin-striped greats as Joe DiMaggio, Charlie Keller, Red Ruffing, George Stirnweiss, and Bill Dickey. The extended family of the Yankees are well represented. And there is another great ballplayer there, Mutt Mantle's favorite player, a legend of another generation, a Hall-of-Famer, and Mickey Mantle's namesake: Mickey Cochrane.

166.   Aug. 28   Kansas City   Art Ditmar   Stadium(n)   4–0, NY   17,304

Mickey powers a three-run, line drive that just carries over the railing of the right field bullpen in this rain-abbreviated contest.

167.   Aug. 29   Kansas City   Jack McMahan   Stadium   6–4, NY   8,882

Mickey launches a prodigious, 410-foot solo shot into the left field grandstand and collects two other safeties, highlighting his climb back up the hitting ladder. Mickey's batting average has moved up to .367 and the Yankees retain a substantial eight-game lead over the rest of the American League.

168.   Aug. 31   Wash.   Camilo Pascual   Wash., D.C.(n) 6–4, NY   15,325

With President Dwight Eisenhower once again on hand, this time on a surprise visit, the two main actors meet on their respective stages, Ike in world affairs and Mickey in the world of baseball. As the two principal players shake hands before the game, the smiling Ike advises, "I hope you hit a home run tonight, but I hope the Senators win." Mickey's fortuitous long-range pokes have been amazingly synchronized to Eisenhower's many appearances at games in which Mantle and the Bombers have played. Mickey considers Ike his "good luck charm."

In the seventh frame, Mantle homers over the right field wall, putting him four games ahead of Babe Ruth's 1927 pace. In a sidelight of the game, slugging out-fielder Jim Lemon, the string-bean slugger of the Washington Nats, has accounted for all of Washington's four runs by clubbing three home runs off Whitey Ford on this day. In the bottom of the ninth, with two runners on and two outs, Lemon comes to the plate to face Ford when Stengel walks to the mound. From center field, Mickey watches as Stengel and Ford carry on a long discussion. Stengel wants Ford to call it a day. Whitey resists, telling the "Ol' Perfesser" that he can get Lemon. Let him pitch to this guy. Casey looks at Lemon and looks at Whitey, ponders his response carefully, and then simply blurts out, "Are you friggin' crazy? The guy already hit three home runs off you." Stengel gives Ford the hook in favor of Tom Morgan, who comes in to get the tall slugger out. The Yankees win the game, 6–4, on Mickey's timely, game-winning blow.

For the first ten days in September, Mantle will be mired in a deep batting slump that will yield a mere five hits in 33 at-bats, with no home runs and no RBIs.

169.	Sept. 13	Kansas City	Tom Gorman		Kansas City	3–2, NY	10,904

Mantle breaks out of his September slump when he collects two hits including a long blast over the left-center field wall. Mantle's longball wins the game for the Bombers.

170.	Sept. 16	Cleveland	Early Wynn		Cleveland	4–3, Cle	39,651
	(second game)						

In the previous game played this day, the first game of the twin bill, the Yankees had beaten the Indians and eliminated the Tribe from the pennant race. Celebrating this feat, Mantle poles a long home run into the right field upper deck during the second tilt.

171.	Sept. 18	Chicago	Billy Pierce(LH)		Chicago(n)	3–2, NY	31,694
						(in 11)	

The 3–2 victory which clinches the pennant for the Yankees is paced by the young slugger's home run that sails over the high roof of the two-tiered left-center field grandstand of the old and massive ballyard. The ball is estimated to have traveled 550 feet in the air and is deemed the "longest ball ever hit in Comiskey Park." Mantle's out-of-the-park heroics is a feat accomplished previously only by one ballplayer, Hall-of-Famer Al Simmons. Staying down on one of Pierce's low curves, Mickey swings and connects for a "tape-measure" clout that wins the game and the pennant for the Bombers. Pressing hard for the Triple Crown, this night game's moon shot also represents Mantle's 50th home run of the year and the 12th time in the history of baseball that this plateau has been reached. This landmark blow also makes Mantle the only Yankee besides Ruth who has ever connected for 50 home runs in a single campaign. The 11th-inning, game-winning, pennant-clinching solo shot also represents the 182nd team home run—which ties the American League record for team home runs in a single season. It is a feat that had been accomplisheded by the 1936 Yankees.

Mantle will be pulled from the lineup for four days after pulling a muscle on the left side of his groin. Stengel wants to give the young slugger a rest for the Series.

Responding to questions about the potential threat to Mickey's chances at pulling off the Triple Crown by sitting on the bench, Stengel reasons, "I'd like to see the kid win all the titles, but I gotta think of the World Series. His being hurt in the last one cost us plenty and we lost it, remember? I don't want to go into another Series without him."

| 172. | Sept. 21 | Boston | Frank Sullivan | Boston(n) | 7-6, Bos | 24,616 |

Mickey wallops a 480-foot home run into the center field bleachers at Fenway Park. In this night game, the ball lands in the second-to-last row of the most rearward wall of the baseball edifice, situated to the right of the scoreboard. Yankee teammate and right-handed hurler Tom Sturdivant recalls the ball as being hit harder than any ball he has ever seen hit. The ball had reached its distant spot of descent with such rapidity that Sturdivant would claim he had never seen a ball that was hit that far "move so fast," banging against the back wall of the center field bleachers. The home run also represents the 183rd for the Yankees team establishing a new American League record for home runs by a team in a single season. In a fascinating aside, the Triple Crown is acutely jeopardized by the presence of the great Ted Williams, who is battling Mantle for the batting title. On this day, the aging yet still graceful "Splendid Splinter" collects two hits and is currently hitting .356. Mantle, meanwhile, has gone 3-for-5 and is now batting .353.

September 22, 1956: At Fenway Park in Boston, Don Larsen of the New York Yankees "experiments" with a no-windup delivery when he pitches to the plate. It serves Larsen well in this day's game with the Red Sox. In a period of 16 days, this new pitching form will serve the big righthander once more very nicely when he tries it out on the Brooklyn Dodgers in this year's Fall Classic.

| 173. | Sept. 28 | Boston | Bob Porterfield | Stadium(n) | 7-2, NY | 16,760 |

Mantle's final home run is also his 188th and the last base hit of his Triple Crown–winning year with his league-leading .353 batting average. Mantle will lead all major league hitters in batting average, home runs, and RBIs. It is only the fourth time in baseball history that a ball player has had Triple Crown figures in the three hitting-for-power categories that were higher than any player in either league. Only Rogers Hornsby, Lou Gehrig, and Ted Williams had accomplished such scintillating Triple Crown statistics. Mantle is still capable of gaining additional safeties with his legs, as Ted Williams himself will note when recalling this year. The wise Williams will point out the fact that Mantle had legged out 48 hits from sheer speed. When asked about having been beaten out by the "Commerce Comet," Williams will say, "If I could run like that sonofabitch, I'd hit .400 every year." Mickey Mantle becomes the first switch-hitter in modern history to win a batting title.

THE 1956 NEW YORK YANKEES

First Place: with a 97-57 record under Manager Casey Stengel.

The 1956 Yankees belted out 190 home runs, which established a new team record for home runs, unseating the 1936 Yankees as the previously most prolific homer-happy team in franchise history.

Yankee Stadium Attendance: 1,491,594

1956 Awards: Mickey Mantle is voted on *Sporting News'* All-Star Major League Team as an outfielder; American League MVP; *Sporting News'* Major League Player of the Year; Associated Press' Athlete of the Year; the Sid Mercer Player of the Year Award of the New York Baseball Writers Association; the Art Griggs Memorial Award of the Oklahoma Sports Writers; the Hickok Professional Athlete of the Year Award, along with its $10,000, diamond-studded, gold-buckled belt that is given to each year's Hickok recipient. Finally, Mickey Mantle is voted on the All-Star Major League Team as an outfielder.

Mickey Mantle's League-leading Categories: Triple Crown-winning Mickey Mantle with a .353 batting average (led majors), 52 home runs (led majors), 130 RBIs (led majors), a .705 slugging average (led majors), 376 total bases (led majors), 132 runs scored (led majors), and the highest average number of home runs per 100 at-bats with 9.8 (led majors). Mickey Mantle has also set an American League record for the most RBIs by a switch-hitter in a single year—130. Mantle's .705 slugging average is the highest all-time slugging average ever attained by a switch-hitter. And, it is still another major league record for switch-hitters, as Mantle collects the most total bases ever—376. Mantle also collects the most long hits by a switch-hitter ever, with 79 long hits.

MICKEY MANTLE'S 1956 HITTING RECORD

G	AB	R	H	2B	3B	HR	HR%	RBI	SA	BB	SO	SB	AVE.
150	533	132	188	22	5	52	9.8	130	.705	112	99	10	.353

In 1956, Mickey Mantle hit .353 while the major leagues averaged .258 with both teams scoring an average 8.90 runs per game and both teams hitting 1.85 home runs per contest. During the 150 games that Mickey Mantle appeared in for 1956, he played in the outfield 144 times. He also appeared in six games as a pinch-hitter.

Mickey's 1956 Salary: $32,500

World Series Winning Share: $8,714

Injuries or Operations: tonsillectomy

Number of Games in Which Mantle Homered: 45

Winning Record When Mickey Mantle Homered: 30-15 a winning percentage of .667

THE 1956 WORLD SERIES

October 3, 1956: The President of the United States has come to Flatbush to take in the Opening Game of the 1956 World Series. At Ebbets Field in Brooklyn, part of the Opening Game proceedings allows for President Eisenhower to meet members of both the Brooklyn Dodgers and the New York Yankees at home plate. This includes the young Yankee slugger, who becomes the first Triple Crown winner ever to compete in a World Series in the same year of his slugging heroics.

In the first inning off Sal Maglie, after Enos "Country" Slaughter singles, Mickey powers a home run over the SHAEFER scoreboard in rightcenter field for a 2–0 Yankee lead. Once again, the good luck presence of Eisenhower inspires yet one more longball off the bat of Mickey Mantle. The Yankee lead will not hold, however, as the Dodgers prevail against Whitey Ford and ultimately pull off a 6–3 comeback triumph.

October 5, 1956: In the second inning of Game Two of the World Series, for the fifth time in Series history, Yogi Berra connects for a grand-slam home run. It is to no avail, however, as the Dodgers wear out seven Yankee pitchers in a 13–8 slugfest. The Dodger arsenal is highlighted by Duke Snider's three-run home run. The nine-inning, fence-busting marathon lasts three hours and 26 minutes, the longest in Series history, as the Dodgers take a two-game-to-zero lead.

October 7, 1956: At the Stadium in Game Four of the Series, played this day in the Bronx, the New York Yankees win on Billy Martin's fourth-inning single. Tom Sturdivant masterfully scatters six hits to upend the Dodgers. Leading off the sixth inning, Mantle uncoils from his slightly crouched batting stance and blasts righthander Ed Roebuck's pitch high and far towards the right-center power alley. The ball is propelled so powerfully deep and high towards the Ballantine Beer sign atop the right-center field bleachers that it lands midway up the bleachers, carrying some 440 feet away. Snider gives up the chase as the ball sails high over his head and over the right field auxiliary scoreboard. Hank Bauer's two-run home run off Don Dryads in the seventh ends the scoring and ices it for the Yankees. The Bombers win, 6–2, and the Series is even in games won, two to two.

October 8, 1956: At Yankee Stadium, before 64,519 nail-biting fans attending Game Five, Yankee hurler Don Larsen pitches the first perfect game in World Series history. During the game, key defensive gems will preserve Larsen's perfection. Leading off the second inning, Dodger Jackie Robinson rips a low, line shot that skips towards Yankee third baseman Andy Carey. The Bomber third baseman gets a glove and a foot on it, which makes the ball ricochet towards shortstop Gil McDougald. The veteran infielder will then field the diverted ground ball cleanly and throw a strike to first baseman Joe Collins nipping the speeding Robinson at first.

The Yankees score their first run in the fourth frame. Indeed, the "Brooklyn Barber" had also been perfect in setting down all of the Bombers until facing "The Kid" from Oklahoma with two outs in the fourth. At this point, Mantle's powerful swing uncoils, ripping a bullet, line-drive lazer that is destined to land in foul territory unless it reaches the fair pole first. The rocket shot curls fair around the foul pole in right field before it disappears. The screaming liner then viciously dips deep into the lower, rightfield bleacher seats of the flag-draped grandstand, amid the echoes of great cheers ringing among the overhanging rafters. The Yankees go up, 1–0.

Mickey will contribute to his teammate's pitching perfection when he would combine his speed and agility to preserve "Goony Bird" Larsen's masterpiece. One particular offering among Larsen's 97 pitches rocketed off the bat of Gil Hodges in a long trajectory towards Yankee Stadium's vast left-center field sector of its immense "Death Valley." Yankee centerfielder Mickey Mantle will take off at the crack of the bat, run down the ball as it comes back down to earth about 430 feet away from home plate and make a back-handed, back-to-the-infield, no-hit-saving catch of Hodges' long drive. The left-handed hitting Sandy Amoros would also blast a long drive that would sail into the rightfield stands, but is foul. As Yankee rightfielder Hank Bauer will later relate, the ball curved into foul territory missing being fair "by inches."

In the seventh, Gilliam skips a ball to Gil McDougald who, in another difficult chance, comes up with the resourceful putout. And in the eighth inning, Gil Hodges hits another difficult chance to third baseman Andy Carey, who spears the ball inches off the ground. Larsen completes his perfection when Plate Umpire "Babe" Pinelli raises his right hand with a generous "Strike Three" call against pinch-hitter Dale Mitchell, the 27th Dodger up, the 27th Dodger down. Don Larsen has pitched a 2–0 gem, and a perfect game, the only one in the glorious annals of World Series competition. It is also the turning point in the Series itself, as the Bombers now pull ahead, three games to two.

October 10, 1956: After the Dodgers manage a Game Six game victory behind the courageous, 10-inning, shutout-pitching performance of Clem Labine, the Yankees will come back again to Ebbets to play in Game Seven. The finale will never be in question as the Yankees would spring out in the first inning to a two-run lead. After this initial burst, the Yankees will pile ahead without looking back. In the mean-time, the Dodgers cannot do a thing with Johnny Kucks, who holds the Bums to three hits and no scoring threats. In the seventh, "Moose" Skowron caps the scoring with a long-ball drive to right field with the bases loaded. For the sixth time in Series history, the ball had disappeared into the stands, which gives Skowron a World Series grand-slam home run. The Yankees become world champions of baseball once more and for the fourth time in the last six years.

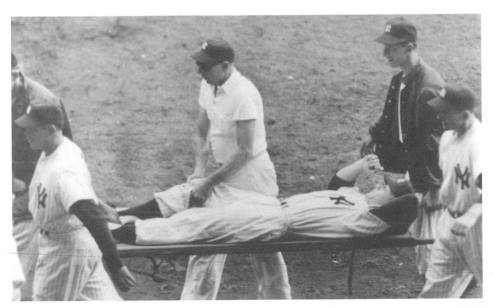

Mantle's long plight with pain and injury would be traced back to the 1951 Game Two injury of the World Series.

Chapter Six

THE HARBINGERS OF PAIN

—1957, 1958 & 1959—

In the Nation and the World: In 1957, America's budding civil rights movement stepped up its momentum when black teenaged children desegregated Central High School in Little Rock, Arkansas. The movement's cause was guaranteed by the President of the United States, who sent troops into Arkansas to enforce the order of the Supreme Court.

Meanwhile, in the continuing Cold War, the Soviet Union launched Sputnik, mankind's first artificial satellite. The U.S. race for space with the Soviet Union had now been inaugurated; however, start-up operations were plagued by very inauspicious beginnings at Cape Canaveral, Florida. On a different, more terrifying front, the U.S.S.R. had now developed the H-Bomb technology.

Back home, disturbing revelations came to light when a special Appalachian conference of Mafia mobster bosses was raided by police. As a result, the Senate Rackets Committee on Capitol Hill was formed; two members, Senator John F.

Kennedy, and his brother, Bobby, would help steer the Committee toward the most ambitious investigation ever conducted into Mob activities. Singer Elvis Presley was inducted into the U.S. Army. And science made another breakthrough discovery with the revelation of DNA.

In 1959, the international ramifications of Cold War politics were showcased when Vice-President Richard Nixon staged a famous exchange in his "kitchen debate" in Moscow with Soviet Premier Nikita Khrushchev. Meanwhile, another significant development was unraveling in the Caribbean as Fidel Castro ousted his antagonist, Batista, on the island of Cuba. In 1959, Hawaii became the 50th state in the union.

It was also a time when, at Cape Canaveral in Florida, Mercury astronauts were selected for the U.S. space program to challenge the Soviet Union, which by now had developed a substantial lead in the race for space. Meanwhile, in American homes, 86 percent of the American people owned a television.

Fads: In 1957, among the younger Baby Boomers, silly putty and a wiry toy called Slinky were the rage. In the meantime, Dick Clark's *American Bandstand* made its television debut in Philadelphia, where a dance called the bunny hop was practiced by couples on nationally televised hookups. The hula hoop made its first sensational appearance as the newest craze. And bowling and Frisbees enjoyed a marked increase in popularity all over the land. Fashion-conscious ladies also adorned themselves with stylish "sac" dresses.

The following year, a new form of diversion was developed nationwide as a sport called water-skiing took over leisure activity in harbors, rivers and ocean fronts, throughout the country. And, in 1959, the last year in this chapter of the Mantle story, the country welcomed a new sport for youngsters called go-karting. Fashion, meanwhile, welcomed the sexy introduction of black leotards among the gentler sex in the United States, and parachuting was introduced as a new sport in the nation. Last, as if to create ways to organize their own fantasies for emulating Mickey Mantle and other baseball heroes in the National Pastime, the younger generation created a massive network of proliferating baseball leagues for the young only.

The Little Leagues flourished in the late Fifties in unprecedented numbers, embracing millions of American boys eager to play the game. This fact was reflected by Little League participation multiplying to more than seven times from its genesis in the early part of the decade—the earlier 776 leagues had grown to 5,700 by the end of the Fifties. Baseball among the Baby Boomers had exploded across the national landscape, millions of youngsters took their "Mickey Mantle" model bat and their Mickey Mantle ball gloves to bed with them at night, dreaming what it must be like to lead as glorious a career as Mickey did with the New York Yankees.

Innovations and First Appearances: In 1957, the Ford Edsel made its ghastly appearance on the American driving scene. And pocket-size transistor radios seemed to pop up everywhere. 1957 also saw Volkswagen sell 200,000 Beetles to economy-minded American driver-consumers. In 1958, SWEET 'N' LOW made its first appearance in American kitchens and restaurants everywhere. The first PIZZA HUT began doling out its circular-shaped pizza pies by the millions. The BANKAMERICARD and American Express were born, giving new meaning to the words "credit" and "plastic." And, the UPI for the first time established a firm footing in the world of mass-media communications. In the following year, 1959, transparent bags for the transport of one's clothes were developed, and weather stations enjoyed a proliferation of mass communications, radar, and the ability to speedily update the science of weather forecasting.

Movies: In 1957, not only did moviegoers increase at the box office as Baby Boomers partook in weekend matinees by the millions, but more exciting cinematic fare was released as Hollywood enjoyed the boom of American prosperity. Movie madness brought such movie hits as *The Gunfight at the OK Corral, Silk Stockings, The King and I, The Bridge on the River Kwai, Heaven Knows, Mr. Allison,* and *Sayonara.* The following year reflected more of the same, as Americans went in record numbers into the darkened houses of cinematic fantasies to enjoy the following spectacles: *Gigi, South Pacific, Indiscreet,* Walt Disney's *Old Yeller, Auntie Mame, The Vikings, Cat on a Hot Tin Roof, The Young Lions, Damn Yankees, No Time for Sergeants,* and *Houseboat.* The pattern of increasing box office receipts continued to dramatically rise as Baby Boomers got old enough to attend movies regularly without having to go with their parents. In 1959, releases included such mega-hits as *Ben-Hur, Pillow Talk, A Hole in the Head, Suddenly Last Summer, Li'l Abner, Porgy and Bess, The Young Philadelphians, Operation Petticoat, Some Like It Hot,* and Alfred Hitchcock's *North by Northwest.*

Television: In 1957, television fare showed a marked swing toward action Westerns that excited the country's increasing viewership with episodes such as *Bachelor Father, The Loretta Young Show, Wagon Train, Sergeant Preston of the Yukon, Cheyenne,* and *Sugarfoot.* The following year, 1958, prime time reflected similar patterns as more Westerns were developed. Simultaneously, a family called the Cleavers was created who lived through the trials of American suburbia. Americans everywhere tuned into other, new TV standards that also gave Americans the first opportunities to take in a new TV phenomenon called "re-runs." *Trackdown, 77 Sunset Strip, Yancy Derringer, Wanted Dead or Alive,* and *Leave It to Beaver* made their first appearances on the tiny screen this year. And in 1959, *Gunsmoke, Playhouse 90, The Rifleman, The Lawrence Welk Show,* and Dick Clark's *American Bandstand* were some of the shows that gained wide popularity.

The Juke Box: 1957 began a new wave of dominance by rock 'and' roll in popular music as its chief devotees, the Baby Boomers, started to spend their allowances for the newest 45 RPM records celebrating teen hits. Such "oldies, but goodies" as "Teddy Bear," "Jailhouse Rock," and "All Shook Up" by Elvis, "Day-O" ("The Banana Boat Song") by Harry Belafonte, "Bye Bye Love" and "Wake Up, Little Susie" by the Everly Brothers were filling the nation's air waves. In addition, "It's Not For Me to Say," and "Chances Are" by Johnny Mathis, "Diana" by Paul Anka, "Great Balls of Fire" by Jerry Lee Lewis, "Honeycomb" and "Kisses Sweeter than Wine" by Jimmie Rodgers, "Little Darlin'" by the Diamonds, "At the Hop" by Danny and the Juniors, "Round and Round" by Perry Como, Fats Domino's "I'm Walkin'," and "Stood Up" by Ricky Nelson also cluttered *Billboard*'s Top 40 hits.

The following year, 1958, showed an increasing foothold for the new form of "Doo Wop" music as millions of dollars were spent by Boomers, increasing their rock 'n' roll record libraries and keeping up with the latest hits they heard every week on their transistor radios: hits like "Dede Dinah" by Frankie Avalon, "Sugar Time" by the McGuire Sisters, "Chantilly Lace" by the Big Bopper, "I Gotta Feeling" by Ricky Nelson, "Oh-Oh, I'm Falling in Love Again" by Jimmie Rodgers, "I Wonder Why" by Dion and the Belmonts, "Johnny B. Goode" by Chuck Berry, "Just a Dream" by Jimmy Clanton, "All I Have to Do Is Dream," and "Bird Dog" by the Everly Brothers "Big Man" and "26 Miles (Santa Catalina)" by the Four Preps, "Maybe Baby" by Buddy Holly and the Crickets, Paul Anka's "You Are My Destiny," "Tequila" by the Champs, The Crests' "16 Candles," "Tom Dooley" and "M.T.A." by the Kingston Trio.

It was more of the same in 1959 as the new releases focused on the far-flung musical tastes of the Baby Boomers snapping their fingers to "Tucumcari" by Jimmie Rodgers, "Lipstick on Your Collar" by Connie Francis, "Way Down Yonder in New Orleans" by Freddie Cannon, "What'd I Say" by Ray Charles, "Charlie Brown" and "Poison Ivy" by the Coasters, "La Bamba" by Ritchie Valens, "Dream Lover" by Bobby Darin, Patti Page's "Fever," Paul Anka's "Put Your Head on My Shoulder" and "Lonely Boy," "Venus" and "Ginger Bread" by Frankie Avalon, "High Hopes" by Frank Sinatra, "Hushabye" by the Mystics, "Mack the Knife" by Bobby Darin, "Lonely Street" by Andy Williams, "There Goes My Baby" by the Drifters, Jackie Wilson's "Lonely Teardrops," "Love Potion Number Nine" by the Clovers, " "Misty" by Johnny Mathis, "Come Softly to Me" and "Mr. Blue" by the Fleetwoods, "Dance With Me" by the Drifters.

Deaths: In 1957, America paid its last respects to polar explorer Admiral Richard Byrd and Big Band leader Jimmy Dorsey. Meanwhile, Senator Joseph McCarthy died of acute alcoholism, and Arturo Toscanini, Humphrey Bogart, and Ezio Pinza saddened Americans at their passing. Indeed, rock 'and' roll stars J.P. "The Big Bopper" Richardson, Ritchie Valens, and Buddy Holly were tragically killed in a plane crash, a crushing tragedy to the youth of America, who wept at the loss of the rich heritage that their brief, but brilliant music reflected on this, the "Day That the Music Died."

In 1958, baseball mourned the passing of diamond immortals Mel Ott and Tris Speaker. And in fashion, Christian Dior had released the last of his trend-setting styles. In the world of movies and make-believe, cinematic giants like actor Robert Donat, W. C. Handy, Louis B. Mayer, actor Tyrone Power, Mike Todd via a plane crash, and actor Ronald Coleman all crossed over. In 1959, Hollywood and the arts mourned the collective loss of many more of the best that ever were, including actress Ethel Barrymore, singer Billie Holiday, author Raymond Chandler, producer/director Cecil B. DeMille, and actor Errol Flynn. American politics lost General George C. Marshall, who slipped into U.S. history as one of the country's greatest wartime military commanders, and the genius of architectural innovation, Frank Lloyd Wright, vanished when the great builder passes away.

Sports: In 1957, great strides were made in sports history when Althea Gibson became the first black tennis star ever to win the Wimbledon Tennis Tournament Championships. And in 1958, the NFL and the country were introduced to one of the league's greatest, most inspirational, and most courageous sports performers on any field of professional athletic endeavor: a pro quarterback named Johnny Unitas, who led the Baltimore Colts to the first-ever "sudden death" 23–17 victory over the New York Giants. Meanwhile, in pro hoops, the NBA Championship was won by the St. Louis Hawks over the Boston Celtics, four games to two. And in the following year, 1959, pro boxing was shocked to watch Ingemar Johanson kayo Floyd Patterson to become the first foreign heavyweight champion in a quarter of a century. In pro football, the American Football League, the pre-merger progenitor of the American Football Conference, was formed. And the Baltimore eleven repeated as world champions of professional football when they manhandled the New York Giants, 31–16. Professional basketball saw the Boston Celtics dominate the Minneapolis Lakers, four games to none, which secured for Beantown its second NBA championship.

Baseball Transitions: The powers-that-be in major league baseball directed that American League batters wear plastic protective helmets at all times when taking their cuts at the plate. Meanwhile, Ted Williams broke the $100,000 salary barrier, becoming the second ballplayer in history to earn six figures, Joe D. being the first. Meanwhile, key personnel changes had been taking place all over the American League. Cleveland lost Al Rosen and Herb Score, but picked up a rookie outfielder named Roger Maris. Boston signed up Frank Malzone. And Detroit landed the services of the future Hall-of-Famer, Jim Bunning. As for the New York Yankees, some personnel adjustments were made when the Bombers let Jerry Coleman go again. In addition, Joe Collins was released and Billy Martin was traded. But the Yanks did pick up Bobby Richardson, Tony Kubek, and Enos Slaughter. The Yankees also traded away Irv Noren, Billy Hunter, Tom Morgan, Mickey McDermott, Rip Coleman, and minor league prospect, Jack Urban. In return, the Yanks received Art Ditmar, Bobby Shantz, and minor league infielder, Clete Boyer.

Meanwhile, the "landscape" of baseball underwent a permanent change, marking a turning point in the major leagues when the interests of big business prevailed over the pedestrian interests of loyal, local fans. After the '57 season, both the New York Giants and the Brooklyn Dodgers made similar earthshaking announcements revealing that both clubs had set their sights on California. The New York Giants would now be ensconced at Seals Stadium by the Bay and would call themselves the San Francisco Giants. The "Bums" from Flatbush would move their operations to Los Angeles, where they would host the rest of the National League in the newly-refitted L.A. Memorial Coliseum with its 42-foot-high screen perched in left field, some 251 feet away from home plate. On a sadder note, in November of 1958, the car that Dodger All-Star catcher Roy Campanella was driving would slide into a telephone pole near his home on an icy night. The three-time National League MVP would emerge tragically from the crash, a helpless, lifelong quadriplegic. It marked the immediate and premature conclusion to a glorious baseball career.

The following year, 1958, roster changes for the Chicago White Sox would dictate the loss of Jack Harshman and Bob Keegan. The Chi Sox would, however, pick up the formidable talents of Early Wynn. Boston bid farewell to Mickey Vernon, but welcomed the batting skills of Pete Runnels. The Cleveland Indians traded away Gene Woodling, but re-signed Larry Doby. The Tribe also mourned their All-Star pitching tandem of Bob Lemon, Early Wynn and Mike Garcia when it was ingloriously dismantled. And, The Baltimore Orioles lost the services of George Kell, but gained the fielding wizardry of Brooks Robinson. Meanwhile, in 1958, the Bronx Bombers lost Tom Sturdivant, said goodbye to Enos Slaughter, but picked up Norm Siebern. The Yanks released Tommy Byrne once again, but picked up Ryne Duren.

The following year, 1959, Pirate southpaw Harvey Haddix would accomplish what no man has ever done, before or since. Haddix would pitch 12 perfect innings against the Milwaukee Braves in what is arguably the best game ever pitched by anyone, if not outright, the most hard-luck no-hitter of all-time. The slick heroics of the slight, but tenacious "Kitten" aside, Haddix lost the game after the Don Hoak bobble of the Felix Mantilla groundball at third. Eddie Matthews then sacrificed Mantilla to second. Hank Aaron then was walked intentionally. The next batter, slugging firstbaseman Joe Adcock, homered to right-center field. Haddix, who had labored long and perfect, now suffered defeat by permitting a solitary hit that lost the game for himself and his teammates, 1–0. The discrepancy between the final score and Adcock's apparent three-run home run was the result of a base running snafu by Aaron. While running out his home run, Adcock had inadvertently passed Aaron on the bases. With Henry on first, and after the burly first sacker slammed his home run, "Hammerin' Hank" had believed that Adcock's stroke was a ground-rule double and, after having touched second base, he merrily ran to the clubhouse, knowing the game was over with the Mantilla run. By that time Adcock, however, had completed his circuit of the basepaths, and had passed Aaron on the base paths unwittingly, while Felix Mantilla, who had reached on the error, scored the game's only run, which ended the game. When Adcock, touched third base, he had officially passed Aaron, who was declared out. This dynamic simultaneously credited Adcock with a game-winning, run-scoring double.

Other AL personnel changes prevailed. The Cleveland Indians would lose Bobby Avila, but would acquire Billy Martin. The Tribe would bid farewell to the great Larry Doby, but pick up Jimmy Piersall. Detroit would lose Billy Hoeft, but would pick up Don Mossi. Boston traded away Dave Sisler, but enlisted the services of Bill Monbouquette. Washington forfeited Eddie Yost, but acquired the slugging Harmon Killebrew. The Senators would also release Albie Pearson, but would welcome the versatile Bob Allison. And, finally, the 1959 Yankees would trade away Jerry Lumpe, Tom Sturdivant, Johnny Kucks, and Andy Carey, but gained the valuable Hector Lopez and the distinguishing promise of Ralph Terry.

1957 SPRING TRAINING

The Yankees welcome a contingent of new rookies which includes Tony Kubek, Woodie Held, Norm Siebern, Bob Martyn, Jerry Lumpe, Marv Throneberry, Ralph Terry, and Al Cicotte. Mickey Mantle will recall these times as the days when "the old Yankee look was changing. Those days of sitting and staring at Joe DiMaggio were gone."

THE 1957 REGULAR SEASON

34 HOME RUNS

April 20, 1957: In a 10–7 slugfest at Fenway Park won by the Yankees, slugging first baseman Bill "Moose" Skowron of the New York Yankees smashes a "tape-measure" blast that sails to the right of the center field flagpole and out of Fenway Park. "Moose" would connect another time as well and knock in three runs. For his part, Mickey contributes mightily in a supporting role, going 3-for-6, pounding out two doubles, with two RBIs of his own and one run scored. Billy Martin, Mickey's running buddy also drives in two runs. Much later, Mickey and Billy are out on the town when they arrive back at the hotel after violating curfew. As they approach the entrance, they both note the presence of Casey Stengel, who is holding court with a handful of reporters. Sneaking down a side alley, the two delinquent ballplayers make their way to the back door, that they find locked. Returning to the alley, the two Yankees note that they are under their window some six floors up and that, if they can reach the fire escape, they can walk up to their room and climb in through the window.

The two begin to stack trashcans on top of each other so that they can reach the fire-escape ladder. Mickey has on a brand-new sharkskin coat, the style of the day, and becomes a tad agitated when Martin climbs up on his shoulders and begins to waver tenuously, standing atop Mickey's frame, on which dirt and scuffmarks begin to multiply. Finally, Billy gains a grip on the ladder, pulls his way up and, like a dart, flies up the fire escape and moves into their room through the window. Mickey then waits and waits and waits. After a seeming eternity, Billy returns to the window and yells down in a loud whisper that Casey has locked the door from the outside and that he's going to bed and will see Mickey in the morning. Now the young Mantle begins to panic. He stacks the trash cans on each other to reach the high ladder. At one point, attempting to balance on the pile of cans, they begin to tremble and he goes down, falling to the ground and tearing his new sharkskin coat. Again the small tower of trashcans is fashioned and another fall results. At another point, as he manages a tentative balance atop the cans—that are spilling over with garbage— Mickey's shoes "...sink into the goop. I smelled worse than the toilet from all the rotten vegetables."

Finally, Mantle scales the height, goes up the fire escape ladder, through the window, and into the hall, where he throws the door open to their room. Into the suite Mickey bursts, only to find Martin feigning snores, as if he was asleep. Meanwhile, Mantle's proud new sharkskin coat is in complete ruin and he is enraged. He yells, "Wake up!" Billy, rubs his eyes and asks "Wha... Wha..." Mickey fumes, "Look at all this crap over me! You couldda reached down and got me, you sonofabitch!" Telling Herb Gluck the story years later, Mickey would say, "Billy only laughed, turned over, and went to sleep."

| 174. | Apr. 22 | Wash. | Chuck Stobbs(LH) | Wash., D.C.(n) | 15–6, NY | 16,054 |
| 175. | Apr. 24 | Baltimore | Connie Johnson | Stadium | 3–2, NY | 12,974 |

In the eighth inning, Mantle's bat explodes, propelling the ball into the right-center field bleachers for the game-winning blow in a 3–2 victory.

| 176. | May 5 | Chicago | Billy Pierce(LH) | Chicago | 4–2, NY | 41,304 |
| | (first game) | | | | | |

One of Mickey's three hits includes a "tape-measure" shot that lands in the top tier of the left field grandstand at Comiskey Park.

May 7, 1957: At Municipal Stadium in Cleveland, it is the first inning of the game when Yankee infielder Gil McDougald approaches the plate with one out. After unleashing a knee-high fast ball, fireballing Herb Score sets in his follow-through, awaiting the result of his pitch. Meanwhile, McDougald connects solidly with a deadly liner right back at Score, who is still uncoiling with his follow-through. The blinding shot escapes Score's instant reflex, smashes into his right eye, fracturing three bones in his face and almost killing him. After impacting against the bridge of Score's nose and right eye, the ball then caroms towards Indian third baseman Al Smith, who makes the stop.

Smith first makes a hurried throw to first base to retire McDougald, who has barely moved out of the batter's box when he sees what happened. After making the reflexive putout that ballplayers make in the heat of the action, Smith then moves rapidly to the mound to see to his stricken teammate. Rushing there, Smith finds Score in a crumpled, fetal-positioned heap. Cleveland pitching ace Herb Score has sustained an extremely serious eye injury after being hit by this vicious line drive off the bat of the Yankee infielder. The injury, which will permanently affect Score's vision, will curtail the promising fireballing southpaw's career considerably. Not only is the brilliant potential of Herb Score never realized, but regarding McDougald, Yankee Manager Casey Stengel will later note that both men, Score and McDougald, one of his most valuable and versatile Yankees, were "never the same after that." The consequences of this split second in baseball history seemed not only to take the hop out of Score's incredible fast ball, but seemed to extinguish the fire in McDougald's play as well. Mickey will draw the similar conclusion in later memoirs, stating that basically this was the end for both players.

177.   May 8   Cleveland   Early Wynn   Cleveland(n) 10–4, Cle   15,629

Mantle wallops a three-run, 440-foot home run into the center field bleachers. Only Vic Wertz, Gene Woodling, and rookie Roger Maris have reached this distant section of this massive old ballpark. It is also during this contest that Roger Maris belts out a round-tripper. It is the first time that Maris and Mantle will ever reach the seats in the same game, this first occurrence coming as rivals.

178.   May 12   Baltimore   Hector "Skinny" Brown   Balt.   4–3, NY   20,893

Mickey connects for the game-winner.

179.   May 16   Kansas City   Alex Kellner(LH)   Stadium(n)   3–0, NY   11,081

Mickey pounds out a home run that gives the Yankees the first and winning run in a Bob Turley four-hit shutout. The blow is a game-winning home run into the left field seats. This particular run comes on the day after a public fight with drunken bowlers at a joint birthday bash for Yogi Berra and Billy Martin who were accompanied by a host of other Yankees and their wives at the Copacabana. In the wee hours of the night before, it seems, blows with drunken and abusive bowler-patrons and the Yankees land Billy Martin, Hank Bauer, Whitey Ford, and Mantle in Casey's doghouse. After the game, Stengel will speak with reporters who ask about the possible ramifications that will result from this incident. He'll tell of his disappointment in all of the Yankees there; but with respect to Mantle, he'll say, "I'm mad at him too for being out late, but I'm not mad enough to take a chance on losing a ball game and possibly the pennant." Today's particular round-tripper marks the 11th time in the last 12 at-bats that Mantle has reached base safely.

| 180. | May 19 | Cleveland | Bob Lemon | Stadium | 6–3, NY | 28,103 |

Mantle connects off a Bob Lemon curve for another very long and towering drive that lands in the top tier of the right field grandstand.

| 181. | May 25 | Wash. | Pedro Ramos | Stadium | 8–1 NY | 11,750 |
| 182. | May 26 (first game) | Wash. | Camilo Pascual | Stadium | 9–7, Wash | 22,782 |

Mantle belts another high, arching drive that carries into the top tier of the right field grandstand before disappearing into one of the upper-deck exit tunnels.

| 183. | May 29 | Wash. | Pedro Ramos | Wash., D.C. Ladies' Day | 6–2, Wash | 11,693 (3,115 pd.) |

Mickey clouts a ninth-inning, 438-foot shot that caroms off the right-center fence to the right of the flagpole before bounding into the center field bullpen at Griffith Stadium. In this year, 1957, Pedro Ramos will surrender 43 home runs—a figure in the history of the Fifties that no American League pitcher will ever equal. Two have come off Mantle's bat in these past five days in May. In his career, Mickey will pound Ramos 12 different times for some of his longest "tape-measure" jobs. Some of the shots are so impressive and so memorable, simply by the nature of their sheer prodigiousness.

| 184. | June 2 (second game) | Baltimore | Hector "Skinny" Brown | Stadium | 4–0, NY | 25,321 |

Mantle's home run is part of a back-to-back scenario with Yogi Berra. The ball lands in the top tier of the right field grandstand and provides the game-winning margin in the second game of the twinbill.

| 185. | June 5 | Cleveland | Early Wynn | Cleveland(n) | 13–3, NY | 22,221 |

Mickey's left-handed wallop translates into a 450-foot "tape-measure" shot to right field.

| 186. | June 6 | Cleveland | Mike Garcia | Cleveland | 14–5, NY | 7,361 |
| 187. | June 7 | Detroit | Jim Bunning | Detroit(n) | 6–3, Det | 43,474 |

In the first inning of a Detroit night game, Mantle belts a long-range, towering shot that lands atop the right field roof of Briggs Stadium off one of the AL's two 20-game winners this year. The ball has been rocketed onto the top of the roof of the 110-foot-high press box, and once again only ooohs, ahhhs, and gasps are heard from the largest crowd of the year, some 43,474 astonished Tiger fanatics seated in the old ballpark. Detroit wins the game, 6–3.

| 188. | June 10 | Detroit | Frank Lary | Detroit | 9–4, Det | 17,644 |
| 189. | June 11 | Chicago | Jim Wilson | Chicago(n) | 3–2, NY | 49,114 |

The battered ball lands in the upper tier of the rightfield grandstand at Comiskey Park.

| 190. | June 13 | Chicago | Jack Harshman(LH) | Chicago(n) | 7–6, Chi | 40,033 |

Before the game begins, Mantle stumbles into the locker room, his clothes disheveled, his eyes bloodshot, and his demeanor decidedly "sloshed" from a night of boozing. His concerned teammates take him to their bosom, hide him from Stengel, and place him on the training table so he can sleep it off, however briefly. Mickey recovers from his nocturnal and all-day partying, suits up for the game, and takes his place in the outfield. Facing Harshman, Mantle puts his wayward ways behind him and belts out a round-tripper for the Bombers.

| 191. | June 13 | Chicago | Bob Keegan | Chicago(n) | 7–6, Chi | 40,033 |

Mickey connects again, this time left-handed off the right-handed Keegan for a long, towering blast that soars into the center field bullpen at old Comiskey Park. It is also the fifth time that Mantle has hit home runs from both sides of the plate in the same game. It is Mantle's seventh home run in the last eight games. Both of the young belter's blasts in this marathon contest come at the beginning and the conclusion of this very long contest. Though the "Mick" goes 4-for-5 with four runs batted in, the Yankees still manage to lose the tilt, 7–6.

The game is marred somewhat when a full-scale brawl is ignited between angry members of the visiting Yankees and the hometowners. One of the more active, combative participants, the strapping, robust Walt Dropo of the White Sox, had taken on the aging Enos "Country" Slaughter of the New York Yankees, who will emerge from the fray appearing the worst for the wear indeed, ripped to bloody shreds.

| 192. | June 14 | Kansas City | Gene Host(LH) | Kansas City(n) | 10–1, NY | 24,639 |

This particular home run during this nocturnal contest represents another landmark for Mickey as he belts out the 100th career home run on-the-road for the Yankees. Mickey greets Gene Host who has come in to relieve for the Sox with a robust longball.

June 16, 1957: Playing in his first game as a new Kansas City A, Billy Martin, traded the day before by the Yankees, now finds himself facing his new team's opposing starting pitcher, Whitey Ford, a bosom buddy and now a former teammate. The two good friends, along with Mickey, their constant companion and Third Musketeer, had discussed this moment the night before. As Mickey listened, the two old friends had plotted together. Whitey will give Martin a pitch to hit. There are two catches, however. The Yankees must have a safe lead against the lowly A's and Martin cannot hit a home run. It is agreed that before delivering the pitch, if Ford stands straight up when he starts his motion to the plate, he will be throwing a fast ball. If he starts his motion bent over, it will be a curve ball. Now, on this day, Martin is standing in the batter's box as the newest member of the Kansas City Athletics. With the Yankees safely ahead in the game, Martin peers at the crafty southpaw, who is standing straight up. Ford lets go with the fast ball, and Martin clobbers it into the stands for a home run. All the way around the bases, Martin cannot stop laughing. ERA league leader and 19-game winner this year, Whitey gets in the last word. In Martin's next at-bat, Ford levels Martin with a fast ball under his chin, sending his old friend sprawling and giving him a message.

| 193. | June 22 | Chicago | Jack Harshman(LH) | Stadium | 6–5, NY (in 13) | 39,544 |

Mickey slams an opposite-field shot into the right-center field bleachers.

| 194. | June 23 (second game) | Chicago | Dick Donovan | Stadium | 4–3, Chi | 64,936 (63,787 pd.) |

After going 4-for-5 in the first game of the twin bill, Mantle launches another Herculean shot that carries high and far until it crashes into the upper-deck filigree of the rightfield grandstand. An eyewitness and *Baseball Digest* editor, John Kuenster, will later relate that the ball "was hit with such force that the ball banged against the overhang almost before Donovan could turn his head." Donovan will later call this particular blow the hardest ball ever hit against him. The righthander also estimates that the ball would have traveled 550 to 575 feet if the stadium's structural impediments had not been in the way.

| 195. | July 1 | Baltimore | George Zuverink | Balt.(n) | 3–2, NY (in 10) | 45,276 |

Mantle launches a tenth-inning game-winner high into the rightfield bleachers.

July 3, 1957: At Yankee Stadium, the hometown pinstripers are led to victory over the touring Bosox by Yogi Berra, who goes 3-for-5, including a home run. Berra's master batsmanship this day accounts for eight runs batted in. In addition, the Yankee backstop would single twice in this 10–0 slaughter of the Red Sox. Berra's second single is a milestone for the batty backstop, the 1,000th hit of his career.

THE 1957 ALL-STAR GAME

SPORTSMAN'S PARK IN ST. LOUIS, MISSOURI
JULY 9

The selection process for those elite ballplayers who constitute the 1957 All-Star Game has been contaminated by suspicious ballot-stuffing procedures in Cincinnati that have ostensibly elected Redleg outfielders George Crowe, Gus Bell, Wally Post, and a host of other Redleg ballplayers for participation in this year's midsummer classic. Because of the voting fiasco, all eight starting positions in the All-Star Game for the National League are members of the Cincinnati Reds. Baseball Commissioner Ford Frick makes a command decision, vacating the voting results and making appropriate selections for the National League All-Stars himself. Commissioner Frick chooses perennial All-Stars like Willie Mays, Stan "The Man" Musial, and Henry Aaron. As for the game itself, the contest proves to be one of the most exciting games since the classic's inception. Before 30,693 National League rooters alongside the Mississippi River, Jim Bunning of the Detroit Tigers shines on the mound, retiring nine batters in a row. Mickey goes 1-for-4 with a scratch single along the first base line in the first, and also scores a run and walks once. In another at-bat, Clem Labine strikes Mickey out. Among the great consistencies in Midsummer Classics in the Fifties and the Sixties are not only Mantle's perennial presence among the game's greats, but his number of mounting All-Star Game strikeouts. The American League wins the star-filled competition, 6–5.

196.	July 11	Kansas City	Tom Morgan	Kansas City(n) 3–2, NY	20,115
				(in 11)	

Mickey connects for an 11th-inning, 465-foot game-winner over the left field wall.

197.	July 12	Kansas City	Ralph Terry	Kansas City(n) 4–2, KC	23,721
198.	July 21	Cleveland	Ray Narleski	Cleveland 7–4, Cle	51,670
	(second game)				

Mickey's wallop is the only hit he will get this day. Cleveland's strategy is to pitch around the dangerous slugger, opting instead to walk him six times. The plan appears to work as the Tribe emerges victorious.

199.	July 23	Chicago	Bob Keegan	Stadium(n) 10–6, NY	42,422

Mantle hits for the cycle, smacking a single, double, a triple, and a 465-foot home run. It is the first time in AL history that a switch-hitter has accomplished this feat. Mickey's third-inning titanic clout ultimately descends into the next-to-last row of the right-center field bleachers situated to the right of the massive Ballantine Ale and Beer scoreboard. This long, monumental wallop impacts into a sea of outstretched Bronx hands. It is the closest that any aspiring ballplayer has ever come to leaving the ballyard in this, remote section of Yankee Stadium. "The Mick's" bases-loaded triple proves to be the game-winner. His four RBIs provide the winning margin in a 10–6 victory.

| 200. | July 26 | Detroit | Jim Bunning | Stadium(n) | 3–2, Det | 31,812 |

Mickey unleashes a high, opposite-field fly ball that hugs the left field foul line all the way into the seats for a home run.

| 201. | July 31 | Kansas City | Wally Burnette(LH) | Stadium | 2–0, NY | 15,709 |
| | (first game) | | | | | |

The ball lands in the opposite-field, upper-deck boxes of the right field grandstand at Yankee Stadium.

| 202. | Aug. 2 | Cleveland | Don Mossi(LH) | Stadium(n) | 3–2, NY | 36,599 |

This particular home run is a lazer shot that does not exceed a height of 15 feet for the entire course of its bullet-like flight until it rockets into the left field seats.

| 203. | Aug. 7 | Wash. | "Tex" Clevenger | Stadium | 3–2, Wash | 10,039 |

After fouling off a pitch on his right foot, painfully dropping him to the ground, Mickey gets up, brushes himself off, and prepares for the next pitch from Clevenger. On the next pitch, Mantle crashes a home run into the right field seats.

| 204. | Aug. 10 | Baltimore | Ray Moore | Baltimore(n) | 6–3, NY | 36,366 |

As 36,366 rabid Oriole fans settle down in their seats to watch the game, Mickey Mantle connects on a pitch from Ray Moore in the first inning that brings everyone in Memorial Stadium to their feet. Mantle propels the horsehide to a point in the stadium that no player has ever reached. The ball clears the fence some 425 feet away from home plate and soars over the 10-foot-high hedge some 30 feet beyond, until it finally comes back down, bouncing against the distant right-center field scoreboard, approximately 475 feet away. "The Mick" is the first player ever to reach this distant point. Leading the Yankees to a 6–3 victory, Mantle goes 4-for-5, including this prodigious two-run drive that is the slugger's 31st of the year.

| 205. | Aug. 13 | Boston | Frank Sullivan | Boston(n) | 3–2, NY | 35,647 |

With this particular round-tripper, Mantle has now hit a home run in every American League park this season. The homer proves to be the game-winner before the largest big league crowd in Beantown this year.

| 206. | Aug. 26 | Detroit | Frank Lary | Detroit | 5–2, Det | 23,550 |

At Briggs Stadium, Mickey Mantle belts out his 33rd home run of the year, connecting off Detroit's Frank Lary. The ball sails deep into the old ballpark's upper deck of the centerfield grandstand some 440 feet away, another patented "tape-measure" shot by Number Seven.

207.   Aug. 30   Wash.   Chuck Stobbs(LH)   Stadium   4–2, Wash.   9,235

Mantle's shot sails to the opposite field over the low railing of the right field wall. It also represents the 100th career home run that Mickey has belted at Yankee Stadium.

Mantle will miss most of the next and last month due to what the Yankee front office deems a bad case of shin splints, which is precisely what Mickey had told them had happened. In fact, it is not what really happened. In a golfing match with his friend and teammate Tom Sturdivant on one particular game day, Mickey had lost his temper over a bad hole and took a wild swing at a tree limb with his putter. It snapped in two, flew off at the handle, and crashed into his own shin. Mickey and Sturdivant cover up the truth and invent a different, more acceptable "accident." Mantle is forced to take ten days off. Injuries will begin to play a more important role in Mickey's game of play in the American League. Mickey Mantle will hurt his right shoulder during the latter phase of the season, an injury which will be compounded in Game Three of the World Series. Mantle will bring his shoulder ailments to spring training along with his aching right knee, which will haunt him in the beginning of the baseball season of 1958 and will continue to do so until the end of his career.

September 19, 1957: Two days before, Ted Williams had pinch-hit and walked. Then, on September 18th, he took the day off. Today, he appears once more at the plate in the second game of the Yankee Stadium series. Facing Whitey Ford in a pinch-hitting role in the first game of a double-header, Williams hits a long ball to right field that barely clears the short right-field railing. Even down seven runs, Bosox slugger Williams recognizes a mistake when a pitcher makes one, even by so great a pitcher as Whitey Ford. It is the only high curve ball that Ford will ever throw to Ted Williams in the great hitter's career. Later, in the second game of the double-header played this day, Williams poles his 13th career grand-slam home run off "Bullet Bob" Turley. "Teddy Ballgame" also walks in three plate appearances the rest of the day. Mantle and Williams, meanwhile, are battling it out once again for the American League batting championship. Mickey goes 1-for-1.

September 20, 1957: At Yankee Stadium, Ted Williams of the Boston Red Sox appears in the ninth inning as a pinch-hitter to face Yankee righthander Bob Grim. The Yankees win the game, 7–4, but Ted still pounds out a home run that keeps alive his streak for reaching base in consecutive plate appearances as well as connecting for two consecutive home runs in two successive official at-bats.

September 21, 1957: In the next-to-final game of the stadium series with the Yankees, Ted Williams walks while facing Yankee starter Tom Sturdivant. In his next at-bat, Williams poles another home run, his third in as many games and in as many official at-bats. "Teddy Ballgame" also singles and walks again. Williams has now reached base safely in 16 consecutive plate appearances—a major league record. Prior to the game, in a personally significant aside, Mickey Mantle is honored by Francis Cardinal Spellman for the young ballplayer's charitable work for research in the fight against Hodgkin's disease, the disease that claimed his father and so many of the male members of his family.

September 22, 1957: Before 34,186 clamoring fans at Yankee Stadium, Ted Williams of the Red Sox slams his fourth home run in his fourth successive game, tying a major league record. The fourth-inning blow underscores a perfect day at the plate for Williams, who goes 2-for-2 with two walks. During the streak, Williams had also worked the opposing pitchers for four bases on balls. The Red Sox win the game, 5–1, thanks to the offensive support of their "Splendid Splinter," who is currently hitting .383. The Thumper from Beantown will add five points to his average before the season ends, which gives him a finishing average of .388, some 23 points ahead of second-place-finishing Mickey Mantle, who will hit .365.

THE 1957 NEW YORK YANKEES

First Place: with a 98-56 record under Manager Casey Stengel Yankee Stadium attendance: 1,497,134

Awards: American League MVP (only the third time in history that an American League ballplayer has ever won back-to-back MVPs, accomplished by Jimmie Foxx and Hal Newhouser); Mickey Mantle is voted on *Sporting News'* All-Star Major League Team as an outfielder.

Mickey Mantle's League-leading Categories: Mickey Mantle with 146 walks (led majors) and 121 runs scored (led majors). It also establishes a major league record for switch-hitters, his 146 bases on balls in a single season. This establishes a major league record that still stands. Mantle establishes another major league record by hitting for an all-time high batting average of .365 for switch-hitters in the modern era. And, in a special noteworthy accomplishment, between his hits and his walks, Mickey reaches base for the entire season more than half the times he comes to the plate to hit.

MICKEY MANTLE'S 1957 HITTING RECORD

G	AB	R	H	2B	3B	HR	HR%	RBI	SA	BB	SO	SB	AVE.

| 144 | 474 | 121 | 173 | 28 | 6 | 34 | 7.2 | 94 | .665 | 146 | 75 | 16 | .365 |

In 1957, Mickey Mantle hit .365 while the major leagues averaged .258, both leagues scoring an average 8.61 runs per game and both hitting 1.78 home runs per contest. During the 144 games that Mickey Mantle appeared in for 1957, he played in the outfield 139 times and appeared in five additional games as a pinch-hitter.

Mickey's 1957 Salary: $65,000

World Series Losing Share: $5,606

Number of Games in Which Mantle Homered: 33

Winning Record When Mickey Mantle Homered: 20-13, a winning percentage of .618

THE 1957 WORLD SERIES

October 2, 1957: In Game One, played this day at Yankee Stadium, the Milwaukee Braves arrive in the Big Apple sporting their new 1957 patch of a bronzed-face Indian on their sleeves to play the defending world champions of major league baseball. With one out in the sixth inning, Yankee third baseman Andy Carey knocks out Braves ace Warren Spahn with a clutch run-scoring single. Jerry Coleman adds an insurance run when he squeezes in a third run in the game.

The real story, however, is Whitey Ford, who spins a five-hitter against the awestruck Braves, many of whose players are playing in the majestic old ballyard for the first time. The Yankees win the opener, 3–1.

October 3, 1957: Over their awe of the historic ballyard and without facing Whitey Ford, the Braves, veterans of the National League pennant wars the last two years, have come to play. In the second inning of Game Two of the World Series, played this day at Yankee Stadium, Mantle misjudges a long Henry Aaron poke off Yankee lefthander Bobby Shantz. The ball Aaron hits is a rising line drive that just seems to go further and further, directly at the pin-striped centerfielder. As Mickey's feet and body get tangled up backpedaling after the 445-foot drive, the ball finally clears a last-second flick of Mantle's glove to snare the ball. Aaron's long-range drive eludes the normally gifted outfielder and plays into a triple. Mantle has always had trouble with the line-drive hit directly at him. This is not to take away anything from "Hammering Hank" who tagged the ball, a clout normally good enough for a home run anywhere in the big leagues. But this is Yankee Stadium's "Death Valley," and 445 feet is just not enough. Shortly thereafter, Aaron ambles home on a Joe Adcock single for the Braves' second run of the game. The Braves prevail, 4–2, behind the seven-hit pitching of Lew Burdette, some fine defensive support from Wes Covington in left field for the Braves, and a clutch home run by Johnny Logan. The Braves win Game Two and even the Series at one game apiece.

October 5, 1957: In Game Three of the World Series, the first ever played in Milwaukee, leadoff batter Hank Bauer of the New York Yankees bounces back to Brave starter Bob Buhl. The next batter, Tony Kubek, homers, and the Yankees are off to the races, outscoring the hometown nine in clumps.

After reaching first base on a first-inning single, Mickey advances to second, and is leading off ready to go home on a safety as the Braves righthander prepares to pitch. Then, suddenly, with a quick turn toward center field, a wild pick-off try is attempted by Bob Buhl on Mickey at second base. The ball is thrown wild of the bag and into center field and Mickey dives back to second. In the subsequent collision between Mantle and second baseman "Red" Schoendienst that the attempt will produce, a Series-ending injury occurs. As Mickey himself will later recall, when the Braves veteran infielder loses his balance, he falls on Mantle's right shoulder "with his full weight." Mantle will describe the pain, stating, "It was as if someone had dropped a sack of cement on me and the wonder is that no bone cracked." Mickey will finish the game, collect a single and a home run off Gene Conley powered into the Milwaukee bullpen to the right of straightaway center field, the deepest part of the park.

But after the game, stiffness in his right arm will occur during the evening hours that will prevent Mantle from even lifting a bat with his right shoulder where he has torn a ligament. Ol' Casey himself said that this career-lingering injury would result in producing "'a hitch' in his swing. He became too much of a lift hitter. His swing wasn't level enough."

As for now, Mickey is effectively finished for the Series. Indeed, he will later admit, "I was never quite the hitter I had been from the left side of the plate."

After his collision with Schoendienst. Mantle, it is noted, will collect 329 home runs from this point in his career until his final game in 1968, with 228 coming from the left side of the plate.

His injuries are beginning to mount, however. Dr. Sidney Gardner will later give his assessment of Mantle's injury-ridden body and his approach to the burden of playing by overcoming pain. "Mickey Mantle," the good doctor will say, "has the capacity to stand pain more than any man I have ever known; it is truly remarkable that Mantle played 18 years with those crippled legs and especially when he wasn't expected to last five years!" As for the Series, the Yankees have now taken the lead, two games to one, but will have to go the rest of the way with a hampered Mantle, or with no Mantle.

As for Game Three on this day, the Yankees never look back as Tony Kubek adds another home run to the onslaught. Kubek becomes the 15th player ever in Series history to pound out two home runs in the same game. Nevertheless, working over six Milwaukee hurlers, the Yankees trounce the hometown Braves, 12–3, in County Stadium. The only real Brave's highlight comes when Henry Aaron connects for a two-run smash off Bob Turley in the fifth.

The Braves will pull out the Series with a home run in the 10th inning of Game Four, which evens the Series. The next afternoon will see a 1–0 pitcher's duel fall to Series MVP Lew Burdette, who outclasses both Ford for seven innings and Turley in relief. With a split back in the Bronx, the Milwaukee Braves take the Series and are crowned baseball's newest World Champions. Mantle has had a disappointing Series and another brush with critical injuries. And this newest injury, to his right shoulder, will alter the future for the young slugger; he will never hit with the same kind of left-handed power that he has enjoyed thus far in his career. Mickey returns to his family in Oklahoma and an off-season for resting his sore shoulder, rehabilitating his weary knees, and enjoying some fishing and hunting.

THE 1958 REGULAR SEASON

42 HOME RUNS

H.R.#	DATE	OPPONENT	PITCHER	SITE	SCORE	ATTND.
208.	Apr. 17	Boston	Tom Brewer	Boston	3–1, NY	15,033

Mantle connects for a fifth-inning game-winner over the "Green Monster" in left-center field.

209.	May 9	Wash.	Pedro Ramos	Stadium(n)	9–5, NY	18,604

Mickey launches a prodigious, 450-foot, inside-the-park to dead center field in the third inning.

210.	May 18 (first game)	Wash.	Pedro Ramos	Wash., D.C.	5–2, NY	27,704

With Vice-President Richard M. Nixon in attendance, Mantle powers a high, opposite-field poke that keeps carrying deep to left field. Disgusted with the result of his at-bat, Mickey slams his bat down into the ground. His anger, however, turns to surprising glee when his high drive to left field disappears into the grandstand.

211.	May 20	Chicago	Dick Donovan	Chicago(n)	5–1, NY	36,167

This particular nighttime explosion is rocketed to the left-center field gap for an inside-the-park home run.

212.	June 2	Chicago	Jim Wilson	Stadium(n)	3–0, NY	12,641

The first and winning runs driven in for the Yankees come on Mickey's first-inning clout.

213.   June 3   Chicago   Dick Donovan   Stadium(n)   13–0, NY   30,970

Mantle launches a first-inning, three-run line drive home run into the right field grandstand. It gives the Yankees all that the team needs for victory.

214.   June 4   Chicago   Billy Pierce(LH)   Stadium   7–2, NY   8,582

Mickey clubs another of his "tape-measure" drives, a sixth-inning, 475-foot, three-run clout that lands 20 rows deep in the left-center field bleachers, sailing over the barrier well to the right of the visitors' bullpen and deep towards the back wall of the stadium's structure.

215.   June 5   Chicago   Early Wynn   Stadium   12–5, NY   14,102
        (first game)

Mantle's home run cuts the two Chisox outfielders in two in right-center field for an inside-the-park round-tripper.

216.   June 6   Cleveland   Dick Tomanek(LH)   Stadium(n)   6–5, NY   35,422

Mantle's night game shot caroms off the front railing of the left field upper deck. This blow duplicates the long-range accomplishments of only six other players, including Andy Carey, Gus Zernial, Hank Greenberg, and Jimmie Foxx. Only Joe DiMaggio has accomplished the feat twice.

217.   June 6   Cleveland   Dick Tomanek(LH)   Stadium(n)   6–5, NY   35,422

Mickey connects for another Bunyanesque drive that sails into the left field bleachers. The blow represents "the Mick's" sixth home run in the last six games.

218.   June 8   Cleveland   Jim "Mudcat" Grant   Stadium(tn) 5-4, Cle   40,903
        (second game)
219.   June 13   Detroit   Billy Hoeft(LH)   Stadium(n)   4–2, Det   35,660

Mantle powers the ball deep into the lower left field grandstand.

220.   June 24   Chicago   Early Wynn   Chicago(n)   6–2, NY   27,845

Mickey slugs a 420-foot home run into the center field bullpen.

June 26, 1958: On a day in Kansas City when Hector Lopez pounds out three home runs in the A's 8–6, 12-inning victory over the Washington Senators, the New York Yankees are in Chicago playing the White Sox. In the game itself, Mantle will knock out one hit, score one run, and drive in another in their 4–3 victory. But what sets the 18,214 Chicago folk buzzing is the pre-game batting practice session. Mickey puts on a clinic in long-ball prowess when, batting left-handed, he powers three balls out of the massive Comiskey Park and over the double-decked, right field grandstand roof. The foul line stretches some 352 feet down the line and extends to 400 feet in right-center field. All three of Mantle's batting practice monsters have soared out of the old ballyard at both these points and between, hushing the crowd and players alike as Mantle's naked power reveals itself.

221.	June 29	Kansas City	Ralph Terry	Kansas City	12–6, KC	30,606
222.	July 1 (first game)	Baltimore	Connie Johnson	Balt.(tn)	7–5, Balt	33,292

Mantle slams an opposite-field drive that carries over the left-field wall.

| 223. | July 1 (second game) | Baltimore | Jack Harshman(LH) | Balt.(tn) | 2–1, NY | 33,292 |

Mickey breaks the tie in the eighth inning with a game-winning home run to center field.

| 224. | July 3 | Wash. | Russ Kemmerer | Wash., D.C. | 11-3, NY | 4,452 |

Mantle's titanic long-ball clears the 31-foot-high wall over the 372-foot marker in right-center field and is still rising when it clears an advertising sign and the ballyard some 450 feet from home plate in the old Washington ballyard. The shot also carries the day for the Bombers, giving the Yankees the winning edge.

| 225. | July 3 | Wash | Russ Kemmerer | Wash., D.C. | 11-3, NY | 4,452 |

Mickey wallops a tremendous opposite-field shot that carries some two-thirds of the way up the distant left-center field grandstand bleachers.

226.	July 4 (second game)	Wash.	Chuck Stobbs(LH)	Wash., D.C.	13–2, NY	20,688
227.	July 5	Boston	Dave Sisler	Stadium(n)	3–3, tie	43,821
					(tie because of curfew in the 10th inning)	

Mantle homers off the son of Hall of Famer George Sisler with the ball carrying into the top tier of the right-field grandstand. The clout ties the game in the bottom of the ninth inning. The contest is stopped to adhere to the American League rule that no game can move past midnight and into the Sabbath. Thus, at 11:59P.M., the announcement is made that the game is suspended with the score deadlocked at three's.

| 228. | July 6 | Boston | Ike Delock | Stadium | 10–4, Bos | 33,195 |

Mickey triggers his swing, connects, and propels the ball deep to right-center field until it descends into the scoreboard bleachers.

THE 1958 ALL-STAR GAME

MEMORIAL STADIUM IN BALTIMORE, MARYLAND
JULY 8

Before 48,829 Baltimore boosters of the American League, Yankee slugger Mickey Mantle starts for the American League in center field. Bob Cerv of the Kansas City Athletics starts in left field with Jackie Jensen of the Boston Red Sox in right. The trio of All-Star flyhawks are the American League's starting All-Star outfield. All three young men some six years before had competed for the honor of replacing Joe DiMaggio in center field. In the game itself, Mickey goes 1-for-2. Both Bob Friend of the Pittsburgh Pirates and Dick Farrell of the Philadelphia Phillies walk "The Mick." The American League wins the star-spangled contest, 4–3.

July 9, 1958: After Yankee Manager Casey Stengel, Ted Williams, Mickey Mantle, and others testify before Congress on the question of baseball anti-trust, the old man and his slugging protégé fly back to New York City for a night game with the visiting Cleveland Indians. On this night, before a stunned assembly of 17,796 rabidly disappointed Bomber boosters, Mickey Mantle gives one offering a tremendous ride as he connects for a long, towering fly towards the wide expanse of the stadium's center-field playing area—the ballyard's massive graveyard for longballs. With the sound of the bat, the flashy, mercuric Indian outfielder Larry Doby takes off like a bullet for the center field flagpole and the distant center field bleachers beyond. The speedy Doby eventually catches up with the gargantuan shot until he flies halfway up the high wall of the center field bleachers some 461 feet away. Doby makes a brilliant leaping catch with his back against the wall. The Yankees win the tilt, 12–2.

| 229. | July 11 | Cleveland | Ray Narleski | Stadium | 11–3, NY | 8,973 |

Mickey connects for a towering drive that carries eight rows deep into the top tier of the right field grandstand at Yankee Stadium.

| 230. | July 14 | Chicago | Early Wynn | Stadium(n) | 5–0, NY | 15,311 |

Mantle powers a 400-foot, opposite-field home run to left field.

231.	July 15	Detroit	Frank Lary	Stadium	12–5, Det	15,614
232.	July 23	Detroit	Bill Fischer	Detroit(n)	16–4, NY	39,644
233.	July 24	Detroit	Paul Foytack	Detroit	10–7, NY	25,704

After getting shellacked by the Tigers ten days before, as of this day's game, at a site no less impressive than Detroit itself, the Yankees have whipped the Tigers five straight times. This the Yankees have done with an able assist from Number Seven. As a result of this morale-breaking drubbing and the four others in succession that lead to it, the Tigers will fold their tents for this year and dream of pennants another day. On this day, Mickey goes 3-for-4, including connecting for the game-winning home run in the eighth inning.

| 234. | July 28 | Kansas City | Dick Tomanek(LH) | Kansas City(n) 14–7, NY | 19,984 |

Mickey lifts a long, opposite-field drive to right-center field over the 387-foot marker at Municipal Stadium.

| 235. | July 28 | Kansas City | Ray Herbert | Kansas City(n) 14–7, NY | 19,984 |

Mickey muscles up on a Ray Herbert offering that soars over the 375-foot sign in left-center field. It is also the sixth time that Mantle has belted home runs from both sides of the plate in the same game.

| 236. | Aug. 4 | Baltimore | Charley Beamon | Baltimore(n) 9–4, NY | 26,685 |
| 237. | Aug. 5 | Baltimore | Connie Johnson | Baltimore(n) 4–1, NY | 22,333 |

Mickey pounds out a three-run, game-winning home run in the third inning.

| 238. | Aug. 9 | Boston | Dave Sisler | Stadium | 9-6, Bos | 67,916 |

On Old Timers Day and with Hall-of-Famer George Sisler watching his son pitch in the majors for the first time, Mantle pounds out a towering home run high into the right field upper deck in Yankee Stadium.

| 239. | Aug. 11 (second game) | Baltimore | Connie Johnson | Stadium(tn) | 9–3, Balt | 14,572 |
| 240. | Aug. 12 | Baltimore | Ken Lehman(LH) | Stadium | 7–2, NY | 11,168 |

Mickey connects for a towering, 430-foot belt into the left-field stands adjacent to the remote left field bullpen in Yankee Stadium.

| 241. | Aug. 16 | Boston | Tom Brewer | Boston | 7–4, Bos | 24,925 |

Mickey's high-arching smash lands in the right-center field bleachers behind the Red Sox bullpen.

| 242. | Aug. 17 | Boston | Ike Delock | Boston | 6–5, Bos | 30,501 |

Mickey pounds out a home run high and deep into the center field bleachers at Fenway Park.

| 243. | Aug. 22 | Chicago | Early Wynn | Stadium | 8–5, NY | 12,527 |
| 244. | Aug. 27 | Kansas City | Tom Gorman | Stadium | 11–7, NY | 19,865 |

Mantle poles a home run into the right field seats down the line.

| 245. | Sept. 2 | Boston | Dave Sisler | Stadium(n) | 6–1, NY | 23,770 |

Mickey teams with Yogi Berra on back-to-back home runs with the Yankee backstop's proving to be the game-winner.

246.   Sept. 3   Boston   Frank Sullivan   Stadium   8–5, NY   13,627

Mickey propels a lazer shot into the right field stands.

247.   Sept. 9   Cleveland   Cal McLish   Cleveland(n) 9–2, Cle   8,638

Mantle unloads a tremendous 410-foot clout over the distant center field wall.

248.   Sept. 17   Detroit   Jim Bunning   Detroit   5–2, Det   2,973

At Briggs Stadium, Mickey Mantle is facing Tiger righthander Jim Bunning in the third inning when he swats one of Bunning's deliveries in a long, towering, arching drive towards the right field roof and the auxiliary press box. The ball clears everything before it hits a building on the other side of Trumbull Avenue. On the fly, the prodigious shot had been powered more than 500 feet away. Not since 1939, when Ted Williams poled his famous shot over the right field roof has a player reached this distant point along the right field foul line. It is the 41st home run this season for this year's home run king in the American League. The blast comes three days after the Yankees would clinch the 1958 American League pennant in Kansas City.

September 20, 1958: Playing at Memorial Stadium in Baltimore, before 10,941 thrilled Oriole rooters, Hoyt Wilhelm faces the visiting New York Yankees. Oriole knuckleballer Wilhelm has fared badly as a starter, going 0-6 thus far this season. On this day, Wilhelm joins the team's regular pitching rotation for the first time in the year. To celebrate his promotion, the Oriole pitches a no-hitter against the New York Yankees, blanking the pin-striped powerhouse, 1–0. It is the first no-hitter ever thrown by a Baltimore Oriole pitcher in the history of the franchise in this century. The only run comes as a result of Wilhelm's backstop, Gus Triandos, who homers in the game. In the Mantle Era, Hoyt Wilhelm is only the second of two pitchers in Mickey's career who pitches a no-hitter against the New York Yankees.

249.   Sept. 24   Boston   Tom Gorman   Boston   7–5, NY   10,020

After Number Seven connects, the abused ball disappears over the left-center field portion of the fabled "Green Monster" some 380 feet away, for a game-winner for the Bombers.

THE 1958 NEW YORK YANKEES

First Place: with a 92–62 record under Manager Casey Stengel. Yankee Stadium attendance: 1,428,438

Mickey Mantle's League-leading Categories: Mickey Mantle with 42 home runs, 307 total bases, 129 bases on balls (led majors), 127 runs scored (led majors), and 120 strikeouts which tied for the major league lead. This latter mark establishes a new Yankee club record, exceeding his own mark.

MICKEY MANTLE'S 1958 HITTING RECORD

G	AB	R	H	2B	3B	HR	HR%	RBI	SA	BB	SO	SB	AVE.
150	519	127	158	21	1	42	8.1	97	.592	129	120	18	.304

In 1958, Mickey Mantle hit .304, while the major leagues averaged .258 with both leagues scoring an average 8.56 runs per game and both hitting 1.81 home runs per contest. During the 150 games that Mickey Mantle appeared in for 1958, he played in the outfield 150 times.

Mickey's 1958 Salary: $75,000

World Series Winning Share: $8,759

Injuries or Operations: Though missing only four games throughout the season, the semi-crippled athlete received painful, debilitating radiation treatments. Often, during the year, recalls teammate Bob Turley, Mantle's shoulder pain was "so intense that he ended up swinging one-handed many times while still connecting for game-winning hits or home runs."

Number of Games in Which Mantle Homered: 38

Winning Record When Mickey Mantle Homered: 26–12 and one tie a winning percentage of .605

THE 1958 WORLD SERIES

October 2, 1958: In Game Two of the World Series, played this chilly day at County Stadium, the Milwaukee Braves establish a Series record by scoring seven runs in the opening inning. In fact, the Yankees have had a good idea what was coming when Bill Bruton became the seventh player ever to hit a home run leading off a game. The lethal, seven-run assault on Yankee starter Turley and long reliever "Duke" Maas will be capped by a home run belted by Milwaukee starting pitcher Lew Burdette himself. Burdette becomes the sixth pitcher in Series history to belt out a home run in a World Series game. The Yankees now face an uphill battle for the rest of the game.

Meanwhile, on the Yankee side of the ledger, Mantle, in an attempt to keep the Bronx Bombers in the game, poles two home runs off the Braves' right-handed ace.

It is the 16th time that this feat has occurred in Series history. The Yankee slugger becomes the 13th player ever to participate in a World Series to hit two home runs in the same Series tilt. With respect to the game, however, Mickey is the only Yankee to solve the problem of Lew Burdette, who resumes where he left off in 1957 with the Yankees. It is the fourth consecutive victory that Burdette has engineered against the Bronx Bombers, the pride of the American League. The Braves win the game, 13–5. Now, in the Series, the Yankees are down two games to none.

October 4, 1958: In the 55th World Series contest ever played at Yankee Stadium, Game Three of the 1958 Series, it is the fifth inning when Hank Bauer comes through to break the scoreless deadlock with a clutch two-run single. The bases had been jammed after Milwaukee hurler Bob Rush walked three Yankee batters in the same frame. Later, in the seventh frame, Bauer's two-run home run would ice the game. Bauer has knocked in the entire scoring output of his team's vaunted offense, which gives the Bombers a 4–0 triumph. It is the first notch in the Series win column for the Bronx Bombers.

October 5, 1958: In Game Four of the Series, played again at Yankee Stadium, with the score knotted at zeros, Mickey Mantle, to no avail, goes long once with a 425-foot shot that does not make the seats, slamming instead against the remote left-center field bleacher wall for a triple. With Mickey on third base, only a re-markable fielding play orchestrated by "Red" Schoendienst would prevent the Mantle tally. The Redbird second baseman makes a tumbling-fumbling stop of a soft, loop-ing, line-drive daisy over the head of the Braves infielder, hit by Yogi Berra, prevent-ing the Yanks from scoring. The ball slaps the ground as Schoendienst sprawls on the turf, scrambles over to the wayward sphere, picks up the rock and fires to first. As Mickey crossed the plate, Berra is nipped at first base, vacating the score. The run will not count and the game will remain tied. Only Mickey's triple and Bill Skowron's single in the seventh are all that the Yanks can muster off the masterful Warren Spahn, who will spin a nifty, two-hit, 3–0 shutout. The Braves have now taken a commanding 3–1 lead in the Series.

October 8, 1958: In Game Six of the Series, played this day at County Stadium, the respective pitching staffs collar their respective foes to two runs apiece, moving into the 10th inning. Gil McDougald belts a tie-breaking home run in the top of the frame. Singles by Elston Howard, Yogi Berra, and "Moose" Skowron add another. The Braves answer the Yankee rally with one run, but fall short by one, with the bases loaded. The final out made in Game Six, the Yankee "must" victory, is realized when Red Schoendienst's fly ball falls into Mickey Mantle's glove in center field. The putout promises a Game Seven, and culminates in one of the greatest comebacks in the history of the World Series. Having faced Series elimination, the Yanks have struggled back to even the Series at three games apiece.

October 9, 1958: In Game Seven at County Stadium, Bob Turley will come in to relieve Don Larsen in the third inning. "Bullet Bob" will slam the door shut on the Braves. The Yankees have come back all the way, down three games to one, to win the championship. It is the first time that such a comeback has been orchestrated since 1925, when the Washington Senators came back to topple the front-running New York Giants. The operative frame comes in the eighth inning, when the Yankees collect four runs to break the 2–2 tie. Elston Howard will break the tie with a run-scoring single and "Moose" Skowron will cap the scoring with a home run. The Yankees, on the brink of extinction, have come back to snatch victory from the jaws of defeat. The Bombers will take the Series and capture the fifth World Championship of the Mickey Mantle Era.

THE 1959 REGULAR SEASON
31 HOME RUNS

H.R.#	DATE	OPPONENT	PITCHER	SITE	SCORE	ATTND.
250.	Apr. 21	Wash.	Pedro Ramos	Wash., D.C.(n)	11-4, NY	13,297

Facing the Cuban-born righthander, Pedro Ramos, who sports the new Senators patch designed by satirist Zang Auerbach from his original cartoon caricature of "Mister Senator," the left-handed-hitting Mantle booms a towering drive to dead-center off the Senator hurler into the distant bleachers of Griffith Stadium.

April 22, 1959: In a night game at Griffith stadium, before 7,337 hearty Washingtonians enduring the chill, Bill Skowron of the New York Yankees blasts a home run that wins the 14-inning, 1–0 thriller. It is the longest game in American League history ever settled by a home run with a 1–0 score. Mickey goes 0-for-5.

H.R.#	DATE	OPPONENT	PITCHER	SITE	SCORE	ATTND.
251.	Apr. 23	Wash.	Russ Kemmerer	Wash., D.C.	3-2, Wash	2,932
252.	Apr. 29	Chicago	Ray Moore	Chicago	5-2, NY	11,724

Mantle lifts a long fly that carries into the right field grandstand.

May 3, 1959: In the first game of a Sunday double-header at Briggs Stadium, before 43,438 exhilarated Tiger boosters, Charley "Paw Paw" Maxwell of the Detroit Tigers goes 2-for-4, including the poling of a ninth-inning home run at the old Detroit ballyard against the Yankees for a 4–2 victory.

Maxwell's Sunday performance is not completed, however. In his first three at-bats in the second game, Maxwell hits three more home runs that tie the major league record for hitting four consecutive home runs and match the American League record for home runs in a double-header. This sterling performance by Maxwell moves him into the exalted ranks of Ted Williams, Jimmie Foxx, Bobby Lowe, Lou Gehrig, Hank Greenberg, Bill Nicholson, and Ralph Kiner. Maxwell is to put a string of Sunday performances together for the Detroit Tigers the likes of which have never been duplicated. He will bring new meaning to the phrase "Sunday punch." Mickey will come to the plate only once in the twin bill, walking in a pinch-hitting appearance in the first game. The Tigers take the second tilt as well, polishing off the Yanks, 8–2.

May 7, 1959: In a special candle lit ceremony at the Los Angeles Memorial Coliseum, the New York Yankees and the Los Angeles Dodgers have arranged to play a special mid-season exhibition game, the purpose of which is to honor the tragically stricken, quadriplegic Roy Campanella, the legendary Brooklyn catcher. A crowd of 93,103 baseball fans will honor the great Dodger and Hall of Fame bound backstop. "Campy" had been tragically paralyzed in a wintertime 1957 automobile crash months before the Dodgers made their permanent move to Los Angeles, in 1958. It is the largest crowd ever to watch a major league baseball game. Mickey does not play in the exhibition game. Before the start of the contest, while confronting a battery of microphones set up near second base, "Campy" tells the massive crowd, "I want to thank each and every one of you from the bottom of my heart for this wonderful tribute—and I thank God that I'm here—living to be here to see it." The Yankees win the unofficial contest, 6–2.

In batting practice on May 8th, an open date, Mickey is taking his cuts with "Duke" Maas, on the mound throwing batting practice. Mickey waits a fraction too late to swing the bat at one of Maas's offerings and takes the pitch flush on his right index finger, where he chips a bone. Batting right-handed is not as large a problem as hitting left-handed. Merely holding the bat, while hitting from the left-hand side of the plate, induces extreme pain. 1959 will be one of the longest seasons, with respect to injuries, that Mickey will endure in his 18-year career. But still the fear of Mantle's great power, injured or not, haunts his American League opponents. Teammate Gil McDougald will later speak of Mickey's long-ball reputation and how it affected Yankee fortunes, stating, "We always knew how bad he was hurt, but the other guy's pitchers didn't. They were afraid of him, and his presence always affected a pitcher's attitude toward us. When he was out, they relaxed and mowed us down."

253.	May 10	Wash.	Chuck Stobbs(LH)	Stadium	6–3, NY	21,769
	(first game)					

Mantle launches a prodigious, towering, 410-foot shot into the left field bullpen at Yankee Stadium. Meanwhile, after completing this day's game without erring, Yankee catcher Yogi Berra has established the major league record for consecutive chances accepted by a catcher without committing an error. Berra's streak extends back in time to when the streak started, almost two years before, on July 28, 1957. In that same time frame, Berra has handled 950 chances without making an error.

| 254. | May 12 | Cleveland | Cal McLish | Stadium(n) | 7-6, Cle | 34,671 |

Not too soon after his right forefinger heals from its chipped bone, Mickey sprains an ankle. It will give him a limp for weeks to come. Mickey's physical deterioration moves Chisox Manager Al Lopez to say, "I don't like to say this, I think Mickey is on his way down. I don't think he'll last very long, what with all his injuries."

| 255. | May 20 | Detroit | Frank Lary | Stadium | 13-6, Det | 11,053 |

Even while rounding the bases on his home run, Mickey Mantle is lustily booed as the fans continue to show their disgust with the sinking fortunes inherent of the Yankees' woeful season. On this very day, Mantle and his Yankee teammates sink to their lowest depths since May 25, 1940, when the Bombers last fell into the American League cellar.

May 21, 1959: With a record of 12 wins and 19 defeats, the New York Yankees, the winner of nine pennants in the last decade and currently the defending world champions, slip into the cellar of the American League.

| 256. | May 23 | Baltimore | George Zuverink | Baltimore | 13-5, Balt | 15,787 |
| 257. | May 24 (first game) | Baltimore | Billy O'Dell(LH) | Baltimore | 9-0, NY | 34,180 |

Mantle poles a booming home run over the 410-foot center field barrier at Memorial Stadium.

| 258. | May 30 (first game) | Wash. | Dick Hyde | Wash. D.C. | 11-2, NY | 26,046 |

Mickey rips a two-run opposite-field blast into the left-center field bleachers. Mantle adds three singles to his afternoon's labors.

The New York Yankees are in last place in the American League. On May 29th in a game at the stadium, Mantle strikes out three times in succession as the Yankees continue to flounder. Mickey, too, is faring poorly, batting a microscopic .228. And then, as if to pick up personally the sagging fortunes of his stricken teammates, Mickey goes on a hitting binge. Shaking the batting lethargy of the last few weeks, Mantle's bat starts to come around in unprecedented form as he bats .522 over the next seven games.

May 31, 1959: Before a discouraged gathering of 8,721 fans at Griffith Stadium in the nation's capital, "Bullet Bob" Turley of the New York Yankees pitches a two-hit shutout of the Washington Senators. While the Yankees win the 3–0 contest, Mantle goes 1-for-4 with a double and scores when Bill "Moose" Skowron poles the three-run home run that wins the game. But the real buzz in the stands still is loosed when Mickey connects high and long to center field, only to watch as Bob Allison flags down the ball for the out at the 438-foot marker.

259.	June 3	Detroit	Ray Narleski	Detroit(n)	6–5, NY	43, 146

Having muscled a long drive for a game-winning home run, Mantle's scorching clout sails into the lower right field stands. Mickey has now set off on a home run tear that begins to set opposing American League pitching ablaze.

260.	June 9	Kansas City	Murray Dickson	Stadium(n)	9–8, NY	23,707
					(in 13)	

Mantle slams a whistling line drive that rockets deep into the lower left field grandstand.

261.	June 11	Kansas City	Ned Garver	Stadium	9-5, KC	7,548
262.	June 13	Detroit	Jim Bunning	Stadium	6–4, NY	25,530

Mantle connects for a home run off one of the star righthander's deliveries that carries into the right field stands on this rainy day.

263.	June 17	Chicago	Ray Moore	Stadium	7–3, NY	11,078

A banged-up Mickey Mantle launches a second-inning, three-run game-winner that lands ten rows beyond the upper deck facing, high in the right field upper deck. Mickey calls the blow "one of the best drives I've had in the last two years."

264.	June 18	Chicago	Jerry Staley	Stadium	5-4, NY	12,217
					(in 10)	

Mantle launches a 10th-inning game-winner into the lower right field stands. As Mickey rounds the bases, fans pour out of the stands to pound the young slugger's back in congratulations and awe-inspired hero worship.

265.	June 22	Kansas City	Ray Herbert	K. C.(n)	11–6, NY	21,451
266.	June 22	Kansas City	Bob Grim	K. C.(n)	11–6, NY	21,451

Mickey also collects a triple and six RBIs.

267.	June 23	Kansas City	Rip Coleman(LH)	K. C.(n)	10–2, NY	22,259

Mantle slams the ball into the left field bleachers.

June 29, 1959: Mantle injures his right ankle. Two days later, he injures his right shoulder, twisting it out of place. Through most of July, 1959, Mantle will hobble through this period on a bad ankle. The injury to his right shoulder will continue to nag the slugging outfielder. Every time Mantle swings left-handed at a high pitch and misses, stabbing pains shoot through his shoulder. Asked about the grimaces on Mantle's face every time he swings at a ball from the left-hand side of the plate and why he doesn't complain, Casey Stengel can only say, "He knows he's got to play, crippled or not. So he don't bother to complain."

July 4, 1959: In the second game of a Yankee Stadium double-header, "Bullet Bob" Turley of the New York Yankees is working on a no-hitter against the Washington Senators when he moves into the ninth inning. With no outs in the frame, Turley surrenders a hit to the Senators when Julio Becquer loops a short fly down the left field foul line that Norm Siebern cannot get to in time. Turley wins the one-hit shutout, 1-0, thrilling 30,276 Bronx rooters. Mickey collects a double in the contest, but does not figure in the scoring.

THE 1959 ALL-STAR GAME

FORBES FIELD IN PITTSBURGH, PENNSYLVANIA
JULY 7 (FIRST GAME)

At Forbes Field in Pittsburgh, with 35,227 Buc boosters rooting for the National League, Vice President Richard M. Nixon throws out the first ball to the midsummer classic. The National League All-Stars play host to the visiting American League All-Stars. It is the second time in history that two All-Star Games will be scheduled in the same season.

The first game goes to the National League. The Nationals' key rally comes in the eighth, when Henry Aaron singles in two runs. Willie Mays then follows with a triple that scores Aaron with the classic's winning run. Mantle's participation in the game is brief as he pinch-runs for Gus Triandos in the eighth inning. The Nationals win, 5–4.

268.	July 16 (first game)	Cleveland	Gary Bell	Stadium	7–5, NY (in 10)	36, 130

Yogi Berra ties it in the ninth inning, with Mickey winning it in the 10th inning with his timely, two-out blast that lands in the third deck of the old ballyard. Fans pour out of the stands and pat his back, shake his hand, and cheer their hero home as he trots towards the plate with the game-ending blow.

269.	July 19 (second game)	Chicago	Billy Pierce(LH)	Stadium	6–4, NY	57,057

THE 1959 ALL-STAR GAME

LOS ANGELES MEMORIAL COLISEUM IN CALIFORNIA
AUGUST 3 (SECOND GAME)

Before 54,982 avid National League boosters, Mickey Mantle goes 1-for-3. Mickey is also walked by the Dodgers' side-whipping Don Drysdale. The Yankee basher also goes down swinging, off Sam "Toothpick" Jones of the San Francisco Giants.

| 270. | Aug. 4 | Detroit | Frank Lary | Stadium(n) | 4–3, Det | 32,972 |
| 271. | Aug. 5 | Detroit | Don Mossi(LH) | Stadium | 3–0, NY | 10,202 |

New York plays Boston at Fenway Park while fighting it out for the pennant with the Chicago White Sox. Welcoming the arrival of the visiting Bosox to the Big Apple, the Yankees are in a position to make a run. It is not to be, however. In the first two games, the Red Sox crush them, 11–6 and 12–4. After losing five straight games, including three to the Red Sox, the hopes for another Yankee title are dashed.

| 272. | Aug. 16 | Boston | Jerry Casale | Stadium | 6–5, Bos | 46,041 |
| | (first game) | | | | | |

In addition to Mantle's upper-deck home run into the right field grandstand, another ball hit by Mantle this day, in this initial tilt, bangs into the 461-foot marker in center field, crashing into the wall so hard and so quickly that it bounces back to centerfielder Gary Geiger, who throws the ball back into the infield, holding Mickey to a double.

| 273. | Aug. 16 | Boston | Bill Monbouquette | Stadium | 6–5, Bos | 46,041 |
| | (second game) | | | | | |

Mantle poles a first-inning, two-run game-winner that lands in the upper deck of the right field grandstand and arrests the Bombers' five-game losing streak.

| 274. | Aug. 26 | Cleveland | Gary Bell | Cleveland(n) | 5–4, Cle | 31,800 |
| 275. | Aug. 29 | Wash. | Hal Griggs | Wash., D.C. | 9–5, NY | 10,229 |

Mickey connects for a 400-foot home run.

| 276. | Sept. 7 | Boston | Jerry Casale | Boston | 12–4, Bos | 19,995 |
| 277. | Sept. 10 | Kansas City | Ray Herbert | Stadium | 12–1, NY | 11,695 |

Mickey collects five straight hits, going 5-for-6, launching the 277th home run of his career, plating three runs, and driving in one.

| 278. | Sept. 13 | Cleveland | Jack Harshman(LH) | Stadium | 2–1, NY | 40,807 |
| | (first game) | | | | (in 11) | |

The Yankees beat the Cleveland Indians as "Bullet Bob" Turley pitches ten scoreless innings. In the top of the 11th inning, the Tribe pushes across a run to take a 1–0 lead. In the home half of the inning, however, clutch-hitting Mickey Mantle pounds out a two-out, two-run, game-ending home run into the left field seats that gives the Bronx Bombers a 2–1 victory.

| 279. | Sept. 15 | Chicago | Billy Pierce(LH) | Stadium | 4–3, Chi | 8,714 |

Mantle's opposite-field clout sails into the right field bullpen.

| 280. | Sept. 15 | Chicago | Bob Shaw | Stadium | 4–3, Chi | 8,714 |

Mantle powers the 6'2" righthander's pitch halfway up into the right-center field bleachers. It is also the seventh time in his career that Mickey has connected for home runs from both sides of the plate in the same game. It is "the Mick's" 100th home run of his career at Yankee Stadium—batting left-handed.

September 19, 1959: At the grand old ballyard, before 24,005 appreciative fans, the Yankee family holds "Yogi Berra Day" for their celebrated catcher. Other "Days" in the history of Yankee Stadium include those occasions given for former players Babe Ruth, Lou Gehrig, Joe DiMaggio, Phil Rizzuto, and Charlie Keller. During the ceremonies at home plate, Yogi is presented with 58 separate gifts, including $9,800 in cash for a scholarship fund to be established that will provide $550 each year for a deserving youth at Columbia University in Yogi's name. For providing the Bronx fans so many clutch-filled and thrilling achievements on the diamond, Yogi this day will receive among other things a silver tray, a swimming pool, a new station wagon, a year's supply of coffee, gold cuff links, 50 pounds of sirloin steaks, a hunting rifle, a vacuum cleaner, a fishing rod, a bathroom scale, new hats for his wife, and a watch especially presented to the legendary catcher by Joe DiMaggio.

As for the game itself, a contest with the Boston Red Sox, Yogi goes 0-for-4 and the Yankees win the game, 3–1, behind another fine pitching effort by Whitey Ford. Mickey Mantle goes 2-for-4, but does not figure in the scoring. As the season winds down, the Yankees' record of 79-75 with a winning percentage of .513, reflects the lowest winning percentage for a Yankee team in 34 years.

THE 1959 NEW YORK YANKEES

Third Place: with a 79-75 record under Manager Casey Stengel. Yankee Stadium attendance: 1,552,030

Mickey Mantle's League-leading Categories: Mickey Mantle with 126 strikeouts, which leads the majors and which also represents an all-time major league record for the most strikeouts by a switch-hitter in a single season. It also establishes a new club record by beating his own mark by six. This club record will stand for 16 years, until both Reggie Jackson with 133 and Bobby Bonds with 137 will break the Mantle mark.

MICKEY MANTLE'S 1959 HITTING RECORD

G	AB	R	H	2B	3B	HR	HR%	RBI	SA	BB	SO	SB	AVE.
144	541	104	154	23	4	31	5.7	75	.514	94	126	21	.285

In 1959, Mickey Mantle hit .285 while the major leagues averaged .257 with both leagues scoring an average 8.77 runs per game and both leagues hitting 1.82 home runs per contest. During the 144 games that Mickey Mantle appeared in for 1959, he played in the outfield 143 times as well as played in one game as a pinch-hitter. Mantle also managed to lead the league in fielding percentage at his position. In addition, Mantle has led the majors throughout the Fifties with 994 runs scored and with 893 bases on balls. As for his own league, no one hit more home runs than Mantle's 280 roundtrippers. Though "The Mick" had missed the entire year of 1950, only "Duke" Snider in all of major league baseball, with his 326 home runs, surpassed the amount tallied by the pin-striped slugger.

Mickey's 1959 Salary: $72,000 Mickey Mantle missed ten games during the year due to a right thigh injury, among many other ailments.

Injuries or Operations: Broken finger, right thigh, right shoulder

Number of Games in Which Mantle Homered: 29

Winning Record When Mickey Mantle Homered: 19–10, a winning percentage of .652

The Mantle-Maris combination in the Yankee attack of the early Sixties would produce the most power-dominated tandem in the history of the game.

Chapter Seven

THE SUMMIT SEASONS

—1960 & 1961—

In the Nation and the World: In the year 1960, a charismatic John F. Kennedy ran successfully for the Presidency of the United States against the foiled bid of Vice-President Richard M. Nixon. Civil rights sit-ins began to take place in the South. A significant Cold War incident occured when an American U-2, a CIA-financed "spy plane" piloted by Gary Powers, was shot down over Russia. This volatile event, in turn, torpedoed the Geneva superpower summit. The year ended with Soviet Premier Nikita Khrushchev disrupting United Nations proceedings by banging his shoe on the dais during a Security Council meeting.

In the following year, 1961, the U.S. moon shot program began in the White House under the young and dynamic President who faced Cold War crises: in Cuba with the unsuccessful invasion by U.S.-backed anti-Communist Cubans at the Bay of Pigs; in East Germany with the construction of the Berlin Wall; and in Southeast Asia with an American commitment to the Vietnam Conflict. In the meantime, the Soviet Union placed a man in orbit around the earth for mankind's first manned space flight. On the domestic front, President Kennedy established the Peace Corps with an eye towards promoting American goodwill to poverty-stricken Third World countries.

Fads: Diversions in 1960 included a slew of comedy records designed to humor America's masses. "Ken," the male counterpart to the Barbie Doll, was manufactured for the first time. And folk-singing in coffee houses began to flourish with social-conscious messages and themes for mass consumption. In the following year, 1961, yo-yo's enjoyed a boost among the Boomers, who were moving into their teens in great waves.Meanwhile, guitars experienced a huge increase in manufacture and sales.

Innovations and First Appearances: In 1961, the McDonald's tag and logo were purchased by wealthy Ray Kroc, who set his sights on a nationwide chain of hamburger stops. And "soul" music, embodied by James Brown, enjoyed a wide acceptance across the country. Meanwhile, Xerox copy machines were developed for the first time. Motown Records distributed its first megahits from coast to coast, while Astroturf was developed as a precursor for use as artificial grass in ballparks across the land. Individually owned bomb shelters proliferated across the country in a wide-scale response to the growing fear of nuclear war between Cold War superpowers.

Certificates of deposit were purchased for the first time, locking up funds and producing higher interest rates. Meanwhile, electric toothbrushes made their first appearances in U.S. households, and minimum wages increased from $1 an hour to $1.25 an hour.

Movies: In 1960, the march of movie madness continued to engulf the thrill-seeking, enjoyment-fulfilling, and diversion-minded. Moviegoers poured into cinema houses to be entertained by such flicks as *North to Alaska, Spartacus, Can-Can, Butterfield 8, Who Was That Lady?, Psycho, The Alamo, The Unforgiven, Spartacus, Exodus, Walt Disney's Pollyanna, Please Don't Eat the Daisies, Ocean's Eleven,* and *The Magnificent Seven.* In 1961, the same wave of theatergoers moved in record numbers into moviehouses to be mesmerized by such fare as *Judgment at Nuremberg, King of Kings, Pocketful of Miracles, One-Eyed Jacks, The Hustler, The Misfits, The Guns of Navarone, West Side Story, Breakfast at Tiffany's, A Hole in the Head,* and *The Apartment.*

Television: Escapism in America's living rooms was reflected by higher and higher ratings in 1960, as the everyday American enjoyed such light fare as *Maverick, The*

Many Loves of Dobie Gillis, The Untouchables, Perry Mason, Have Gun Will Travel, and *Candid Camera.* In 1961, Americans enjoyed newly developed programs that brought even more diversion for the working stiffs who came home to gather around the television to laugh and cry at such shows as *What's My Line?, The Dick Van Dyke Show, My Three Sons, Checkmate, The Andy Griffith Show, Dr. Kildare, The Bob Cummings Show,* and *Rawhide.*

The Juke Box: In 1960, Baby Boomers snapped their fingers to, stomped their feet at, and hummed the melodies of such new standards as "Cathy's Clown" by the Everly Brothers, "It's Now or Never" and "Are You Lonesome Tonight" by Elvis Presley, "The Twist" by Chubby Checker, "Mr. Custer" by Larry Verne, "Save the Last Dance for Me" by the Drifters, and "Georgia on My Mind" by Ray Charles. The following year welcomed the two-and-a-half-minute hit tunes that, via the radio airwaves, sweep across the nation. Hit songs like "Will You Love Me Tomorrow" by the Shirelles, "Pony Time" by Chubby Checker, "Surrender" by Elvis Presley, "Blue Moon" by the Marcels, "Mother-in-Law" by Ernie K-Doe, "Michael" by the Highwaymen, "Take Good Care of My Baby" by Bobby Vee, "Hit the Road Jack" by Ray Charles, "Big Bad John" by Jimmy Dean, "The Lion Sleeps Tonight" by the Tokens, and "Please Mr. Postman" by the Marvelettes peppered the weekly TOP 40 lists reflecting the increasing sales to the millions of Baby Boomers who were showing for the first time the weight of their massive purchasing power.

Deaths: In 1960, Americans mourned the passing of the musical genius of Oscar Hammerstein II, whose Broadway and movie musical scores uplifted all who were fortunate to hear the exquisite lyrics of the noted songwriter. Aly Khan died. And Boris Pasternak would write no more. The watchguard of etiquette, the venerable Emily Post, passed. In the following year, 1961, baseball took note of the fact that one of its greatest immortals, Ty Cobb, had passed on. And in the Queen City, one of it's most beloved baseball owners and greatest innovators, Powel Crosley, Jr., had died. Hall-of-Famer Dazzy Vance drew his last breath. And in the world of art, the beloved Grandma Moses passed and author Ernest Hemingway took his own life. UN Secretary General Dag Hammarskjold perished in a plane crash in Africa while on a peace-seeking mission. And Marion Davies, actress and former mistress to publishing tycoon William Randolph Hearst, was gone, as well as Dr. Carl Jung. Movie zany, Chico Marx, died and author Richard Wright lost his battle for life. In addition, Hollywood mourned the loss of movie giants Clark Gable and Gary Cooper.

Sports: In the 1960 Rome Olympics, U.S. Olympics sprinter Wilma Rudolph won three Gold Medals. Meanwhile, in the cool autumn air of Philadelphia football, the NFL Championship was won by the underdog Eagles, driven to glory by quarterback

Norm Van Brocklin, and beating Vince Lombardi's Green Bay Packers, 17–13. In professional basketball, the NBA championship was won again by the Boston Celtics when the Shamrock Five nipped the Los Angeles Lakers, four games to three. In 1961, in the NFL, the professional football championship was won by Vince Lombardi's Green Bay Packers who crushed the New York Giants, 37–0. In the NBA, the Boston Celtics punctuated their pre-eminence in professional hoops by beating the St. Louis Hawks, four games to one.

Baseball Transitions: In 1961, nostalgia-minded purists everywhere in the land wept as Ebbets Field was demolished to make way for an apartment project in Flatbush. Ted Williams played a last time for the Red Sox as he homered in his final plate appearance, to give history one of baseball's most memorable and fitting exits. Meanwhile, Baltimore lost Bob Boyd, but picked up the slugging talents of Jim Gentile. The O's released Hoyt Wilhelm, but welcomed the arrival of a talented righthander named Chuck Estrada. The Chicago White Sox lost Earl Torgeson, but picked up the ageless services of Minnie Minoso. Cleveland let Rocky Colavito go, but enlisted the nifty, experienced bat of Harvey Kuenn. Detroit released Ray Narleski, but subsidized the slugging services of Norm Cash. And as for the New York Yankees, Hank Bauer and Norm Siebern departed the Big Apple, while Clete Boyer arrived. The Yankees gave up on Don Larsen, but gained the pitching services of Luis Arroyo. Later in the year, Bill Stafford joined the pin-striped ranks, and in the most significant transaction in years for the Bombers, Roger Maris became a Yankee via the Kansas City underground.

In 1961—a most historic season for major league baseball—for the first time in 60 years two metropolitan centers were given major league franchises as the American League accepted and instituted a permanent expansion. The Los Angeles Angels were given official AL sanction and the old Washington Senators moved to Minnesota. The expansion phenomenon would be repeated by the National League in the following year. Meanwhile, "The M & M Boys" were teamed together for the first time. The Detroit Tigers lost Charlie Maxwell, but bought the contract of National League castoff Bill Bruton. The Chicago White Sox lost Dick Donovan to the expansion draft, but signed up Juan Pizarro. Boston lost the legendary Ted Williams, but garnered the services of future legend Carl Yastrzemski. The Yankees bade farewell to the valuable Gil McDougald, but promoted Johnny Blanchard to the parent club. The pin-stripers lost the services of Bob Turley to injury and traded away Art Ditmar; but still, the Bombers were able to cultivate the talented moundsmanship of rookies Bill Stafford and Roland Sheldon.

THE 1960 REGULAR SEASON

40 HOME RUNS

April 19, 1960: At Fenway Park, the Boston Red Sox are playing their first game at home this season while playing host to the New York Yankees. The Red Sox faithful rejoice at the presence of a future Hall-of-Famer, the "Splendid Splinter," the indomitable Ted Williams. Responding to the occasion that this game marks the first game at Fenway Park of his final year. Williams responds in characteristic style by belting out a home run. The milestone blow, coming off Jim Coates in the eighth frame, gives Williams 494 career four-baggers, which push him ahead of Lou Gehrig, No. 4 on the all-time home run list. Only Babe Ruth, Jimmie Foxx, and Mel Ott have hit more career home runs than Williams. "Teddy Ballgame's" heroics, however, are not enough.

After playing through a miserable exhibition season, the Bombers demonstrate that there are two aspects to consider. One is that spring training results do not matter since this day marks the real beginning of the year when everything counts. There is an important second factor: This is the first ball game which Roger Maris plays as a member of the Yankees. And on this day, Ted Williams, grand master of the longball and a legendary power-hitting champion, and Roger Maris, the young slugger who joins his team of destiny, face off against one another. For the Yankees, it is an opportunity to offset a miserable team performance in spring training.

The Bombers make the most of it. The 1960 New York Yankees explode for an impressive Opening Day victory over the Beantown nine, beating the Crimson Hose, 8–4, and ushering in a new phase of the Mantle Years in the fabled history of the pin-striped franchise. "The Mick" contributes a 400-foot double to center field, two runs scored, and an RBI. As for Maris, in his first day with the Bombers, dressed in travel grays, the young slugger takes his bats in the lead-off position. In his first plate appearance as a Bronx Bomber, the strong rightfielder belts out a long double. After coming to the plate four more times during the contest, Maris will single and connect twice for home runs, score two runs, and knock in four.

H.R.#	DATE	OPPONENT	PITCHER	SITE	SCORE	ATTND.
281.	Apr. 22	Baltimore	Hoyt Wilhelm	Stadium	5–0, NY	35,645

Mickey Mantle rips a towering shot that carries into the right-field upper deck at Yankee Stadium.

H.R.#	DATE	OPPONENT	PITCHER	SITE	SCORE	ATTND.
282.	May 13	Wash.	Jim Kaat(LH)	Wash., D.C.(n) 7-3, NY		14,205

Mickey pounds a high drive to the opposite field for a home run over the right field wall.

283.   May 17   Cleveland   Gary Bell   Cleveland(n)   7–6, Cle   14,642

Mantle lights up the 23-year-old hurler when he laces a longball over the left-center field fence at Municipal Stadium. The opposite-field blow represents another landmark shot for "The Mick", as he collects the 100th left-handed-hitting home run of his career belted on-the-road.

284.   May 20   Chicago   Early Wynn   Chicago(n)   5-3, Chi   40,970

Earlier in the game when Ted Kluszewski had belted a home run for the home team, the new exploding scoreboard lighted up in a frantic celebration of noise and lights. When Mickey belts his, the scoreboard stands ominously quiet.

285.   May 28   Wash.   Jim Kaat(LH)   Stadium(n)   5–1, NY   32,581
                                                                  (27,508 pd.)

After watching his batting average slip to a career low of .226, Mantle launches an opposite-field, 400-foot home run into the right-center field bleachers.

286.   May 29   Wash.   Hal Woodeshick(LH)   Stadium   6–4, NY   21,516
                                            (in 11)

Mickey lifts a long fly to the opposite field that sails into the right field bleachers.

May 30, 1960: The Yankees have just earned a split in a Memorial Day twin bill with the Washington Senators. In the bottom of the eighth inning, Mickey will score the tying run on Yogi Berra's game-winning home run. Now, in the ninth inning, Mantle is trotting off the field after having made the catch for the final out in the double-header. While exiting the field, Mantle is surrounded by a sparse flock of some of the 42,927 fans who have attended the game. This over-zealous group, which had just stormed the field, would envelop the young slugger. The well-wishing scenario would soon become a free-wheeling melee as the fans begin to grab at Mantle's Yankee ballcap, spiriting it away. Then they grab for his uniform. With flailing hands all around his face, Mickey fears injury to his eyes and begins to speed up his exit. Before too long, Mickey is bulling his way through the horde of grasping fans. Before He can reach the sanctuary of the clubhouse, one of the rooters amid the mob surrounding him, punches him in the face, bruising his jaw and cheek. Taken completely off guard, Mantle takes the punch without a chance to react.

For the next four days, Mantle will not miss any playing time. He will, however, order softer food from the menu in this very brief spate of time. Because of this incident, the Yankees announce that, in the future, "bouncer-type" ushers using ropes will escort Mickey off the field in a flying-wedge kind of interference, the same security tactic that the Yankees utilized in escorting Joe DiMaggio off the field in his heyday.

287.	June 1	Baltimore	Hal "Skinny" Brown	Baltimore(n)	4–1, Balt	23,762
288.	June 5	Boston	Tom Brewer	Stadium	5–4, NY	37,211
	(first game)					

In an interesting aside, while facing Yankee righthander Ralph Terry at Yankee Stadium, slugging leftfielder Ted Williams of the Red Sox blasts the 495th home run of his career.

| 289. | June 8 | Chicago | Bob Shaw | Stadium(n) | 6–0, NY | 30,420 |
| 290. | June 8 | Chicago | Ray Moore | Stadium(n) | " | " |

For the first time as teammates, Mickey Mantle and Roger Maris belt out back-to-back home runs as pinstriped teammates.

| 291. | June 9 | Chicago | Frank Baumann(LH) | Stadium | 5–2, NY | 12,588 |

Mantle's two-run game-winner settles matters for the Yankees when their third run is scored in the fourth inning off Mickey's home run into the Yankee bullpen in right field.

| 292. | June 10 | Cleveland | Dick Stigman(LH) | Stadium(n) | 4–3, NY | 46,030 |

Before the largest crowd of the year thus far, gimpy Mantle, pained by a spill taken earlier in the contest, blasts the game-winner in the eighth inning into the left field stands off the rookie southpaw before the largest crowd to date this year. The crowd applauds Mickey's heroics as he trots lamely, but gamely around the bases. It is "The Mick's" fourth round-tripper in three games.

| 293. | June 17 | Chicago | Turk Lown | Chicago(n) | 4–2, NY | 43,320 |
| 294. | June 18 | Chicago | Bob Rush | Chicago | 12–5, NY | 34,640 |

Mantle unleashes a fourth-inning, two-run blast that is smoked into the distant center field bullpen at Comiskey Park. The fashion of the blow is back-to-back with Roger Maris. The Mantle round-trippers over the two games highlight a four-game sweep of the Chisox and solidify the Yankees' grip on first place in the American League. This day's clout actually proves to be the blow that will settle the affair—the game-winner.

| 295. | June 21 | Detroit | Frank Lary | Detroit(n) | 6–0, NY | 39,311 |
| 296. | June 21 | Detroit | Frank Lary | Detroit(n) | " | " |

Maris has hit behind Mickey consistently in the lineup now, and has given Mickey a relief in pressure as pitchers serve up more good pitches to Mantle for fear of facing Maris, Berra, and "Moose" Skowron, batting behind "The Mick." On this day, Frank Lary has been ruffled so badly by Mantle's home run-hitting prowess that after each of Mickey's blasts, he will walk Maris. In the contest, Mantle has produced a 3-for-5 evening, with three runs scored, and three RBIs.

One day after his field day against Lary, Mantle complains to the Yankee trainer that his right knee is hurting him severely.

297.   June 28   Kansas City   Bud Daley(LH)   Stadium(n)   5–2, NY   20,002

Mantle's drive into the left field seats is his 11th home run for the month of June.

298.   June 30   Kansas City   Bob Trowbridge   Stadium   10–3, NY   8,513

Mantle connects high and far to right-center field, where it carries into the Yankee bullpen. It is Mantle's 12th round-tripper of the month.

299.   July 3   Detroit   Pete Burnside(LH)   Stadium   6–2, NY   50,556
        (second game)

Mantle's three-run home run in the fifth proves to be the game-winner.

300.   July 4   Wash.   Hal Woodeshick(LH)   Wash.   9-8, Wash   16, 913

Mantle's right-handed clout is the 300th home run of his career. At this point in time, there have only been 18 major leaguers who reached this exalted level of home run production. Mickey's blow is manifested by a three-run home run in the first inning.

THE 1960 ALL-STAR GAME

MUNICIPAL STADIUM IN KANSAS CITY, MISSOURI
FIRST GAME—JULY 11

Before 30,619 American League rooters, the National League wins, 5–3. Mickey gets two walks, one from Pittsburgh's Bob Friend and another from San Francisco's Mike McCormick, and fails to register even one official at-bat as a result.

THE 1960 ALL-STAR GAME

YANKEE STADIUM IN NEW YORK, NEW YORK
SECOND GAME—JULY 13

In the seventh inning of this year's second midsummer classic, played this day at Yankee Stadium before 38,362 Big Apple baseball boosters, Stan "The Man" Musial comes to the plate to pinch-hit. Facing Gerry Staley, Musial connects for a long drive into the seats of the lower level of the right-field grandstand. Shortly thereafter, Ted Williams comes to the plate as a pinch-hitter in the bottom of the inning. Williams singles sharply. It is the last time that these two baseball legends, Williams and Musial, will play in the same game.

The National League beats the Americans, 6–0. Mickey Mantle goes 1-for-4, collecting an eighth-inning single, and strikes out once against Stan Williams of the Los Angeles Dodgers.

301.	July 15	Detroit	Don Mossi(LH)	Detroit(n)	8–4, Det	45,714
302.	July 18	Cleveland	Dick Stigman(LH)	Cleveland(n)	9–2, NY	23,513
303.	July 20	Cleveland	Gary Bell	Cleveland(n)	8–6, Cle	27,353
304.	July 24	Chicago	Russ Kemmerer	Stadium	8–2, NY	60,002
	(second game)					
305.	July 26	Cleveland	Dick Stigman(LH)	Stadium(n)	6–1, NY	37,632

Mickey's belt settles the affair against the visiting Tribesmen.

306.	July 28	Cleveland	Jim Perry	Stadium(tn)	4–0, NY	39,812
	(first game)					
307.	July 31	Kansas City	Johnny Kucks	Stadium	5–2, KC	29,012
	(first game)			(in 11)		

Mickey's clout soars into the right-center field bleachers.

August 8, 1960: Before 48,323 excited South Siders, the largest crowd ever to attend a day game at old Comiskey Park, the Chicago White Sox play host to the on-the-road New York Yankees. Mickey goes 1-for-2, but the Chisox prove victorious. Billy Pierce, Sox left-handed ace, pitches a masterful four-hitter, facing a bare minimum of 31 batters, excluding the four Bombers who manage insignificant safeties and a walk. Pierce wins the contest, 9–1, for the hometown nine.

August 14, 1960: Up to this point in the season, Mickey has made some bonehead errors in his play. For instance, the day before, Mickey had been daydreaming when he struck out, and failed to notice that the catcher had dropped the third strike. Mickey had merely walked back to the dugout as the catcher threw him out at first base for the putout. Another time, Mickey had been on first base when he took off for second when one of his teammates had lifted a routine fly ball to the outfield. Mantle's lack of awareness will result in a double play as the outfielder's throw to first doubles up Mickey, still running out the ball. His lame excuse is only that he believed that there had been two outs instead of the actual one-out count in the inning. On this day, Mickey's distracted approach to the game and its resounding consequences will prove to be the topper.

Roger Maris had connected for 35 home runs by the first week in August and is ahead in the pace to catch Babe Ruth's single season mark of 60 home runs. To make matters worse, in the fourth inning of this day's contest, Mantle hit a ground ball that starts an inning-ending double play executed by Washington's infield. Having been distracted all day by the Senator bench and thinking there were two outs, Mickey remains stationary after hitting the ball and watches the play unfold. In the ensuing action, Maris would hurt himself trying to break up the double play, while Mantle will remain stationary near the plate, making nary a step towards first base. Subsequently, Mickey will not run, believing the force out of Maris at second ended the inning. Immediately, a rain of abuse from the fans would descend on the pin-striped slugger who had watched helplessly as the Senators completed the throw to first base notching the double play and retiring the side. By this time, Mickey had barely started even a trot towards first. Enraged, Casey Stengel will order Mantle out of the game immediately, replacing him with Bob Cerv, as the echoing disgust of the New York assembly fills the hallowed walls of the storied stadium. Mantle merely hangs his head and walks to the bench.

Meanwhile, out at second base, Maris is down. Having attempted to break up the double play, Roger has piled hard into second base. Now he will be taken out of the game because of a rib injury that had resulted in the collision at second base. Maris will be absented from the lineup, missing 18 crucial games. To make matters worse, the Senators reign this day by sweeping the Yanks.

| 308. | Aug. 15 | Baltimore | Jerry Walker | Stadium(n) | 4–3, NY | 24,233 |

Booed lustily by the fans who had heard about last night's bonehead play against the Senators that got Roger Maris injured, Mickey Mantle believes this round of re-sounding jeers to be the loudest he has ever heard in his career. Mantle comes to the plate in his second at-bat and lines a long drive to right-center field.

The ball travels to the furthest reaches of right field, smashing into the second wire fence of the bullpen. The rocketed 420-foot line drive, and a two-run home run, account for the Yankees' first two runs. In one of the rarest gestures made in his entire career by the shy, but contrite Mantle, the forgiven slugger will tip his cap to the appreciative crowd.

| 309. | Aug. 15 | Baltimore | Hoyt Wilhelm | Stadium(n) | 4–3, NY | 24,233 |

Later, representing the winning run at the plate, Mantle will account for all of the Yankees' four runs against the hot Orioles, who are tied for first place with the Chicago White Sox. Interestingly, on one of Wilhelm's fluttering offerings in this at-bat, Mickey pops up behind home plate. The combative, bespectacled O's catcher, Clint Courtney, is camped under the ball when the foul pop starts its descent. Wear-ing an over-sized glove, that helps the backstop bottle up the knuckleballer's more difficult, dancing deliveries, Courtney drops the ball. On the next pitch, Mantle blasts the ball into the right field upper deck. The Yankees take over first place as a result.

| 310. | Aug. 26 | Cleveland | Jim Perry | Stadium(tn) | 7–6, NY | 56,508 |
| | | | | (first game) | | |

The ball clears the right-center field auxiliary scoreboard over the 407-foot marker.

311. Aug. 28 Detroit Phil Regan Stadium 8–5, NY 47,971
(second game)

Besides his home run, a back-to-back job with Yogi Berra, Mantle adds another hit to this game's production that includes two runs scored and four runs knocked in.

312. Sept. 6 Boston Billy Muffett Stadium 7–1, Bos 12,865

The ball slams into the seats of the lower right field grandstand. Mantle's round-tripper is one of only three hits the Yankees generate during the contest. In an interesting sidelight of the same game, Ted Williams belts his 518th career home run.

313. Sept. 10 Detroit Paul Foytack Detroit 4–1, NY 10,815

On his 2-and-0 count delivery to the plate, Tiger righthander Paul Foytack in the seventh inning is greeted by the booming bat of the powerful Mickey Mantle. Though Mantle goes 2-for-4 with three RBIs, his home run is as memorable in flight as it is important in the outcome of the game. The blow is a gargantuan shot, perhaps the longest ever by the legendary switch-hitter, that sails over everything, leaving a point in the old ballyard that is at least 110 feet above the 330-foot sign at the base of the right field wall at field level. The ball rockets high over the head of future Hall-of-Famer Al Kaline, bulleting through the metal trappings of the rooftop light standards clean and untouched, and sailing clear out of the ancient ballyard, over the outlying Trumbull Avenue on the fly, until it comes to land in the parking lot of a lumberyard across the street and adjacent to the ballpark. Veteran observers estimate that the Herculean blast over the roof has traveled between 560 and 643 feet in the air. Only four batted balls have ever cleared the roof of Briggs Stadium in right field, including one foul, since the Red Sox's Ted Williams did it in 1939, and Mantle has all of them. The 15-year veteran George Kell, a former Tiger great, and Hall of Fame performer in the big leagues, is on this day one of the Tiger team of broadcasters, and describes the wallop as "the longest ball he has ever seen."

314. Sept. 11 Cleveland Carl Mathias(LH) Cleveland 3–2, NY 33,403
(second game) (in 11)

Mickey pounds out an eleventh-inning game-winner.

September 17, 1960: As the Yankees begin to play a series with the Orioles, the great Tyrus Raymond Cobb pays a pre-game visit in the Yankee clubhouse. The Hall of Fame flyhawk meets the awe-filled Mickey Mantle. Cobb attempts to educate "The Mick," saying, "Don't be upset when the fans boo you. That has happened to all of us. The good ones survive the booing."

315. Sept. 17 Baltimore Chuck Estrada Stadium 5–3, NY 39,656

Mantle connects high into the seats of the right field upper deck.

| 316. | Sept. 20 | Wash. | Jack Kralick(LH) | Stadium(n) | 2–1, NY (in 11) | 13,129 |

Mickey propels the ball in a long, towering, fourth-inning drive to the opposite field that carries over the 407-foot marker on the right-center field wall with room to spare.

| 317. | Sept. 21 | Wash. | Pedro Ramos | Stadium(n) | 10–3, NY | 6,868 |
| 318. | Sept. 24 | Boston | Ted Wills(LH) | Boston | 6–5, NY (in 10) | 30,061 |

Mantle's blast represents a 10th inning game-winner over the 407-foot marker of the "Green Monster" and carries well over the Wall and onto Lansdowne Street beyond. The blow provides the winning margin for the visiting Bombers.

September 25, 1960: For the final time in his career with the New York Yankees, Casey Stengel is assured his 10th pennant as the skipper of the pin-striped Bronx Bombers. The clincher comes as the "Ol' Perfessor" oversees the 4–3 triumph over the visiting Boston Red Sox before 32,420 strutting Bronx boosters. In a close race all year, the Yankees have cruised to the pennant by winning their last 15 games. The Yankees win the game behind the strong-arm pitching of Ralph Terry, who has yielded a measly two runs in his last 22 innings pitched. In this particular pennant-winning contest, Mickey goes 0-for-4.

| 319. | Sept. 28 | Wash. | Chuck Stobbs(LH) | Wash., D.C.(n) | 6–3, NY | 5,519 |
| 320. | Sept. 28 | Wash. | Chuck Stobbs(LH) | Wash., D.C.(n) | 6–3, NY | 5,519 |

It is Mickey's 40th and final home run of the year that leads all American League sluggers. Twenty of Mickey's 'taters have either won games or set up Yankee wins. The blast also gives the Yankees 190 team home runs for the year, which ties the American League record that had been set by the 1956 Yankees. The season is four days short of its conclusion and will give the Bombers enough time to establish a new record for team home runs in the American League.

The Yankees finish the year on a 15-game winning streak as they prepare to meet the astonishing Pittsburgh Pirates, who have captured the National League flag in 1960. Mickey Mantle wins his fourth and final home run title of his career. The Yankees also establish a new team record for home runs in a single season, belting out 193 home runs for the year and breaking their own team mark of 190 in 1956.

THE 1960 NEW YORK YANKEES

First Place: with a 97–57 record under Manager Casey Stengel.

Yankee Stadium Attendance: 1,627,349

Mickey Mantle's League-leading Categories: Mickey Mantle with 40 home runs (fourth and final home run crown), 294 total bases, 119 runs scored (led majors), and 125 strikeouts.

MICKEY MANTLE'S 1960 HITTING RECORD

G	AB	R	H	2B	3B	HR	HR%	RBI	SA	BB	SO	SB	AVE.
153	527	119	145	17	6	40	7.6	94	.558	111	125	14	.275

In 1960, Mickey Mantle hit .275, while the major leagues averaged .255 with both teams scoring an average 8.63 runs per game and both teams hitting 1.72 home runs per contest. As a team, the Yankees establish a new league record for team home runs in a single season, with 193. During the 153 games in which Mickey Mantle appeared in 1960, he played in the outfield 150 times as well as appeared in three games as a pinch-hitter.

Mickey's 1960 Salary: $65,000

World Series Losing Share: $5,214

Number of Games in Which Mantle Homered: 36

Winning Record When Mickey Mantle Homered: 28–8, A winning percentage of .778

THE 1960 WORLD SERIES

October 5, 1960: In the first inning of Game One, Roger Maris becomes the seventh player ever in Series history to connect for a home run in his first World Series at-bat. The fortuitous blow by the American League's Player of the Year is struck to no avail, however, as the Pirates score three in the first to take a lead they do not relinquish. Bill Mazeroski's two-run home run in the fourth frame guarantees the victory for the Pirates as Vernon Law and Elroy Face stick their fingers in the dyke of the filling dam. Though the Yankees out-hit the home team, 13–8, and despite Elston Howard's pinch-hit home run in the ninth, the Pirates take the opener, 6–4.

October 6, 1960: In Game Two of the Series, played this day in the cavernous Forbes Field, before 37,308 stupefied Steeltown boosters bucking for their Buccaneers, the gray-flanneled Bronx Bombers explode. As the Pirate fans watch the game unfold, the New York Yankees shell the Pittsburgh pitching staff, 16–3. For his part, Mickey is hoping to make up for striking out three times the day before in the Yankee defeat. Indeed, Mantle not only leads the way, but does so in spectacular fashion. Number Seven becomes only the fourth player to belt out two home runs in the same Series game *twice* in his career.

In the explosive sixth frame, while batting right-handed against rookie hurler Freddie Green, Mickey is hoping merely not to strike out when he faces the nervous southpaw. The powerful Mantle propels a monster home run towards the right-of-straightaway center field canyon. Ultimately, the ball disappears over the distant wall's 436-foot sign, landing in the green grass of Schenley Park situated outside the ancient structure. As the 500-foot clout sails out of the massive ballyard, Buc centerfielder Bill Virdon will later take a mental note of the monumental rip. From the astonished Pirate fielder's vantage point, Mantle's blow "went at least 50 feet above the fence and was still going when I last saw it. The ball went to the right of the [spot where they stored the] batting cage, over the monuments, [and] over straightaway centerfield." It is the first time a right-handed hitter has ever hit a ball out of the park at that particularly remote section of Forbes Field. In the same sixth inning, Elston Howard will become only the 10th player ever to collect two base hits in the same inning. In short order, Bobby Richardson becomes the 11th player ever to collect two hits in the same inning, and the Yankees become the only team in history with two players each collecting two safeties together in the same inning.

In the seventh frame, following the Yankee seven-run detonation the inning before, Mickey comes to the plate to face yet another Pirate portsider, the unlucky Joe Gibbon. As Gibbon releases his pitch towards the outside corner of the dish, about thigh-high in Mickey's strike zone, Mantle reaches out and drives the ball on a screaming line to the opposite field. The ball rockets to right field and clears the right-field barrier 375 feet away with split-second speed.

Though he also walks twice and strikes out twice, Mickey Mantle has ignited the thundering offensive of the booming Bomber bats, giving Bob Turley the pitching victory in a cruise. Mickey bats in five runs, which ties a World Series record. This mark will soon be broken by the most unlikely of candidates, second baseman Bobby Richardson. Though the Buc bats combine for 13 hits on this day against "Bullet Bob," the Yankees pound the shell-shocked Pirate staff for 19 other hits. In their opponent's own backyard, the Yankees have collected an ego-deflating 32 base hits in two games against the Pittsburgh Pirate pitching staff, owner of the National League's third best team ERA. The Bronx Bombers have now decidedly evened matters with the Bucs.

October 8, 1960: Before a restless throng of 70,001 Bronx rooters, gathered together for Game Three in the Series, the New York Yankees rout the Pittsburgh Pirates, 10–0. Batting against Freddie Green, Mickey Mantle pounds out a home run into the lower left field grandstand bleachers. The ball carries over the 402-foot sign and impacts some ten rows back as the speeding spheroid disappears into a sea of outstretched hands of Yankee boosters. In an October classic that will showcase the equivalent or fall of many Series records, this game will not disappoint the many Bronx rooters gathered to root for their Bombers. In the first inning, Bobby Richardson will blast a grand-slam home run and, for the game, will knock in six runs. The grand slam ties a Series record. His RBI output in the tilt establishes another. Bob Cerv will also place his name in the books by collecting a record-tying third pinch-hit in his World Series career. And Whitey Ford will shut out the Bucs on four hits. Whitey's mastery begins a Series record-setting streak of scoreless innings pitched. Indeed, on this day the "Chairman of the Board" begins living up to his nickname by scattering four hits and blanking the Buccaneers. The power-laden Yankees have laid the Pirates to waste twice and now lead the Series, two games to one.

October 10, 1960: In Game Five of the Series, played this day at Yankee Stadium before 67,812 worried Yankee devotees, Mantle walks three times, twice by Harvey Haddix and once by Elroy Face. In the meantime, Roger Maris homers, but still the pinstriped Bombers can only manage to score twice. The Bucs win, 5–2, and forge ahead of the Yankees by taking an unlikely 3–2 advantage in the Series.

October 12, 1960: Returning to Forbes Field, the Yankees have their backs against the wall, forcing Professor Stengel to schedule his "money" pitcher, Whitey Ford, to oppose the Pirates. Ultimately, Ford limits the Pirates to seven ineffectual base hits, whitewashing Pittsburgh for the second time in a row and giving him the first Series pitching victory of his career away from Yankee Stadium. Once again, the Yankees throttle the embattled Pirate staff, led by Bobby Richardson's record-tying two triples in this game. The clutch-hitting second sacker also knocks in three of his teammates, which gives him a Series record-setting total of 12 RBIs. The Bombers tag six Pirate pitchers for 17 hits, which drive across 10 Yankee tallies. Mickey scores two of the Yankee runs after walking once and singling once. He also manages to knock in two runs.

October 13, 1960: It is Game Seven of the World Series, crunch time in Pittsburgh, and what is about to unfold will truly become one of the greatest, most thrilling, dizzying contests ever played in baseball, let alone for the World Series championship. Before the Yankees can blink, they are down, 4–0, after two innings of play. In the bottom of the first, Rocky Nelson will belt a two-run home run. In the next frame, Bill Virdon strokes a long two-run single to right-center field that will give the Bucs a 4–0 lead. The Yankees finally get on the board, however, when Bill Skowron lines a long fly ball to right field that barely makes the seats, just fair, for a home run. The score is now 4–1, Pittsburgh.

In the sixth inning of this, the Series decider, Vernon Law faces two Yankee batters before being lifted. Bobby Richardson would single to center and Tony Kubek will walk on a 3–2 count. Buc Forkballer Elroy Face then comes in to face Roger Maris. The Yankee rightfielder fouls out to third baseman Don Hoak. It is at this point in time that Mickey Mantle then finds the seam up the middle with a ground single just past the lunging form of shortstop Dick Groat. It scores Bobby Richardson and moves Kubek to third. Yogi Berra is the next batter. Greeting Face, the National League's premier fireman, Bomber backstop Berra smashes a three-run home run into the upper deck of the right field grandstand, giving the Yankees a 5–4 lead.

In the eighth, after scoring two runs in the top half of the inning, the Yankees are leading 7–4. In their half of the inning, the Pirate respond. Pirate pinch-hitter Gino Cimoli leads off with a single. The Pirates' next batter, Bill Virdon, then strokes a perfect double-play ground ball to Tony Kubek. The sharply-hit bounder takes a bad hop, viciously tearing into his Adam's apple, and downing the All-Star Yankee shortstop. The bad-hop single opens the door for the Bucs. With the lead now at 7–4, Yankees, Jim Coates comes in to relieve for Bobby Shantz. After getting two outs, the Pirates have runners on second and third, with the always dangerous Roberto Clemente coming to the plate.

Working the Latin batting legend carefully, Coates coaxes Clemente to dribble a slow roller to Bill Skowron at first base. "Moose" makes the play and looks to toss the ball to the Yankee pitcher covering first base. But Coates arrives late and Clemente beats the southpaw to the bag with Virdon scoring the Pirates' fifth run. The Yankees now lead, 7–5. The next batter, Pirate catcher Hal Smith, then clobbers a long, high fly to left field. The ball clears the wall for a three-run home run. As the smoke clears in this wild eighth frame, five Pirate runs have scored, capped by the clutch four-bagger by reserve catcher Smith. Yankee lefty Jim Coates's failure to make the routine cover play at first may have cost the Yankees the World Series championship. Now, the Pirates are back on top, 9–7.

In the top of the ninth, while facing Bob Friend and elimination, Bobby Richardson and Dale Long place singles back-to-back, putting Yankees at first and third. The next batter, Roger Maris, then hits a high, foul pop-up behind the plate, which Hal Smith cradles for the out. Now, with one out, Mickey lines a single to rightcenter off Harvey Haddix, knocking in Richardson and reducing the Yankee deficit to one run, 9–8. So, with the Yankees two outs from being eliminated, Mickey is on first base and Gil McDougald, who is running for Dale Long, is dancing on third with the potentially tying run. Now batting: Yogi Berra. Facing Harvey Haddix, Yogi grounds sharply to Pirate first baseman Rocky Nelson.

Nelson's first reaction is to take his eyes off Mantle to field the ball, go to the bag for the putout of Berra, and then pivot quickly for the throw to second base and the potential final out of the Series by doubling up Mickey at second. Sensing Nelson's strategy, Mickey does not attempt to advance to second, but opts instead to return to first base. Nelson, meanwhile, had, after touching first base, wheeled to throw the ball to Pirate shortstop Dick Groat, who had moved over to second base to cover the bag. Before realizing Mickey's counter-ploy, a startled Nelson reacts too late in checking his throw and moves a fraction too slow to tag Mantle who is diving head-long back to first base safely as Gil McDougald crosses the plate with the tying run. The scoreboard in left field now reads 9–9.

In the bottom of the ninth inning, Ralph Terry faces Bill Mazeroski, who leads off the home half of the inning. On Terry's first pitch to the Pirate second baseman, a high slider misses. Then, on the second pitch, delivered precisely at 3:35 P.M., Terry fires another high slider on a 0-and-1 count. Following the ball hurtling to-wards the plate, Mazeroski takes his cut and connects, belting the fateful Ralph Terry offering 420 feet towards left field. The fateful ball sails over the head of Yan-kee leftfielder Yogi Berra and clears the ivied, left field wall, just to the right of the Longine's scoreboard. It is the first home run ever in the 56-year history of the World Series to end the competition. The Pirates win the game and the World Se ries, and the city of Pittsburgh erupts. The World Championship of baseball belongs to the underdog Buccaneers.

In a note of final irony, Bobby Richardson will be voted the Series MVP. It is the only time in history that a member of the losing team will ever be accorded the award. For Mickey Mantle, who has enjoyed his most productive World Series ever, it is worse than ironic.

It was feast or famine for Pirate pitching in this Series. Unfortunately for the Yankees, though there was a bit more feast than famine with their bats, the Yankees feeding on Buc hurlers in an awesome display of offensive voraciousness, the Pi-rates still prevailed. After the Series had run through its seven-game course, the Buc pitching staff would reflect a shameful, collective ERA of 7.11, the poorest showing ever by any Series pitching staff in history. In fact, Yankee bats generated a mon-strous team Series batting average of .338 in the seven-game series, scoring 55 runs, while collecting 91 hits, including 27 for extra bases. No team has ever had a higher batting average in the World Series than the '60 Yankees, win or lose. No team has ever scored more runs in a World Series than the '60 Yankees, win or lose. No team has ever collected more base hits in a World Series than the '60 Yankees, win or lose. In fact, up to this point in time, by collecting 91 base hits, the 1960 Yankees had out-hit all participating Series teams combined, throughout all the previous World Series in history, 28 different times; that is, half of all participating Series teams combined with each other could not match the offensive prowess of the 1960 Yankees.

Mickey Mantle will later reflect on this grossest of disproportionate showings, remarking, "It was terrible. I'd been with the Yankees 10 years at that time and I cried all the way home on the airplane. I just couldn't quit, you know. It's the worst I ever felt in my life. It's the only time that we ever played in the World Series where I felt like that the best team got beat."

1961 SPRING TRAINING

In spring training this year, Ralph Houk, the new manager of the New York Yankees, asks two things of Mickey Mantle. First, the new Yankee field general asks Mickey to bat fourth in the lineup so that Roger Maris, being groomed for Mantle's familiar spot in the Yankee lineup, will be hitting third in the batting order. This adjustment in the lineup will give Maris more good pitches to hit. The second thing that Houk requests is that Mickey become the team leader. In addition, 1961 would be the year when the American League will expand to 10 teams, two more than the traditional eight. As Al Lopez, the manager of the Chicago White Sox, will observe, with regarding the league-wide dynamics of the expansion, "We all lost seven players in the draft, but the Yankees were hit the hardest....[In addition,]...Anyone who loses Casey Stengel is losing a great manager." With respect to players, the Yankees lose Dale Long, Bob Cerv, Bobby Shantz, Eli Grba, and Duke Maas, who will ironically be traded back to the Yankees early in the season. In return, the Yankees fill these vacancies with Lee Thomas, Jack Reed, Danny McDevitt, Rollie Sheldon, and Fritz Brickell who will later be lost in a trade. Meanwhile, in the first year of his stewardship, Ralph Houk has overseen a miserable spring season, winning nine games while losing 19 of the exhibitions. On the eve of beginning his 11th year in major league baseball, Mickey has connected seven times in the grapefruit league. For the young Mantle, there have been 10 seasons, eight league pennants, and five world championships. Composing an article entitled "M for Murder," the elegant and fabled storyteller Jim Murray of the *Los Angeles Times* writes about Mantle with the perspective of a sage, scripting, "For an ordinary mortal, Mantle's ten-year achievements in baseball—307 lifetime average, 993 runs batted in, 323 home runs, 1,611 base hits—are perfectly astonishing. For a man with osteomylitis, they are incredible."

THE 1961 REGULAR SEASON

54 HOME RUNS

In the first 14 days of the 1961 season, nine Yankee games will be postponed either by rain or by cold weather. It's the calm before the storm.

H.R.#	DATE	OPPONENT	PITCHER	SITE	SCORE	ATTND.
321.	Apr. 17	Kansas City	Jerry Walker	Stadium	3–0, NY	1,947

Mickey crushes the ball, which slams against the facing of the upper deck of the right field grandstand. The first-inning game-winner is the first of the Yankees' three runs, all of which Mantle accounts for. This he does before the smallest crowd in Yankee Stadium in seven years.

H.R.#	DATE	OPPONENT	PITCHER	SITE	SCORE	ATTND.
322.	Apr. 20 (first game)	Los Angeles	Eli Grba	Stadium	7–5, NY	7,059

Mantle poles another towering home run. It sails into the 12th row of the right field upper deck at Yankee Stadium. The home run gives the Yankees their first lead, 2–0, in the game.

H.R.#	DATE	OPPONENT	PITCHER	SITE	SCORE	ATTND.
323.	Apr. 20 (first game)	Los Angeles	Eli Grba	Stadium	7–5, NY	7,059

Mickey launches his second home run in the game, another upper-deck shot into the right field grandstand, some ten rows behind the third-deck railing. Mantle accounts for the first five of the Yankee runs in the 7–5 victory.

H.R.#	DATE	OPPONENT	PITCHER	SITE	SCORE	ATTND.
324.	Apr. 21	Baltimore	Steve Barber(LH)	Baltimore(n)	4–2, NY	12,368

In the spacious Memorial Stadium, a tough home run park, Mickey Mantle blasts another "tape-measure" shot that soars in a tremendous trajectory slightly to the right of straightaway center field off Steve Barber, the Oriole southpaw fireballer. Only two home runs have ever reached the center field scoreboard. This one is the second such blast, and sails over the right-center barrier, striking the scoreboard on a hop, 470 feet away after hitting the distant cinder track situated immediately in front of the massive Oriole board. Four years before, Mantle had accomplished the feat batting left-handed. On this day, he does it again, this time batting right-handed off the hard-throwing portsider. This particular blast is the fourth home run in four days and proves to be the game-winner. A Baltimore newspaper makes the first public note that Mickey Mantle is eight days ahead of "The Babe" during Ruth's 1927 record pace of 60 home runs.

Mantle is amused over this premature heralding of his assault on Ruth, since the Yankee season is only into its sixth game.

| 325. | Apr. 23 | Baltimore | Chuck Estrada | Baltimore | 4–1, O's | 18,704 |

Mantle's 390-foot home run ties the game in the fifth inning, but "The Mick" leaves the game in the eighth inning with a badly swollen knee, the result of impacting with the outfield fence in the game played the day before. Mickey's physical woes, so inherent in his game, are haunting him again. He moves into the clubhouse as his right knee begins to swell up. So early in a new season, and once again Mantle must cope with ever-present pain.

| 326. | Apr. 26 | Detroit | Jim Donohue | Detroit | 13–11, NY | 4,676 |
| | | | | | (in 10) | |

The greatest individual run on home runs ever made in the history of baseball begins in obscurity. Starting late, now in the 11th game of the season, Roger Maris blasts his first home run en route to a record-shattering 61-home run season. In Babe Ruth's case, in the record-setting year of 1927, the "Bambino" began his record year by hitting his first home run of the season in the fourth game. In Babe's record run, from the time he started hitting them, the powerful Ruth would take 150 games to hit 60 home runs. In 1961, using the same starting point, Roger Maris will take 149 games to duplicate Ruth's standard. As for the magic 61st home run, Maris will take 152 games to surpass the great "Babe." On this day, the day of his first round-tripper in this historic season, Maris propels a fast ball off Detroit right hander Paul Foytack into the grandstand bleachers at Tiger Stadium.

For his part, Mickey launches an eighth-inning, two-run home run into the upper deck of the right field grandstand off Donahue that ties the game in a Yankee come-from-behind effort. For the first time in 1961, in the same game, Mickey's home run is coupled with that of his teammate, Roger Maris, in the Yankee cause.

| 327. | Apr. 26 | Detroit | Hank Aguirre(LH) | Detroit | 13–11, NY | 4,676 |

In this same wild game, Mickey will follow with another home run, the game-winner, and now with the two teammates paired together for the first time with home runs in the same box score, the stage is set for a historic dual run at Ruth in the 1961 season. Mickey approaches reliever Luis Arroyo, who is slated to go out to the mound in the next frame. Leaning down, Mickey asks the Yankee ace reliever, "How you feeling?" Arroyo admits, "I'm a little tired." Mantle assures the southpaw, "Don't worry about it. I'm the next batter, this game's over." Mantle steps into the batter's box, faces the veteran Tiger lefthander, and awaits the pitch. With the winning run on base, Hank Aguirre goes into his stretch and then delivers. Striding towards the pitch, the switch-hitter unleashes his powerful swing and clouts his second home run in the same contest—a two-run, game-winning, tenth-inning job off the southpaw that sails into the upper deck of the left-field grandstand. It is the great switch-hitter's 10th home run of the year, and his seventh home run in the last eight games. It is also the eighth time in his career that Mantle has connected for home runs from both sides of the plate in the same game—already a major league record. This home run gives Mickey the fastest start he has ever had in his career. The Yankees win the high-scoring contest, 13–11. Mickey's timely four RBIs have paced the Yankee attack.

April 27, 1961: At Yankee Stadium, before 8,897 elated fans, Mantle booms a triple to left-center field against the Cleveland Indians' Johnny Antonelli. It paces the Yankee attack and saves Art Ditmar's first and final, complete-game triumph of the season. Mantle also makes a game-saving catch when, with two outs in the ninth and a runner aboard, the Yankee centerfielder "lunged, slipped, and skidded" for a glove-handed snatch of the ball inches off the ground. It is the final out of the game. Mickey's timely catch preserves the Yankee 4–3 victory.

| 328. | May 2 | Minnesota | Camilo Pascual | Minn. | 6–4, NY (in 10) | 16,669 |

In their first foray into the state of Minnesota to play a major league baseball game, the Yankees prove successful, as Mantle belts a 10th-inning, game-winning grand-slam home run. The Mantlesque clout sails 430 feet, carrying high over the 402-foot marker fronting the center-field bleachers.

Mantle's timely blast is the first of two consecutive games in which Pascual will surrender a grand-slam home run to an opposing batter. This dubious honor ties a major league record. For Mickey, it is the "Switcher's" sixth grand-slam home run of his stellar career.

| 329. | May 4 | Minnesota | Ted Sadowski | Minn. | 5–2, NY | 18,179 |

Mantle's round-tripper clears the right field fence and helps Mickey extend his hitting streak to 16 straight games.

May 7, 1961: The Los Angeles Angels are playing the franchise's first home schedule at Wrigley Field in Hollywood, California, for the entire year. On this day, the Angels are playing the New York Yankees. The Angels welcome 19,722 of the fans—the largest day-game crowd ever to watch an Angel game at Wrigley. The last-place expansion Angels beat the New York Yankees two out of three times in this series, including 5–3 in today's game. The Yankees had come to Hollywood three days before, tied with the Detroit Tigers in first place. Tonight, they leave town two and a half games out of first place. Mickey went 0-for-4.

May 12, 1961: Before a bustling throng of 23,556 disappointed Bronx night rooters, it is the New York Yankees versus the Detroit Tigers at Yankee Stadium. During the contest, native Knickerbocker Rocky Colavito is playing for the visiting Tigers.

Colavito's father is in the stands, having arrived to watch his son play the Yankees. A disturbing incident occurs in the stands that catches Colavito's attention and the ballplayer runs into the stands to protect his father. The elder Colavito is under some pressure in the grandstand from some of the Yankee fans. As a result of the fracas, Colavito is ejected from the game. Still, the Tigers beat the Yanks, 4–3. Mickey, meanwhile, will walk in a pinch-hitting appearance in the eighth.

May 13, 1961: In his first day back from his ejection, Rocky Colavito of the Detroit Tigers pounds out two home runs and goes 4-for-5 while driving in half of the Tiger scoring output and tallying four himself. New Yorkers have now learned not to rock "The Rock's" dad. Mickey goes 0-for-2. The Tigers beat the Yankees, 8–3.

| 330. | May 16 | Wash. | Hal Woodeshick(LH) | Stadium(n) | 3–2, Wash | 10,050 |

May 17, 1961: In a game against the Washington Senators, before a brassy crowd of 6,197 disappointed rooters, Mickey goes 1-for-4 and scores a run. Roger Maris, however, pounds out his fourth home run of the season. It is Maris' first homer at Yankee Stadium in what will soon develop into a banner year not only for him, but for Mickey as well. Indeed, the "Dynamic Duo" will begin to electrify a baseball-mad country. Both Roger Maris and Yankee teammate Mickey Mantle are poised to make an unprecedented parallel run at Babe Ruth's sacrosanct record for the most home runs, 60, in a single season. Roger's first 1961 home run at Yankee Stadium this day will also begin one of the hottest, most sustained streaks in the individual slugging of home runs in the history of the game. In the next 38 games, from this day forward until June 22nd, Maris will pole an unbelievable 24 home runs.

May 20, 1961: With the exception of "Whitey" Ford, whose record is at 4–1, Yankee pitching is struggling somewhat as their starting rotation has not yet stabilized. As a result, the Bombers are dallying five games behind the front-running Detroit Tigers. From this point onward, however, to the middle of September, because of the solidification of the Yankees' starting pitching and the sizzling hot bats of Roger Maris and Mickey Mantle, the Yankees, from this early point in the season onward, will win nearly 75 percent of the games remaining in their schedule.

| 331. | May 29 | Boston | Ike Delock | Boston(n) | 2–1, Bos | 21,804 |

The President of the United States is coming to Boston. John F. Kennedy is 44 years old on this very day. The young President, who is on the eve of summiting with Soviet Premier Nikita Khrushchev, is ensconced at Hyannis Port, Massachusetts, preparing to fly to Vienna with his wife, Mrs. Jacqueline Kennedy, to meet with Khrushchev to discuss Cold War issues.

JFK will miss the tilt at Fenway between the Yankees, the hot-slugging tandem of Roger Maris and Mickey Mantle, and the Beantown nine. The American leader's absence notwithstanding, at the old, storied ballyard, Whitey Ford and the Yankees lose to the Bosox, 2–1, but it is Mickey Mantle's home run into the right-center field Red Sox bullpen in the second inning that will grab a headline as "The Mick" returns to his home run hitting form, belting out a solo four-bagger, his first in two weeks. In his final plate appearance, Mickey propels a pitch to the deepest portions of right-center field that falls into the glove of a resourceful Red Sox outfielder registering the last out of the game. The Yankees are in third place five games out of first.

| 332. | May 30 | Boston | Gene Conley | Boston | 12–3, NY | 19,592 |

On Memorial Day of this, the "Year of the Home Run," Mantle unleashes a three-run shot in the first inning some 380 feet into the right field seats, as does Roger Maris two innings later in the same game. Indeed, Mantle, Maris, and Bill Skowron of the New York Yankees will each hit a pair of home runs against the Boston Red Sox in this game. It is the second time in American League history that three players on the same team will belt out two home runs apiece in the same game.

| 333. | May 30 | Boston | Mike Fornieles | Boston | 12–3, NY | 19,592 |

Mantle's second blast sails into the center field bleachers above the 420-foot mark at Fenway Park. With the able assistance from Maris of two home runs, another two blasts from Bill "Moose" Skowron, and a solo shot from Yogi Berra, the Yankees tromp the Red Sox. Maris, Mantle, and Skowron have accomplished with their six home runs what only has been accomplished once before in major league history. Berra contributes one of his own as the Yankees pepper the Red Sox pitching staff, 12–3. Maris has now poled 10 home runs for the year. "The "Mick" has reached the seats 13 times.

| 334. | May 31 | Boston | Billy Muffett | Boston(n) | 7–6, NY | 17,318 |

Mickey launches a 400-foot home run into the right-center field Red Sox bullpen. Though Roger Maris adds one of his own in this same game, Mantle's round-tripper is the blow that settles matters. In an important aside, *The New York Times* forecasts what will become a source of national fascination when it refers to the "M & M Boys," now engineering a twin attack on the Ruthian seasonal standard for home runs.

| 335. | June 5 (first game) | Minnesota | Don Lee | Stadium(tn) | 6–2, NY | 23,103 |

Mickey poles a 420-foot home run into the right-center field bleachers.

| 336. | June 9 | Kansas City | Ray Herbert | Stadium(n) | 8–6, NY | 22,418 |

Mantle belts out an opposite-field home run into the lower left field grandstand bleachers. Maris also poles a home run in the game, making this the third occasion that both the "M & M Boys" have connected in the same game in this record-setting season.

337.	June 10	Kansas City	Bill Kunkel	Stadium	5–3, NY	18,665
338.	June 11	L.A.	Eli Grba	Stadium	5–1, NY	37,378
	(second game)					

Grba, the Angel right hander, will not only contribute three home runs to the litany of booming longballs in 1961 belonging to Mantle—one this very day, a three-run special, one of Mickey's trademark upper deck shots to right—but he will serve up two to Roger as well. Grba, a pre-expansion Yankee, has now given up five home runs to the "M & M Boys." For Grba, he has his own nickname for the twin terrors, calling them "Thunder and Lightning."

339.	June 15	Cleveland	Jim "Mudcat" Grant	Cleveland(n)	3–2, NY	23,350
				(in 11)		

At Municipal Stadium in Cleveland, before 23,350 boisterous Cleveland spectators, the New York Yankees open up a three-game series with the Cleveland Indians who, after winning 21 of the last 25 games, have moved into first place, one game ahead of the Yankees. This particularly crucial series results in two wins for the Bombers.

340.	June 17	Detroit	Paul Foytack	Detroit(n)	12–10, Det	51,509

Mantle's home run is paired with one off the bat of his teammate, Roger Maris. It is the only time in the 14 games this year in which both Yankee sluggers will hit home runs in the same game that the Yankees lose.

341.	June 21	Kansas City	Bob Shaw	Kansas City(n)	5–3, NY	19,416

Batting left-handed, Mickey Mantle of the New York Yankees blasts two prodigious home runs in one game at Kansas City's Municipal Stadium against pitcher Bob Shaw. In the first inning with two teammates aboard, the first of these monstrous shots rockets 525 feet, rising beyond the fence upwards over the slanting grassy incline in right-center field, where it slams into the top of the scoreboard.

342.	June 21	Kansas City	Bob Shaw	Kansas City(n)	5–3, NY	19,416

Mantle's second moonshot travels between 475 and 500 feet in a towering, "tape-measure" monster of an arc, clearing the 353-foot right field fence, spanning the 50-foot-long grassy incline, while soaring over the second, deeper, 30-foot-high right field barrier atop the turfed slope until it lands on Brooklyn Avenue outside the stadium. This feat has been accomplished four times: once by Larry Doby, once by Harry "Suitcase" Simpson, and once before by Mantle himself. Mantle's five RBIs account for all of the Yankee runs in the pinstripers' triumph.

June 22, 1961: In a personal, searing display of the most intense, surging 37-day home run assault in baseball history, Roger Maris of the New York Yankees has belted out 24 homers in 38 games. It is what baseball scholar Robert Creamer calls "an example of sustained, unrelenting achievement." This night's home run at Municipal Stadium in Kansas City represents Roger Maris' 27th of the season. He will also add two doubles and a single and drive in four runs before 17,254 fellow Missourians. One game before, as logged, Mickey had poled two home runs himself, giving him 22 thus far this season. In this same period, Mantle has crushed 12 round-trippers.

The stage is now set for both pin-striped sluggers to wage a dual-pronged, double-barreled assault on one of the most vaunted baseball records of all time. Maris and Mantle who will set a mutually torrid pace, have together begun to legitimately and independently challenge "The Babe." There have only been four days in the past 26 that both sluggers were prevented from reaching the seats. New York Yankee fans everywhere rejoice and all eyes in the baseball world begin to turn to New York and the slugging, Mel Allen-dubbed "M & M Boys." After this evening's game, an 8–3 victory over the Kansas City A's, Roger Maris, beginning to feel the burden of a prying press, is asked by Joe Trimble of the *Detroit Free News* whether he believes he can catch "The Babe." Private by nature, Maris becomes impatient and perturbed. With the intensification of unwanted media attention, Maris is resentful for, first, having been thrust into the spotlight. Nor has he received any insulation from the media or protection from the press by the Yankees. Consequently, to Trimble's query about Roger and "The Babe," a growingly embittered Maris, already disagreeable with reporters so early in a long season still to come, replies curtly and vulgarly, "How the fuck do I know?"

343.	June 26	L.A.	Ken McBride	L.A.(n)	8–6, NY	18,870

Mickey connects for a 412-foot blast over the center field wall.

344.	June 28	L.A.	Ryne Duren	L.A.(n)	5–3, LA	14,674
345.	June 30	Wash.	Dick Donovan	Stadium(n)	5–1, NY	28,019

Mantle skirts around the bases for an inside-the-park home run standing up after belting the ball over the massive "Death Valley" of the stadium's center field playing space and all the way to the 461-foot marker on the fly. The ball slams so hard against a point very near the top of the 20-foot-high center field wall that it rebounds halfway back to the infield.

The Yankee victory puts Whitey Ford's pitching record at 14–2. Meanwhile, the Yankees are hot, sporting a 22–10 record for the month.

346.	July 1	Wash.	Carl Mathias(LH)	Stadium	7–6, NY	24,144

Mantle muscles the ball after his whipping bat connects for another of his "tape-measure" shots, sailing ten rows deep just to the left of the 457-foot sign and 10 rows deep into the left-center field bleachers—a 485-foot rocket shot. It is the second time in his career that Mantle has reached the distant left-center bleachers. This long-range feat permits Mantle to join the exclusive ranks of Moose Skowron and Joe DiMaggio, who have also reached this remote target looming on the left-center horizon twice in their careers. Mantle also celebrates this home run by driving in the 1,000th RBI of his career during this contest.

347.   July 1   Wash.   Carl Mathias(LH)   Stadium   7–6, NY   24,144

The Switcher bombs a prodigious right-handed drive, that lands deep in the lower deck of the left field grandstand. Maris also adds a home run in this game. Washington had been leading, 6–5, in the bottom of the ninth when Roger's round-tripper wins the game, a two-run shot down the right field line.

348.   July 2   Wash.   Johnny Klippstein   Stadium   13–4, NY   19,794

After walking four straight times in his first four plate appearances, Mantle connects for his 29th home run of the year. The ball soars into the right field upper deck. It is Mantle's fourth home run in the three-game series against the Senators. Meanwhile, Maris has poled two on this day. In today's game, the first home run hit by Maris, his 29th for the year, had hit high up on the right field foul screen. His next home run, No. 30, was an upper deck shot into the right field grandstand. Mantle homers in his only official at-bat. Number 7 scores twice on the walks and once on his home run. Completing this day's game ends a three-game sweep as the Yankees connect five times for home runs in this tilt. Maris has hit two home runs, Mantle has hit another, Elston Howard yet one more, and Bill Skowron still another. Skowron's home run is another milestone for him as he reaches the distant left-center field bleachers for the third time in his career. Only Joe DiMaggio and Mickey Mantle have done it twice, Mickey's second one coming the day before. As for the "M & M Boys," in this series with the Senators, the dangerous duo has thrashed Senators' pitching, combining for seven home runs and 17 RBIs, while batting .619 (13–21) and scoring 12 runs between them in three games. Mickey's particular home run on this day ties Roger's for the league lead in home runs for the season, with 30. Both historic clubbers are now tied with each other, halfway to the mark, halfway through the season. Besides the spirit of the chase, the feat is fascinatingly, statistically impressive. American baseball fans, from sea to shining sea, are in heaven.

July 4, 1961: In a Yankee Stadium doubleheader with the visiting Detroit Tigers, the New York nine attracts a large holiday crowd of 74,246 clamoring spectators, the largest stadium crowd since 1947. The Yankees win the first game, 6–2. The Tigers win the second, 4–3, in 10 innings.

Maris hits his 31st home run. The Tigers remain one game ahead of the Yankees.

349.   July 8   Boston   Tracy Stallard   Stadium   8–5, NY   23,381

Mantle launches a soaring drive into the upper deck of the right field grandstand. This timely blow represents the 10th time this year that Mickey has homered with Whitey Ford on the mound. The home run also supplies his good friend with the winning run.

THE 1961 ALL-STAR GAME

CANDLESTICK PARK IN SAN FRANCISCO, CALIFORNIA
FIRST GAME—JULY 11

In the All-Star Game in windy San Francisco, performing before an appreciative assembly of 44,115 Bayside boosters, the 165-pound Giants' reliever Stu Miller gets blown off the mound by a robust gust of wind at Candlestick Park and is called for a balk as a result. In fact, despite the balk, Miller's 1⅔ inning relief stint at Candlestick will earn him the win in the extra-inning affair. The National League proves victorious, 5–4, despite a record number of All-Star Game errors by both teams— six.

There is an interesting sidelight to the game, a secret drama, that unfolds in the first inning of the midsummer classic. Mickey Mantle and Whitey Ford and the owner of the San Francisco Giants, Horace Stoneham, had made a wager the day before that would be settled in the opening frame of the game this day. Mr. Stoneham had bet Whitey that he could not get Willie Mays out in his first at-bat, which appeared to be a sucker's bet designed to take advantage of the Yankee All-Stars. The day before the All-Star Game, the Stonehams—Giant owner Horace and his son, Peter—had offered Mickey and Whitey a round of golf at their country club with arrangements made for the famous Yankee visitors to sign Stoneham's name to their tab. Mickey and Whitey, however, had gone a bit overboard, running up a bill of $400 for the round of golf, while padding the tab with the purchase of sweaters, golf shirts, and other golf sundries. Later that evening at a pre-All-Star Game cocktail party, the two Yankees had met with Stoneham to tell him that they got carried away. After apologizing, Ford hands the Giants owner his and Mickey's $400 for the extraordinary bill. Rejecting the cash, Stoneham, a chronic sportsman at heart, comes up with another idea. He is willing to make a double-or-nothing wager that Whitey cannot get Willie Mays out in his first at-bat in the next day's classic. If he does, he will forget the money. But, if Willie gets a hit, then the two Yankees owe Stoneham $800.

Whitey goes for the bet. Mickey, meanwhile, is appalled and starts to stall. First, $800 is a lot of money, and second, Mays owns Whitey Ford, having gone 6-for-7 against the "Chairman of the Board" in All-Star competition over the years. The two pin-striped friends have bittersweet memories of Mays' dominance of Ford in their various All-Star confrontations—bittersweet in the sense that Ford achingly remembers its agony, while Mickey rubs it in gleefully. But Whitey, who has been rightfully nicknamed "Slick" for precisely these kinds of occasions, is able to convince Mickey to accept the bet since he is sure he can get the fabled "Say Hey Kid" out.

Finally, the first inning arrives and the confrontation takes place, as a nervous Mickey Mantle watches the fateful face-off from his position in center field. After getting two strikes on the storied slugger, Whitey breaks off a wicked "spitter," that dazzles Mays, droping sharply into the strike zone for the third strike and the end of the inning. After Ford fans the legendary Mays, a relieved Mickey leaps into the air laughing, clapping, cheering, and expressing total elation. To everyone watching at Candlestick Park and the millions of eyes observing the All-Star game in their living rooms and taverns, it appears as though Mickey is behaving inappropriately as if the final out of the World Series had just been made. To others, it looks like he is showing up Willie. On the contrary, the "Kid from Oklahoma" can barely contain himself with "Slick" having saved them $800 and being one up on the owner of the San Francisco Giants. Just for a second, and having nothing to do with his good friend, the great Willie Mays, with whom Mantle has always been so accepting and cordial, Mickey unthinkingly and blatantly applauds his teammate's wizardry. Indeed, only "Whitey," Mickey, and Horace Stoneham are aware of the real reason behind Mickey's unbridled elation—the $400 double-or-nothing side bet. As for the game itself, the contest is a game of long balls. Home runs in this All-Star Game will electrify the appreciative crowd. Long-range taters would be provided by Harmon Killebrew, George Altman, Elston Howard, and Bill "Moose" Skowron.

Meanwhile, as is his constant habit in these annual showcase exhibitions, Mickey goes 0-for-3 with two strikeouts.

350.	July 13	Chicago	Early Wynn	Chicago(n)	6–2, NY	43,960

Resuming the season after the All-Star break, the Yankees are playing the White Sox in a Comiskey Park night game when the Yankees beat Early Wynn and the Chisox, 6–2. As a result, the visiting pinstripers nudge the Detroit Tigers out of the lead and take sole possession of first place. It is another of Mickey's "tape-measure" blasts, that carries on a line some 500 feet into the center field upper deck above the field-level bleachers. The titanic blow comes in back-to-back fashion with Roger Maris, who preceded Mantle with the initial burst of another of their rat-a-tat-tat home runs. The Mantlesque blow also proves to be the game-winner for the Bombers.

351.	July 14	Chicago	Juan Pizarro(LH)	Chicago(n)	6–1, Chi	43,450
352.	July 16	Baltimore	Steve Barber(LH)	Baltimore	2–1, NY	28,847

At a soggy Memorial Stadium, Mantle's home run to left-center field ties the game with the Yankees' first run. Later, in the ninth inning, with the game on the line, Mickey doubles in the winning run.

| 353. | July 17 | Baltimore | Milt Pappas | Baltimore(tn) 5–0, NY | 44,332 |
| | (first game) | | | | |

This home run comes in the first game of a scheduled twinight doubleheader and represents "The Mick's" fourth long shot in the last five games. In their race with Babe Ruth, Roger Maris has clubbed 35 home runs and is 19 games ahead of "The Babe's" record-setting pace of 1927. The maturing Mickey Mantle has, meanwhile, throttled 33 home runs and is eight games ahead of the Ruthian schedule. Before the second game starts on this drizzly day in Baltimore, an announcement is made between games that Tyrus Raymond Cobb, the greatest base-hitter in the history of baseball, has died in California. In the second game of the twin-bill, both Mantle and Roger Maris power home runs off the Orioles pitching early in the game, as does Clete Boyer. For this game, however, the rains come and wash away the contest and all of the game's statistics.

| 354. | July 18 | Wash. | Joe McClain | Wash., D.C.(n) 5–3, NY | 17,695 |
| 355. | July 18 | Wash. | Joe McClain | Wash., D.C.(n) 5–3, NY | 17,695 |

Mantle's longball production this day reflects a blazing consistency, characteristic of this year's "M & M" twin tater-terrors. Mickey now has tied Roger Maris at 35 home runs for the year and this day's output represents eight home runs in the last nine games, including Baltimore's "rained-out" home run. In the "M & M Boys" race, Mantle has belted the last six home runs between the two sluggers. This had allowed a hot Mantle to overtake the current home run sluggishness of Roger Maris.

In the meantime, the hounds of the press are frothing at the mouth, covering the long-ball antics of the "M & M Boys." Because of having gone through this kind of onslaught in 1956 when he, too, chased "The Babe," Mickey points the way for Roger. The simple, country-boy, new-to-the-big-time Maris is being crushed by the daily deluge of demands and aggressive requests from increasingly insensitive sportswriters. To help insulate Roger from this constant siege, the two stars, good friends with one another, would decide to share an apartment with teammate Bob Cerv. They would live together, cook together, and basically stay inside their apartment together. Gone for Mickey this year, because of Roger's predicament with the media, and difficulties with the Big Apple in general, are the long nights of drinking binges that were the hallmark of his characteristic "night-rider" life with his drinking buddy Billy Martin.

| 356. | July 19 | Wash. | Dick Donovan | Wash., D.C.(tn) 12–2, NY | 27,126 |
| | (second game) | | | | |

The "M & M Boys" are drawing crowds in record numbers wherever they go to play ball. Consequently, Mantle and Maris take the field before the largest attendance figure for any Capital crowd ever to attend a twinight doubleheader with the newest version of the Washington Senators. The expansion Senators, who are in their first year of existence, are playing their first year's home stand at old Griffith Stadium as they await the construction and opening of D.C. Stadium, scheduled to be completed next year. Meanwhile, this day's crowd, some 27,126 Senator fans have poured into the stands at Griffith Stadium to see the "M & M Boys" ply their trade, while pursuing their sensational quest of catching "The Babe." They are not to be disappointed as Mickey Mantle poles a home run off Senator pitching that gives him 36 for the year and one round-tripper ahead of Roger Maris. It is Mickey's eighth home run in nine official games.

Ford Frick, the Commissioner of Baseball and a proud and long time friend of Babe Ruth's, makes a fortuitous announcement this day and which will forever resound through the rest of his days and beyond, which will neither serve him nor his memory well. Commissioner Frick, Babe's former ghostwriter, decides arbitrarily to diminish any home run record accomplished by anyone, but principally threatened by Mantle and Maris, should that record occur after 154 games, the same number of games utilized by the "Great Bambino" in 1927 when he established the record. With this slant on things, thus is born the infamous "*" (asterisk). Accordingly, Frick states, Any player who may hit more than 60 home runs during his club's first 154 games will be recognized as having established a new record. However, if the player does not hit more than 60 home runs until after his club has played 154 games, there would have to be a distinctive mark in the record books to show that Babe Ruth's record was set under a 154-game schedule and the total of more than 60 was compiled while a 162-game schedule was in effect.

This "distinguishing mark"—an asterisk in the record books alongside the 154-game mark by Babe Ruth—whether intended or not, serves somehow to trivialize the magnitude of a new record should it occur. To many of the baseball purists, a record in an expanded season will signify a blemish on the new mark since it takes an extra eight games to accomplish it. When asked to comment about the ruling, Maris keeps his response simple: "A season's a season." Mantle agrees with Roger, stating later how ludicrous this edict was, and in a future interview decrying the ruling, declaring "a lot of guys have tried since and no one has come close."

357.   July 21   Boston   Bill Monbouquette   Boston(n)   11–8, NY   32,186

The "M & M Boys" are knotted at 36 home runs apiece when Maris poles a round-tripper in the first inning of the first game of a doubleheader. Mantle forges back ahead when he follows Roger with the tail end of back-to-back blasts. It is Mantle's ninth home run in the last ten games. However, moving into the ninth inning, the Yankees are trailing the Bosox, 8–6, as they seek to overtake the Red Sox in the last frame. In the meantime, in the top of the ninth inning with two outs, Yankee Manager Ralph Houk sends Johnny Blanchard up to pinch-hit for Clete Boyer. The Yankee catcher replacement hits a pinch-hit grand-slam home run. Luis Arroyo comes in to put down the Red Sox in the home half of the inning, which gives the Yankees an 11–8 decision.

July 22, 1961: Once again playing against the Boston Red Sox at Fenway Park, before 25,089 Beantowners, Johnny Blanchard of the New York Yankees clouts his second successive pinch-hit home run in two days, a solo shot, that helps pace the Bombers to another hard-fought, 11–9 victory.

| 358. | July 25
(first game) | Chicago | Frank Baumann(LH) | Stadium(tn) | 12–0, NY | 46,240 |

Mantle's fourth-inning home run on this day is once again of the back-to-back variety with Roger Maris as his blast bounces off the left field foul pole. Still, the real story is Maris. In the Yankee Stadium doubleheader against the Chicago White Sox, Yankee slugger Roger Maris crashes four home runs in a display of the most productive day in this, his and baseball's most productive season. The twinbill performance by the young power hitter ties an American League record. Just as impressive, the four clouts by Maris come off four different White Sox hurlers. Maris collects his 37th home run off Frank Baumann, his 38th off Don Larsen, his 39th off Russ Kemmerer, and his last home run of the night, his 40th of the year, off Warren Hacker. Maris' home run count now stands at 40 home runs, the soonest in a season that any major league batter has reached the 40-home run plateau in a single season. This places the crewcut Maris 25 games ahead of Babe Ruth's 1927 pace.

| 359. | July 26 | Chicago | Ray Herbert | Stadium | 5–2, NY | 22,366 |

Mantle's 39th home run of the year soars into the right-center field bleachers, where it disappears into a sea of outstretched hands some 15 rows deep. The mighty blow puts Mickey 22 games ahead of Ruth's 1927 pace. At this point, Maris has 40 home runs and is 23 games ahead. In addition, it is the third consecutive game in which back up catcher Johnny Blanchard of the New York Yankees has appeared. Blanchard belts out two home runs in his first two at-bats, which, in combination with his last two successive at-bats when he belted two pinch-hit home runs in a row against Boston, represents four home runs in a row—which equals a major league record. The Yankees are still sizzling, winning this month's slate of games at a 20–9 clip.

THE 1961 ALL-STAR GAME

FENWAY PARK IN BOSTON, MASSACHUSETTS
SECOND GAME—JULY 31

In the second All-Star Game of the year, tied at 1–1 at Fenway Park, a monstrous downpour prevents the game from continuing that produces the only tie in All-Star Game history. A drenched Beantown assembly of 31,851 American League rooters are treated to a damp, defensive-oriented-duel of All-Star pitchers. Mickey goes 0-for-3, striking out twice, fanning against Sandy Koufax and Stu Miller, while also drawing a base on balls.

| 360. | Aug. 2
(second game) | Kansas City | Jim Archer(LH) | Stadium(tn) | 12-5, NY | 23,616 |

Mickey's towering shot plows into the upper right field deck, that is a familiar destination for his arching blows.

| 361. | Aug. 6
(first game) | Minnesota | Pedro Ramos | Stadium | 7–6, NY
(in 15) | 39,408 |
| 362. | Aug. 6
(first game) | Minnesota | Pedro Ramos | Stadium | 7–6, NY | 39,408 |

In this game alone, Mickey's home run production gives him career totals which ties and surpasses the career total of Joe DiMaggio's glittering long-ball-laden career. Mickey has been busy in this first contest, going 4-for-6, scoring three runs while driving in another tray. Mantle's wallops also place him ninth on the all-time home run list in baseball.

| 363. | Aug. 6
(second game) | Minnesota | Al Schroll | Stadium | 3–2, NY | 39,408 |

Mantle has enjoyed a field day at the plate in this double—dip, going 5—for-9, smashing three home runs and a double, driving in four runs, scoring five times, and drawing three walks. Meanwhile, Roger Maris establishes a major league fielding record by accepting no fielding chances in the longest of one day's duty in the outfield. Maris has played a doubleheader that would last 24 innings without getting one ball hit in his direction. On offense, meanwhile, Maris has cooled off in his record pursuit. The left-handed power-hitting outfielder will go a full week without homering. At the same time, during the same twin bill, as noted, Mickey Mantle gets hot beginning this day when he pounds out his 39th, 40th, and 41st home runs of the year. The Bronx Bombers, as a consequence, are also hot, on the verge of completing the current home stand with a spectacular 15–4 winning record.

364.   Aug. 11   Wash.   Pete Burnside(LH)   Wash., D.C.(n) 12–5, NY   22,601

At Griffith Stadium, newly expanded Senators set their one-year record for a night game's attendance when 22,601 Washingtonians watch the Senators play the New York Yankees as the "M & M Boys" pursue their dedication to homering against American League pitching. This evening's fare for Maris and Mantle's long-ball appetites equates with the worst staff pitching in the league. For his part, Maris ends a brief home run-drought when he lifts a long ball in the fifth inning for a home run, his 45th of the year. Mickey Mantle add his own four-bagger in the eighth, his 44th of the year, a 400-foot shot into the center-field bleachers.

August 12, 1961: At Griffith Stadium in the nation's capital, Roger Maris connects for his 43rd home run off Dick Donovan of the Washington Senators.

365.   Aug. 13   Wash.   Bennie Daniels   Wash., D.C.   12–2, Wash   27,368
     (first game)

Roger Maris, Mickey Mantle, and the rest of the record-setting 1961 New York Yankees play the expansion team Washington Senators in a Griffith Stadium doubleheader. Yankee home runs seem to be raining down on the Senators. In the first game, Maris belts a long line drive deep into the distant right-center field bullpen, the furthest location in the park without going out of the yard completely. Both Maris and Mantle are now tied at 44 home runs for the season. One inning later, Mickey pounds out another long blast in the same remote bullpen, that gives the pin-striped "tape-measure" legend his 45th of the year and once again the lead. Maris has collected 45 home runs in 117 games. In 1927, the "Great Bambino" had not hit his 45th until his 132nd game. In the second game of the twin bill, Maris poles yet one more home run out of the playing confines of Griffith, an historic baseball landmark that is in its last year of service to the Washington Senators and the American League. The "M & M Boys" are now tied at 45 home runs apiece.

August 15, 1961: In the searing home run race between Roger Maris and Mickey Mantle, both members of the New York Yankees, the Yankee rightfielder moves ahead of "The Mick" by belting out his 46th home run off Juan Pizarro of the Chicago White Sox. During what Maris considers a post-game confrontation with the media, the question is asked whether Maris believes himself to be a great man since Babe Ruth was a great man. Maris, growing increasingly unforgiving of the probing press, answers almost spitefully, "Maybe I'm not a great man, but I damned well want to break the record. And feller, I don't like your goddamn questions. Get outta here." This comment will inspire one journalistic reaction in Chicago alleging that Maris was "cracking under pressure."

August 16, 1961: Before 29,728 deliriously happy Yankee rooters, in a game against the White Sox, Maris pounds out his second home run of the game which gives him his seventh home run in six consecutive games—a feat that matches the American League record for the most home runs, seven, ever hit by a player in six consecutive games.

366.	Aug. 20 (first game)	Cleveland	Jim Perry	Cleveland	6–0, NY	56,307

At Municipal Stadium, in the greatest crowd of the year, are some 56,000 Indians fans; it is some 20,000 more spectators than the next-highest Cleveland attendance figure at home this year. Yankee sluggers Roger Maris and Mickey Mantle each contribute a home run to the Yankee cause, helping beat the Indians in the process. Mickey's first-inning blow is the decider, his game-winner knocking in three Yankee runs.

For the remainder of the game, Mickey collects two more hits and knocks in another run. For Maris, it is his 49th home run of the season; for Mickey, his 46th. Both sluggers receive a welcome and generous roar of approval from the bipartisan if momentarily happy clutch of "M & M Boys" rooters who are cheering the slugging teammates towards their historic goal of overtaking "The Babe." The dual race against Ruth proceeds with increased intensity. It is the 14th time this year that the "M & M Boys" have connected in the same game. The twin tandem in slugging power, the most awesome twosome in baseball history, have accounted for 35 home runs in those 14 games that have contributed to a 13–1 record for the Bronx Bombers in those same contests.

August 22, 1961: At Wrigley Field in Los Angeles, Roger Maris of the New York Yankees becomes the first player ever in baseball history to hit his 50th home run while it's still the month of August. The left-handed slugger connects off California Angels' Ken McBride in a 4–3 loss. The blow is unleashed before the largest L.A.-based Wrigley Field crowd ever to watch an Angel night game, an excited brace of 19,930 thrilled Tinsel Town touters. It is the earliest point in any season in baseball history that a player has reached this hallowed plateau in home run legend. To Maris, the earliest time anyone prior to Maris reaching 50 home runs was September 4th, a date shared by George Herman "Babe" Ruth and Jimmie Foxx. Maris shatters their record by 13 days. Maris is only the ninth player ever to hit 50 home runs in a single season.

August 26, 1961: Roger Maris blasts his 51st home run against Kansas City pitcher Jerry Walker, giving the Yankee slugger more home runs than anyone in the majors. No one has ever reached this impressive plateau of home run production so soon in a season.

August 27, 1961: In Kansas City, before the largest crowd ever assembled at Municipal Stadium to watch a day game, 34,065 excited Athletics boosters have poured through the turnstiles to catch the "M & M Boys" traveling show. The Maris–Mantle fever is spreading all over Baseball America, which is maintaining an intense and fascinating vigil on this tandem threat to one of the most sacred records in all of sports.

367.   Aug. 30   Minnesota   Jim Kaat(LH)   Minnesota(n) 4–0, NY   41,357

After belting his 47th clout of the year, Mantle chides Maris later in the locker room, saying with a smile and affording a quote to the prying media within earshot of his remarks, "Well, I caught my man. Now Roger has to catch his." Mickey is referring to 1927, when Babe set the record, and Lou Gehrig, Ruth's main challenger and slugging teammate, belted out 47 in that historic year. Mickey's shot in this game was another of his signature longballs, soaring halfway up the distant left field bleachers, an estimated 425 feet. What made the home run even more impressive, was that the veteran basher had been so badly fooled by the pitch. Even though Kaat's offering would have bounced in the dirt before it reached the plate, Mickey had over committed on unleashing his powerful swing and had no choice but to go through with completing it. After the contest, reporters had asked about the pitch, to which Mantle replied, "I shouldn't have gone for it. I was expecting a fast ball, and when that slow pitch came up I just couldn't stop the swing and had to go through with it. I haven't been so surprised all season."

368.   Aug. 31   Minnesota   Jack Kralick(LH)   Minnesota   4–3, Minn   39,985
                                                                     Ladies' Day   (33,709 pd.)

Mickey pounds out a towering home run, No. 48, though the Yankees drop the tilt to the Twins. As the "M & M Boys" continue with their torrid stretch of homers, the Yankees, as a team, are also proceeding to flail at their American League opponents, scorching them while winning 22 of 31 games. After the game, Mickey Mantle is talking with Dick Young of the New York Daily News when he is asked about the condition of his legs. Mickey responds, saying, "Not too bad. But don't count on me [breaking Ruth's record]. I don't want to think about Ruth's record. I'm just concerned with the team's record. But if anyone breaks the record, it will be Maris."

September 1, 1961: At Yankee Stadium, the pin striped pack begins a crucial three-game series against the Detroit Tigers, who are one game behind the league-leading Yankees. In the bottom of the ninth inning of the first contest, Tiger lefthander Don Mossi retires Maris and Mantle, to seemingly emerge out of the heart of the fearsome Yankee lineup. But, Mossi gives up singles to Elston Howard, Yogi Berra, and Moose Skowron and the Yanks win the series opener, 1–0. In this season of personal sensations, Roger Maris will recall this game as the game that made him most proud to be a Yankee. Both sluggers had contributed nothing to winning the contest, but still their teammates came through without them, stressing what both bashers have contended all year: that winning the pennant takes the work of all 25 men on the roster playing in unison.

September 2, 1961: At Yankee Stadium, in the second game of the showdown series of the season with the Detroit Tigers, the Yankees face their chief Tiger nemesis Frank Lary, the reputed "Yankee killer" and the immediately pending, proud holder this year of a 23–9 pitching record. In Maris' first at-bat, Lary throws four balls in a row, giving the Yankee outfielder a base on balls. Tiger pitcher Lary gets roundly booed for passing Maris. In his second plate appearance, in the fourth, with the Yankees trailing 2–1, the next pitched ball from Frank Lary sails wide of the strike zone, producing more boos, whistles, and catcalls from the Bronx fans, who want Lary to pitch to Maris. On the next pitch, the first strike Maris sees in the game, the classic swing is unloosed and the ball is launched for a double to right-center field. Maris moves to third base on the mishandling of the ball.

Meanwhile, Mickey has, earlier in the game, pulled a muscle in his forearm, having checked one of his mighty cuts in the first inning. Afterwards, while sitting on the bench with Yankee Manager Ralph Houk watching the game progress, Mickey mentions that he just pulled a muscle in his forearm. The Yankee field general asks Mickey what he wants to do. Mickey assures the coach, "I'll stay in the game. The Tigers don't know I'm hurt. I'll bunt instead of swing." Houk says, "It could get embarrassing for you. They'll boo you." Looking out at the field from the bench, Mantle replies, "I'm used to it." In Mickey's next at-bat, with Roger on third, the veteran slugger lays down a perfect drag bunt for a hit while Maris scores the tying run.

Later, with two outs in the sixth, Maris connects on a 3-2 pitch from Lary, propelling the ball into the right field stands. The Yankees now lead the game, 3-2. In the eighth, Maris connects once more, blasting a 450-foot shot that ties the game going into the ninth inning. In the bottom of the ninth, Elston Howard belts a three-run home run that skins the Tigers for good and produces a 7–2 victory. The Yankees are now enjoying a 4 ½-game lead over Detroit.

| 369. | Sept. 3 | Detroit | Jim Bunning | Stadium | 8–5, NY | 55,676 |

At Yankee Stadium, before 55,000 hearty New York fans, Mickey Mantle of the New York Yankees prepares to take the field, despite a forearm so sore that Houk has already decided not to play his centerfielder. In fact, the concerned manager tells Mickey that he wants to rest him for two days. But after taking some careful practice swings in the training room, Mickey informs the Yankee manager that he can play.

As a result, Mantle lifts a powerful longball to right field for a home run, his 49th of the season. Mantle is followed to the plate by Yogi Berra who fashions a back-to-back home run down the right field line.

| 370. | Sept. 3 | Detroit | Jerry Staley | Stadium | 8–5, NY | 55,676 |

The attendance for this three-game set with Detroit has established a new Yankee Stadium record for a three-game series with 171,503 paying patrons. Later, in the ninth, trailing the Tigers by a run, Mantle leads off the inning by smashing his second home run of the game, electrifying the frenzied crowd, tying the game, and recording his 50th home run of the campaign. Mantle's 50th circuit blast of the year keeps the Bombers alive as he energizes the crowd with still another clutch bolt off his bat. The milestone blast, a 450-foot shot into the right-center field bleachers, allows Mantle to join the rarefied exclusivity of the likes of Babe Ruth (54 in 1920, 59 in 1921, 60 in 1927, and 54 in 1928), Jimmie Foxx (58 in 1932 and 50 in 1938), Ralph Kiner (51 in 1947 and 54 in 1949), and later Willie Mays (51 in 1955 and 52 in 1965) and Mark McGwire (52 in 1996 and 58 in 1997): the only sluggers in history ever to generate two or more seasons in their careers connecting for 50 or more home runs in a single year. This most impressive feat is even more magnificent since it marks the only time in the history of the game when two teammates reach the 50-home run plateau in the same year.

Five batters later, Elston Howard ends the game when he crashes a towering blast that leaves the field, beats the Tigers, 8–5, and crushes all pennant hopes for Detroit, now 4½ games back.

September 4, 1961: Mickey Mantle misses this day's Labor Day twin bill with a pulled muscle in his forearm that has now turned swollen and purple. Even on this day, after belting two home runs the day before, the extent of his injury had actually been compounded by Mantle's long-ball activity. Now the revivification of the injury will require the Yankee slugger to recuperate for a day, will involve missing a doubleheader. In the sixth inning of the game two days earlier, Mickey Mantle had been batting immediately behind Maris's home run when he checked his swing of the bat so hard that he pulled a muscle in his left forearm. Since yesterday, the pain has intensified to the point that he able to swing the bat without great pain. The injury will cause Mantle to miss the Labor Day doubleheader with the Washington Senators. Giving up two games to injury while chasing history is agonizing for Mantle.

During this critical juncture in this historic year, Mickey Mantle is chatting with sportswriter Roger Kahn, when the journalist asks the Yankee leader, "What do you tell Maris?" After many years of dealing with a hounding press, and after selecting a mere few of the media-types as close confidants with whom he actually communicates, Mickey tells the scribe that what he tells Maris is "what you heard me tell him. That he's gotta put up with the horseshit. That he's gonna make some real money. And don't make such a big deal out of every fucking thing. I have been through the writers' stuff myself."

| 371. | Sept. 5 | Wash. | Joe McClain | Stadium(n) | 6–1, NY | 16,917 |

Beginning this day, one day after missing a doubleheader because of the painful forearm injury, another surge in the tandem home run prowess of Roger Maris and Mickey Mantle is registered against American League opponents. The two Yankee terrors go on a home run binge with such a ferocity that each slugger is seriously touted to shatter the Ruthian mark. Today Mickey Mantle hits his 51st home run, teeing off on McClain, propelling the ball deep into the right field upper deck at Yankee Stadium, some six rows beyond the front railing of the upper tier, and gives the Yankees a 1–1 tie. Mickey is only two home runs behind the hot-hitting Maris in their paired pursuit of "The Babe". It is precisely at this point in the race, however, that Mantle's chances begin to fade, burdened by sheer numbers alone and by the mounting injuries that are once again beginning to plague him.

September 6, 1961: On this day at Yankee Stadium, Roger Maris hits his 54th home run off righthander Tom Cheney of the Washington Senators.

September 7, 1961: The performance of Roger Maris on the field is nothing short of remarkable. His off-the-field demeanor, however, is beginning to show signs of dissembling. In one of the pressure-cooked press conferences that are intensifying with every passing day, Maris snaps at yet another idiotic query by a member of the press who wants to know why he laid down a bunt to advance a runner at a crucial moment in that day's game instead of trying for a home run. His patience wearing thin with questions that challenge his instincts as a ballplayer and his integrity as a team member, Maris reacts testily, snapping, "Trying to win the game, you stupid cocksucker! Why do you think?" The reporter had also failed to acknowledge that in the at-bat after the bunt, Maris had hit his 55th home run.

| 372. | Sept. 8 | Cleveland | Gary Bell | Stadium(n) | 9–1, NY | 41,672 |

Mickey connects for his 52nd home run of the year, a long drive deep into the lower right field seats. This particular circuit blast is not as significant as is the crowd's response. Mantle's trot around the bases shows that the slugger is truly ailing. Having recently banged up his left shin, his jog takes on the character of a wounded man attempting to canter gingerly, limping all the way as he circles the basepaths. As he rounds first base, the stadium spectators unloose one of the greatest standing ovations Mickey will ever experience. As Mantle continues his impaired lope, the noise of the excited assembly increases in volume until the din becomes deliriously loud. It is the fans' salute to Mickey's courage that sends shock waves through the rafters of the majestic ballyard. The commotion will not die down until Mantle has crossed the plate and disappeared into the dugout. After the game, Mantle will be asked about this spectacular salute and simply reply, "They've been like that for about a week, but never so...so loud and long. Maybe it's because I'm kind of an underdog now, trailing Rog by three homers yet. People always seem to root for the guy who's behind."

September 9, 1961: At the stadium in the Bronx, on "Whitey Ford Day," Roger Maris of the New York Yankees connects against Jim "Mudcat" Grant of the Cleveland Indians for his 56th home run of the season. This home run, together with Mickey Mantle's own total of 52, gives the two teammates 108 home runs in a single season, surpassing the phenomenal 1927 record of Ruth and Gehrig and establishing the major league record for teammate production in home runs. It is during this same game that Luis Arroyo, the Yankee's chief fireman, comes in from the bullpen to secure his 12th relief triumph in a row. In this year of record-breaking performances, this pitching feat establishes an American League record.

373.	Sept. 10	Cleveland	Jim Perry	Stadium	9–3, NY	57,826

(first game)

Before an adoring hometown crowd of 57,826 at Yankee Stadium, during the first game of a doubleheader with the Cleveland Indians, Mickey Mantle belts the 53rd home run of this most exciting year of longballs. In the doubleheader with Cleveland, the Yankees had, by this game, pushed 1,657,031 frenetic fans through the turnstiles, its highest annual attendance in ten years.

As the Yankees move into Chicago for a three-game set, Roger is close to experiencing a nervous breakdown because of his intensified relations with the mobbing press. He complains endlessly about the constant series of face-offs to which he is becoming increasingly adverse and more frequently subjected. Maris has been asked to pose for the same photos, asked to answer the same questions over and over again, and questioned on every strategy he has utilized as a hitter and as a contributor to the Yankee cause. The wholesome slugger has even been asked if he has cheated on his wife when he was on the road. Even in this very town, the most famous of the Midwest's "Toddlin' Towns," Roger's reply to one question is presented in the papers as a "gripe;" he complains that Mickey should concede that he is out of the race in catching "The Babe." In truth, Maris believes that they are both still in the race. Somehow this had degenerated into a new round of press debate that the two friends had been having a running feud over the home run race. It would be at this point in his colloquy with the press that Maris would again flare, implying that once again they have gone too far. His eventual disgust with the press stemmed over what he was saying, what was reported, and how misinterpreted and distorted it became. It is at this point in time when Roger decides not to answer any more questions from the press. At one point with Mickey, in a private moment, after the latest of the unending waves of aggressive queries, rawer and ruder, and decidedly increasing and unwanted press attention, Roger comments with his head in his hands, "I can't take this anymore." Mickey retorts, "You got to."

September 15, 1961: At Detroit, the Yankees are playing a doubleheader with the Tigers which produces no home runs from either Maris or Mantle. But it does provide the showcase of the team's unprecedented, record-setting power as Yogi Berra connects to tie the all-time team record for home runs in a season. Moose Skowron adds his own round-tripper in a later frame; it proves to be the record-making 222nd team round-tripper. This team accomplishment establishes a new major league record.

September 16, 1961: At Detroit's Tiger Stadium, facing "Yankee killer" Frank Lary, Roger Maris lifts a long fly to right-center field that disappears over the head of center fielder Bill Bruton, deep into the lower level of the right-center field grandstand, and into a sea of outstretched hands of delighted Detroit fans. Maris has now connected 57 times in his historic chase after "The Bambino's" ghost. The Tiger partisans actually boo their own hometown hurler when he walks Maris on four pitches in the first inning.

September 17, 1961: Still in Detroit, Roger Maris will approach the plate in the seventh inning. Again the pitch, an offering delivered by relief artist Terry Fox, and Maris swings and connects off the Tiger relief ace for a long drive to the right. The descending ball finally crashes high off the wall for a triple will would drive in the go-ahead run. The Detroit Tigers would come back to tie the game, which would send the contest into extra innings. In the top of the twelfth, as Tony Kubek stands on second base for the Yankees, Roger Maris is preparing to hit once more against Fox when something high over the ballfield catches the attention of the lonely slugger. A long and elegant, V-shaped pattern of Canada geese is flying overhead when its southerly route takes them in a graceful glide over the right-center field grandstand. For a very long moment, Maris stands outside the batter's box and takes off his batting helmet. For another long moment, Maris stares at the spot in the heavens situated over the hallowed walls of Tiger Stadium, his gaze following the beautiful formation of southerly-flying geese. Maris has been transported back to a calmer, more serene Fargo, North Dakota–like existence, a quieter time of contemplation. For a simple, quick moment, Roger Maris has divorced himself from his physical environment and is at ease—no media, no pressure, no hype—and, paradoxically, standing in the middle of a brimming Tiger Stadium before a packed assembly, all eyes on him, waiting breathless at this, a dramatic pause. In the meantime, Terry Fox, the Detroit reliever, is getting somewhat antsy, waiting for Maris to get into the batter's box. So is Plate Umpire Nestor Chylak, who is getting a little nervous himself. Finally, after watching the aesthetic formation of 250-odd geese soar overhead and out of view from the historic ballyard, Maris fits his helmet back onto his head and steps back into the box.

On the first pitch from Fox after the delay, Maris reacts quickly, triggering once again the classic, fluid nature of his compact swing, and—CRACK—the ball meets the powerful bat and is launched into a high trajectory towards a spot high and upward towards the right-center field façade, in fact towards the distant spot below where Maris had admired the geese. The ball's rapid ascent climbs highward in a rising arc until the soaring white sphere crashes against the facing of the second deck. Home run! The ball slams against the second deck and bounces back onto the playing field. This prodigious clout registers the 58th home run of this sensational season for Roger Maris.

September 20, 1961: At Memorial Stadium in Baltimore, the birthplace of Babe Ruth, it is the 154th game of the regular schedule, the deadline date in Baltimore. Commissioner Ford Frick's "moment of truth" for Roger Maris has arrived. Yesterday, in a doubleheader, the intensely pressured Maris went 1-9 in the two games, managing a mere single in his last at-bat. Today's game is the 154th the like game number Babe Ruth had when he set the 60 home run standard. Connecting off a low fast ball thrown by righthander Milt Pappas, Yankee outfielder Roger Maris connects for his 59th home run of the year against the Oriole nine. The ball is catapulted high and long towards right field, where it sails over the 380-foot sign. In a later at-bat, as recalled by teammate Bob Cerv, Maris "hit one even better than he hit No. 59. But the wind had changed and it hung up there, and they caught it against the wall. I used to kid Roger, 'That was the ghost of Ruth that blew that ball back in.'" Another of Maris' drives also sailed over the fence but had left the playing field in foul territory as it curled ten feet to the right of the right field foul pole. Almost framed as a minor sidelight, the Yankees beat the Orioles, 4–2, and clinch the American League pennant.

| 374. | Sept. 23 | Boston | Don Schwall | Boston | 8–3, Bos | 28,128 |

At Fenway Park, Yankee slugger Mickey Mantle collects his 54th and final home run of the season, poling a tremendous shot to right-center field that lands in the bleachers behind the Red Sox bullpen. It is the last home run Mantle will hit this season. A debilitating hip abscess will curtail the season for the disappointed Oklahoman. In '27, Ruth and Gehrig had set the combined home run record between two teammates at 107. In '61, Maris and Mantle have shattered that record by eight home runs. As for the game itself, Whitey Ford will leave the game in the fifth, leading 4–1, which secures his final victory of the year, his 25th. Whitey Ford has had a sensational year for the Bombers. Even more significantly, Whitey has been the stopper for the Yankees, running up a 12–0 string of victories, a phenomenal record for each of those starting assignments that comes after a Yankee loss. In all games that Whitey started after a Yankee loss, the Yankee record, as a team, had been 17–1. Ford had stopped two game-losing streaks eight different times. As for this day, the Yankees win, 8–3. It is a landmark home run giving Mickey Mantle the major league record for the most home runs, 30, on the road ever made by a switch-hitter in a single season.

September 24, 1961: Mickey Mantle, the rest of the Yankees, and the premier broadcaster of Yankee baseball, Mel Allen, are taking the train back to New York City when Mantle and Allen confer over his latest row of physical impairments. Mantle has been fighting off the flu and coping with his ailing legs. Allen gives Mantle the name of an uptown doctor off Central Park West named Dr. Max Jacobson, a celebrity feel-good doctor with questionable methods, who concocts strange mixtures of steroids and animal fluids, that he has used to inject into a long list of star–studded personalities around New York City, Washington, D.C., and the country. Dr. Jacobson, who will later lose his medical certification and license to practice medicine, treats Mantle with one of his unorthodox concoctions. The doctor administers the injection high on the ballplayer's right hip. Jacobson does so with an unsterilized needle that, in turn, infects Mantle's system. The quack's "treatment" is painful. After receiving his injection, Mantle is told by that his discomfort is temporary and that it will pass. Jacobson tells Mickey not to be alarmed and that he should not even bother to take a cab back to the hotel, but just walk the short distance to it. It will do him some good. When Mantle gets down to the street, the pain is so intense, that he almost blacks out, collapsing on the sidewalk, where he gets help and is immediately transported to the hospital.

September 26, 1961: In the 158th game of the season against the Baltimore Orioles, the Maris challenge on the Ruthian record proceeds. Mickey Mantle attempts to play, but Dr. Max Jacobson's strange concoction has backfired badly and has infected Mickey's vulnerable system. Mantle plays one inning before coming out of this evening's game, unable to continue. In the interim, in the first inning of the game, played this night at the stadium before 19,401 excited fans, Maris singles. Later, with two outs in the third inning and no one on base, facing Oriole righthander Jack Fisher, New York Yankee slugger Roger Maris connects on a high curve ball, hitting the 60th home run of the season, that crashes high over the facade of the third deck of the upper grandstands and against the fourth row of seats before it rebounds back onto the field. The Maris blow ties him with all-time slugger George Herman "Babe" Ruth with 60 home runs in a single season. The long upper deck blow had been propelled off one of Fisher's hanging curve balls and had left the field of play six feet fair. The shot will depart the field so fast and go so far that Maris will stand at the plate, the bat still in his right hand leaning towards the ground. As he admires No. 60, Maris watches the rocketing, record-tying slam crash over the concrete facade of Yankee Stadium's rightfield grandstand. The bellow of the exhilarated Yankee fans resonates around the concreted canyon, deemed so aptly the "House That Ruth Built." The continued cheering of the frenzied crowd brings a sheepish Maris out of the dugout for a short bow. Reluctantly, the crew-cutted slugger complies. Mrs. Babe Ruth is on hand to congratulate the shy and bashful basher.

Mickey Mantle will miss the rest of the regular season from September 26th onward—some five games—after receiving the dubious "medical treatment." The injection is so damaging that it will immediately infect the thigh and buttock area of Mickey's right leg. In fact, Mantle will watch the rest of the regular season from his bed in the Lenox Hill Hospital. Mickey is cheering on his roommate as Maris pursues the historic, record-breaking home run, in this fabled year of the longball, which will push Roger past the "Bambino."

September 29, 1961: Roger Maris has been free for a couple of days, which included an off-day and one actual game in order to get some rest. Maris is desperate to spend some relaxing, stress-free time with his wife, who has just arrived in town, and regain some respite from the constant day-to-day stress. Roger will spend the time out at his old friend, Whitey Herzog's, Baltimore home. Now, on this day, when a rested Roger returns to take up the hunt, the Yankees manage to beat the Boston Red Sox, 2–1. Roger scores the winning run in the ninth. Afterwards, Maris and his wife will visit Mickey, who is still laid up in Lenox Hill Hospital in Manhattan and sitting out the rest of the regular season. At this point, although Mickey's fever has been broken, the pain and injury done to him and the disastrous medical ramifications stemming from Dr. Max Jacobson's quackery give Mickey the slimmest hopes of participating at any level for the rest of the year. Characteristically, Mantle resists this kind of thinking, insisting that he will be able to regroup for the upcoming World Series with the Cincinnati Reds.

September 30, 1961: On the second-to-last game of the year, the Yankees manage a victory over Boston, Maris managing to go 1-for-3. The Yankees, scintillating at home this year, will close out the month having won 21 out of the 29 games played. As Saturday moves into Sunday, Roger's quest for the Ruthian mark has come down to one game, one final game to set a new standard, a last chance at immortality, the ultimate one-game opportunity to beat "The Babe."

October 1, 1961: Before 23,154 rabid Roger rooters in Yankee Stadium and millions of eyes and ears in the baseball world riveted on Yankee Stadium in the Bronx, New York radio and television broadcaster Phil "The Scooter" Rizzuto describes the action of the fourth-inning. Roger Maris stands at the plate to face Tracy Stallard of the Boston Red Sox who winds up and delivers a 2–and–0 offering. At 2:43P.M. (EST), Rizzuto's commentary follows the pitch from Stallard as "The Scooter" calls the action, transforming the tenor in his voice with split-second urgency as the drive off the bat of Maris takes off on a high and deep arc towards the right field bleachers adjacent to the Yankee bullpen. The Yankee broadcaster, a shrill, high–pitched stridency seizing his narration, describes the drive in flight, exclaiming, "…fast ball hit deep to right.…This could be it!…Way back there.…Holy Cow, he did it. Roger Maris,…Holy Cow! What a shot!"

The ball sails over the head of the Red Sox rightfielder Carroll Hardy and disappears into the cheering throng seated in the right field grandstand. It is the 61st home run of the season for Roger Maris. After circling the bases, Maris calmly trots slowly into the dugout, where he is engulfed by his teammates. Shortly afterwards, when the deafening din of the stadium fails to subside, it is evident that the ovation will not stop until Maris can once again regain the spotlight. As he steps back out from below to take a reluctant bow from the highest dugout step, he takes off his hat and waves it to the crowd, grinning shyly in this curtain call for his phenomenal deed. Phil Rizzuto reports, "Another standing ovation for Roger Maris.…" As the Yankee faithful cheer for Roger, smothering the shy ballplayer with acclaim, covering him in glory, Maris' teammates, led by Bill Skowron, push him further out of the dugout to acknowledge the crowd.

Somewhat drained by the weight of this singular moment in baseball history, "Scooter" Rizzuto speaks into his microphone, narrating the experience: "One of the greatest sights I have ever seen here at Yankee Stadium." As to the outcome of the game, Roger's home run fittingly stands alone in the game's scoring, allowing the Yankees to emerge from the game victorious, 1–0. The home run is also the final home run hit by his team, the 1961 New York Yankees. Among other things, the Maris right field blast establishes a team record of 240 home runs, the highest single-season standard for team production in home runs. It is also the final home–game victory for the record-making New York Yankees who have now fashioned 65 victories at home while accumulating a mere 16 defeats. The winning-at-home percentage for the New York pinstripers has been a whopping .802 winning percentage, another major league record.

THE 1961 NEW YORK YANKEES

First Place: with a 109–53 record under Manager Ralph Houk The Yankees' winning percentage of .673 is the highest ever for any team playing a 162-game schedule. This record will be tied in 1969 by the Baltimore Orioles.

Yankee Stadium Attendance: 1,747,725

Awards: Mickey Mantle is voted on *Sporting News'* All-Star American League Team as an outfielder.

Mickey Mantle's League-Leading Categories: Mickey Mantle with a .687 slugging average (led majors), 132 runs which ties teammate Roger Maris for the major league lead, 126 bases on balls (led majors), and the highest average number of home runs per 100 at-bats with 10.5 (led majors). It is a landmark year for Mantle for other feats. Mantle's last home run of 1961 establishes the pin-striped "Clutch of Clout" as the greatest home run producer ever in back-to-back years by a switch-hitter, 94 round-trippers—40 in 1960 and 54 in 1961. It is also the most extra bases on long hits by any switch-hitter in the history of the game, with 190 in a single season.

MICKEY MANTLE'S 1961 HITTING RECORD

G	AB	R	H	2B	3B	HR	HR%	RBI	SA	BB	SO	SB	AVE.
153	514	132	163	16	6	54	10.8	128	.687	126	112	12	.317

In 1961, Mickey Mantle hit .317 while the major leagues averaged .258 with both leagues scoring an average 9.05 runs per game and both leagues hitting 1.91 home runs per contest. During the 153 games that Mickey Mantle appeared in for 1961, he played in the outfield 150 times as well as appearing in three games as a pinch-hitter.

Mickey's 1961 Salary: $75,000

World Series Winning Share: $7,389

Number of Games in Which Mantle Homered: 47

Winning Record When Mickey Mantle Homered: 39-8, a winning percentage of .830

THE 1961 WORLD SERIES

October 8, 1961: Before the start of Game Four of the World Series, Mickey feels well enough to take batting practice. As the baseball-mad denizens of Cincinnati pour into the small, neighborhood ballpark, they are treated to a typical Mantlesque display of prodigious long-ball power that simply stupefies the Queen City gathering. Batting right-handed, Mickey belts the first four pitches thrown to him over the left field fence. The fifth pitch is then slammed against the left field barrier. The next two pitches are then smashed against the 58-foot high scoreboard in left-center field. After a short breather for the players, the game begins. Now, while toiling against the Cincinnati Reds, Whitey Ford establishes a World Series record for consecutive scoreless innings pitched.

Then, leading off the fourth inning, Roger Maris draws a base on balls that brings Mickey Mantle hobbling to the plate. With literally no ability to run at all, Mickey rips into a pitch from lefthander Jim O'Toole, that carries to the base of the 58-foot-high scoreboard. Because of his painful incapacitation, Mickey's clout can only be translated into a single. The ball had been a scorching line drive like an electrified power line, yet Mantle is restricted in movement so severely that he can barely move without excruciating pain. Mantle can barely walk to first with his painful abscessed hip—a wound really, which amounts to a deep hole the size of a half-dollar, protruding downward two inches into his leg. The puncture prevents Mantle from running the ball out at all. The best he can do is amble lamely down to first base. In fact, as a result of this plate appearance, Mantle has begun to bleed through his dressings, bandages, and his gray New York travel flannels. This magnificent thoroughbred can barely move. Manager Houk immediately sends Hector Lopez into pinch-run for the injured slugger. As Mantle exits the game, his right hip is bleeding so profusely that his right pant leg is saturated with his blood, now flowing freely.

In the sixth inning with the game proceeding and Mickey in the clubhouse lying down on the training table, Whitey Ford joins his old friend, having been taken out of the game holding a 2–0 lead after five innings of scoreless pitching.

As their Yankee teammates are scoring two more runs in their half of the inning, the two friends chat amiably. Mickey congratulates his old friend for having officially broken "Babe" Ruth's scoreless inning streak of 29$\frac{2}{3}$ innings. Indeed, Whitey has amassed 32 of his own. In terms of their respective participation in the Series, both men are finished. But it is only now that Whitey sees his buddy's hip wound. After eyeing Mickey's infection, oozing pus from that deep hole in his hip, Ford almost gets sick to his stomach. Whitey's exit had been necessitated by a foot injury he gave himself when he fouled two balls off his lower digits in his third-inning at-bat. Now looking at Mickey, he forgets about his foot. Ford thinks to himself, "There is [not] another player who would have attempted to play in the pain that Mickey was in."

The Yankees will win the game, 7–0, and take a three-game-to-one advantage in the Series. But they will finish without Mickey. The final at-bat by Mantle in the October classic on this day will be his last appearance in the championship competition. Mickey had hit a paltry .167 for the Series, going 1-for-6, but his courage has been immeasurably more evident than anyone else's in the Series. The next day, using a lineup filled with second-stringers, the New York Yankees will batter the National League pennant winners mercilessly, pounding out a 13–5 thrashing of the Reds, and securing the seventh world championship for the New York Yankees in the Mickey Mantle Era.

Mickey Mantle's experience in the World Series represents one of the most glittering post-season careers ever witnessed in the game.

Chapter Eight

THE LENGTHENING SHADOWS OF OCTOBER

—1962, 1963 & 1964—

In the Nation and the World: The nation, in 1962, was moving through a time of glory and trauma, through triumph and trial, through crisis and crowning moments. During the year, U.S. Astronauts John Glenn, Scott Carpenter, and Wally Schirra would orbit the earth in three separate launches. As the 1962 World Series ended, the Cuban Missile Crisis would begin. The following year, 1963, the youth of America welcomed a revolutionary group of young British musicians called the Beatles, who would appear in the United States for the first time and mark the onset of the British invasion in rock 'n' roll music. Meanwhile, on the less pleasant side of national concerns, the Birmingham civil rights crisis erupted. But the March on Washington took place, lending dignity to the civil rights struggle and catapulting Dr. Martin Luther King, Jr. into national prominence.

Meanwhile, President Kennedy visited the Berlin Wall in Germany to extol the virtues of liberty and freedom behind the barriers of Communism. The American leader also staged a nostalgic visit to the homeland of his forefathers in Ireland before touring an electrified populace in Italy who riotously cheered his appearance. The young and dynamic President also made a trip to Dallas, Texas, from which he would not return alive—instead the victim of assassination at the hands of a demented nobody named Lee Harvey Oswald. And because of the tragedy of Kennedy's assassination in Dallas, Lyndon Johnson became the 36th President of the United States.

In 1964, the Vietnam Conflict entered into a phase of higher escalation as a result of the Gulf of Tonkin incident. In the presidential election, LBJ was elected over the conservative candidate, Senator Barry Goldwater. President Johnson launched the War on Poverty. Red China exploded its first A-bomb. And on the volatile civil rights battlefield, three civil rights workers were murdered in segregated Mississippi shortly after arriving to help black Americans secure their voting rights. In the meantime, Dr. Martin Luther King, Jr., won the Nobel Prize for Peace for applying his principles of nonviolence to the civil rights movement.

Fads: American diversions in 1962 included the wholesale success of novelties and collectibles underscoring the wide popularity of the young President in the White House, among these JFK books and JFK phonograph albums. In addition, worry beads became the rage. In the following year, Beatlemania was widespread as the four mop-heads became the most popular singing group in the history of popular music. A year later, in 1964, mini skirts became a fashion statement for the young women in America. The Sexual Revolution and the "pill" were born. Beatle items became collectors' items. Prince Valiant hairdos began appearing in increasing numbers, making long hair on men a source of reluctant, yet widespread acceptance. And G.I. Joe dolls and toys became a hit on the market.

Innovations and First Appearances: In 1962, Diet Rite and Tab would offer significant competition for the first time in the Cola wars. Polaroid color film allowed Americans to enjoy the fruits of their photographic labors instantaneously. K-Mart began to flourish at hundreds of supermarket sites all over the land. In the following year, CBS dazzled millions of TV sports addicts by introducing the ultimate in vicarious viewer participation: the instant replay. The Beatles were introduced to U.S. television audiences, while appearing nationally on *The Ed Sullivan Show.*

Meanwhile, the Kodak Instamatic was developed for the first time, giving Americans the ability to instantly develop their own pictures. And push-button telephones would begin replacing the obsolescent rotary dial models. In the following year, 1964, public health would take a giant step forward in civic responsibility when, for the first time, the Surgeon General issued the mandatory warning that cigarette smoking could lead to cancer and that that warning must be affixed to every pack.

A new, innovative, almost immediate classic-type automobile was designed when the Ford Mustang was sold across America for the first time. Zip codes were developed to help streamline and modernize postal delivery service. Meanwhile, the Kennedy half-dollar became so popular that Americans everywhere refuse to spend the coins, hoarding them instead for their personal collections.

Movies: In 1962, American moviegoers continued to fill their Saturday nights with trips to the cinema to enjoy such theater fare as *The Music Man, Mutiny on the Bounty, The Longest Day, That Touch of Mink, To Kill a Mockingbird, Advise and Consent, Gypsy, Two for the Seesaw, Lawrence of Arabia,* and *The Miracle Worker.* The following year, 1963, pleased cinematic patrons with such diverse films as *Cleopatra, Hud, The Ugly American, Tom Jones, The Birds, Bye, Bye Birdie, The Great Escape, Donovan's Reef, The Prize, PT-109, Dr. No, Lillies of the Field,* and *Move Over, Darling.* In 1964, Americans by the millions began to pay higher admission charges in order to take in the latest wave of film efforts; included were: *Mary Poppins, Goldfinger, From Russia with Love, Dr. Strangelove, Becket, Fail-Safe, Seven Days in May, The Pink Panther, My Fair Lady, Charade, Robin and the Seven Hoods, The Unsinkable Molly Brown,* and *Send Me No Flowers.*

Television: In 1962, Johnny Carson began his long run on late-night television as the new host of *The Tonight Show* on NBC. Prime-time situation comedies and tear-jerking dramatic episodes like *Ben Casey, The Jackie Gleason Show, McHale's Navy, Hazel, Mr. Ed,* and *Combat* began to compete for American viewers. In the following year, 1963, new standards in white-picket fence sitcoms began to project the innocence of the times, portraying America and family values in popular programs of the day. Included were: *The Donna Reed Show, My Favorite Martian, The Twilight Zone, Outer Limits, Route 66,* and *The Fugitive.* A year later, a lighter fare gave Americans escape in their own living rooms as laughter and humor prevailed over more thought-provoking dramatic choices. Such patterns in TV viewing were reflected in the higher ratings given the more popular shows, such as *Beverly*

Hillbillys, Petticoat Junction, The Man From U.N.C.L.E., The Andy Griffith Show, The Munsters, The Addams Family, Gilligan's Island, The Farmer's Daughter, Daniel Boone, and *Bewitched.*

The Juke Box: In 1962, America's teeny-boppers and their favorite kind of rock 'n' roll were not to be denied as billions of dollars were spent by Baby Boomers bent on humming and dancing to the tunes of the day. Hits included: "The Peppermint Twist" by Joey Dee and the Starlighters, "Johnny Angel" by Shelley Fabares, "Good Luck Charm" by Elvis Presley, "Soldier Boy" by the Shirelles, "I Can't Stop Loving You" by Ray Charles, "Roses are Red" by Bobby Vinton, "Breaking Up is Hard to Do" by Neil Sedaka, "The Locomotion" by Little Eva, and "Sherry" by the Four Seasons. The following year produced more of the same, with such snappy hits and love ballads as "Go Away Little Girl" by Steve Lawrence, "Hey Paula" by Paul and Paula, "Walk Like a Man" by the Four Seasons, "He's So Fine" by the Chiffons, "It's My Party" by Lesley Gore, "So Much in Love" by the Tymes, and "My Boyfriend's Back" by the Angels. 1964 would mark the first full year for the widespread appreciation of such early Beatle standards as "I Want to Hold Your Hand," "She Loves You," "Can't Buy Me Love," and "A Hard Day's Night." Meanwhile, Broadway hits such as "Hello, Dolly!" by Louis Armstrong made a comeback. And rock 'n' roll TOP 40 hits flourished with Boomer favorites like "Rag Doll" by the Four Seasons, "Where Did Our Love Go?" and "Come See About Me" by the Supremes, "Leader of the Pack" by the Shangrilas, "I Get Around" by the Beach Boys, and "Mr. Lonely" by Bobby Vinton.

Deaths: America would watch with fascination as television coverage of, first, the capture, then the trial, and finally, the privately held execution in 1962 of Adolf Eichmann. Meanwhile, America mourned the tragic premature loss of comic Ernie Kovacs, who died in a fatal car crash. Actor Charles Laughton passed away after a glorious career in Hollywood. One of America's most beloved First Ladies and distinguished women of the ages, Mrs. Eleanor Roosevelt, left us; and authors James Thurber and William Faulkner died. Baseball's Hall-of-Famer Mickey Cochrane would perish in relative obscurity as his namesake, Mickey Mantle, stared in yet another World Series. Marilyn Monroe died of an "accidental" drug overdose that sent Hollywood spiraling. In 1963, the world mourned the tragic passing of the martyred young President, John F. Kennedy, assassinated in Dallas. The baseball world, meanwhile, was saddened at the news that two of the game's immortals, Rogers Hornsby and Frank "Home Run" Baker, had passed away.

The roll call would go on in 1963 when America lost one of its treasures, poet Robert Frost. In the meantime, W.E.B. DuBois, Aldous Huxley, and Senator Estes Kefauver expired. And movie giants Monty Woolley and Dick Powell also came to their respective ends. 1964 marked the end of the road for Gracie Allen, 007 author Ian Fleming, Eddie Cantor, General Douglas MacArthur, actor Alan Ladd, Harpo Marx, President Herbert Hoover and Cole Porter.

Sports: In the 1962 world of sport, new faces and new names began to make their presence known. Jack Nicklaus won his first professional golf tournament, taking the U.S. Open. In pro tennis, Rod Laver won the Grand Slam, taking the titles at the Wimbledon, the Australian Open, the U.S. Open, and the French Open. The NBA Championship was once more secured by the Boston Celtics, who beat the Los Angeles Lakers, four games to three. And, early in 1962, Wilt Chamberlain of the Philadelphia Warriors scored 100 points in a single professional basketball game for an all-time scoring, single-game output of points. In addition, the Green Bay Packers won the professional football championship when Vince Lombardi's green-and-gold defeated the New York Giants, 16–7.

The following year, the Chicago Bears beat the New York Giants, 14–10, for the NFL Championship; while, in professional round ball, the Boston Celtics once again won the NBA when the Beantown five toppled the Los Angeles Lakers, four games to two.

In the last year of the final glories of "The Mickey Mantle Era" in Yankee baseball, 1964, the United States won the Tokyo Olympics, led to glory by particularly sterling individual performances in the track and field events, such as Bob Hayes in the 100 meters, Henry Carr in the 200 meters, Billy Mills in the 10,000 meters, Dallas Long in the shot put, and Al Oerter in the discus. These champions and others won gold for America. In swimming, the sensational performances of Don Schollander pulled down four gold medals for the United States. And in boxing, "Smoking Joe" Frazier (before he became "Smoking Joe") won the gold medal by dominating the heavyweight division in boxing.

Meanwhile, the Cleveland Browns' Jim Brown became the first NFL running back to attain 10,000 rushing yards in a stunningly spectacular career on the professional gridiron. And, in professional boxing, the cocky Cassius Clay upended Sonny Liston in a stunning upset defeat, wresting the champion heavyweight's crown rudely from his head. The pro football world acknowledged the Cleveland Browns as a dominant force in the NFL when they won the championship game by defeating the Baltimore Colts, 27–0. In the NBA Championship, the Boston Celtics smothered the San Francisco Warriors, four games to one. It was the seventh world basketball championship in eight years for the Celtics.

BASEBALL TRANSITIONS: In 1962, former Yankee manager Casey Stengel took over the managerial reins of the new expansion team named the New York Mets. In the meantime, the Yankees lost the services of Tony Kubek, who fulfilled his military obligation. The following year, the season would see Pete Rose of the Cincinnati Reds collect the first hit of his major league career: a triple to left field off Pittsburgh's Bob Friend. It would also hail the farewell tour of the legendary Stan "The Man" Musial, who retired with 3,630 base hits in his spectacular career. 1,815 of those hits were at home, 1,815 of his remaining hits came on the road.

In 1963, the American League underwent a considerable facelift among its rosters. The Detroit Tigers, for example, made changes such as bidding farewell to Paul Foytack and Don Mossi. But they did place a substantial down payment on their future, promoting Mickey Lolich and Denny McLain to the parent club and the Tiger starting rotation. Meanwhile, Boston lost Pete Runnels, but picked up Dick Stuart. The Red Sox pitching absorbed the loss of Mike Fornieles and Gene Conley, but gained the rookie sensation Dave Morehead. In the Buckeye State, the Cleveland Indians dropped Jim Perry and Sam McDowell, but acquired Jerry Walker and Jack Kralick. The White Sox did not retain Early Wynn, but they added Gary Peters to their pitching staff. The Baltimore Orioles said goodbye to Chuck Estrada, Billy Hoeft, and Hoyt Wilhelm, but increased their number with Mike McCormick, Dave McNally, and Stu Miller. In the meantime, the Yankees lost Moose Skowron to a trade with the Los Angeles Dodgers, but they picked up Joe Pepitone as his replacement. The Bombers also lost Jim Coates and Luis Arroyo, but they gained the pitching talents of Steve Hamilton and Al Downing.

In 1964, highlights on the diamond would include Sandy Koufax pitching the third no-hitter of his career; Jim Bunning hurling a perfect game on "Father's Day" against the New York Mets; and the Yankees losing Yogi Berra as a player, but retaining him as their new manager. Pitcher Mel Stottlemyre was acquired. The White Sox finally said goodbye to the anchor of their infield for 14 years, the 37-year-old second baseman Nellie Fox, but they welcomed Al Weis in his stead. The Orioles traded away Jim Gentile and waived farewell to Mike McCormick. But they gained the services of Wally Bunker and Harvey Haddix. The Detroit Tigers traded Jim Bunning and Gus Triandos to the Phillies and Rocky Colavito to the Kansas City Athletics. Still, The Tigers received Dave Wickersham as part of the deal in return;

they also signed Gates Brown. The Minnesota Twins lost Vic Power, but signed Tony Oliva. And the Boston Red Sox signed the rookie homegrown slugger Tony Conigliaro.

THE 1962 SPRING TRAINING

The relationship between Roger Maris and Mickey Mantle will come to full fruition by the time of this year's spring training and will help Mantle mature as a result. Mickey will, especially after the sensational year before, never be the young man-about-town he had been as a youth. But like it or not, want it or not, the Yankee mantle of leadership will be Mickey's for the rest of his career.

THE 1962 REGULAR SEASON

30 HOME RUNS

H.R.#	DATE	OPPONENT	PITCHER	SITE	SCORE	ATTND.
375.	Apr. 10	Baltimore	Hoyt Wilhelm	Stadium	7–6, NY	22,978

Mantle's eight-inning, 400-foot home run to right field ties the score.

| 376. | Apr. 19 | Baltimore | Chuck Estrada | Baltimore(n) | 3–1, NY | 16,376 |

Mantle's drive to right-center field soars over the 380-foot mark.

| 377. | May 5 | Wash. | Marty Kutyna | Stadium | 7–6, NY | 13,291 |

The ball sails high and 14 rows deep into the right field upper deck at Yankee Stadium.

| 378. | May 6 (first game) | Wash. | Dave Stenhouse | Stadium | 4–2, Wash | 23,940 |

Mantle pounds out a colossal home run deep into the right-center field bleachers, sailing so far that it will slam into the 32nd row, the last row of the bleachers separating the elated, if disbelieving, spectators from the rearward exterior wall of Yankee Stadium.

| 379. | May 6 (second game) | Wash. | Pete Burnside(LH) | Stadium | 8–0, NY | 23,940 |

Mickey poles an opposite field blow over the right field wall while hitting from the right side of the plate. Mantle's clout comes right behind a four-base blow delivered by Roger Maris in back-to-back form.

| 380. | May 6 | Wash. | Jim Hannan | Stadium | 8–0, NY | 23,940 |
| | (second game) | | | | | |

For the third successive at-bat over two games, Mantle poles another home run over the right field wall. It is the 10th time in Mantle's career that he has hit home runs from both sides of the plate in the same game. It has been a great day and Mickey, Jr., Mantle's eight-year-old boy, has seen it and reveled at the great cheering from the Yankee throngs. Later, Mickey Jr. will become confused when the same crowd will boos his father; the lad retreats to the clubhouse. The Yankees sweep the series with the Senators and move into first place.

| 381. | May 12 | Cleveland | Barry Latman | Cleveland | 9–6, NY | 8,694 |

Mantle powers the ball into the right field bullpen.

May 18, 1962: Forced out of the lineup with injuries once more, Mantle will miss a little less than a month of play when, on this day, he tears an adductor muscle in his right thigh trying to beat out an infield, one-hop smash to the shortstop Zoilo Versailles of the Minnesota Twins. When Mantle pulls his muscle, he is running at full speed when, suddenly, his right knee goes pop, which, in turn, tears ligaments and some of the cartilage in his left knee, the bedraggled Mantle's good leg. Mickey recalled the moment later, stating to an interviewer, "...the basepath came up to meet me. I went down like a slaughtered steer and I could feel the jolt when I hit the grass....As I went down, I felt the stab of pain in my other knee too." After Mickey goes down so suddenly and, in a heap, his Yankee teammates rush to the top step of the dugout and look back into the stands believing that someone has shot Mickey with a rifle. Mantle will not return to the field of play until June 13th, when Manager Ralph Houk writes Mickey's name into the lineup. Mantle will play six innings before he is taken out of the game for some much-needed rest.

May 22, 1962: Playing in a 12-inning night contest, before 13,135 patient Bronx rooters, Roger Maris of the New York Yankees will be given four intentional walks in the same game something that will establish an American League record. At the stadium, the Yankees would finally win the game, 2–1, on a sacrifice fly in the final inning. Maris has learned that good offerings from pitchers to hit were a rare commodity, rare indeed, without Mickey Mantle in the on-deck circle. After the game, Roger telephones Mickey, checking on his medical condition, urging him on to a complete recovery, and imploring him to return to the lineup as quickly as possible. As for the game itself, the Yankee pitching staff will enjoy a brilliant, red-letter day, one-hitting the Angels over 12 frames.

May 23, 1962: Tying a major league record in a contest played at Yankee Stadium on this day, first baseman Joe Pepitone of the New York Yankees would blast two home runs in the eighth inning, knock in four, and pace the Yankees to a 13–7 triumph over the Kansas City A's. Mickey is still laid up on crutches, but is present in the dugout, watching the game, and cheering on his teammates.

| 382. | June 16 | Cleveland | Gary Bell | Cleveland | 10–9, Cle | 50,254 |

(21,208 pd.)

Mantle belts an eighth-inning, three-run, 400-foot pinch-hit home run to right-center field that sails over the railing, fronting the Indian bullpen. For Mickey, it is a special moment as the large Cleveland assembly erupts in frenzied delirium, exploding into a huge ovation for the famous slugger. Mickey later recalls this moment, "The way those fans stood up and roared really took hold of me as no applause ever had before. I could feel the skin getting tight on my neck as I hobbled around the bases. It was like being a kid again and hearing the stands screaming for a run I had made in a football game. Those fans yelled and yelled and pounded their hands long after I reached the dugout. It more than made up for every boo or catcall that had ever been thrown at me. I was so choked up over it I could not speak but just grinned foolishly as the guys [who] pounded my back in the dugout....It's one of the things that makes the game so great."

June 23, 1962: Mantle returns to the regular line-up on this day. From this point in the season to July 25th, The Yankees, inspired by Mickey's presence, will generate a 22–9 showing.

| 383. | June 23 | Detroit | Paul Foytack | Detroit(n) | 5–4, Detroit | 38,150 |

June 24, 1962: Before 35,638 weary but ecstatic Tiger fans, the New York Yankees and the Detroit nine tie an American League record, playing for 22 innings in the third-longest regulation game ever played in the history of the league. Detroit wins the game, 9–7. Additionally, Bobby Richardson ties a major league record when he goes to the plate 11 times in the game. For his part, Mantle will go 1-for-3, score one run, and knock in two. Mickey would not finish the marathon, still wobbly on his shaky legs, and will be substituted for in the seventh frame. Meanwhile, the contest will end as a result of utility outfielder Jack Reed's 12th-inning round-tripper. On the Detroit side of the ledger, Rocky Colavito bumps his batting average up 17 points because of the sensational day that he enjoys at the plate. Rocky goes 7-for-10, including a triple, one run scored, and another knocked in.

| 384. | June 28 | Minnesota | Jack Kralick(LH) | Stadium | 4–2, NY | 14,814 |

Mantle wallops a 400-foot, opposite field home run to right-center field.

| 385. | July 2 | Kansas City | Ed Rakow | Stadium(n) | 8–4, NY | 16,653 |

Mantle drives the ball in a high, towering arc halfway to the top of the upper deck of the right field grandstand.

| 386. | July 3 | Kansas City | Jerry Walker | Stadium | 8–7, NY | 13,378 |

Mickey lifts a powerful drive high into the upper deck of the right field grandstand.

| 387. | July 3 | Kansas City | Gordon Jones | Stadium | 8–7, NY | 13,378 |

Mickey powers a back-to-back home run with Roger Maris that is lasered into the lower right field seats. The timely blast in the sixth inning proves to be the game-winner.

| 388. | July 4 (second game) | Kansas City | Dan Pfister(LH) | Stadium | 7–3, NY | 27,901 |

Mantle slams the ball over the 407-foot marker in right-center sailing into the distant bleachers.

| 389. | July 4 (second game) | Kansas City | John Wyatt | Stadium | 7–3, NY | 27,901 |

Mickey's home run comes after Maris' round-tripper in a back-to-back, lightning-like strike. Mantle's towering home run reaches the upper deck of the right field grandstand at Yankee Stadium. In this game, the day's after piece, Mickey's two home runs are exploded in his final two at-bats in the contest. His two homers keep alive a streak that is still on track. The Yankees win the contest with the scrappy A's, 7–3.

| 390. | July 6 | Minnesota | Camilo Pascual | Minn.(n) | 7–5, NY | 40,994 |

Mantle's longball slams into the right field stands in back-to-back fashion with Roger Maris. Both have connected off Camilo Pascual, a hurler at the peak of his career and en route to his first 20-win season. It is Mantle's third home run in a row over two games. Fashioning a throwback to last year's scintillating season, Mickey's blast, when paired with Roger's in the same game, represents the seventh time this season that the two have powered home runs in the same game and the third time in four games that both have hit roundtrippers in succession.

| 391. | July 6 | Minn. | Camilo Pascual | Minnesota(n) | 7–5, NY | 40,994 |

In his next at-bat, Mickey Mantle ties a major league record by hitting four consecutive home runs in successive at-bats over two games. This impressive feat also translates into eight home runs in nine days.

THE 1962 ALL-STAR GAME

D.C. STADIUM IN WASHINGTON
FIRST GAME—JULY 10

Before the start of the midsummer classic, Yankee slugger Mickey Mantle watches President Kennedy, who is in attendance, chat with Stan "The Man" Musial. The young American leader tells the legendary Stan, who is nearing the end of his brilliant career with the St. Louis Cardinals, that even though they are the same age, the critics tell him the Cardinal great is too old for the game, and that he is too young. Meanwhile, during the All-Star Game in the nation's capital, 45,480 Washingtonian baseball fans watch as Maury Wills, Dodger speedster, dominates the game with his legs. In the sixth inning, Wills steals second base and scores on a single. Two innings later, the slap-hitting shortstop singles, moves daringly to third base on a single to left field, and scores on a sacrifice fly to short right field. Mickey goes 0-for-1, walks once, and fans once against Don Drysdale.

July 13, 1962: Playing before the largest crowd in Dodger Stadium history, 53,591 happy Los Angelenos, the first ever to watch a night game, the Los Angeles Angels play host to the visiting New York Yankees. Mickey goes 2-for-5 in the contest with two singles. The Angels beat the defending World Champions, 5–2.

July 15, 1962: At Municipal Stadium, the Kansas City Athletics play host to the New York Yankees before the largest crowd ever to watch a doubleheader in the ballpark, 34,865 excited A's fans. Mickey gets a hit in both games, but manages only two singles, while scoring three runs. On the other hand, the hometown boy, Roger Maris, will do himself proud, enjoying a very good day at the plate, homering twice in the initial contest with four runs batted in, while tripling in the second. The Yankees sweep the A's, 8–6 and 11–3.

| 392. | July 18 | Boston | Galen Cisco | Boston | 14–3, NY | 23,855 |

Mantle slams a 400-foot-plus home run into the right field bleachers.

| 393. | July 20 | Wash. | Steve Hamilton(LH) | Stadium(n) | 3–2, NY | 20,255 |

Mickey unleashes another Mantlesque rocketshot, a towering, prodigious drive, that will be estimated to have carried 530 feet before the assaulted spheroid bangs high against the steel structure. The ball reaches a point where it crashes into the facing of the third tier of the left field copper green grandstand, slamming so hard into it that it will bound back onto the field of play. Steve Hamilton will later describe this shot as the hardest ball ever hit off him in his entire pitching career. The lean portsider would describe the blast, declaring that it "would have left the county had the stands not gotten in the way." In the game itself, though, the Yankees can only manage six hits, the slugging Mantle collecting three of them. The Yankees will still win, 3–2.

| 394. | July 25 | Boston | Earl Wilson | Stadium(tn) | 4–2, Bos | 24,772 |
| | (first game) | | | | | |

Mickey pummels an Earl Wilson delivery far and long into the right-center field bleachers.

| 395. | July 28 | Chicago | Eddie Fisher | Stadium | 4–3, NY | 52,038 |

The ball flies into the right field bleachers, giving the Yankees cause for celebrating Mickey's 200th home run in Yankee Stadium.

July 29, 1962: It will be at this point in the campaign when Mickey Mantle reinjures his knee. Shortly thereafter, five days later, Mantle will wrench his knee. Four days after that, August 7th, Mantle would return to action.

THE 1962 ALL-STAR GAME
WRIGLEY FIELD IN CHICAGO, ILLINOIS
SECOND GAME—JULY 30

Playing the midsummer classic at Wrigley Field, before 38,359 Windy City baseball wags, the American League snuffs out the NL Stars, 9–4, led by roundtrippers by Pete Runnels, Leon Wagner, and Rocky Colavito. Mickey's thigh injury keeps him from participating.

July 31, 1962: At D.C. Stadium, comprising the largest crowd ever to watch the expansion Washington Senators in a night game, 30,421 excited Senator's rooters have come to the game this evening to cheer on the home team. The hapless Senators have picked up the gauntlet thrown by the visiting New York Yankees. With Mickey on the bench, his wrenched left knee still stiff, the Yankees manage to generate a 9–5 victory without him. The Yankee effort is paced by Moose Skowron's grand-slam home run, that carries over the 31-foot high right-center field barrier at the 378-foot marker.

August 1, 1962: Last night, more Washingtonians had watched a night game rooting for the expansion Senators in the nation's capital than ever had in the past. This evening, that record is shattered when 48,147 screaming citizens cheer on the Senators as they play a twinight doubleheader against the visiting New York Yankees. Mickey does not play.

| 396. | Aug. 17 | Kansas City | Bill Fischer | K.C.(n) | 7–2, K.C. | 23,110 |

Mantle poles a 400-foot drive to left-center field for an opposite field Municipal Stadium clout.

| 397. | Aug. 18 (first game) | Kansas City | Diego Segui | K.C.(tn) | 5–4, K.C. | 35,147 |

At Municipal Stadium, the Kansas City Athletics produce the largest attendance in the history of the Kansas City franchise, 35,147 cheering fans, watching the game between the A's and the visiting New York Yankees. For the entire day, Mantle collects a solitary hit, a fourth-inning, solo home run in the first game, as the Athletics split with the Bombers. Mantle will lead off the fourth by unleashing a wicked swing and bashing a long, towering, 420-foot wallop over the left-center field barrier. The Athletics had taken the opener, 5–4, while the Yankees bounced back in the afterpiece, slugging it out with three home runs by Dale Long, Bobby Richardson, and Clete Boyer. The Yankees beat the A's, 11–7, to secure the split.

| 398. | Aug. 19 | Kansas City | Jerry Walker | K.C. | 21–7, NY | 29,274 |

Mantle pounds out a grand-slam home run, the seventh of his career, and knocks in seven runs. Mantle has also doubled and singled. In addition, "The Mick" has managed to steal second and third base in the third inning of this brilliant contest. Unbelievably, Elston Howard has superseded Mantle's RBI output with eight of his own, giving the two gray-flanneled teammates 15 RBIs between them.

| 399. | Aug. 28 | Cleveland | Jim "Mudcat" Grant | Stadium(n) | 2–1, NY | 31,819 |

On a 3-and-2 count, Mickey connects for a two-run game-winner that sails into the right-center field bleachers in the rain-shortened contest.

September 4, 1962: Mantle is sidelined with a stomach pull for the next seven days.

| 400. | Sept. 10 | Detroit | Hank Aguirre(LH) | Detroit(n) | 3–1, NY | 22,810 |

Muscling up on one of the slim southpaw's fast balls, Mantle connects for a 450-foot shot into the lower center field stands at Tiger Stadium. It ties the game.

| 401. | Sept. 11 | Cleveland | Pedro Ramos | Cleveland(n) | 5–2, NY | 13,411 |

Mantle connects off his old right-handed rival for a three-run, 400-foot game-winner over the right-center field wall. It is also Mickey's 200th career home run belted on-the-road.

| 402. | Sept. 18 | Wash. | Tom Cheney | Wash. D.C.(n) | 7–1, NY | 16,824 |

The first-inning, three-run smash off the lean right-handed hurler is belted high off the right-center field scoreboard and settles matters for another game-winner.

| 403. | Sept. 18 | Wash. | Tom Cheney | Wash. D.C.(n) | 7–1, NY | 16,824 |

Mantle's second shot gives him five RBIs for the game.

| 404. | Sept. 30 | Chicago | Ray Herbert | Stadium | 8-4, Chi | 14,685 |

In his final at-bat of the year, Mickey Mantle's circuit shot comes off the hard-throwing righthander Ray Herbert, who is en route to a 20-9 winning record this year. It is also the eighth straight year that the 31-year-old Mantle has hit 30 or more home runs in a single season, which ties him with the great Babe Ruth. Only Jimmie Foxx with 12, and Lou Gehrig, Eddie Mathews, and later with Mike Schmidt with nine, have surpassed this amazing record of consistent, year-by-year, home run production. In the hitting department, Mantle completes the year batting .321, finishing second behind the league-leading Pete Runnels, who hit .326.

THE 1962 NEW YORK YANKEES

First Place: with a 96–66 record under Manager Ralph Houk.

Yankee Stadium Attendance: 1,493,574. On the road, the Yankees draw 2,215,659 paying patrons who mob their hometown ballparks to see the travel-gray Bronx Bombers. This enormous figure in on-the-road attendance establishes a major league record.

Awards: American League MVP; *Sporting News'* American League MVP; Mantle is also voted to *Sporting News'* All-Star American League Team as an outfielder; Mantle receives 1962 Gold Glove Award for American League outfielder.

Mickey Mantle's League-Leading Categories: Mickey Mantle with 122 bases on balls (led majors); .605 slugging average.

MICKEY MANTLE'S 1962 HITTING RECORD

G	AB	R	H	2B	3B	HR	HR%	RBI	SA	BB	SO	SB	AVE.
123	377	96	121	15	1	30	8.0	89	.605	122	78	9	.321

In 1962, Mickey Mantle hit .321 while the major leagues averaged .258 with both leagues scoring an average 8.92 runs per game and both leagues hitting 1.85 home runs per contest. During the 123 games that Mickey Mantle appeared in 1962, he played in the outfield 117 times as well as appeared in six games as a pinch-hitter. Mantle missed 31 games as a result of his knee injury in May. Unbelievably, Mickey Mantle only struck out 78 times, an incredible reversal of his usual strikeout trend. Mickey will tell Bob Smith later that in 1962, "...it was my best season for getting on base. Every other time I went to bat I made it to first base, or farther."

Mickey's 1962 Salary: $82,000

World Series Winning Share: $9,882

Number of Games in Which Mantle Homered: 25

Winning Record When Mickey Mantle Homered: 18–7, a winning percentage of .720

THE 1962 WORLD SERIES

October 4, 1962: Mickey's teammate Whitey Ford wins the World Series Opener, 6–2, played this day at Candlestick Park, but watches helplessly as Jose Pagan squeezes home Willie Mays with the Giants' first run in the Series and the first run given up by Ford in World Series competition since Game Six of the 1958 championship set. Whitey's Series record for consecutive shutout innings has now been stopped, and the new record established at 33 1/3rd innings. Ford's ten pitching victories in the World Series makes the crafty southpaw the winningest hurler in Series history. In the game itself, Clete Boyer's home run breaks the 2–2 tie in the seventh and with another two tallies in the eighth the Yanks emerge with the Game One win. The 1962 World Series will produce another World Championship for New York, the seventh in the Mantle Era of Yankee history. But Mickey's production numbers for this particular October classic have been anemic, hitting .120, lining a double, stealing two bases, scoring three runs, and knocking in no one. An argument can be made that it was a pitchers' Series, with the Yankees batting .199 and the Giants hitting for a team average of .226. But the fact of the matter is that Mickey's Series performance in his final MVP season is completely forgettable. This World Series championship will be the final title for the New York Yankees in Mickey's career.

THE 1963 REGULAR SEASON

15 HOME RUNS

H.R.#	DATE	OPPONENT	PITCHER	SITE	SCORE	ATTND.
405.	Apr. 10	Kansas City	Ted Bowsfield(LH)	Kansas City	5–3, NY	3,855

Batting right-handed against the A's portsider, Mantle slams the ball over the left field wall.

406.   Apr. 11   Baltimore   Milt Pappas   Stadium   4–1, Balt   29,772

On this chilly afternoon, Mickey poles a home run into the right field bullpen for another of his 400-foot belts.

In what will become one of the most injury-ridden seasons in an injury-laced career, Mickey aggravates a right rib and side injury in an attempt to make an impossible try for a line drive and will remain out of the lineup for two weeks.

407.   May 4   Minn.   Jim Kaat(LH)   Minnesota   3–2, NY   31,667

Mickey connects for an opposite field shot that soars 407 feet to right-center field.

408.   May 6   Detroit   Hank Aguirre(LH)   Detroit(n)   10–3, NY   18,423

Mickey powers the Aguirre delivery high and long into the left field upper deck. Mickey's stats on this day reflect a 3-for-3 showing, with three RBIs to boot.

409.   May 11   Baltimore   Milt Pappas   Baltimore   13–1, NY   12,171
410.   May 15   Minnesota   Camilo Pascual   Stadium   4–3, NY   7,013

Mickey's left-handed stroke catapults the ball high and far into the upper right field deck of the Stadium's right field grandstand, where it disappears through an upper deck exit opening, the third exit tunnel from the extreme left edge of the right field grandstand.

411.   May 21   Kansas City   Orlando Pena   Stadium(n)   7–4, NY   11,795

Mickey scorches a hot liner into the lower right field seats.

412.   May 21   Kansas City   Diego Segui   Stadium(n)   7–4, NY   11,795

Mantle launches a two-run game-winner in the fifth that is the first in a back-to-back sequence of roundtrippers with Roger Maris as the ball sails into the right field bullpen.

413.   May 22   Kansas City   Bill Fischer   Stadium(n)   8–7, NY   9,727
                                                                 (in 11)

Poised and with bat cocked, Mantle is bearing down, looking for his pitch when righthander Bill Fischer delivers the ball. Mickey slams the pitch for a dramatically prodigious, irrepressibly monumental blast, an 11th-inning game-winner that soars high in a towering arc until it slams against the uppermost right field facade. The ball, in a spectacular climb, is still rising from the force of Mantle's breathtaking blow when the spheroid pounds off the top edge of the roof of the massive 40-year-old stadium. On this foggy, muggy night, its flight, an immense and majestic trademark shot, soars to a point some six feet from clearing the roof and is still rising when it crashes against the uppermost facade of the great ballyard. The ball itself has carried some 500 feet away and more than 108 feet, one inch, higher above the field. It collides with such incredible force against the filigree that it rebounds all the way back to Jerry Lumpe, the opposing second baseman and former Yankee teammate situated in the right-hand portion of the infield. Another former Yankee teammate and current Athletics Manager Eddie Lopat will later admit that he did not see the flight of the ball. The old lefthander knew, from experience what had happened when he heard the sound of Mantle connecting. In his years as a Yankee, he had heard the sound of Mickey's bat impacting against a pitch when there was no doubt that Mantle had the ball exactly measured. Just from the sound of the bat, Lopat knew that it was "outta here." This was such an occasion. Yankee coach Frankie Crosetti calls the clout "the hardest I've ever seen anybody hit a ball, Jimmie Foxx, Ruth, anybody. I don't believe a man can hit a ball harder. It went out like it was shot out of a cannon."

Mantle will later say that it is the only time that he felt that any ball that he hit in the great ballyard had a chance to clear the stadium. A scientist, Dr. James McDonald, computes that the ball must have been travelling at a speed of 235 feet a second when it hit the uppermost partition of the stadium. McDonald believes, therefore, that it would have spanned an incomprehensible distance of 650 to 700 feet: the longest, hardest-hit home run of all time. Only Babe Ruth had hit a baseball such distances with such frequency as has Mickey Charles Mantle. Mickey will later reflect in an interview that he believed this particular supersonic shot had a real chance of leaving the ballyard, the first fair ball ever to clear Yankee Stadium. He later claimed that connecting with the pitch had produced "as hard a ball as I had ever hit in my life."

414.   May 26   Wash.   Don Rudolph(LH)   Stadium   7–1, NY   18,332
   (first game)

Mickey wallops a long drive to the opposite field that carries into the right field bleachers.

415.   June 4   Baltimore   Steve Barber(LH)   Baltimore(n) 3–1, Balt   37,137

Mantle slams the ball to the opposite field into the right field bleachers off one of the AL's premier hurlers now enjoying a 20-13 season.

June 6, 1963: On this rainy night in Baltimore, while chasing a long drive by Oriole third baseman Brooks Robinson to left-center field in Memorial Stadium, Mantle will crash into the center field fence breaking a bone in the instep of his left foot. He must be carried off the field on a stretcher. The Yankee outfielder had caught his spikes in the wire cyclone fence, colliding awkwardly with the chain-links. This tragic contact will cause a loosening of the cartilage and ligaments in his left knee. Mickey will miss 61 games as a result, unable to return to action until August 4th, and then only as a part-time pinch-hitter.

THE 1963 ALL-STAR GAME
MUNICIPAL STADIUM IN CLEVELAND, OHIO
JULY 9

Though unable to play because of the broken bone in his foot, Mickey Mantle receives the highest of tributes by still being voted by the players as the American League's starting centerfielder.

416.   Aug. 4   Baltimore   George Brunet(LH)   Stadium   11–10, NY   39,432
        (second game)   (in 10)   (38,555 pd.)

It is the second game of a doubleheader, with the first game having gone the way of the visiting Orioles. After a two-month layoff, the hobbled Mickey Mantle returns to action for the first time since injuring himself this past June. As soon as he emerges from the dugout to prepare for entering the game, the Golden Boy in the Golden Age of Baseball receives the loudest standing ovation ever enjoyed by the "switcher" at Yankee Stadium. In this sterling moment in a phenomenal career, Number Seven comes off the bench to pinch-hit during the seventh inning.

Walking from the dugout, Mantle steps towards the on-deck circle to prepare for his first at-bat in two months. The ovation thunders over the field, its rumbling echoes pounding against the historic girders of the magnificent ballpark. The boisterous tribute emanating from the packed assembly electrifies the moment. Mickey will recall this moment as "one of the loudest ovations I'd ever heard. It was the first time in my life I ever got goose pimples." Mantle had rehabbed for 61 days from a broken instep of his left foot and another injury to one of his plagued knees. Now, No. 7 strides gingerly to the plate to make a pinch-hitting appearance against Oriole lefty George Brunet. Down one run, Mantle takes his place in the batter's box for first time from two months on the mend. Selecting his pitch carefully, the right-handed-batting Mick swings on the second pitch, a curve, and connects for a line-drive, pinch-hit home run that just barely clears the left field railing, leaving a jet trail as it disappears into the mass of frenzied spectators seated in the lower seats of the left field grandstand. As he trots around the bases, "The Mick"'s gimpiness shows. Mantle actually limps while rounding the basepaths, making his tortured circuit arduous but satisfying. This clutch shot ties the game for the New York Yankees, who ultimately engineer a turnaround victory by taking the tilt in extra innings.

Mantle is still not ready for full-time duty as he attempts to get back into playing shape. For the rest of the month of August, Mantle will come to the plate a mere seven times, all in pitch-hitting assignments, with no additional success at the plate: three walks and no hits.

| 417. | Sept. 1 | Baltimore | Mike McCormick(LH) | Baltimore | 5–4, NY | 24,073 |

Still nursing a broken bone in his foot, which has not completely healed, Mickey comes to the plate to pinch-hit. As of the day before, Mantle had not even been on the active list That changes this very day without Mickey knowing anything about it. Nursing a hangover from a wild night the night before at the farmhouse of one of Mickey's friends, a shivering Mantle had awakened this morning on a porch swing. Believing there was no way he would be playing in this day's game, Mickey is catching some shut-eye on the bench during the game, when in the eighth inning, he is awakened by Manager Ralph Houk to pinch-hit for the pitcher. Approaching the plate and hitting right-handed, Mantle swings at the first pitch he sees from McCormick, a high fast ball that the woozy slugger belts for a long two-run home run over the same center field wall where he injured his left foot and right knee, almost three months before. The Yankees are back in the game at 4–3. As Mickey rounds second base, barely able to trot, he aims his troubled gait towards third base, where he finds future Hall of Fame third baseman Brooks Robinson standing on the bag, his hands on his hips and shaking his head in disbelief. The game will eventually be won with a two-run, Tom Tresh home run.

Mantle returns to the everyday lineup on September 2nd.

| 418. | Sept. 11 | Kansas City | Eddie Rakow | Kansas City(n) 8–2, NY | 14,834 |

Mickey settles matters early when he belts a three-run game-winner in the first inning that hugs the right field foul line until it descends into the lower right field seats.

| 419. | Sept. 21 | Kansas City | Moe Drabowsky | Stadium | 5–3, KC | 15,081 |

For the year, Mickey Mantle will miss the most games in one season to injury, 96, that he will ever have in his career. For the six-year remainder of Mickey Mantle's Hall-of-Fame career, he will miss 146 more games to the schedule because of injury. More important, Mantle will never play another game without great pain and, as a result, an increasingly taxing and physical deterioration of his phenomenal combination of skills and gifts will take place, even accelerate, taking its toll on his once magnificently gifted body.

THE 1963 NEW YORK YANKEES

First Place: with a 104–57 record under Manager Ralph Houk.

Yankee Stadium Attendance: 1,308,920

MICKEY MANTLE'S 1963 HITTING RECORD

G	AB	R	H	2B	3B	HR	HR%	RBI	SA	BB	SO	SB	AVE.
65	172	40	54	8	0	15	8.7	35	.622	40	32	2	.314

In 1963, Mickey Mantle hit .314 while the major leagues averaged .246 with both leagues scoring an average 7.89 runs per game and both leagues hitting 1.67 home runs per contest. During the 65 games that Mickey Mantle appeared in 1963, he played in the outfield 52 times as well as appearing in 13 games as a pinch-hitter.

Mickey's 1963 Salary: $100,000

World Series Losing Share: $7,874

Number of Games in Which Mantle Homered: 14

Winning Record When Mickey Mantle Homered: 11–3, a winning percentage of .786

THE 1963 WORLD SERIES

October 6, 1963: In Game Four of the World Series, played this day at Chavez Ravine before 55,912 sun-drenched spectators, Whitey Ford allows a scant two hits, both of them coming off the bat of Frank Howard. The Dodger slugger contributes mightily to the Dodger cause when, fooled slightly by a sharp-breaking Whitey Ford curve ball, the slugging behemoth swings one-handed, but still connects, propelling the ball in a towering, 430-foot arc towards a distant destination never before reached at Dodger Stadium. The ball lands high in the uppermost left field tier of the West Coast ballpark. This phenomenal poke gives the Dodgers a 1–0 lead.

In the top of the seventh, for a brief moment, Mickey Mantle solves Sandy Koufax, timing perfectly one of his letter-high, fast ball deliveries, crashing the ball on a high trajectory towards the bleacher section of the left-center field pavilion. The ball sails into the stands and the game is knotted at one run apiece. The home run ties Mantle with the great Babe Ruth for the most World Series home runs ever hit by a Series competitor.

In the bottom half of the inning, Yankee fortunes once again take a dip. When Junior Gilliam hits a ground ball to third baseman Clete Boyer, the ball is stopped by the hot corner slickster, who then throws the ball to first base for the potential putout. The throw, however, blends into the white-shirted background of the Dodger crowd seated alongside the third-base line. First baseman Joe Pepitone loses the flight of the ball thrown by the Yankee hot corner artist allowing the ball to get by him. This error will permit Junior Gilliam, the batter, to reach third on Boyer's error. With Gilliam on third, Willie Davis will hit a fly ball to Mickey in center field that will score Gilliam with the final run that puts the Dodgers ahead to stay.

In the ninth inning, it is up to Sandy Koufax to nail down the World Series Championship. This he proceeds to do when he strikes out Tom Tresh and Mickey Mantle, giving the Dodgers the title. Koufax has struck out eight Yankees for a two-game total of 23 whiffs in 18 innings. For the potential final out of the Series, Koufax gets Elston Howard to ground to Maury Wills, who tosses to Dick Tracewski covering second base for the forced out. But Tracewski fumbles the ball and all hands are safe. Then, with the tying run on second and the go-ahead run on first, Koufax gets Hector Lopez to ground to Maury Wills, who throws to Bill "Moose" Skowron for the putout and a World Series sweep of the Bronx Bombers. The Los Angeles Dodgers are the World Champions of baseball. Mickey Mantle's performance, even with his record-tying home run, has been frightful, as it had been with the rest of the Yankees. Mickey's only other hit had come off Don Drysdale in the righthander's masterful three-hitter in Game Three, when he bunted safely. In four games, the Yankees had admittedly been pathetic, scoring a paltry four runs, while striking out 37 times in 36 innings. The Bronx Bombers had never enjoyed one lead in all that time. After their pitiful showing, the Yankees break ranks and scatter for their off-season destinations.

At the end of yet another championship season, Mickey loses one of his most stellar teammates: Yogi Berra retires from baseball. The two Yankee teammates had combined to hit 702 home runs while playing together for the New York Yankees, a total that ranks fifth all-time for baseball's best home run duos and the second best ever in the American League.

1964 SPRING TRAINING

Mickey Mantle has undergone surgery on his left knee to correct the damage done to ligaments and cartilage which occurred the year before in Baltimore.

THE 1964 REGULAR SEASON

35 HOME RUNS

From April 27th and for the next ten days of the season, Mantle misses playing time due to bothersome muscle pulls in both legs. Mickey will not return to the everyday lineup until May 6th.

H.R.#	DATE	OPPONENT	PITCHER	SITE	SCORE	ATTND.
420.	May 6 (first game)	Wash.	Bennie Daniels	Wash.(tn)	9–2, NY	32,026

Mickey tattoos the righthander's pitch, fashioning a back-to-back sequence of home runs with Hector Lopez.

H.R.#	DATE	OPPONENT	PITCHER	SITE	SCORE	ATTND.
421.	May 6 (second game)	Wash.	Bob Meyer(LH)	Wash.(tn)	5–4, Wash	32026
422.	May 8	Cleveland	Tommy John(LH)	Cleveland(n)	10–3, NY	20,877

Mantle's opposite field blow sails into the right field seats for a first-inning, three-run home run.

H.R.#	DATE	OPPONENT	PITCHER	SITE	SCORE	ATTND.
423.	May 9	Cleveland	Pedro Ramos	Cleveland	6–2, NY	8,106

| 424. | May 16 | Kansas City | Moe Drabowsky | Stadium | 10–6, NY | 24,007 |

Mickey's long-range poke slams into the left field seats just beyond the 402-foot sign. Mantle's 410-foot blast is not the longest ball he hits in this game. One ball that he belts travels 440 feet, ending up being caught by Athletics outfielder Nelson Mathews in center field. The home run, however, knocks in the Yankees' seventh and eighth runs for the game's-winning blow.

| 425. | May 17 (first game) | Kansas City | John O'Donoghue(LH) | Stadium | 11–9, NY | 24,942 |

Mickey clobbers a long fly ball to the opposite field that falls into the lower right field grandstand.

| 426. | May 23 | Los Angeles | Jo Belinsky(LH) | Stadium | 9–5, NY | 12,412 |

Mickey lifts a long, opposite field, 420-foot shot into the right-center field bleachers.

| 427. | May 24 (second game) | Los Angeles | Fred Newman | Stadium | 8–5, NY | 21,294 |

Mantle connects for another of his towering shots that carries into the upper deck of the right field grandstand. From this point on, nagging muscle pulls keep Mantle out of the lineup until June 10th.

| 428. | June 11 | Boston | Bill Monbouquette | Bos.(n) | 8–4, NY | 28,494 |

After a two-week layoff, Mantle returns to the lineup to clout the ball high and far on to the right field runway off last year's 20-game winner still at the peak of his skills.

| 429. | June 11 | Boston | Bill Monbouquette | Bos.(n) | 8–4, NY | 28,494 |

Mickey connects, powering yet another ball into the right field bleachers.

| 430. | June 13 | Chicago | Don Mossi(LH) | Stadium | 6–3, NY | 15,531 |

The fabulous Switcher connects right-handed for an opposite field shot that soars into the right field grandstand seats. Reflecting his equitable approach to unloading his longball, Mickey's 430 home runs break down accordingly: 215 home runs belted in Yankee Stadium and 215 roundtrippers smashed on-the-road.

| 431. | June 17 | Boston | Dick Radatz | Stadium | 4–3, Bos (in 12) | 9,668 |

Mickey swings at the pitch and lifts a fly ball to right field. Believing he has missed the ball badly, Mantle throws down his bat in disgust as he starts to run to first base. The clout, however, mirroring Mickey's great strength, keeps carrying further and further towards the right field barrier until it sails into the stadium's right field seats.

| 432. | June 21 | Chicago | Juan Pizarro(LH) | Chicago | 2–0, NY | 39,316 |
| | (first game) | | | | | |

On Father's Day, Mantle powers a paternal shot into the upper deck of the left field grandstand of the antiquated ballyard.

| 433. | June 23 | Baltimore | Chuck Estrada | Baltimore(n) | 9–8, Balt | 31,860 |

Mickey connects for a grand-slam home run to right field.

| 434. | June 27 | Detroit | Denny McLain | Stadium | 5–4, NY | 25,065 |
| | | | | | (in 10) | (17,224 pd.) |

Mickey powers the ball into the right field seats.

| 435. | July 1 | Kansas City | John O'Donoghue(LH) | Stadium | 5–4, KC | 7,588 |
| | | | | | | (in 11) |

Mantle connects for a first-inning two-run shot.

| 436. | July 4 | Minnesota | Al Worthington | Stadium | 7–5, NY | 30,685 |
| | | | | (first game) | | |

Mickey pounds out one of his signature upper-deck shots into the right field grandstand down the line for a two-out, game-winning, three-run home run.

THE 1964 ALL-STAR GAME

SHEA STADIUM IN NEW YORK, NEW YORK
JULY 7

In the bottom of the ninth inning of the All-Star Game played this day at Shea Stadium, the game had just been tied, 4–4, when Orlando Cepeda will single in Willie Mays. Shortly thereafter, following a walk to the Reds' Johnny Blanchard, Johnny Callison will belt's a three-run home run into the upper deck of the right field grandstand off Bosox hurler Dick "the Monster" Radatz. The timely blow, when added to the earlier National League belts by Billy Williams of the Chicago Cubs and Ken Boyer of the St. Louis Cardinals, helps the National League even matters with the

American League. With 50,844 partisan fans cheering on the American League, Mantle does little, going 1-for-4, scoring a run, and striking out twice, once apiece confronting Don Drysdale of the Los Angeles Dodgers and once by Dick Farrell of the Philadelphia Phillies. In the 31-year history of the midsummer classic, the overall record now stands at 17 American League wins to the National League's 17 wins and one tie.

| 437. | July 13 | Cleveland | Gary Bell | Cleveland(n) | 10–4, NY | 18,427 |

Mickey scorches a line-drive home run into the right field seats that drives in the fifth, deciding, and game-winning run.

| 438. | July 24 (first game) | Detroit | Hank Aguirre(LH) | Det.(tn) | 10–5, NY | 51,044 |

| 439. | July 28 | L.A. | Dean Chance | L.A.(n) | 2–1, LA | 35,976 |

The ace Angel righthander holds the Yankees to two hits, but one of them is Mantle's 390-foot shot over the 14-and-a-half-foot high center field wall, the longest of the safeties off this year's 20-9 performer. In the Sixties, Dean Chance will lead the American League in allowing the fewest home runs in a given year, that year being this year—7—one of which is clouted by "The Mick" on this day.

| 440. | Aug. 1 | Minnesota | Dick Stigman(LH) | Minn. | 6–4, NY | 36,288 |

Mantle hits a 3–0 pitch some 415-feet over the center field screen.

| 441. | Aug. 4 | Kansas City | John O'Donoghue(LH) | Kansas City(n) | 5–1, KC | 18,232 |

Mantle muscles a 400-foot line drive over the left-center field wall at Municipal Stadium.

| 442. | Aug. 11 (second game) | Chicago | Juan Pizarro(LH) | Stadium | 8–2, Chi | 25,203 |

Mickey launches a final at-bat, opposite-field home run with two outs in the ninth inning that soars into the lower right field seats.

| 443. | Aug. 12 | Chicago | Ray Herbert | Stadium | 7–3, NY | 16,945 |

It is in the fourth-inning that Mantle launches one of his trademark "tape-measure" shots, a 500-foot home run over the 461-foot sign in center field. It is only the second time in the history of the stadium that any major league player has reached the most remote of the straightaway center field bleachers. The ball actually spans the field, soaring over the head of Chisox centerfielder Gene Stephens, who is standing at the base of the 22-foot, five-inch, barrier between the two field-level exit signs and the 461-foot marker. It will then crash into the empty bleacher seats 15 rows beyond the top of the wall. A voice over the loudspeaker "with controlled wonder," as described by *New York Times* sports reporter Joseph Durso, announces that "efforts are being made to compute the distance." The noted computation, given one hour later, sets the distance at "just over 500 feet." Mickey is hot, hitting the longball, and has now walloped three dingers in his last five at-bats, while collecting six hits in his last 11 trips to the plate. Mantle had been in an 0-for-17 slump and had chose yesterday to emerge from this dire slump. Mel Stottlemeyer hurls his first major league pitching victory.

| 444. | Aug. 12 | Chicago | Frank Baumann(LH) | Stadium | 7–3, NY | 16,945 |

Connecting to the opposite field, Mantle hits a 350-foot home run to right field. It is also the 10th time in his career that Mantle has hit home runs from both sides of the plate in the same game; at this point in time it represents a major league record. Even with his other baseball skills fading because of injury and the inevitable march of time's, "The Mick" can still, once in the groove, get power-hot. It is the 32-year-old Mantle's third home run in his last five times at bat over the past two games. It is also at this point in time that Mantle re-injures his left knee and will not return to the lineup until August 21st.

| 445. | Aug. 22 | Boston | Jack Lamabe | Bos.(d-n) | 8–0, NY | 19,958 |
| | (second game) | | | | | |

Breaking a Yankee losing streak, Mickey hammers a long home run into the Red Sox bullpen in right-center field at Fenway Park. Mantle's two-run, first-inning shot drives in the first two runs of the game and the game-winners for the Yankees.

446.	Aug. 23	Boston	Earl Wilson	Boston	4–3, NY	26,518
447.	Aug. 29	Boston	Pete Charton	Stadium(tn)	10–2, NY	37,672
	(first game)					

In the third-inning of the second bill, Mickey Mantle looks at a third strike, fanned by righthander Earl Wilson for the 1,330th time in his career, which ties him for the all-time major league lead in career strikeouts with the "Great Bambino." Mickey has accomplished this ignominious feat in 1,853 ball games, some 650 games sooner than "The Babe" had needed.

448.	Sept. 4	Kansas City	John O'Donoghue(LH)	K.C.(n)	9–7, NY	9,900
						(in 10)

Mickey and Elston Howard orchestrate back-to-back home runs.

449.	Sept. 5	Kansas City	John "Blue Moon" Odom	Kansas City(n)	9–7, NY	18,759

Feasting on one of the righthander's fast balls in the first inning, Mantle wallops an opposite field, three-run shot over the left field fence at Municipal Stadium. The blow is Mantle's 30th home run of the year and represents the ninth time in his career that he has banged out as many as 30 home runs in a year.

450.	Sept. 17	Los Angeles	Bob Duliba	Stadium(n)	6–2, NY	10,957

In addition to his home run, it is in the sixth inning of this game that Mantle collects his 2,000th hit: a line-drive single to center field off Fred Newman.

451.	Sept. 19	Kansas City	Diego Segui	Stadium	8–3, NY	9,458

Mickey connects for a high, towering blast, the ball soaring deep into the furthest reaches of the Yankee bullpen.

452.	Sept. 22	Cleveland	Dick Donovan	Cle.(tn)	8–1, NY	22,557
	(second game)					

Mantle slams the ball into the seats for a first-inning, two-run game-winner.

453.	Sept. 27	Wash.	Bennie Daniels	Wash. D.C.	3–2, Wash	14,985
					(in 11)	

Mickey unleashes a game-tying home run in the seventh-inning.

454.	Sept. 30	Detroit	Mickey Lolich(LH)	Stadium(tn)	7–6, NY	15,243
	(first game)					

THE 1964 NEW YORK YANKEES

First Place: with a 99–63 record under Manager Yogi Berra. It is the final year in 39 straight seasons, a major league record, that the New York Yankees have finished in the first division.

Yankee Stadium Attendance: 1,305,638

MICKEY MANTLE'S 1964 HITTING RECORD

G	AB	R	H	2B	3B	HR	HR%	RBI	SA	BB	SO	SB	AVE.
143	465	92	141	25	2	35	7.5	111	.591	99	102	6	.303

Awards: Mickey Mantle is voted on *Sporting News'* All-Star American League Team as an outfielder.

In 1964, Mickey Mantle hit .303 while the major leagues averaged .250 with both leagues scoring an average 8.07 runs per game and both leagues hitting 1.69 home runs per contest. During the 143 games that Mickey Mantle appeared in 1964, he played in the outfield 132 times while appearing in 11 games as a pinch-hitter. Mantle missed 19 games to injury, appearing almost exclusively hurt in all of his pinch-hitting assignments.

Mickey's 1964 Salary: $100,000

World Series Losing Share: $5,309

Number of Games in Which Mantle Homered: 33

Winning Record When Mickey Mantle Homered: 25–8, a winning percentage of .758

THE 1964 WORLD SERIES

October 10, 1964: In the second inning of Game Three at Yankee Stadium, with Elston Howard on first base after singling, lefty Curt Simmons comes in to Clete Boyer with an inside strike when the light-hitting third baseman doubles down the third-base line, knocking in Howard, and giving the Yankees a 1–0 lead. Later, off Yankee rookie righthander Jim Bouton, Redbird catcher Tim McCarver will single to right field, but Mickey misplay's the ball in right allowing McCarver to speed to second base. Dal Maxvill's ground out to Richardson moves the Cardinal catcher to third base. Cardinal pitcher Curt Simmons then line's a shot off Boyer's glove at third, which permits McCarver to score an unearned but game-tying run.

In the well-pitched game, both teams fail to score through the next three frames. In the ninth, after setting down the Cards, the Yankees come up in their home half of the inning in the hopes of settling matters. With Simmons pulled in favor of a pinch-hitter in the ninth, knuckleballer Barney Schultz has come in to face the Yanks. As the knuckleballer warms up on the mound, the Yankee scouting reports are consulted for any apparent weaknesses. Mickey Mantle is to lead off the inning. As Schultz continues his warm-up pitches, Mantle walks over to Elston Howard in the on-deck circle to share a thought. He leans over and tells the Yankee backstop, "You might as well go on back to the clubhouse because I'm going to hit the first pitch out of here for a home run."

Schultz completes his warm-ups and readies himself to face the switcher. Barney had joined the club with 59 games left in the season, appearing in 30 games, more than half of the contests that were left to be played. The flutter-ball artist had been the Cardinals' "money" pitcher, coming out of the bullpen in the crucial '64 pennant race, and he belonged right where he was—tight game, right man—that is, until today's first pitch. While he is warming up, Schultz is relieved to feel that he has his stuff moving well today.

Mantle leads off the bottom of the ninth. Destiny dictates that Game Three will be decided on the last pitch of the game and that final pitch the only pitch in the game made by reliever Barney Schultz is served up to Mickey. After completing his warm-up, Schultz prepares to offer his first pitch. As the Cardinal knuckleballer lets go of the ball, a fluttering knuckleball is approaching the plate without its flutter. Mantle triggers his swing, slams the ball, and pulls the Schultz hanging spinner in a prodigious belt. The ball would carries high and deep into the upper deck of the right field grandstand, one of Mantle's patented trademark "tape-measure" drives. Years later, Mickey will recall, "...I knew instantly the ball was gone. It landed in the third deck of the right field; another few feet and it would have cleared the roof." This home run pushes Mantle ahead of "The Babe" for the most lifetime home runs in World Series competition. Even more important, the "Clutch of Clout" has tattooed the game-winning, game-ending home run. The Yankees win the game, 2–1, as a sustained crescendo of deafening roars ring off the rafters. Later, in the clubhouse, Cardinal Manager Johnny Keane is asked if Barney Schultz's knuckleball pitch "did anything." The boss of the Cards replies, "Yes. Once Mantle got involved with it."

October 14, 1964: In Game Six of the Series, played this day at Sportsman's Park, the "M and M Boys" connect for back-to-back home runs in the sixth inning. Roger belts a rooftop shot just inside the foul pole. The next batter, Number Seven, pastes a Curt Simmons fast ball, propelling the ball high and far to the opposite field. Mickey's swat is a line-drive wallop that also lands on the roof of the right field pavilion. Veteran southpaw Curt Simmons becomes only the fourth pitcher in Series history to yield back-to-back home runs to his opponents—in this case, the "M &

M Boys" from the Bronx, the historical slugging team of Mickey Mantle and Roger Maris. The Yankees now lead, 3–1. Off Gordon Richardson, Yankee first baseman Joe Pepitone adds an eighth-inning grand-slam home run that assures the Bombers an 8–3 victory. Pepitone becomes only the 10th player in history to connect for a grand-slam home run.

In a footnote to the Mantle legacy in October, Mike Shannon of the Cardinals strikes out in this game for the fifth straight time in the Series, sharing this particular Series mark with Mickey Mantle and others.

October 15, 1964: At Sportsman's Park in St. Louis, pitching his second complete game, Cardinal ace Bob Gibson outduels five Yankee hurlers, striking out nine batters and beating the Yankees, 7–5, despite three Yankee home runs. The long-ball barrage includes Mickey Mantle's three-run, opposite-field shot in the sixth. The Yankee power game is, to a degree, offset by the element of speed and astonishing surprise. In the home half of the fourth, Ken Boyer starts things off with a single to center. With Boyer on first base, Dick Groat also walks on four straight pitches, putting Cardinals runners on first and second with Tim McCarver due up. The Yankee starter Mel Stottlemyre then gets McCarver to bounce a perfect double-play ball to Bobby Richardson at second base who flips the ball to rookie shortstop Phil Linz. Linz then fires the ball to first base in his try to nab the slow-footed Cardinal catcher. The ball is wide, however, and rolls to the wall behind first, which scores Boyer. The Cards lead, 1–0.

The next batter, Mike Shannon, then singles, sending McCarver scampering to third. The Cardinals will win this game by two runs, an eventual 7–5 score, and a superbly heroic pitching effort by a tired Bob Gibson, who keeps summoning that something extra in tight spots. The two runs, the margin of victory, can be traced to a double steal in this frame, which involves two of the slower ballplayers on the team, players who, between them, have stole six bases during the season: burly Mike Shannon and catcher Tim McCarver. Now hooked up in this tight pitching duel, Card Manager Johnny Keane had decided to shake things up with a double steal. With one out and Mike Shannon on first base, the burly outfielder takes off for second base with Tim McCarver dancing on third. When Yankee backstop Elston Howard realizes Shannon is on his way, he double-pumps before throwing down to second base in a late attempt to get the over-ambitious Shannon. As the throw sails past the head of Yankee righthander Stottlemyre, McCarver breaks for home in an attempt to steal a run. Richardson's relay throw back to Howard arrives late and wide of the plate as McCarver slides into home for Game Seven's second run. In the process, Tim McCarver becomes the 13th player in Series history to steal home.

Then, with Shannon on second base, Dal Maxvill singles him home, giving the Cardinals a three-run lead.

Meanwhile, Bob Gibson has held the Yankees scoreless for five innings. In the bottom of the fifth, with Al Downing on the mound for the Yankees, Lou Brock wallops a 400-foot drive onto the roof of the right-center field pavilion. Slugging first baseman Bill White then singles to center, followed by a Ken Boyer double to right. Downing is then replaced by Roland Sheldon. Greeting the new Bomber reliever, Dick Groat grounds to the right side of the diamond where Bobby Richardson, having no play at home for White or for Boyer who advances to third, tosses the ball to Joe Pepitone to retire Groat. The next batter, the ubiquitous McCarver, then lifts a fly to the right scoring Boyer and giving the hometown Cardinals a 6–0 lead.

As the Cardinals start to pull away from the Yankees, the Redbirds appear to be this year's team of silver-lined destiny. Indeed, a big part of the Cardinals' glory in the Series has belonged to Bob Gibson, who will establish a Series record for whiffing 31 Yankees. One Yankee, Mickey Mantle, then comes to the plate to face a tiring Bob Gibson—who is pitching his heart out with every pitch. Mantle, as with his other Yankee teammates, has not been able to solve Gibson. In this plate appearance in the sixth, the former long-ball glories of the past are soon revisited by the legendary switch-hitter. Mickey hits a high drive, left, deep to the opposite field towards Lou Brock. Brock drifts back further and further until he runs out of room. Mickey's three-run blast carries well into the seats, over the head of Lou Brock and over the 379-foot marker, landing halfway up the left field bleachers that stretch up to the prominent, red-bedecked BUDWEISER scoreboard dominating the left-field bleachers 81 feet above field level. The Cardinal six-run lead has now shrunk to three, thanks to Mickey Mantle who once more, as he has done all season and throughout his career, puts the Yankees back into the game. The Redbirds lead, 6–3.

As the game is played out, a unique feat occurs during this contest which has, by now, embraced the final home run of the most productive World Series home run belter of all-time. Still, in a most unique display in this Series play, two brothers playing on opposing sides each connect for home runs in the same Series game for the first time. The Boyer brothers each belt out home runs in the game, ironically passing each other from their respective positions at third base. As each Missouri-born Boyer circled the bases, each trots by the other, getting a very unobtrusive, and private congratulations from the other. Clete's round-tripper for the Yankees combines with another by Phil Linz, helping the Bombers draw within two runs in the final frame, but Bob Gibson, as tired as he is, still proves too tough for the travel-gray Yankees.

The Yankees' Bobby Richardson has once again excelled in the game's most visible showcase and now embodies the Yankees' last hope. The experienced veteran of seven October Classics, and a high-profile Series achiever, has been a wonder in his post-season career. Not only in 1960 did he compile a .367 batting average, with eight runs scored and 12 runs batted in, but in 1961 he batted .391. Still figuring in the high-stakes drama a year later, it was Bobby who made the clutch, Series-saving 1962 spear of Willie McCovey's vicious line drive for the final out of Game Seven. And in this Series, Richardson once again shines, batting .406 and setting a new World Series record with 13 base hits.

For Mickey, meanwhile, this will be his last World Series. The collision between "The Mick" and World Series destiny has run its course. Mickey Mantle bows out of the history of post-season championship play watching as Bobby Richardson prepares to face the forbidding Gibson. While the final shadows begin to darken in the visitor's dugout, obscuring Number Seven for the last time, it is his twelfth championship October in the last 14 seasons. With Richardson facing Gibson, Mickey approaches the bat rack to ready himself for what could be another opportunity to hit. As his last chance begins to recede into history amid the lengthening shadows of Sportsman's Park, the fabled slugger grabs his bat and begins to grip the same Louisville bludgeon he has used for so long. Stepping on the top step of the third base visitor's dugout, "The Mick" is one at-bat removed from having homered off Bob Gibson, his final home run of his championship career. Now, he is ready to face the fates once more; but it is not to be. For Bobby Richardson, the Yankee sparkplug of prior Bomber rallies, faces Gibson, who, in turn, coaxes a pop-up off the bat of the battling second baseman. Watching the final out of his World Series career, Mickey Mantle waits at the top step of the dugout, choking a Louisville slugger which is resting on his shoulder, short-swinging the bat, still preparing for another final at-bat.

Mickey Mantle is still the image of lightning-like power that has devastated so many of the opposing National League pitching staffs over the years. His bat, however, is now immobile, still leaning on his left shoulder. As Richardson's pop-up descends to earth to settle into Julian Javier's glove for the final putout of the Series, the damages caused by Mickey's World Series booming home runs are to be no more. Mickey Mantle is in a state of animated suspension, a ghost of October glories past. He will never again be seen in a World Series. The end has come with Roger Maris "on deck" and Mickey Mantle "in the hole" in a St. Louis dugout.

In 1963 action, with Mickey framed by the Monuments of Yankee Greatness, the legendary Switcher will earn his own niche in this same sacred nook of the Stadium's "Death Valley" spaces in this, the greatest of big league ballyards.

Chapter Nine

THE TWILIGHT OF FADING GREATNESS

—1965, 1966, 1967 & 1968—

In the Nation and the World: In 1965, President Lyndon Johnson launched the "Great Society." In the conflict in Southeast Asia, LBJ commited U.S. "combat troops" to South Vietnam for the first time. Meanwhile, in the skies above, U.S. Astronaut Ed White spent 20 minutes "walking" in outer space tethered to the orbiting space capsule. The Voting Rights Act of 1965 is passed.

In the following year, as the Mantle Era began to ebb towards its conclusion, the country saw 43 race riots explode in our major cities. And the war continued to escalate as President Johnson resumed the bombing of North Viet Nam.

The following year, 1967, became the "Year of the Hippie." Ghetto violence peaked in Newark and Detroit. In education, college enrollment has almost doubled since 1960.

Meanwhile, in the U.S. space program, U.S. Astronauts Roger Chafee, Virgil Grissom, and Edward White were killed during a test launch in the Apollo when a fire swept through their capsule. In the Middle East, the Six-Day War between Israel and the Arabs resulted in the smashing of the Arab forces by the Israelis. In medicine, meanwhile, Dr. Christian Barnard performed the first heart transplant.

The following year, 1968, was a year of tumult and turmoil: North Koreans seized the U.S.S. *Pueblo*; the Tet Offensive was unleashed in South Vietnam; and college students initiated anti-war demonstrations and Richard Nixon was getting elected by an eyelash. In civil rights, riots occurred in 125 American cities in the wake of Dr. Martin Luther King's assassination. The total number of U.S. casualties in the conflict in Southeast Asia (30,8567 dead) exceeded the number suffered in the Korean Conflict. The Soviet Union invaded a rebelious Czechoslovakia. And during the Democratic Nominating Convention in Chicago, violence erupted when "Yippies" led major riots in the "Windy City."

Fads: In 1965, as liberal attitudes began to dominate popular choices, a freer, more widely accepted sexual permissiveness began to take hold across the nation. Trivia contests became the rage, as did computer dating. And James Bond toys were popular. In 1966, skateboards, which had been a required diversion for California youth in the early Sixties, were now meeting wide acceptance throughout the country. "Underground newspapers" underscored the rebelliousness of the times; and Batman toys and accessories made their first appearance. Meanwhile, Ouija boards, astrology, and Tarot cards became a new and highly profitable industry. In the following year, 1967, jogging became the rage. Mickey Mouse watches were a runaway best-selling source of nostalgia, and a large wave of protest buttons embracing all causes expressed this new age of rebellion. In addition, psychedelic art became a popular diversion.

Innovations and First Appearances: In 1965, domed stadiums came into vogue among aspiring architects. Mini skirts continued to enjoy their widespread popularity. In the nation's refrigerators, Diet Pepsis continued to multiply as Americans begin to watch their waistlines. Sony home videotape recorders also made their first appearance.

In the next year, 1966, Medicare ID cards appeared on the scene for America's elderly. Tape cartridges were manufactured for the first time on a widespread basis, making yet another form available for expressing the popular music sweeping the country. Instant credit took a mighty upturn when the new Bank Americard was introduced. In 1967, as Mickey Mantle's career began to wind down, the UHF-VHF combination on TV sets was introduced, giving American viewers more choices in selecting their entertainment fare. And the compact microwave was discovered and developed for use in American kitchens.

In 1968, enzyme detergents were developed. And for the first time, when the Cold War seemed to be lessening its tensions, a direct airlines service from the United States to the U.S.S.R. was established. In the United States, for the first time, four permanent three-day holiday weekends were selected for the national calendar to celebrate: Washington's Birthday, Memorial Day, Columbus Day, and Veterans Day.

Movies: In 1965, moviegoers crowded into the theaters to catch this year's releases from Hollywood, which among other hit titles included *The Sound of Music*, *Cat Ballou*, *The Yellow Rolls Royce*, *The Spy Who Came in from the Cold*, *The Greatest Story Ever Told*, *Thunderball*, *Doctor Zhivago*, and *The Cincinnati Kid*. In 1966, Saturday-night dates revolved around dinner and the following movie fare: *The Bible*, *The Russians Are Coming–The Russians Are Coming*, *Who's Afraid of Virginia Woolf?*, *Nevada Smith*, *Hawaii*, *Harper*, *Born Free*, *The Blue Max*, *A Man for All Seasons*, *Is Paris Burning?*, and *Alfie*.

The following year, 1967, saw cinematic epics such as *The Dirty Dozen*, Walt Disney's *Jungle Book*, *Thoroughly Modern Millie*, *Barefoot in the Park*, *Bonnie and Clyde*, *Funeral in Berlin*, *To Sir With Love*, *The Taming of the Shrew*, and *Dr. Doolittle* released for the enjoyment of millions of American moviegoers. In 1968, Americans were ushered to their seats in darkened theaters to enjoy *Oliver*, *Ice Station Zebra*, *Funny Girl*, *The Lion in Winter*, *Planet of the Apes*, *Romeo and Juliet*, *Where Were You When the Lights Went Out?*, *Anzio*, *2001: A Space Odyssey*, and *The Thomas Crown Affair*.

Television: In 1965, sitcoms and humor ruled the TV sweepstakes with such new standards as *I've Got a Secret*, *The Patty Duke Show*, *I Spy*, *Green Acres*, *The Defenders*, *Gomer Pyle, U.S.M.C.*, *F Troop*, and *The Smothers Brothers Show*. In 1966, Americans were enjoying their living-room fare watching *The FBI*, *Big Valley*, *Bonanza*, *I Dream of Jeanie*, *Lost In Space*, and *Mission: Impossible*. It was more of the same in 1967, when Americans settled down in their dens, snuggling with the kids watching episodes of *The Virginian*, *The Carol Burnett Show*, *Star Trek*, *Judd for the Defense*, *That Girl*, and *The Flying Nun*. The programs for 1968 showed a marked upswing in dramatic renderings that unfolded thrilling, hour-long plot lines of episodes of *It Takes a Thief*, *The Avengers*, *Here's Lucy*, *60 Minutes*, *Hawaii Five-O*, *Ironside*, *Name of the Game*, *Get Smart*, and *Mannix*.

The Juke Box: Musical fare in 1965 reflected the rock 'n' roll tastes of the Baby Boomer generation, touting such standards as "Wooly Bully" by Sam the Sham and the Pharoahs, "(I Can't Get No) Satisfaction" by the Rolling Stones, "King of the

Road" by Roger Miller, "Ferry Cross the Mersy" by Jerry and the Pacemakers, Petula Clark's "Downtown," and Sonny and Cher's "I Got You Babe." In 1966, deeper themes for thought and memorable melodies crowded the TOP 40: such hit tunes as "The Ballad of the Green Berets" by Barry Sadler, Frank Sinatra's "Strangers in the Night," "The Last Train to Clarksville" by the Monkees, "Eleanor Rigby" by the Beatles, Simon and Garfunkel's "Scarborough Fair," "Cherish" by the Association, "Reach Out, I'll Be There" by the Four Tops, "Monday, Monday" by the Mamas and the Papas, and the Righteous Brothers' "You're My Soul and Inspiration."

The musical strains of 1967 mirrored the "California Sound," while inspiring millions to loosen their wallets for purchasing tapes that included hot-selling numbers like the Four Tops' "The Letter," "The Beat Goes On" by Sonny and Cher, the Beatles' "Lucy in the Sky With Diamonds," "Windy" by the Association, and "Light My Fire" by the Doors. Moreover, in 1968, social themes in a time of turmoil and melancholic complexities crowded the billboard list of top-selling songs which included such standards as "(Sittin' on) The Dock of the Bay" by Otis Redding, "Stoned Soul Picnic" by the Fifth Dimension, Herb Alpert's "This Guy's in Love With You," "Midnight Confessions" by the Grass Roots, and "Love Child" by Diana Ross and the Supremes.

Deaths: The passing of America's most well-known personalities in 1965 included Adlai Stevenson, Nat King Cole, T.S. Eliot, Bernard Baruch, silent screen actress Clara Bow, Judy Holliday, Stan Laurel, Helena Rubinstein, Malcolm X, Edward R. Murrow, Sir Winston Churchill, and Dr. Albert Schweitzer. In baseball, fans mourned this year's passing of Paul Waner, Branch Rickey, and Pepper Martin. In 1966, an entertainment giant passed away as Walt Disney brought tears to the eyes of young people of all ages. Other obituaries of note in the field of entertainment included Lenny Bruce, actor Montgomery Clift, Billy Rose, Sophie Tucker, and actors Ed Wynn and Clifton Webb.

In the following year, 1967, baseball's Jimmie Foxx died when he choked to death on a piece of meat. Jayne Mansfield perished in a car crash. The poetry of Carl Sandburg reached an end when its author died. And Hollywood mourned the loss of actresses Dorothy Gish and Vivien Leigh, as well as actors Ramon Navarro, Basil Rathbone, Robert Taylor, and Spencer Tracy. Finally, in 1968, the last year of Mickey Mantle's career in baseball, America mourned the passing of Langston Hughes, Nelson Eddy, John Coltrane, Ann Sheridan, Alice B. Toklas, John Steinbeck, and Helen Keller. In addition, the nation would be rocked by the tragic assassinations of Robert F. Kennedy and Dr. Martin Luther King, Jr.

Sports: For the year 1965, boxing champion Muhammad Ali retained his crown when Sonny Liston refused to answer the bell in their heavyweight championship rematch. Ali proved successful in the first defense of his heavyweight title and victorious for the first time as a Black Muslim. The NFL Championship belonged once more to Vince Lombardi's Green Bay Packers, who beat the Cleveland Browns, 23–12. In pro basketball, meanwhile, the Boston Celtics won their eighth NBA Championship in a row, and ninth in ten years, by beating the Los Angeles Lakers, four games to one.

In 1966, distance runner Jim Ryun ran a sensational mile time of 3 minutes, 51.3 seconds. And, again in pro basketball, the Boston Celtics defeated the Los Angeles Lakers, four games to three, for still another NBA Championship. In pro football, the Green Bay Packers toppled the Kansas City Chiefs, 35–10, in the first Super Bowl played in the first month of the year at the L.A. Memorial Coliseum, giving the Packers their third straight NFL title. In the following year, 1967, the NFL Championship was once again seized by the Packers, who crushed the Oakland Raiders, 33–14, in Super Bowl II. In addition, the NBA Championship was won by the Philadelphia 76er's, who beat the San Francisco Warriors, four games to two.

Meanwhile, as Mickey Mantle concluded his Hall-of-Fame career in 1968, the Mexico City Olympics was stunned by Bob Beamon's phenomenal 29-foot, 2½-inch leap in the broad jump. The black-fisted protest on the Olympic award stand for the 200-meter winners—by American Olympians Tommie Smith, who won the gold, and John Carlos, who turned in the bronze medal-winning performance—ignited a scurrilous suspension from the games and a raging controversy at home in America. Meanwhile, in pro football, the two leagues, the American Football League and the National Football League, gained parity when the New York Jets upset the heavily favored Baltimore Colts, 16–7, in the third Super Bowl. And in the NBA Championship Series, the Boston Celtics defeated the Los Angeles Lakers, four games to two.

Baseball Transitions: In 1965, major league baseball adopted a practice that would provide momentum towards a sports-wide movement towards parity and the ringing of the death knell for baseball dynasties. The development, replete with certain and immediate ramifications for the dynastic Yankees and the defending American League champions, became manifest with the first amateur rookie draft. As a result, the Yankees would begin one of their most serious downturns in franchise history, finishing this year in the second division for the first time in 40 years. Baseball strategy took a turn as well, as pitching staffs relied more and more on the bullpen, heralding an inclination among managers to get out the hook for their starting pitchers not only earlier in the game, but with more frequency. In addition, the Astrodome opened in 1965 in Houston, creating a completely domed environment for the "Grand Old Game," and Sandy Koufax pitched his fourth no-hitter—a perfect game against the Chicago Cubs.

Personnel changes around the league in 1965 were beginning to show a changing of the guard as the Yankees lost Tony Kubek and Whitey Ford. The Chicago White Sox lost Juan Pizarro and Milt Pappas, but picked up Tommy John and Joel Horlen. Meanwhile, the Baltimore Orioles accepted the retirement of Harvey Haddix, but welcomed the talents of Jim Palmer. Boston bade farewell to Dick Stuart and Eddie Bressoud, but picked up Rico Petrocelli. The Cleveland Indians accepted the loss of Dick Donovan, but received Ralph Terry. The Detroit Tigers lost Bill Bruton, but picked up Willie Horton. And the Washington Senators lost Chuck Hinton, but retained the slugging services of Frank Howard. But 1966 balanced the disappearing veterans with the introduction of new faces, such as at Detroit, when the Tigers waived Don Demeter but signed Jim Northrup. The Orioles lost Jerry Adair to the onset of Davey Johnson's career. Baltimore also let Robin Roberts go, but replaced him with Moe Drabowsky. Cleveland lost Jack Kralick, but picked up John O'Donoghue. And Boston traded Bill Monbouquette, but retained Jose Santiago.

In 1967, the year that Carl Yastrzemski won the Triple Crown, the New York Yankees bade farewell to Mantle's most visible partner in power, the great Roger Maris. The Yanks also lost Jim Bouton, but welcomed Steve Barber and Bill Monbouquette to the pitching staff. Boston lost Don Demeter, but signed the powerful switch-hitting talents of Reggie Smith. The Minnesota Twins lost Earl Battey and Camilo Pascual, but introduced Rod Carew and Dean Chance to the Twin Cities. The Chicago White Sox bid adieu to Juan Pizarro, but added the services of Wilbur Wood. The Orioles lost Jim Palmer temporarily, but anchored their infield with Mark Belanger and retained the pitching prowess of Pete Richert.

1968, the final year of the Mantle Era in Yankee history, revealed that the landscape of AL baseball was modified when the Kansas City team moved to Oakland. In the meantime, the Yankees lost Al Downing. Chicago lost Tommy Agee, but signed on Luis Aparicio once again. Oakland picked up Sal Bando, Joe Rudi, and Reggie Jackson, securing its future fortunes. And the Boston Red Sox, meanwhile, lost Tony Conigliaro to a frightening beanball injury, but picked up the void somewhat with the purchase of Ken Harrelson.

THE 1965 SPRING TRAINING

April 8, 1965: Playing in the first major league baseball game ever played in the Astrodome—the first indoor major league baseball game ever played—the New York Yankees face the old Houston Colt .45s, newly rechristened for this occasion, and for perpetuity, the Houston Astros. Among the 47,876 wild-eyed Texans enjoying the festivities are President and Mrs. Lyndon Johnson. The President and the First Lady leave after eight innings with the game tied at 1–1. Up to this point in the game, the highlight of this special exhibition has been the first home run ever hit in the Astrodome, a long drive for a home run to center field by Mickey Mantle off the Astro's Dick "Turk" Farrell. Although it is not official, Mantle, batting leadoff for the Yankees, connects on the second pitch of the game. Later, in the 12th inning, long after the President and his entourage have left the game, Nellie Fox singles in Astro teammate Jim Wynn with the run that beats the Yankees, 2–1.

THE 1965 REGULAR SEASON

19 HOME RUNS

H.R.#	DATE	OPPONENT	PITCHER	SITE	SCORE	ATTND.
455.	Apr. 17	Kansas City	John Wyatt	Kansas City(n)	5–2, NY	10,589

On the first pitch he is offered in his final at-bat in the game, Mickey connects, propelling the ball over the right field fence at Municipal Stadium. Mantle's home run scores the third and fourth runs which account for the game-winning tallies.

| 456. | Apr. 18 | Kansas City | Moe Drabowsky | Kansas City | 10–4, NY | 9,056 |

Mantle pounds out a home run on the first pitch of his first at-bat in the game. Over two successive games, Mickey has seen two consecutive offerings and blasted both for roundtrippers.

| 457. | Apr. 21 | Minnesota | Camilo Pascual | Stadium(n) | 7–2, Minn | 38,212 |

On Opening Day of the Yankee home schedule, a night game, Mickey launches another of his patented upper-deck shots into the right field grandstand.

| 458. | Apr. 25 | Los Angeles | Rudy May(LH) | Stadium | 1–0, NY | 17,310 |
| | (second game) | | | | | |

Mantle launches a fourth-inning, game-winning home run into the lower left field seats for the only run of the game. Mickey will miss more than eight days of action due to nagging leg injuries. In a game against Kansas City, Mantle's first injury will occur when he slides late into second, hitting his left leg hard on the base.

| 459. | May 10 | Boston | Jim Lonborg | Boston(n) | 3–2, Bos | 11,163 |

Mantle's home run accounts for both Yankee runs. Mickey adds a single and a double, the latter of which comes with two outs in the ninth-inning off the "Green Monster" in deep left-center field. After reaching second base, Mantle is substituted for by Manager Johnny Keane. Retiring from the game, Mickey leaves the field amid the roaring echoes of a Beantown standing ovation. Mickey Mantle's superstar status is becoming more and more appreciated around the league and, in some respects, even more respected than at home in Yankee Stadium.

460.	May 11	Boston	Arnold Earley(LH)	Boston(n)	5–3, Bos	15,444

On a 3–2 pitch, Mickey unleashes a 400-foot home run over the 17-foot-high wall and into the center field bleachers at Fenway Park.

461.	May 15	Baltimore	Dick Hall	Baltimore(n)	3–2, NY	32,338

Mickey propels the ball to the opposite field for a 400-foot game-winner into the left field bleachers in the eighth-inning.

462.	May 30	Chicago	Gary Peters(LH)	Chicago	3–2, NY	33,561
				(in 12)		

Mantle's clout comes off the outstanding southpaw who last year earned the distinction of being one of only two 20-game winners in the American League, finishing with a 20–8 pitching record.

463.	June 5	Chicago	Gary Peters(LH)	Stadium	4–3, NY	15,722
				(in 10)		

With increasing frequency, Mantle's lightning-like reflexes are a millisecond off as he powers the ball once again to the opposite field, carrying it into the right field bleachers. In fact, during his career, Mantle has poled at least 63 home runs to the opposite field. And still, at least half of them have occurred in the last third of his 18-year career.

464.	June 18	Minnesota	Mel Nelson(LH)	Stadium(n)	10–2, NY	22,241

In the first inning, Mickey lifts a long drive to the opposite field that carries high over the short right field wall for a grand-slam home run and into the right field seats for the game-winner.

465.	June 22	Kansas City	John O'Donoghue(LH)	Stadium(tn)	6–2, KC	13,129
	(first game)					

Mantle's ball is crushed into the left-center field bleachers some 460 feet away, making him only the 18th player ever in the 42-year history of Yankee Stadium to hit a ball that carries over the 457-foot sign. Later, in the second tilt of the twinbill, in an attempt to score from third base on a wild pitch, the Yankee slugger pulls a muscle in his left leg.

Three strides from the plate, Mantle's hamstring muscle snaps and he can barely hobble across home plate. The injury forces him to miss 18 games.

466.	July 15	Wash.	Phil Ortega	Stadium(n)	2–1, NY	14,556
				(in 12)		

Mickey's belt ties the game at 1–1 in the sixth inning.

467.	July 25 (first game)	Cleveland	Lee Stange	Cleveland	7–4, Cle	56,634

Mickey powers the ball over the center field wall at Municipal Stadium. Mickey misses three days of action, from this day forward to August 2nd, because of an injured knee.

468.	Aug. 6	Detroit	Mickey Lolich(LH)	Detroit(n)	5–4, Det	33,653

Mickey belts the ball to the opposite field. It hits high on the right field foul screen.

469.	Aug. 7	Detroit	Fred Gladding	Detroit(n)	6–5, NY	34,625

Mickey slices the ball into the lower left field grandstand seats.

470.	Aug. 10	Minnesota	Jim Kaat(LH)	Stadium(n)	7–3, Minn	29,529

Mickey pounds the ball to the opposite field, far to right-center, until it lands deep into the right field bullpen.

471.	Aug. 18	Los Angeles	Dean Chance	Stadium(n)	7–3, LA	12,573

Mantle launches a towering, 425-foot shot over the right-center field auxiliary scoreboard, giving him his privileged trot around the bases. Mantle's gait is somewhat marred by his marked limp as he struggles to complete the circuit.

472.	Sept. 2	L.A.	Marcelino Lopez(LH)	Los Angeles	8–1, NY	5,198

Playing in the last regularly-scheduled Angels game in Dodger Stadium, Mantle propels one of his trademark 400-foot clouts, that carries over the left-center field barrier, driving in the Yankees' first three runs for another game-winner.

473.	Sept. 4 (second game)	Boston	Dennis Bennett(LH)	Stadium(tn)	7–2, NY	18,110

Batting right-handed, Mickey belts a sixth inning, opposite field, 420-foot shot into the right-center field bleachers.

September 18, 1965: On "Mickey Mantle Day" at the stadium, coinciding with his 2,000th career appearance in a game for the New York Yankees, a nervous Mantle approaches the battery of microphones. Mickey has just received a slew of gifts, including a brand-new Chrysler Imperial, two quarter horses, a year's supply of bubble gum for Mickey's four sons, and, from his team, a barbecue grill molded and shaped like a prairie schooner and a six-foot long Kosher salami that weighed 100 pounds. In addition, all money collected would be donated to the Mickey Mantle Hodgkin's Disease Foundation. His wife, Merlyn, receives a mink coat. Among the dignitaries present were Joe DiMaggio and U.S. Senator Robert F. Kennedy, brother of the late John F. Kennedy.

Now the moment has come to address the cheering New York crowd of 50,000 appreciative fans, the paying patrons of his Yankee family. Guy Lombardo and the Royal Canadians have been warming up the crowd with appropriate music. Then, after being introduced by the "Yankee Clipper," Mickey tells to the adoring crowd, "I'm glad to have the greatest ballplayer I ever saw introduce me. I've been very nervous in this ballpark in the past fifteen years but never more nervous than I am now." After a pause, Mickey brings his brief remarks to a close by stating how appreciative he has been of them over the years for their support in his 15-year career. Mickey says, "I just wish I had 15 more years with you."

In the game itself, the Yankees are playing host to the Detroit Tigers. Veteran *New York Times* sports correspondent Arthur Daley describes Mickey's role in the game played on his "Day"; "...He received an ear-splitting ovation the first time he stuck his head out of the dugout and another when he first came to bat. Umpire Bill Haller stopped play and handed Mickey the ball as a souvenir. Then Joe Sparma, the Detroit pitcher, came in off the mound and shook his hand in open admiration. Mickey should have hit a homer. Instead, he flied out." As a result of his appearance, now only Babe Ruth with 2,084 games, Yogi Berra with 2,116 career games, and Lou Gehrig with 2,164 total games have played in pinstripes longer than "The Kid From Oklahoma".

THE 1965 NEW YORK YANKEES

Sixth Place: with a 77–85 record under Manager Johnny Keane.

Yankee Stadium attendance: 1,213,552

MICKEY MANTLE'S 1965 HITTING RECORD

G	AB	R	H	2B	3B	HR	HR%	RBI	SA	BB	SO	SB	AVE.
122	361	44	92	12	1	19	5.3	46	.452	73	76	4	.255

In 1965, Mickey Mantle hit .255 while the major leagues averaged .246 with both leagues scoring an average 7.98 runs per game and both leagues hitting 1.66 home runs per contest. During the 122 games that Mickey Mantle appeared in 1965, he played in the outfield 108 times as well as appeared in 14 games as a pinch-hitter.

Mickey's 1965 Salary: $100,000

Injuries or Operations: Right shoulder and right elbow. Only after a February examination and subsequent surgery to his right shoulder at the Mayo Clinic does the world learn that for at least a decade, dating back to 1955, Mickey labored in the game with a tendon in his chronically sore right shoulder that was deeply inflamed and embedded with multiple pieces of bone fragments.

Number of Games in Which Mantle Homered: 19

Winning Record When Mickey Mantle Homered: 12–7, a winning percentage of .632

THE 1966 REGULAR SEASON

23 HOME RUNS

H.R.#	DATE	OPPONENT	PITCHER	SITE	SCORE	ATTND.
474.	May 9	Minn.	Jim Perry	Minn.(n)	3–2, NY	10,119

Mantle's home run on this day represents the latest in any season when Mickey hit his first home run.

| 475. | May 14 | Kansas City | Fred Talbot | Kansas City(n) | 4–2, KC | 12,258 |

This particular four-master matches the career home run record of Stan "The Man" Musial, seventh on the all-time list. Still later, in the sixth inning, Mantle pulls a leg muscle in his left thigh. This particular injury forces Mickey to miss 11 days of action.

| 476. | May 25 | Cal. | Dean Chance | Stadium(n) | 11–6, NY | 14,327 |

Mantle slams a towering drive deep into the right-field bullpen.

| 477. | May 25 | Cal. | Lew Burdette | Stadium(n) | 11–6, NY | 14,327 |

Mantle lifts a long fly to the opposite field that carries into the left-field box seats.

| 478. | June 1 | Chicago | Juan Pizarro(LH) | Chicago | 6–2, Chi | 21,637 |
| 479. | June 16 | Cleveland | Sam McDowell(LH) | Stadium(n) | 7–6, NY | 12,171 |

Crashing the ball to the opposite field, Mantle's blast off the highly touted Indian lefthander flies into the right field bleachers. Mantle's shot comes off the talented southpaw fireballer who, this very year, produces the third-highest average at this point in time in baseball history for strikeouts every nine innings. Only Sandy Koufax and McDowell himself the year before have ever produced a higher strikeout per nine inning average with 10.42 K's per each nine-inning outing in a single season.

| 480. | June 23 | Baltimore | Jim Palmer | Stadium | 5–2, Balt | 10,640 |

Mickey lifts a towering fly ball high and far to right field until it lands, falling into the first row of the upper deck at Yankee Stadium. The 1966 edition of the Baltimore Orioles sports a new patch, emblazoning on their caps the cartoon version of the Oriole for the first time.

| 481. | June 28 | Boston | Jose Santiago | Boston(n) | 5–3, Bos | 14,922 |

Beginning this day at Fenway Park in Beantown, Mickey begins the hottest streak of his career for belting out home runs. This particular blast, his first roundtripper in this night game, sails into the right field bleachers.

| 482. | June 28 | Boston | Jose Santiago | Boston(n) | 5–3, Bos | 14,922 |

Mickey powers a ball to the opposite field and into the netting of the "Green Monster" at Fenway Park in a losing cause. Mickey is about to unloose a home run rampage of his own that will come at a higher rate, connecting more frequently than any previous rate generated by any player in the history of the American League.

| 483. | June 29 | Boston | Roland Sheldon | Boston(n) | 6–0, NY | 14,614 |

At Fenway Park, in a game with the Boston Red Sox, the pin-striped slugger belts out a home run in his first appearance at the plate. The ball is slammed to the opposite field into the screen atop the "Green Monster" in left-center field. the Mick has now hit three home runs in three straight official at-bats.

| 484. | June 29 | Boston | Lee Stange | Boston(n) | 6–0, NY | 14,614 |

In his next at-bat, his fourth successive opportunity at the plate to hit a home run, Mantle once again connects with the middle round-tripper in a back-to-back-to-back home run sequence with Bobby Richardson and Joe Pepitone. Mantle's heroics equal a major league record for hitting four straight home runs in four straight at-bats. This fortuitous shot equals the major league mark held respectively by Babe Ruth, Jim Bottomley, Charley Maxwell, and Vic Wertz for four consecutive home runs over two games.

| 485. | July 1 | Wash. | Phil Ortega | Wash. D.C.(n) | 8–6, NY | 16,104 |

Mickey lines the ball over the scoreboard in right-center field.

| 486. | July 2 | Wash. | Mike McCormick(LH) | Wash. D.C. | 10–4, Wash | 7,197 |

Just as McCormick winds up to deliver a 3-2 pitch to the plate, Mickey calls time, causing the umpire to declare the ball dead. This brings on a brief argument between the Senators players before play in the game is resumed. On the next pitch, Mantle connects for all his worth, powering the ball some 450 feet into the mezzanine seating area in dead-center field of D.C. Stadium, (later renamed Robert F. Kennedy Memorial Stadium).

| 487. | July 2 | Wash. | Mike McCormick(LH) | Wash. | 10–4, Wash | 7,197 |

Muscling up on another McCormick fast ball, Mickey batters the ball off the scoreboard in right-center field to the opposite field.

| 488. | July 3 | Wash. | Pete Richert(LH) | Wash. D.C. | 6–5, NY (in 11) | 16,760 |

In his first at-bat in this game, the powerful Mantle continues with his current rampage of home runs, propelling the ball to the opposite field over the right field barrier. It is the second time in four days that Number Seven has hit three home runs in three consecutive at-bats over two games. In addition, Mickey Mantle has now hit his eighth home run in six games, belting roundtrippers that, at this point in time, represents the greatest rate in the history of the American League.

| 489. | July 7 | Boston | Don McMahon | Stadium(n) | 5–2, NY | * none |

reported by *The NY Times'* Joseph Durso who covered the game.

After a three-day lull in long-ball production, Mantle lines a two-out, ninth-inning, three-run, game-winning home run into the lower right field stands.

| 490. | July 8 (first game) | Wash. | Dick Bosman | Stadium(n) | 7–6, Wash | 14,863 |

In the third inning, after the Yankees had fallen behind by five runs, Mickey, in his second at-bat, ties the game when the slugging Yankee slices a long fly to left field that finds the grandstand seats for an opposite-field home run. It is Mantle's 10th home run in 11 days.

491.	July 8	Wash.	Jim Hannan	Stadium(tn)	7–5, NY	14863
	(second game)					

In his second at-bat of the second game, Mantle once again crushes the ball for another of his prodigious shots, a 460-foot home run that carries over the 14-and-a-half-foot fence and screen situated to the right of the flagpole in center field. Mickey's blow represents his 11th home run in 11 days, which also translates into 11 roundtrippers in 14 games.

Limping, Mickey Mantle leaves the second game of the July 8th twin bill with Washington. Having pulled his hamstring muscle behind his left knee, Mickey will not play in the All-Star Game or even return to regular play until he pinch-hits on July 18th.

492.	July 23	Cal.	Marcelino Lopez(LH)	Stadium	7–6, Cal	34,042

Mantle slugs the ball far and high to the opposite field, where it sails into the right field upper deck for a grand slam home run to right field. Mickey's participation in this game gives him a tie with Babe Ruth for total games played as a member of the New York Yankees. Mickey adds two safeties to his personal hit parade for his day's efforts.

493.	July 24	Cal.	George Brunet(LH)	Stadium	9–1, NY	23,534
	(first game)					

Mantle's blow is of the milestone variety, tying Lou Gehrig on the all-time list for career home runs. The opposite-field clout carries deep into the lower right field seats.

494.	July 29	Chicago	Bruce Howard	Chicago(n)	2–1, NY	30,364

Mickey's clout surpasses Lou Gehrig on the all-time homer list when the ball sails into the upper deck of the rightfield grandstand.

495.	Aug. 14	Cleveland	Jack Kralick(LH)	Stadium	6–4, NY	31,407
	(second game)					

Mickey Mantle misses 12 days because of a re-injury to his knee. Father Time has given Mickey a difficult year with which to cope. Mantle will move through the rest of the season suffering from a broken toe and a serious injury to one of his fingers.

496.	Aug. 26	Detroit	Hank Aguirre(LH)	Stadium(n)	6–5, NY	14,385

On the second pitch he sees, Mickey connects for a pinch-hit, opposite-field, game-winning home run that clears the right field wall.

September 18, 1966: Before a crowd of 12,315 disgruntled, but hearty souls, it is a tight game between the Yankees and the visiting Minnesota Twins. The game goes ten innings before the Yankees lose, 5–3, on a pinch-hit, three-run home run by Bob Allison. By this time, however, Mantle has retired from the game after jamming his finger while making a fine running catch in the fifth inning. Mickey's solid single in the first inning had led to the Yankees' first run. As a result of Bob Allison's heroics, the Yankees slip into the American League cellar. In his final at-bat in the game, Mantle strikes out. In fact, it is his final at-bat of the year and his final whiff of the campaign. Fanning in his last plate appearance of the year gives Mickey the distinction of becoming the first ballplayer in the history of the game to strike out 1,500 times in his career.

September 22, 1966: At Yankee Stadium, 413 of the most diehard faithful attend a game held by the New York Yankees against the Chicago White Sox. It is believed to be the smallest crowd that ever attended a major league baseball game in the 43-year history of Yankee Stadium. As a result of this all-time low—a legitimately newsworthy item—Yankee broadcaster and future Hall-of-Famer "Red" Barber will direct the television cameramen to pan through the massively vacant graveyard of empty seats. This monumentally meager turnout represents the lowest number of fans ever assembled in the greatest of ballyards. Consequently, Barber will be summarily fired by the Yankee brass for showing such a spectacle to the millions of television viewers tuning in to the game. It is not a proud moment for Yankee management when they fire Barber, who merely broadcast the truth. As if to underscore their bonehead decision, the Yankees finish dead last in the American League for the first time since 1912. Mickey does not play in this contest, won by the White Sox, 4–1.

THE 1966 NEW YORK YANKEES

Last Place: in the 10-team American League with a 70–89 record under Managers Johnny Keane (4-16) and Ralph Houk (66-73).

Yankee Stadium Attendance: 1,124,648

MICKEY MANTLE'S 1966 HITTING RECORD

G	AB	R	H	2B	3B	HR	HR%	RBI	SA	BB	SO	SB	AVE.

| 108 | 333 | 40 | 96 | 12 | 1 | 23 | 6.9 | 56 | .538 | 57 | 76 | 1 | .288 |

In 1966, Mickey Mantle hit .288 while the major leagues averaged .248 with both leagues scoring an average 7.99 runs per game and both leagues hitting 1.69 home runs per contest. The pin-striped slugger became the first ballplayer to strike out 1,500 times. During the 108 games that Mickey Mantle appeared in 1966, he played in the outfield 97 times as well as appeared in 11 games as a pinchhitter.

Mickey's 1966 Salary: $100,000

Number of Games in Which Mantle Homered: 18

Winning Record When Mickey Mantle Homered: 11–7, a winning percentage of .611

THE 1967 REGULAR SEASON

22 HOME RUNS

April 16, 1967: Before 19,290 hearty Bronx baseball bluebloods, the Yankees beat the Boston Red Sox, 7–6, in the 28th-longest game in AL history to date, going 18 innings in the process. Mickey goes 0-for-3 while scoring one run in this five-hour, fifty-minute marathon classic. The Yankees take this lengthy skirmish, 7–6.

H.R.#	DATE	OPPONENT	PITCHER	SITE	SCORE	ATTND.
497.	Apr. 29	Cal.	Jack Sanford	Stadium	5–2, NY	20,318
						(12,126 pd.)

Mickey's game-winning, two-run shot clears the 14 ½-foot wall some three rows deep just to the left of the 407-foot marker in right-center field, where it lands in a sea of outstretched hands among the bleacherites.

498.	Apr. 30	Cal.	Minnie Rojas	Stadium	4–1, NY	47,980
	(first game)					(in 10)

Mantle caps the game for the Yankees when he laces a three-run, 10th-inning, game-winner into the upper-deck seats of the right field grandstand. The blow ties Joe DiMaggio on the all-time hit list for the Yankee franchise. In the second game of the twin bill, the Yankees drop the encounter, 4–2. Picking out his pitch, Mickey comes up to pinch-hit in the ninth inning.

Mantle doubles, giving him his 2,215th career base hit and enabling the one-time "Kid from Oklahoma" to surpass the "Yankee Clipper" with the third most safeties in Yankee history. Only Babe Ruth and Lou Gehrig have collected more hits as a Yankee than has Number Seven.

| 499. | May 3 | Minn. | Dave Boswell | Minn.(n) | 4–3, Minn | 6,545 |
| 500. | May 14 | Baltimore | Stu Miller | Stadium | 6–5, NY | 18,872 |

In the seventh inning, Mickey lines a long drive deep into the lower right field seats of an uproarious stadium. Mickey Mantle is the sixth player to reach the 500-home-run plateau. His brilliant star fading, this milestone round-tripper comes in Mantle's 7,300th career at-bat, making him the fourth earliest player ever to reach this plateau. The milestone clout also wins the game for the Yankees.

| 501. | May 17 | Cleveland | Steve Hargan | Stadium(n) | 8–7, Cle. | 9,772 |

Mantle's blast clears the remote right-center field barrier and flies into the bleacher section of the grand old ballyard.

| 502. | May 19 | Detroit | Mickey Lolich(LH) | Detroit(n) | 4–2, Det | 33,941 |

In the eighth inning, Mickey's home run sails down the left field line until it disappears into the short seats next to the foul pole.

| 503. | May 20 | Detroit | Denny McLain | Detroit | 3–1, Det | 13,164 |

Mickey laces a towering home run to right-center field that carries into the upper grandstand some 40 feet over the 370-foot marker.

| 504. | May 21 (first game) | Detroit | Earl Wilson | Detroit | 9–4, Det | 44,862 |

Mantle's blow comes off one of the league's top performers this year, who will carve out a 22-11 pitching record. This four-master represents his fourth homer in four games and his fifth in the last six contests.

| 505. | May 24 | Baltimore | Steve Barber(LH) | Baltimore(n) | 2–0, NY | 12,449 |

Mickey slams a game-winning, two-run home run in the third inning.

| 506. | May 27 | Cleveland | Sonny Siebert | Cleveland | 5–3, Cle | 12,680 |

Mantle's roundtripper breaks a tie in an eventual defeat.

| 507. | May 28 | Cleveland | Gary Bell | Cleveland | 5–0, NY | 15,197 |

Mantle's poke clears the right field fence and gives "The Mick" eight home runs in 13 games.

508.	June 5	Wash.	Darold Knowles(LH)	Stadium(n)	4–2, NY	8,045

Appearing as a pinch-hitter, Mantle reaches for a pitched ball two feet outside and low, which he hits to the opposite field into the lower right field stands for another game-winning blast.

June 11, 1967: In the first game of a "Bat Day" doubleheader at Yankee Stadium, playing before 62,582 rabid but disappointed fans in the Bronx, a pin-striped Mickey Mantle plays in the 2,164th game of his career, every one of them contests for the New York Yankees. Playing against the Chicago White Sox, Mickey goes 2-for-3, including a double, and knocks in a run. This particular milestone ties the team record for most games played as a member of the New York Yankees, a mark held by Lou Gehrig. In the second game, Mickey is hitless in his only plate appearance, a pinch-hitting assignment, which gives Number Seven participation in more games as a Yankee than any player in franchise history. The Chisox sweep the twin bill, 2–1 and 3–2.

June 12, 1967: Mickey Mantle exceeds the lifetime number of games played as a member of the New York Yankees.

509.	June 15	Wash.	Frank Bertaina(LH)	Wash., D.C.(n)	2–0, NY	9,416

Mantle powers a 462-foot game-winner which crashes into the second row of the left-center field bleachers.

510.	June 24	Detroit	Fred Gladding	Stadium(n)	4–3, NY	18,287

Mickey's power produces yet one more ninth-inning game-winner which sails half-way up the remote right-center field bleachers some 420 feet away. For the year, it is the eighth time that Mantle has knocked in the winning run for the pin-stripers, seven of those come in the ninth inning.

511.	July 4 (first game)	Minn.	Jim "Mudcat" Grant	Minn.(d-n)	8–3, Minn	25,342

Mickey knocks in all three Yankee runs with a 370-foot, opposite-field drive over the left-center field fence. This milestone homer ties Mantle with Mel Ott on the all-time home run list. It also comes off Jim "Mudcat" Grant, who will fashion, this very year, the first 20-win season ever put together by a black pitcher in the American League.

512.	July 4 (first game)	Minn.	Jim "Mudcat" Grant	Minn. (d-n)	8–3, Minn	25,342

Mickey plants the ball over the right-field screen 380 feet away.

THE 1967 ALL-STAR GAME

ANAHEIM STADIUM IN ANAHEIM, CALIFORNIA
JULY 11

Hitting at Anaheim Stadium in the 15th inning of the midsummer classic, while 46,309 rooters are cheering for the longest All-Star Game to be concluded, Cincinnati Red Tony Perez cracks a long home run to left field, which paces the National League to a 2-1 victory. Carl Yastrzemski of the Boston Red Sox adds three hits and two walks to the AL cause. Mickey enters the All-Star Game to appear as a pinch-hitter to face Juan Marichal. In the meantime, Ferguson Jenkins ties an all-time All-Star Game standard by striking out six American League stalwarts. Fergie's victims include Harmon Killebrew, Tony Conigliaro, Jim Fregosi, Rod Carew, Tony Oliva, and Bill Freehan. Indeed, it is a game in which 30 different batters whiff against a domineering battery of pitchers on both sides of the diamond. Guess what Mickey did?

The most impressive story on this day is Mickey's travel arrangements involved to and from the game. On the morning of the game, after starting out at his country club, Preston Trails, in Dallas, Texas, Mickey flies from Love Field to Los Angeles, where he is met at L.A. International by a helicopter that choppers him to Anaheim. From that point, Mickey gets a police escort to Angel Stadium. After arriving at the game, Mickey puts on his uniform alone in the clubhouse while the other players are playing the game. After greeting the other players, former teammates and O's Manager Hank Bauer, the AL field chief asks Mickey if he wants to hit. Mantle tells Bauer that he sure does. Bauer then informs "The Mick" that he will hit for Dean Chance in the fifth inning.

At the appointed time, Mickey faces Juan Marichal of the San Francisco Giants. In a most abrupt manner, Mickey fans against the high-kicking righthander. Mickey then retires from the game, returns to the locker room, changes back into his clothes, takes the police car back to the Anaheim Airport, gets back into another helicopter, flies to LAX, hops a plane, and flies back to Big D. Even before the game completes its 15 innings of play, Mickey has returned to his golf club at Preston Trails, where he surprises his buddies who only a short time before had seen their friend strike out on television.

| 513. | July 16 | Baltimore | Bill Dillman | | Stadium | 2–1, Balt | 21,695 |
| | | | | | | (in 14) | |

| 514. | July 22 | Detroit | Earl Wilson | Detroit | 11–4 ,Det | 25,700 |
| | | | | | | (18,439 pd.) |

Mickey's third-inning, solo bash soars into the upper deck of the right field grandstand, which ties him for eighth place with Johnny Mize on the all-time list for home runs hit by left-handed batters. Before connecting on this particular home run, Mantle had struck out six straight times. The Yankee loss is their sixth in a row, permitting the Bombers to slip into 10th place in the standings.

| 515. | July 25 | Minn. | Jim Kaat(LH) | Stadium(n) | 1–1,tie | 12,320 |
| | | | with rain postponement coming with two outs in the ninth | | | |

inning

Mickey pounds out a prodigious, 450-foot blast over the left-center auxiliary scoreboard which lands 12 rows deep into the distant left-center bleachers. In the 44-year history of the magnificent old ballyard, Mantle's long wallop represents the 19th time that a "tape-measure shot" such as "The Mick's" has reached the distant left-center field bleachers. Mantle has accomplished this four separate times. Later this year, the rainout will be completed with the Yankees winning the game. In this year, with the miracle finish for the Boston Red Sox, the Minnesota Twins will conclude one game behind the Crimson Hose.

July 26, 1967: In the 29th-longest game in the history of the American League, the Yankees lose in 18 innings to the Minnesota Twins, 3–2, in the second game of a twinight doubleheader. Mickey goes 0-for-6. The New York Yankees had taken the second game and split the twin bill played this day before 21,927.

| 516. | Aug. 7 | California | Minnie Rojas | L.A.(n) | 8–4, Cal | 17,836 |

Mickey powers a towering shot to left-center field, which gives the Yankees a 4–1 lead that the Yanks fail to hold.

August 29, 1967: In the eighth-longest game ever played in AL history to date, the Yankees play the Boston Red Sox before 40,314 persevering Bronx boosters in a 20-inning contest in the second game of a twinight doubleheader. The Yankees win, 4–3, after having dropped the opener, 2–1. Mickey does not make an appearance in either game.

| 517. | Sept. 2 | Wash. | Bob Priddy | Stadium(n) | 2–1, NY | 29,155 |

On a 3–2 pitch, Mickey makes the most of his appearance in the game by belting an outside pitch for a pinch-hit, game-winning home run that carries deep into the lower stands of the right field grandstand.

| 518. | Sept. 3 | Wash. | Dick Bosman | Stadium | 6–3, Wash | 14,828 |

THE 1967 NEW YORK YANKEES

Ninth Place: with a 72–90 record under Manager Ralph Houk.

Yankee Stadium attendance: 1,141,714

MICKEY MANTLE'S 1967 HITTING RECORD

G	AB	R	H	2B	3B	HR	HR%	RBI	SA	BB	SO	SB	AVE.
144	440	63	108	17	0	22	5.0	55	.434	107	113	1	.245

In 1967, Mickey Mantle hit .245 while the major leagues averaged .243 with both leagues scoring an average 7.54 runs per game and both leagues hitting 1.42 home runs per contest. During the 144 games that Mickey Mantle appeared in 1967, he played at first base 131 times as well as appeared in 13 games as a pinch-hitter.

Mickey's 1967 Salary: $100,000

Number of Games in Which Mantle Homered: 21

Winning Record When Mickey Mantle Homered: 9–11 and one tie, a winning percentage of .450

THE 1968 REGULAR SEASON

18 HOME RUNS

H.R.#	DATE	OPPONENT	PITCHER	SITE	SCORE	ATTND.
519.	Apr. 18	Cal.	Jim McGlothlin	L.A.(n)	6–1, NY	11,170

Mantle's game-winning shot is powered over the 406-foot sign in center field. It produces the first two Yankee runs in the 6–1 triumph. Mickey strains a tendon in his right knee on April 21st which puts him out of action for one day.

| 520. | Apr. 24 | Oak. | Jim Nash | Oak.(n) | 4–3, Oak (in 11) | 12,536 |
| 521. | Apr. 26 | Detroit | Earl Wilson | Stadium(n) | 5–0, NY | 17,116 |

Mantle powers the ball into the upper deck of the right field grandstand. His towering, two-run drive ends the scoring in the game and ignites a roaring ovation for the

"Switcher". This particular roundtripper ties the Mick with Ted Williams on the all-time home run list with 521 career home runs.

| 522. | May 6 | Cle. | Sam McDowell(LH) | Stadium(n) | 3–2, Cle | 6,237 |

Mickey drives the ball to the opposite field, reaching the lower right field seats. This particular home run moves Mickey past Ted Williams on the all-time list for career home runs.

| 523. | May 30 (first game) | Wash. | Joe Coleman | Stadium | 13–4, NY | 28,197 |

The last time that Mantle faced Coleman, at D.C. Stadium, the Senator righthander had struck out Mickey four straight times. On this day, it is Mickey's turn to show his stuff in this case, a home run against the Washington righthander.

| 524. | May 30 (first game) | Wash. | Bob Humphreys | Stadium | 13–4, NY | 28,197 |

Mickey goes 5-for-5 for the third time in his career, including two home runs, a double, two singles, three runs scored, and five RBIs. For the 45th time in his career, Mickey Mantle has poled two home runs in the same game. The second long-range poke proves to be another game-winner.

| 525. | June 7 (second game) | Cal. | Jim McGlothlin | Stadium(tn) | 8–4, Cal | 19,791 |

On a day when the nation is mourning the fallen figure of the assassinated Robert F. Kennedy—who is lying in state this very day at St. Patrick's Cathedral—the Yankees go ahead with their game against the visiting Angels. Mickey homers for two runs in the first frame in an eventual loss to the California nine.

| 526. | June 11 | Chi. | Joel Horlen | Stadium(n) | 9–5, Chi | 4,825 |

Mantle propels the ball into the right field grandstand.

| 527. | June 16 | Cal. | Clyde Wright(LH) | Cal. | 4–3, NY | 22,176 |

Mickey's long home run, the final game-winning home run of his career, his 118th, sails high and far into the parking lot in left field, giving the Yankees the victory.

| 528. | June 22 | Minn. | Jim Kaat(LH) | Minn. | 5–2, NY | 21,340 |
| 529. | June 29 (first game) | Oak. | John "Blue Moon" Odom | Stadium(tn) | 5–4, NY | 21,434 |

In the second contest, Mickey pinch-hits a double to the furthest reaches of the center field pasture, some ten feet in front of the monuments. It scores the eventual winning run.

THE 1968 ALL-STAR GAME

ASTRODOME IN HOUSTON, TEXAS
JULY 9

Playing the midsummer classic in the Astrodome, Willie "Stretch" McCovey of the San Francisco Giants hits into a double play while teammate Willie Mays crosses the plate with the winning run of the 39th All-Star Game, the solitary run scored in the contest. It is the first All-Star Game ever to be played indoors and the first 1–0 decision in the history of the game's existence. It also stands as the only All-Star Game in history in which no ballplayer will knock in a run. With 48,321 cheering Texans filling the grandstands, Mantle comes to the plate to pinch-hit for Sam McDowell. Mickey fans against right-handed fireballer Tom Seaver of the New York Mets.

July 20, 1968: At Yankee Stadium on "Bat Day," before 38,224 excited Bronx rooters, the hobbling Mickey Mantle is now manning the first-base position as the Bombers take on the visiting Cleveland Indians. The leadoff batter for the Cleveland Indians is second baseman Dave Nelson, who pushes a bunt to the first base side of the mound. After six knee operations, the daily wear-and-tear on his legs for 17 and a half years, an intense, after-hours party life, and the march of time on his injury-wracked body, Mickey attempts to make the play against the first-year speedster. Nelson beats out the hit, primarily on the inadequate coverage provided by the lead-footed, sluggish Mantle, whose legs do not respond. As Nelson speeds over the bag unchallenged and races up the right field foul line, the young second baseman is thrilled to death that he, on this vaunted field, was able to make his drag bunt work. And now, returning to the bag, he is met halfway back to first base by the Indian first base coach. Though not particularly frantic in his tones, the coach gently informs the excited rookie that there is an unwritten rule in the league not to make Mickey look bad or take advantage of his physical incapacities like laying down a bunt that he would have to cover. It is done "out of reverence for him."

The wide-eyed rookie returns to the base, where Mickey has taken his position, to hold him close to the bag. As an awe-filled Nelson stands next to his boyhood idol, he is wary that Mantle may have been offended by his tactic. Nelson steals a glance at Mickey's arms which, to him, look like "tree trunks." Nelson tells himself, "Man, he's gonna pinch my head off." Mantle walks over to the bag to prepare to hold Nelson closer to first when he leads off. The apprehensive Nelson then feels a slight pat on his butt by Mantle, who tells the young ballplayer, "Nice bunt, rook." Relieved, and still more than a little awed, the rookie infielder says shyly, "Thanks, Mr. Mantle." Nelson then steals second base, and is moved to third, before scoring on a sacrifice fly. It is all that Luis Tiant, will need as he hurls a three-hit shutout. The Tribe beats the Bombers, 3–0.

After the game, one of the Yankees' key prospects of the future, Thurman Munson, is waiting inside the clubhouse. He had played a minor league contest in the morning as his Binghampton teammates competed in a morning game at Yankee Stadium against the Waterbury nine. Now the young, starry-eyed minor leaguer awaits the end of the game so he can "meet Mr. Mantle."

| 530. | Aug. 10 | Minn. | Jim Merritt(LH) | Stadium | 3–2, Minn | 36,072 |

On this special day, Old Timers' Day at the Stadium, Mickey Mantle poles an opposite-field blow into the right field bleachers.

| 531. | Aug. 10 | Minn. | Jim Merritt(LH) | Stadium | 3–2, Minn | 36,072 |

Mickey connects for a line shot into the lower seats of the left-field grandstand. It is the 46th and final time that Mantle will hit two or more home runs in the same game. Only Babe Ruth and Jimmie Foxx on the inactive list have accounted for more multiple home run games in a career. On the active list, only Willie Mays and Eddie Mathews have surpassed the Mick in coupling home runs in the same contest.

| 532. | Aug. 12 | Cal. | George Brunet(LH) | L.A.(n) | 5–2, NY | 14,520 |

After fouling off one pitch on his foot, Mantle launches a 400-foot, opposite-field home run over right-center field at Anaheim Stadium.

| 533. | Aug. 15 | Oak. | John "Blue Moon" Odom | Oak.(n) | 4–3, NY | 9,197 |
| 534. | Aug. 22 | Minn. | Jim Merritt(LH) | Minn. | 3–1, Minn | 15,898 |

Mickey swats a pinch-hit home run in the ninth inning which ties the legendary Jimmie Foxx with 534 home runs. Mantle's clout provides the Yankees with their single run in the game as the Minnesota southpaw, Jim Merritt, yields a mere three hits to the traveling Bombers.

August 23, 1968: As 33,880 spectators in the Bronx watch, the Yankees beat the visiting Detroit Tigers, 2–1, in the first game of a twin bill. Mickey goes 0-for-3 in the game. The second game proves to be the 17th-longest game ever played in American League history to date, going 19 innings when the Yankees play the second tilt. The Yankees play the Detroit Tigers to a tie. Mickey has pinch-hit and singled, but will not figure in the scoring. In the highlight of the game, Yankee reliever Lindy McDaniel would retire 21 Detroit Tiger batters in a row, with six strikeouts. In his last three-relief pitching appearances, McDaniel has retired 30 straight batters. The game ends at 1:07 A.M. with 33,880 fans going home disappointed. Mantle will not play in the marathon game.

September 17, 1968: The Detroit Tigers clinch the pennant when they beat the visiting Yankees before 46,512 Motor City maniacs. Don Wert strokes a bases-loaded single with two outs in the bottom of the ninth inning. Wert's safety scores Al Kaline with the run that beats the New York Yankees, 2–1. Joe Sparma starts and completes the game, goes nine frames, and yields a mere five hits. Mantle goes 1-for-4. Mickey's home run output at Briggs Stadium, later renamed Tiger Stadium, has been nothing short of spectacular. In all, Mickey Mantle has pounded out prodigious home runs which, in right field alone, have borne witness to three separate occasions when Number Seven hit the roof and four other times when he cleared the roof altogether.

| 535. | Sept. 19 | Detroit | Denny McLain | Detroit | 6–2, Det. | 9,063 |

Facing 30-game winner Denny McLain of the Detroit Tigers, Mickey Mantle approaches the plate in the eighth inning for his last career at-bat at Tiger Stadium, a rich haven for some of Mantle's most memorable "tape-measure" shots. Calling "Time out," McLain asks catcher Jim Price to join him for a brief conference. The exchange between catcher and pitcher takes place five or six feet away from home plate. With the game apparently out of reach, McLain tells Price that he is going to give Mantle a good pitch to hit since this could be Mantle's last plate appearance in the Motor City. In all Mickey Mantle has powered balls onto the roof three separate times. Four other times he cleared the 110-foot-high right field roof completely, including one that was hit from the right-hand side of the plate to the opposite field, but foul.

Meanwhile, Mantle has been eavesdropping on the conversation between this year's best pitcher and his backstop. When Price returns to his place behind the plate, Mantle asks him whether he heard McLain right. Price tells Mickey that McLain has decided not to work on the Yankee slugger, but only to serve up fast balls. Still unsure that this ploy might not be a trick, Mantle takes a pitch for a strike over the heart of the plate. Nursing a big lead, McLain looks at Mantle quizzically as if to ask, "Well?" Now taking McLain at his word, Mickey waits for the next pitch: a belt-high fast ball over the center of the plate. Mantle fouls it off. Then, on the next pitch, McLain grooves up another perfect strike over the plate that Mantle launches into the upper-deck grandstand in right field.

This longball is Mantle's 535th career home run and permits him to pass Jimmie Foxx on the all-time career home run list. Mickey will never catch Babe Ruth because of his infirmities, and Willie Mays is still adding home runs to his own second-place total, but "Mutt's Boy" passes everyone else in the history of the game at hitting home runs—and every one of them as a Yankee. As Mickey rounds the bases, he characteristically keeps his head down, almost seeming embarrassed, afraid someone may think he is bragging or showboating, circling second and proceeding towards third base. It is evident that the playing days of this legendary slugger are nearing their end as Mickey limps through his circuitous tour. When Mantle rounds third, he looks over at McLain who has walked slightly over towards the third-base line from the pitcher's mound. Mickey gazes at McLain as he heads for home; McLain smiles and winks. Mickey smiles back and shyly aims his gaze back towards the ground that he is covering. After the game, Mantle tells reporters, "McLain has made a fan of me for life."

After Mantle crosses the plate, the next Yankee batter is first baseman Joe Pepitone who has witnessed the courtesy that McLain has accorded Mantle. Pepitone signals out to McLain, holding his extended bare hand over the plate, as if to say, "I'd like mine here." After motioning for a grooved duplicate for himself, Pepitone awaits his pitch from McLain. Winding up and delivering, this year's Cy Young Award Winner lets the next pitch fly. The speeding pitch sails in at Pepitone's coconut head, knocking the playful Pepitone down, forcing the cocky first baseman to an ignominious, "every man for himself," bail-out humility, separating Pepi's head from his helmet and his feet from the earth. McLain's message is received.

McLain wins his 31st game and the Tigers win, 6–2. In the Tiger clubhouse, clamoring reporters want to know whether McLain served the ball up to the fabled slugger on purpose. After denying any such thing, the Tiger righthander will terminate his reply by saying, "But that Mantle—he was my idol." As for Denny McLain, the Tiger hurler becomes, as of this writing, the last pitcher to win 30 games in a single year since Dizzy Dean some 34 years before in the National League and Lefty Grove in the American League in 1930.

| 536. | Sept. 20 | Boston | Jim Lonborg | Stadium(n) | 4–3, Bos | 15,737 |

Mickey Mantle's final home run is manifested as a whistling, curving, top-spinning line drive that carries into Yankee Stadium's right field bleachers for the last time. Pitcher Lonborg is sporting a new Boston Red Sox patch on his ballcap: a white-bordered, red-colored "B" on a solid navy blue cap. Coming as it does, at Yankee Stadium, Mickey's final longball also represents the last of the most lifetime home runs, 266, ever hit by a single player in Yankee Stadium. Mickey Mantle, the "Commerce Comet," now just a shooting star about to disintegrate before its burning brilliance extinguishes itself, has beaten Babe Ruth by four, the number of home runs hit in "The House that Ruth Built." Only Mel Ott at the Polo Grounds (323) and Ernie Banks at Wrigley Field (290) has homered more in one ballyard than

Mickey Mantle has pounded out at Yankee Stadium. Nor has any single slugger in American League history ever hit more home runs in a single ballpark than has the Mick at the Stadium. With respect to the All-Time Home Run list, only Babe Ruth with 714 home runs and Willie Mays with 587 home runs have, to date, hit more total home runs in their respective careers. In a fascinating sidelight, another Hall-of-Famer-to-be, Boston's Carl Yastrzemski, also poles a home run in this contest.

Mantle's baseball abilities have not waned all that much. His crippled legs, however are another matter. Four years from this point in time, the eve of his imminent retirement, Roger Kahn, a prince of the printed word, will be interviewing Mantle in his Dallas home when the retired slugger will show him a tether-ball contraption that Mickey was marketing in his name. The machine is a pitching machine that a batter can set up against. Its mechinations can make adjustments in incremental speeds of more than 90 miles per hour. Taking his place in a batting box for a prolonged series of tethered pitches, Mantle will flail at the ball whizzing by at 90 miles per hour and never miss the ball. Inspired by the spectacle of the batting eye and hitting power of Mickey Mantle, Kahn writes in his memoirs, *Memories of Summer*: "...his batting eye...was phenominal. That and his power. He swung so hard that each swing made him grunt. He hit for ten minutes and never missed. I had never seen anybody swing so hard. As best I could tell, some power came up from the battered legs, but most seemed to flow out of the upper body and the mighty arms and wrists. Swing. Crack. Grunt. His timing meshed arm strength and wrist strength and hand strength into an instant of phenomenally violent contact with the baseball. Again and again and again. It was only 68 degrees, but he was sweating when he limped away. I wanted to cheer."

September 27, 1968: At Fenway Park, facing Red Sox right-hander Lee Stange, Mickey Mantle comes to the dish for the final plate appearance of his storied career. Appearing in his final game, the Mick is batting left-handed when he lifts the ball to left field for an easy putout. In a sterling career, underscored by the relentless threat of a career-ending injury and the constant underpinnings of excruciating pain, it is Mickey Mantle's final farewell to baseball. Gone, but never forgotten.

THE 1968 NEW YORK YANKEES

Fifth Place: with a 83–79 record under Manager Ralph Houk

Yankee Stadium Attendance: 1,125,124

MICKEY MANTLE'S 1968 HITTING RECORD

G	AB	R	H	2B	3B	HR	HR%	RBI	SA	BB	SO	SB	AVE.
144	435	57	103	14	1	18	4.1	54	.398	106	97	6	.237

In 1968, Mickey Mantle hit .237 while the major leagues averaged .236 with both leagues scoring an average 6.84 runs per game and both leagues hitting 1.23 home runs per contest. During the 144 games that Mickey Mantle appeared in 1968, he played at first base 131 times as well as appeared in 13 games as a pinchhitter.

Mickey's 1968 Salary: $100,000

Injuries or Operations: In his career, Mickey Mantle had suffered through and survived six knee operations, which would eventually lead to his contracting Hepatitis C. This latter condition would contribute, in concert, to a serious drinking problem that would not become full-blown alcoholism until after his playing years were behind him. This deadly combination of physiological dynamics would lead to the destruction of his liver and the onset of cancer, the ultimate cause of his death. But when he played, only the injuries could slow him down. They represented setbacks, but they did not defeat him.

To the former Yankee pitching coach Jim Turner, the underlying greatness to Mickey's bountiful talents as a ballplayer lay actually in his tremendous reservoir of courage. The wise and venerable Turner, a nine-year veteran of the American League pitching campaigns which ended with the Yankees, and with just as many years as their pitching coach, remembers, "It's phenomenal that Mickey played in more than 2,400 major league games; he did it on heart. No athlete I've ever known had more competitive fire than Mantle. Any day, any inning, he put everything he could summon into every effort. He just didn't know any other way."

Number of Games in Which Mantle Homered: 16

Winning Record When Mickey Mantle Homered: 8–8 and one tie, a winning percentage of .500

EPILOGUE

Mickey Charles Mantle
("The Commerce Comet")
Born: October 20,1931, in Spavinaw, Oklahoma
Member of the New York Yankees, 1951–1968
Inducted into Baseball Hall of Fame on August 10, 1974
Died: August 13, 1995, in Dallas, Texas

With his own innate shyness and undeniable reserve, Mickey always seemed to have a sense of proportion about himself in the world of major league baseball. But the truth is, every young boy in Baby Boomer America in the Fifties and early Sixties dreamed of being the small-town kid who went to the big leagues to play for a team that played in the World Series. Indeed, Mickey Mantle lived that dream. Indeed, every young boy wanted to be the Mickey Mantle of the booming home runs and his constant, scintillating presence in the crisp autumn days of World Series glory. Throughout the Fifties and the early Sixties, with respect to baseball-world championships, it was the New York Yankees against the best of the National League; and Mickey Mantle *was* the New York Yankees.

Still, Mickey Mantle had a sense of perspective. He would spend the rest of his life telling his listeners that he walked 1,734 times during his career. He also pointed out the fact that he struck out 1,710 times. Mickey would tell amused audiences that if one could count the number of at-bats in a complete season, and accepted that as being at or around 550 at-bats, this would mean, in effect, that for seven years in the majors he never hit the ball. Such is the game of baseball. But what he did with the rest of his career was more than magnificent, it was unprecedented. Without question, no one who ever made it to the Hall of Fame was more battered or more wracked up than Mickey Mantle, for all of the glories he produced.

Many believe that Babe Ruth, Henry Aaron, and Mickey Mantle have been baseball's greatest hitters—left-handed, right-handed, and switch-hitting. Indeed, there are common threads that weave their way through the respective glittering careers of these three superstars. All were teenagers when they began their professional baseball careers. All were poor kids growing up. All had an abiding love of the game. And all did things that were rarely, if ever, duplicated. All became their sport's principal superstars of their time. And all, when at the top of their game, would bring ultimately, a commensurate credit to the National Pastime. Another corollary linking these three legends together for all time was the universally accepted acknowledgment that all were the best there ever was when they were at their best. For Mickey Mantle, however, when it came to be that his best was not good enough, the time had come for him to go.

On March 1, 1969 (the author's 22nd birthday), Mickey Mantle held a brief press conference in Fort Lauderdale, Florida, at the Yankee training camp, to announce to the members of the media that it was all over. Mickey would tell the press, "I just can't play anymore. I don't hit the ball when I need to. I can't steal second when I need to. I can't go from first to third or score from second on base hits when I need to. I just think it's time to quit trying."

Later that year, on June 8, 1969, a bright and sunny spring day at Yankee Stadium, before a massive throng of 61,157 paying patrons, the Golden Boy of the Golden Age of Baseball bowed out of the game. Sports journalists reported that "The Commerce Comet" from Oklahoma has officially called it quits. Confronting the huge crowd, Mickey Mantle said farewell to the baseball-mad bevies of boosters in the history-saturated Bronx.

Each of the various passages of Mickey's Yankee career were represented liberally by the personalities and teammates who had been with him along the way through his years of glory and pain. In attendance on the field, to mark this great occasion, the master of ceremonies, the unparalleled voice of the Yankees for so long, Mel Allen, who introduced Mickey and his extended baseball family to the crowd. The gathered ex-ballplayers and former executives who answered Allen's roll call of honor stood in a clutch behind Mantle, fitted in tailored suits, looking fit and tanned. Present were former Yankee General Manager George Weiss, and former managers Harry Craft and George Selkirk, two of Mickey's minor league tutors. Also in attendance was scout Tom Greenwade who had discovered "The Kid" in the northeastern Oklahoma mining quarries. Of course, former teammate and current Met player Yogi Berra has showed up to honor his friend, having flown in from San Diego. Also present was Whitey Ford, his running buddy in the early days and his friend for life. Former Manager Ralph Houk is also there, as well as 12 of his teammates over the years.

The roster of honored invitees included Joe DiMaggio who would commemorate the day with his presentation to Mickey of his retired Number Seven. The "Yankee Clipper" also announced that a plaque with Mickey's likeness would be adorning the center field wall alongside his own. Mickey himself would also present DiMaggio with his center field plaque. Kiddingly, but characteristically, Mickey suggested that Joe D's should perhaps be hung a little higher than his own. Other teammates and the years they shared with Mickey were also gathered for the ceremony, milling about in the middle of the vast "House That Ruth Built." They included those teammates representing particular pennant teams over the years: Eddie Lopat, Yogi Berra, and Joe DiMaggio of the 1951 Yankees, Gene Woodling of the 1952 Yankees, Joe Collins of the 1953 Yankees, Phil Rizzuto of the 1955 Yankees, Jerry Coleman of the 1956 Yankees, Gil McDougald of the 1957 Yankees, Whitey Ford of the 1958 Yankees, Bobby Richardson of the 1960 Yankees, Elston Howard of the 1961 Yankees, Tom Tresh of the 1962 Yankees, Joe Pepitone of the 1963 Yankees, and Mel Stottlemeyer of the 1964 roster—the last pennant-winning Yankee ballclub of the Mickey Mantle Era. It was a day filled with glorious memories and images, so thick and pervasive under the green-coppered roof in the Bronx that Mickey would have to brush them away with his hand.

Finally, it was Mickey's turn to speak. Approaching the battery of microphones and television cameras, Mickey faced the crowd that filled all of the great upper decks, the mezzanine areas, and the grandstands throughout the great ballyard. Gathering his wits, Mickey addressed the fans who had pour out their love for "The Mick." Touchingly sincere, Mickey said in his easy Oklahoma drawl, "When I walked into the stadium 18 years ago, I guess I felt the same way I feel now. I can't describe it. I just want to say that playing 18 years in Yankee Stadium for you folks is the best thing that could ever happen to a ballplayer. Now having my number join 3, 4, and 5 kind of tops everything."

Yankee Stadium exploded. The applause at this point was deafening as its echoes rebounded and resounded around the rafters of the magnificent ballyard with its hallowed girders and elegant filigreed roof. Speaking once more, Mickey added, "I never knew how a man who knew he was going to die could say he was the luckiest man in the world. I think now I know what Lou Gehrig meant." After more waves of admiration wash down on him, Mickey closed his remarks by saying, "This is a great day for my wife, my four boys and my family. I just wish my father could have been here. I'll never forget this. Thank you all. God bless you and thank you very much."

For eight minutes, Mickey Charles Mantle received the love and adulation of the great mass of gathered Yankee Stadium well-wishers. Mickey would take a final tour of the great ballpark in one of the Yankee golf carts with an especially marked New York license plate marked "MM * 7."

In the vast expanse these days of that which used to be Yankee Stadium's "Death Valley," the roaming grounds of Joe DiMaggio and Mickey Mantle situated beyond the modern-day shortened fences, there lies a bemedalled set of baseball monuments to Yankee immortals. Among them are Babe Ruth, Lou Gehrig, Joe DiMaggio, Thurman Munson, Phil Rizzuto, Managers Miller Huggins, Joe McCarthy, Casey Stengel, and Billy Martin. There are also the Hall-of-Fame likenesses of executives Edward Barrow and Jacob Ruppert. And—there is a plaque for "Mutt's" boy, the son of an Oklahoma miner: Mickey Charles Mantle.

POSTSCRIPT ON COURAGE AND PAIN

There are all kinds of courage. There are all kinds of heroes. There is the courage to face crippling pain with uncomplaining grace, while pursuing athletic excellence. And there is the courage to abandon caution and to imperil oneself for the sake of others. Mickey Mantle was the embodiment of these types of courage.

During his career, Mickey Charles Mantle could not pass an Army physical because of the osteomylitis he contracted in high school. This bone disease left a permanent deformation in his leg, a gap in his left leg that was without some of the bone normally present between one's ankle and leg. Mickey's litany of medical conditions, which he had to deal with while generating a Hall-of-Fame career in major league baseball, were legion.

Mickey had knee surgery in 1951. The next year he coped with a horribly swollen knee, requiring the regular draining of fluid from the puffy, damaged area. In the year following, 1953, Mickey sprained his left knee, tore ligaments in his right knee, and received off-season surgery on the damaged left knee to remove a piece of torn cartilage.

Meanwhile, from 1954 onward, permanent damage had caused an unrecoverable 5 to 10 percent efficiency in his right knee. His problems and pain would continue with his right knee in 1954, the same year that he had a cyst removed. In 1955, he experienced a severe muscle tear in his back. In that year, Mantle also had pulled a lateral ligament behind his right knee. In 1956, the year of the Triple Crown, he was relatively injury-free, only damaging his instep from having a foul ball slam into it. But he also strained lateral ligaments behind his right knee and suffered through a slight neck injury, a pulled left groin muscle, and a tonsillectomy.

In 1957, Mickey incurred a severe shin injury when he accidentally slammed a golf club against his leg, temporarily crippling himself. Meanwhile, ongoing problems with his right knee kept Mantle operating at less than 100 percent. Capping this year, in the 1957 World Series, Mantle's collision with Red Schoendienst left his right shoulder permanently diminished for the rest of his career. Mantle's swing, due to the ever-present pain, was thereafter affected for the duration of the 11 years he had left to play baseball. He later admitted that he never had the power swinging from the left-hand side of the plate that he possesed before 1957.

In 1958, it would all begin again when the ailing slugger had to deal with painful radiation treatments on his right shoulder, a shoulder that gave him constant pain when batting left-handed. In 1959, with the New Year came a new set of medical problems. Mickey would break his finger when he took a batting-practice pitch flush against his right forefinger, chipping a bone inside it. Mickey would also sprain his right ankle and twist his shoulder out of place. He would miss ten games following an injury to his right thigh. The next year, 1960, Mickey would even get slugged in the jaw by a fan as he attempted to leave the field following a Yankee Stadium doubleheader. The fan's assault loosened his teeth and caused his jaw to swell. Later, his right knee became a source of pain so intense that he would miss playing the last two weeks in June.

In 1961, another great year, Mickey pulled a muscle in his forearm that would turn his arm a swollen purple. In late September, Mantle would receive a steroid treatment from a jet-set quack that became infected, necessitating immediate surgery to remove the steroids from his hip. Mickey's deteriorated state required him to suffer through a half-dollar-sized hole in his hip about two to three inches deep. The painful hip surgery would incapacitate him for a final run at Babe Ruth's homer record and the 1961 World Series.

Additional highlights of Mantle's medical history continued early in the 1962 season, when, while running out a hard-hit infield smash, Mickey would tear an adductor muscle in his right thigh that combined to tear ligaments and cartilage from his left knee, the good knee—all on the same play. The multiple injuries cost him a month of games. Later the same year, Mickey would wrench the same knee. Furthermore, in 1962, Mickey missed a week of play with an abdominal muscle pull. The next year, 1963, there was more of the same sad tale of physical woe when Mickey would injure the right side of his rib cage. Later, a more substantial threat occurred when Mantle would break a bone on the instep of his left foot. He also suffered, this year, from loosened cartilage and ligaments in his left knee. Again, as a result of one bad play, Mickey ended up in a collision with a fence while chasing a Brooks Robinson home run. The injury would force his absence from the lineup for two months of games.

In the year that followed—the year of his final World Series participation—the pain would start at the beginning of the year. In early 1964, there was off-season surgery on his left knee. During the season, after surviving a series of early-season muscle pulls, Mantle would re-injure his left knee in the dog days of August. In the following year, 1965, Mickey would miss eight days of action for nagging leg ailments, caused by banging his left leg hard into a bag during a bad slide into second. Later the same year, Mantle would suffer a pulled hamstring muscle, causing him to miss 18 games. A month after that, he re-injured his knee. The year would also subject the suffering Mantle to painful bouts with his right shoulder and right elbow.

The year after, 1966, Mantle missed 11 games due to pulling a muscle in his left thigh. Then, in early July, Mantle would miss the All-Star Game because of another hamstring pull. Next, he missed 12 days because of another injury to his knee; then he broke a toe and suffered serious injury to a finger. Finally, in 1968, his last year in baseball, barely able to hobble, let alone run, Mantle strained a tendon in his right knee, missing one game.

When the smoke to his career had cleared, Mickey had been subjected to six knee operations. One tragic repercussion from these unwanted but necessary surgeries was his contracting Hepatitis C. But to Mickey Mantle pain had become a constant companion.

Besides the pain that had its origins in the physical realm, Mickey also suffered through emotional pain, the kind that comes from living under the specter of a medical curse, the ever-threatening Hodgkin's disease. Dealing with all of this pain and being a macho kind of guy in a macho age that winked at such things as all-night binges of hard-drinking, late hours, and easy women who asked nothing in return, Mickey fell into an unhealthful routine.

The scars of his emotional pain stemmed from his father's tragically premature death as well as that of his son, Billy's, to Hodgkin's disease. Mickey fully expected himself to also be a victim and, consequently, he would attempt to wash away his troubles with drink. He would later admit that his drinking problem did not really take control of his life until after his playing days were over. But then that insidious "disease," fueled by his physical and emotional strains, and by the guilt over the shortcomings he felt he demonstrated as both a husband and a father, would take over his life with a vengeance, slamming into his system like an incessant hammer on the anvil of his being.

Indeed, after his playing days were over, Mickey became a full-blown alcoholic. It was the alcoholism that would eventually destroy his liver. And despite a therapeutic, albeit late, intervention at the Betty Ford Clinic, the years of alcoholism took their toll on the liver of the courageous Mantle, and eventually transformed into cancer. Although Mickey would remain sober the last 18 months of his life, the internal damage done was irreversible. It would lead to an organ transplant and the shopcking discovery of an extremely aggressive cancer that would soon take his life. But once again, Mickey's courage surfaced and he took the precious little time left to him, first to establish an organ transplant foundation and, second, to confront the nation: to brave the slings and arrows, if not outright condemnation, of a judgmental country that was, by and large, ignorant of his desperate medical plight.

On July 11, 1995, looking emaciated and ravaged by the disease that would soon claim his life, Mickey Mantle held a press conference that would launch his foundation and give him the opportunity to thank the thousands of fans of all ages who had sent him letters wishing him a quick recovery. In the conference, a chipper but weakened Mickey addressed the youth of America and denounced his drinking, admonishing himself for his laxity in taking care of himself. He ridiculed himself as one of the icons of his age and implored young people not to follow his example. As for being a role model, the always frank and honest Mickey said he was not that.

The courage that had been rooted in his soul to combat all of the physical pain that impeded his potential as a great ballplayer—that is, the same courage he brought to the baseball diamond. It was also the same kind that led him to face the nation, humble himself, and speak to the merits of clean living and self-respect. With class and dignity, "The Mick," for whom everybody seemed to feel a kinship, bid farewell to the millions of his baseball fans for the last time, addressing their children, at his own expense and at the cost of his own image, on the evils of excessive drinking and reckless behavior.

Thirty-three days later, the legendary Mickey Mantle would be dead, leaving a legacy of not only baseball immortality, but of the selflessness of his own national abasement. For one final time, Mickey Mantle, who had been the centerpiece of a historically showcased big-league baseball team, who had been the "stand-up guy" for 12 American League championship teams, and who had been a magnificent New York Yankee, was once again—for millions of Americans—an undeniable hero. Only this time, he was a hero off the playing field.

THE APPENDICES

APPENDIX I.
YANKEE ERAS

THE LIVELY BALL ERA AND POST 1920 to 1968

THE "BABE" RUTH ERA ("Murderers' Row")

The Yankee teams of the "Babe Ruth Era" (1920 to1934).

— "Babe" Ruth (1920-1934)—667 winning percentage (10 pennants in 15 years and 4 World Championships; a .400 winning percentage).

    Total Ruthian record—1405 wins and 895 losses; a .611 winning percentage.

—Lou Gehrig (1923-1939)—529 winning percentage (9 pennants in 17 years and 8 World Championships; an .889 winning percentage).

    Total Gehrig record—1616 wins and 982 losses; a .622 winning percentage.

THE JOE DIMAGGIO ERA ("The Bronx Bombers")

The Yankee teams of the "Joe DiMaggio Era" (1936-1942,1946-1951).

—Joe DiMaggio (1936-1942,1946-1951)—a .769 winning percentage (10 pennants in 13 years and 9 World Championships a .900 winning percentage in Series titles).

    Total DiMaggio record—1272 wins and 724 losses; a .637 winning percentage.

—Bill Dickey (1928-1943,1946)—647 winning percentage (11 pennants in 17 years and 8 World Championships; a .727 winning percentage in Series titles).

    Total Dickey record—1636 wins and 966 losses; a .629 winning percentage.

THE MICKEY MANTLE ERA ("The Last Great Yankee")

The Yankee teams of the "Mickey Mantle Era" (1951-1968).

—Mickey Mantle (1951-1968)—722 winning percentage (12 pennants in 18 years and 8 World Championships; a .727 winning percentage in Series titles).

    Total Mantle record-1664 wins and 1165 losses; a .588 winning percentage.

—"Yogi" Berra (1946-1963)—-737 winning percentage (14 pennants in 18 years and 10 World Championships; a .714 winning percentage in Series titles).

    Total record—1736 wins and 1056 losses; a .622 winning percentage.

RANKINGS OF ERA NAMESAKES AND MAINSTAYS

Regular Season

1. Joe DiMaggio   (.769 winning percentage).

2. Bill Dickey   (.629 winning percentage).

3. Yogi Berra   (.622 winning percentage).

4. Babe Ruth   (.611 winning percentage).

5. Mickey Mantle (.588 winning percentage).

6. Lou Gehrig   (.529 winning percentage).

World Series Games

1. Joe DiMaggio   (.900 winning percentage)

2. Lou Gehrig   (.889 winning percentage)

3. Mickey Mantle (.727 winning percentage)

4. Bill Dickey   (.727 winning percentage)

5. Yogi Berra   (.714 winning percentage)

6. Babe Ruth   (.400 winning percentage)

Mickey Mantle was the Most Feared Batter in the American League in the Fifties and Sixties and the greatest switch-hitter in the history of the game.

APPENDIX II.
THE MAJOR LEAGUE RECORD OF MICKEY MANTLE OF
THE NEW YORK YANKEES (1951-1968)

Years Played:	18
Games Played:	2,401
At-Bats:	8,102
Runs:	1,677
Hits:	2,415
Doubles:	344
Triples:	72
Home Runs:	536 (eighth place all-time)

At Yankee Stadium:	266

187 left-handed home runs and 79 right-handed home runs

On-the-Road:	270

183 left-handed home runs and 87 right-handed home runs

At the time of his retirement, only Babe Ruth and Willie Mays had collected more home runs in their respective careers. Currently, Mantle is eighth place on the all-time list for home runs.

Home Run Percentage:	6.6% (sixth place all-time)
Runs Batted In:	1,509
Slugging Average:	.557
Base on Balls:	1,734

At the time of his retirement, only Babe Ruth and Ted Williams attained more bases on balls during their respective careers. Currently, Mantle is fifth place on the all-time list for walks.

Strikeouts:	1,710 (ninth place, all-time)
Stolen Bases:	153
Multiple Home Run Games:	46
Both Sides of Plate/Game:	0
Grand Slam Home Runs:	10
Game-Winning Home Runs:	118
Pinch-Hit Appearances:	106
Pinch-Hits:	25
Batting Average:	.298

Mickey Mantle batted over .300 during 10 different seasons.

APPENDIX III.
THE HOME RUN PROFILE
OF MICKEY MANTLE

World Series Home Runs

Ebbets Field (Brooklyn)		5
County Stadium (Milwaukee)		3
Forbes Field (Pittsburgh)		2
Dodger Stadium (Los Angeles)		1
Sportsman's Park (St. Louis)		2
Yankee Stadium (New York)		5
	Total:	18

All-Star Game Home Runs

County Stadium (Milwaukee)		1
Griffith Stadium (Washington D.C.)		1
	Total	2

Regular Season Home Runs

—Right-handed Home Runs		164
—Left-Handed Home Runs		372
—Yankee Stadium Home Runs		266
—On-the-road Home Runs		270
—Home Runs in 278 Day Games		306
—batting righthanded	104	
—batting lefthanded	202	
—Home Runs in 202 Night Games		230
—batting righthanded	60	
—batting lefthanded	170	
—Home Runs in 104 Doubleheaders		125
—batting righthanded	43	
—batting lefthanded	82	

Includes 24 twinight doubleheaders
and 2 day-night games. Mickey also
hit home runs in both ends of a double-

header 11 times in his career.

—Home Runs in 41 Extra Inning Games   44
      —batting righthanded   22
      —batting lefthanded   19
A winning record of 31-10; a
.756 winning percentage.

—Game-Winning Home Runs,   118
including 13 Extra Inning,
Game-Winning home runs

Regular Season Home Runs	536
World Series Home Runs	18
All-Star Game Home Runs	2
Total Major League Home Runs (in all play)	556

A familiar sight in the Bronx. Mickey Charles Mantle hit more home runs, 266, in the "House That Ruth Built" than any player who has ever set foot on its sacred trample.

APPENDIX IV.
MICKEY MANTLE'S WINNING HOME RUN PROFILE

Year	Games in which Mantle Homered		Wins	Losses Winning %
1951	13	11	2	.846
1952	22	4	8	.636
1953	21	15	6	.714
1954	26	21	5	.808
1955	32	27	5	.844
1956	45	30	15	.667

1957	33	20	13	.606
1958	38	26	12	.684
1959	29	19	10	.655
1960	36	28	8	.778
1961	47	39	8	.830
1962	25	18	7	.720
1963	14	11	3	.786
1964	33	25	8	.758
1965	19	12	7	.632
1966	18	11	7	.611
1967	20	9	11	.450
1968	16	8	8	.500

CAREER TOTALS

Years	Total Games	Games Played	Wins w.HRs	Losses	Winning %
18 years	2401	487	344	143	.706

In 18 years of major league play and 2,401 games appearing for the New York Yankees, more games in pinstripes than anyone else in history, Mickey Mantle hit home runs in 20 percent of those contests. In the same number of total Yankee games in which Mickey participated, 14 percent of the time was accentuated by a Mickey Mantle home run in a winning cause.

APPENDIX V.
MICKEY MANTLE IN OCTOBER:
THE WORLD SERIES EXPERIENCE OF
MICKEY MANTLE

The Second-Highest Record of World Series Participation in Baseball History
(1951, 1952, 1953, 1955, 1956, 1957, 1958, 1960, 1961, 1962, 1963, and 1964)

THE WORLD SERIES HITTING RECORD

Year	Opponent	G	AB	H	R	2B	3B	HR	RBI	BB	SO	.BA
1951	vs. New York	2	5	1	1	0	0	0	0	2	1	.200
1952	vs. Brooklyn	7	29	5	10	1	1	2	3	3	4	.345
1953	vs. Brooklyn	6	24	3	5	0	0	2	7	3	8	.208

Year	Opponent	G	AB	H	R	2B	3B	HR	RBI	BB	SO	.BA
1955	vs. Brooklyn	3	10	1	2	0	0	1	1	0	2	.200
1956	vs. Brooklyn	7	24	6	6	1	0	3	4	6	5	.250
1957	vs. Milwaukee	6	19	3	5	0	0	1	2	3	1	.263
1958	vs. Milwaukee	7	24	4	6	0	1	2	3	7	4	.250
1960	vs. Pittsburgh	7	25	8	10	1	0	3	11	8	9	.400
1961	vs. Cincinnati	2	6	0	1	0	0	0	0	0	2	.167
1962	vs. San Francisco	7	25	2	3	1	0	0	0	4	5	.120
1963	vs. Los Angeles	4	15	1	2	1	0	0	1	1	5	.133
1964	vs. St. Louis	7	24	8	8	2	0	3	8	6	8	.333
TOTALS: (12 years)		65	230	42	59	6	2	18	40	43	54	.257

Ebbets Field, the site of Mantle's brush with World Series glory, would be the Flatbush backdrop to five of Mantle's World Series home runs.

APPENDIX VI.
WORLD SERIES RECORDS HELD BY MICKEY MANTLE

The Most World Series Home Runs All-Time: 18 (1951-1964)

The Most World Series with one or more home runs: 9, tied with Yogi Berra (1952, 1953, 1955, 1956, 1957, 1958, 1960, 1963, and 1964)

The Most World Series with two or more home runs: 6 (1952, 1953, 1956, 1958, 1960, and 1964)

The Most World Series with three or more home runs: 3, tied with Babe Ruth. (1956, 1960, and 1964)

The Most Grand Slams in World Series History: 1, tied with 15 others, and the only switch-hitter ever to accomplish this rarest of World Series moments.

The Youngest player ever to hit a home run in World Series Championship competition: On October 6, 1952, the date of his Game Six home run, the Oklahoman kid's first World Series roundtripper, Mickey Mantle is 20 years, 351 days old. This particular World Series record will stand for 44 years until Andrew Jones, age 19, of the Atlanta Braves pounds out his first two home runs during his first World Series game while facing Yankee southpaw Andy Petitte in Yankee Stadium.

The Most World Series Games Played by a Switch-Hitter: 65, (second place all-time to Yogi Berra's 75 games)

The Most World Series RBIs by a Switch-hitter: 40

The Most World Series Games Played by an outfielder: 63

The Most World Series At-Bats ever by a switch-hitter: 230 at-bats (second place all-time to Yogi Berra's 259 career Series at-bats)

The Most Times Led the World Series in Home Runs: 5 times [1953=2, tied with three others; 1956=3, tied with one; 1960=3; 1963=1, tied with four others; and 1964=3]

The Most World Series Total Bases All-Time: 123

The Most Series long hits in a career: 26

The Most Series extra bases on long hits in a career: 64

Most World Series Runs Scored All-Time: 42

Most Runs Scored in a Seven-Game Series: 8 (twice:1960,1964)

The Most World Series Lifetime RBIs: 40

The Most World Series Lifetime Bases on Balls All-Time: 43

The Most World Series Lifetime Strikeouts All-Time: 54

The Most Series games with one or more strikeouts: 12

Most Series with one or more hits: 12, tied with Yogi Berra

Most World Series Base Hits by a switch-hitter: 59, (second all-time behind "Yogi" Berra's 71 highest-number of lifetime hits in the Fall Classic)

Most World Series Base Hits by an outfielder: 59

The joyous bench reaction to Mickey's 1953 grand slam against the Dodgers is one of many joy-filled receptions "The Mick" will receive in his lustrous career.

APPENDIX VII.
THE WORLD SERIES HOME RUN RECORD OF MICKEY MANTLE

1. October 6, 1952: In the eighth inning of Game Six at Ebbets Field, Mantle powers an opposite-field home run to left-center field off Billy Loes which gives the Bombers their winning margin. The blond, crewcutted Mickey Mantle, aged 20, is the youngest World Series performer ever to hit a home run. The Yankees win, 3-2.

2. October 7, 1952: In the sixth inning of Game Seven at Ebbets Field, Mickey Mantle connects off Joe Black sending the ball soaring over the right-center field scoreboard. Mantle's home run proves to be the game-winner as the Yankees beat the Brooklyn Dodgers, 4-2, and win the World Championship of Baseball.

3. October 1, 1953: In the eighth inning of the second game of the World Series, played this day at Yankee Stadium, Mantle powers a change-up off "Preacher" Roe of the Brooklyn Dodgers into the lower left-field bleachers. Mantle's two-run roundtripper is the game-winner. The Yankees win, 4-2.

4. October 4, 1953: In the third inning of Game Five in the "Subway Series" with the Dodgers, played this day in Flatbush, Mickey Mantle connects for an opposite-field home run into the upper deck of the left-center field grandstand at Ebbets Field. Mantle's home run comes off Russ Meyer with the bases loaded and represents the fourth time only in World Series competition that a player has hit a World Series grand slam home run. The blow provides the winning margin as the Yankees beat the powerful Dodgers, 11-7.

5. September 30, 1955: In the second inning of Game Three, played this day at Ebbets Field, Mantle connects off a change-up thrown by Series MVP Johnny Podres for a home run which counts for nothing with respect to the game. The Dodgers win, 8-3.

6. October 3, 1956: In Game One of the Series, with President Eisenhower in attendance, it is the first inning at Ebbets Field with Sal "the Barber" Maglie on the mound for the Dodgers. In his first Series at-bat, Mantle poles a two-run home run off the Dodger righthander that gives the Yankees a lead that they will soon relinquish. The Dodgers win, 6-3.

7. October 7, 1956: In Game Four of the Series, played this day at Yankee Stadium, Mantle pounds an Ed Roebuck delivery in the sixth inning which soars over the right-center field wall landing, some 440 feet away, midway up the bleachers towards the famous Ballantine Beer sign. The Yankees win, 6-2.

8. October 8, 1956: In Game Five of the Series, Sal Maglie and Don Larsen are pitted against each other with the Series even at two games apiece. Don Larsen pitches a perfect game against the Dodgers and Mantle collects the first Yankee hit in the fourth inning when he slashes a curving, line-drive home run into the right-field bleachers just before it bullets into the foul territory of the right-field grand-stand beyond the right-field foul pole. The Yankees lead, 1-0, and Larsen proceeds with his magic afternoon on the mound. With the help of a long, running, backhanded catch, more than 430 feet from the plate by centerfielder Mickey Mantle, Don Larsen completes his perfect game and the Yankees win, 2-0.

9. October 5, 1957: In the fourth inning of Game Three, played this day at County Stadium in Milwaukee, Braves hurler Gene Conley offers up a fast ball to Mickey Mantle who swings mightily and connects. The high-kicking, 6'7" righthander's pitch lands in the distant right-of-center center field bleacher area between the seats and the bullpen that helps sustain the 12-3 annihilation of the Milwaukee Braves.

10 and 11. October 2, 1958: At County Stadium in Game Two of the Series, Mantle connects off 20-game winner Lew Burdette who is turning away the batting power of the hard-hitting New York Yankees. All of Milwaukee is thrilled as the Braves continue to turn out the powerful Yankee bats—that is, except for Mickey Mantle who pounds out another home run to no avail off the otherwise masterful Lew Burdette as the Milwaukee Braves take a 2-0 lead in games. The Braves win, 13-5.

12 and 13. October 6, 1960: At Forbes Field in the fifth inning of Game Two of the Series in Pittsburgh, Mickey Mantle connects from the right-side off Pirate lefty Freddie Green. Green's pitch, low and just outside of the strike zone, is powered by the mighty Mantle on a deep line just to the right of dead center field. The ball is rocketed high and far to the distant right-center alley of Forbes' vast expanse. The ball continues to sail until it traverses the field and carries over the 436-foot sign in right-center field. Only lefthanded power-hitters Stan Musial, "Duke" Snider, and Dale Long, have carried that remote wall in 51 years. No righthanded hitter ever in the long history of Forbes Field has ever hit a ball out of that section of the spacious ballyard. Two innings later in the same game, Mantle faces southpaw Joe Gibbon who throws another fast ball in at the righthanded-hitting slugger. Again Mantle connects and again the ball leaves the great ballyard, sailing over the right-field wall. The Yankees win, 16-3.

14. October 8, 1960: In Game Three of the Series, played this day at Yankee Stadium, Mantle connects off Freddie Green of the Pittsburgh Pirates for a 430-foot home run into the left-field bullpen as the Yankees throttle the hapless Bucs, 10-0.

15. October 6, 1963: At Dodger Stadium in Chavez Ravine, California, Mickey Mantle connects off the fireballing Sandy Koufax in the seventh inning which gives the Yankees their only run in a 2-1 defeat of the New York Yankees, defending World Champions. Mantle's home run ties him with the long-standing mark of the legendary "Babe" Ruth for the most career World Series home runs ever hit: 15.

16. October 10, 1964: At Yankee Stadium in Game Three of the World Series, Mickey Mantle clubs a devastating, towering "tape measure" shot which sails into the upper deck of the right-field grandstand in the ninth inning which ends the game and gives the Yanks a one-run victory. The timely blow came in the bottom of the ninth with Mantle leading off the inning. Before walking to the plate, Mantle had told Elston Howard that he was going to end this game right now. On the first pitch from knuckleball-relieving Barney Schultz, Mantle swung and connected. If it stayed fair, it was long enough to reach the seats. It stays fair and the Yankees win, 2-1. The record for the most home runs ever hit in the World Series now belongs to the "Kid" from Oklahoma.

17. October 14, 1964: In Game Six of the Series, played this day at Sportsman's Park, Mickey Mantle powers a back-to-back home run with Roger Maris on successive pitches in the sixth inning against the hometown Cardinals. It is the fourth time in World Series history that teammates have hit consecutive home runs in a World Series contest. Batting righty against southpaw Curt Simmons, Mantle belts a long blast to the opposite field where it lands atop the right-field pavilion. The Yankees win, 8-3.

18. October 15, 1964: In the decisive Game Seven of the Series with the Cardinals, Mickey Mantle powers a Bob Gibson fast ball high and long into the opposite-field, left-center field grandstand. The three-run shot comes in the sixth inning and proves to no avail as it is a day for the Redbirds and their staff's fireballing ace, Bob Gibson. The St. Louis Cardinals win the contest, 7-5, and the World Series Championship, in front of the delirious hometown crowd.

APPENDIX VIII.
REGULAR SEASON CAREER RANKINGS OF
MICKEY MANTLE

8TH PLACE ON THE ALL-TIME LIST FOR LIFETIME HOME RUNS (as of 1995): 536 (the highest ever for a switch-hitter in major league history. Also the most home runs by any major league ballplayer ever who played his entire career with one team.)

7TH PLACE ON THE ALL-TIME LIST FOR LIFETIME SLUGGING AVERAGE IN BIG LEAGUE HISTORY (as of 1995): tied with Willie Mays with .557 (the highest ever for a switch-hitter in major league history.)

27TH PLACE ON THE ALL-TIME LIST FOR LIFETIME TOTAL BASES IN BIG LEAGUE HISTORY
(as of 1995): 4,511

15TH PLACE ON THE ALL-TIME LIST FOR LIFETIME EXTRA BASES IN BIG LEAGUE HISTORY (as of 1995): 2,096

28TH PLACE ON THE ALL-TIME LIST FOR LIFETIME LONG HITS IN BIG LEAGUE HISTORY (as of 1995): 952

56TH PLACE ON THE ALL-TIME LIST FOR LIFETIME GAMES PLAYED IN BIG LEAGUE HISTORY (as of 1995): 2,401

22ND PLACE ON THE ALL-TIME LIST FOR LIFETIME RUNS SCORED IN BIG LEAGUE HISTORY (as of 1995): 1,677

30TH PLACE ON THE ALL-TIME LIST FOR LIFETIME RUNS BATTED IN IN BIG LEAGUE HISTORY (as of 1995): 1,509

FIFTH PLACE ON THE ALL-TIME LIST FOR LIFETIME BASES ON BALLS IN BIG LEAGUE HISTORY (as of 1995): 1,734 (the highest ever for a switch-hitter in major league history.)

NINTH PLACE ON THE ALL-TIME LIST FOR LIFETIME STRIKEOUTS (as of 1995): 1,710 (the highest ever for a switch-hitter in major league history. Also the most strikeouts by any major league ballplayer ever who played his entire career with one team. With respect to all players, Mickey Mantle will hold the all-time career strikeout record for the American League for 19 years before Reggie Jackson breaks the mark. Mantle's major league record for strikeouts will stand for 11 years until it is broken by Lou Brock.)

21ST PLACE ON THE ALL-TIME LIST FOR MOST STRIKEOUTS PER AT BAT (as of 1990): .211 (the highest ever for a switch-hitter in major league history.)

37TH PLACE ON THE ALL-TIME LIST FOR MOST GRAND SLAM HOME RUNS (as of 1995): 9

APPENDIX IX.
LEAGUE-LEADING HITTING CATEGORIES:

1952—Mickey Mantle with 111 strikeouts in a season (also sets new Yankee club record).

1954—Mickey Mantle with 129 runs scored (led majors) and with 107 strikeouts (led majors). [In fielding, Mantle leads the major leagues with 20 fielding assists from his center field position.]

1955—Mickey Mantle with 37 home runs, 113 walks (led majors), 11 triples which ties teammate Andy Carey for the league lead, and a .611 slugging average.

1956—Triple Crown-winning Mickey Mantle with a .353 batting average (led majors), 52 home runs (led majors), 130 RBIs (led majors), a .705 slugging average (led majors), 376 total bases (led majors), 132 runs scored (led majors), and the highest average number of home runs per 100 at-bats with 9.8 (led majors). Mickey Mantle has also set a major league record for the most RBIs by a switch-hitter in a single year—130. It is another major league record for switch-hitters as Mantle collects the most total bases, 376, ever by a switch-hitter. Mantle also hit the most long hits by a switch-hitter ever with 79 long hits.

1957—Mickey Mantle with 146 walks (led majors) and 121 runs scored (led majors). It is also a major league record for switch-hitters, his 146 bases on balls in a single season. This establishes a major league record that still stands.

1958—Mickey Mantle with 42 home runs, 307 total bases, 129 bases on balls (led majors), 127 runs scored (led majors), and 120 strikeouts (led majors and established a new Yankee club record).

1959—Mickey Mantle with 126 strikeouts which led majors and which also represents an all-time major league record for the most strikeouts by a switch-hitter in a single season.

1960—Mickey Mantle with 40 home runs (fourth and final home run crown, 294 total bases, 118 runs scored (led majors), and 125 strikeouts.

1961—Mickey Mantle with a .687 slugging average (led majors), 132 runs which ties teammate Roger Maris for the major league lead, 126 bases on balls (led majors), and the highest average number of home runs per 100 at-bats with 10.5 (led majors). It is a landmark year for Mantle for other feats. Mantle's last home run of 1961 establishes the pinstriped clutch of clout with the most home runs ever in back-to-back years by a switch-hitter, 94 roundtrippers—40 in 1960 and 54 in 1961. It is also the most extra bases on long hits by any switch-hitter in the history of the game with 190 in a single season.

1962—Mickey Mantle with 122 bases on balls (led majors).

APPENDIX X.
MICKEY MANTLE'S SIGNATURE "TAPE-MEASURE" SHOTS AT YANKEE STADIUM (123 HOME RUNS)

LEFT-FIELD GRANDSTAND (8)

1. May 16, 1951 vs. Cleveland's Steve Rozek: a deep, 420-foot drive into the lower grandstand.

2. May 3, 1956 vs. Kansas City's Art Ceccarelli: 440 feet.

3. July 14, 1956 vs. Cleveland's Herb Score: a clout of 425 feet that settles some 20 feet behind the 402-foot marker adjacent to the visitors' bullpen.

4. August 12, 1958 vs. Baltimore's Ken Lehman: 430 feet, landing at a point left of the left-center bullpen].

5. May 10, 1959 vs. Washington's Chuck Stobbs: a 400-foot plus drive into left-center bullpen.

6. July 1, 1961 vs. Washington's Carl Mathias: a titanic blast deep into the lower grandstand.

7. May 16, 1964 vs. Kansas City's Moe Drabowsky: a 405-foot drive.

8. April 29, 1967 vs. California's Jack Sanford: a drive that carries the 14 and-a-half foot wall over the 407-foot marker.

The overhanging left-field balcony at Yankee Stadium is highlighted in this photo which shows Whitey Ford on the mound in the 1962 Season Opener.

LEFT-FIELD UPPER DECK (6)

1. September 12, 1953 vs. Detroit's Billy Hoeft: a projected 620-foot drive had the ball enjoyed uninterrupted flight. The ball still pounds into the seats some 425 feet away, 80 feet above the playing field, while still rising.

2. May 7, 1954 vs. Philadelphia's Morrie Martin: six rows deep beyond the upper deck railing of the left-field grandstand.

3. July 1, 1956 vs. Washington's Dean Stone: a 525 feet monster deep into the left-field upper tier.

4. August 23, 1956 vs. Chicago's Paul LaPalme: a potential 600-foot drive which impacts 20 rows deep into the third tier of the left field grandstand, missing the roof by only 20 feet.

5. June 6, 1958 vs. Cleveland's Dick Tomanek: off the upper deck facing, bounding back onto the field.

6. July 20, 1962 vs. Washington's Steve Hamilton: a 530-foot clout which crashes into the facing of the upper tier with such force that the ball bounds almost back to the infield.

This aerial overview shows the massive and remote left-center field bleachers which Mickey reached more than any player who ever played in the Grand Old Ballyard, Yankee Stadium.

LEFT-CENTER FIELD BLEACHERS ("Sun Deck") (4)

1. June 4, 1958 vs. Chicago's Billy Pierce: a 475-foot drive into the left-center field bleachers where it impacts some 20 rows deep and to the right of the visitors' bullpen.

2. July 1, 1961 vs. Washington's Carl Mathias: a tremendous clout that clears the 457-foot marker over the deepest portions of the left-center field bleachers and over a 78.3-foot wall. The belt is hit to the remote spot which only Joe DiMaggio and Bill "Moose" Skowron have ever reached twice in their careers.

3. June 22, 1965 vs. Kansas City's John O'Donoghue: a 460-foot drive that clears the 457-foot marker to the deepest portions of left-center field bleachers, becoming only the 18th player to hit this distant spot.

4. July 25, 1967 vs. Minnesota's Jim Kaat: a 450-foot drive that carries 12 rows deep into the left-center bleachers over the auxiliary scoreboard.

This 1964 photo actually shows the flight of the ball that Mantle belted, clearing the deepest portions of the playing field of Yankee Stadium in dead-center. Mantle was the only player who cleared the 461-foot marker multiple times in Stadium history and he did it from both sides of the plate.

CENTER FIELD ("DEATH VALLEY") SHOTS (3)

1. June 21, 1955 vs. Kansas City's Alex Kellner: a 486-foot straightaway clout that clears the 33.83-foot barrier of concrete and wire visibility screen. It is the only home run to date ever to carry into the centerfield bleachers in the 32-year history of the fabled ballpark.

2. May 9, 1958 vs. Washington's Pedro Ramos: a 450-foot inside-the-park home run.

3. August 16, 1959 vs. Boston's Bill Monbouquette: a 461-foot drive that smashes into the 461-foot marker in center field with such force that it rebounds rapidly to the opposing center fielder who is able to rifle a quick throw back into the infield that holds Mantle to a double.

4. June 30, 1961 vs. Washington's Dick Donovan: a 461-foot drive that hits the 461-foot marker in straightaway center field for a standing inside-the-park home run.

5. August 12, 1964 vs. Chicago's Ray Herbert: a scorching 500-foot drive over the 33.83-foot high wall and hitter's screen. It is the second time that anyone has belted a home run into Yankee Stadium's center-field bleachers. Both have come off Mantle's mighty bat.

6. July 8, 1966 vs. Washington's Jim Hannan: a 460-foot home run that sails over the fence to the right of the center-field flagpole.

In this 1956 photograph, the Kansas City A's align themselves in the "Mantle Shift" to defend themselves against the pinstriped slugger. Under the lights, scanning left-to-right, from the scoreboard to the Yankee bullpen located under the light standard atop the right-field filigree, lies the right-center field bleachers, a haven for Mantle's lofted long-balls. Only Mickey Mantle would reach this distant site of descent more than once in the same contest, and he did it three times in one game against the 1955 Detroit Tigers.

RIGHT-CENTER FIELD BLEACHERS (44)

1. June 19, 1951 vs. Chicago's Lou Kretlow.

2. September 8, 1951 vs. Washington's Sid Hudson: 450-foot drive to right-center field bleachers.

3. July 13, 1952 vs. Detroit's Hal Newhouser: a 400-foot opposite-field blast.

4. April 23, 1953 vs. Boston's Ellis Kinder: a 400-footer.

5. April 21, 1954 vs. Boston's Leo Kiely: a back-to-back blast with Yogi Berra.

6. May 21, 1954 vs. Boston's Frank Sullivan: 410-foot drive over right-field auxiliary scoreboard.

7. May 22, 1954 vs. Boston's "Tex" Clevenger.

8. June 6, 1954 vs. Baltimore's Don Larsen.

9. April 13, 1955 vs. Washington's Ted Abernathy.

10. May 13, 1955 vs. Detroit's Steve Gromek.

11. May 13, 1955 vs. Detroit's Steve Gromek.

12. May 13, 1955 vs. Detroit's Bob Miller.

13. June 22, 1955 vs. Kansas City's Art Ditmar: a 415-foot game-winner.

14. September 4, 1955 vs. Washington's Pedro Ramos.

15. May 10, 1956 vs. Cleveland's Bob Lemon.

16. July 18, 1956 vs. Detroit's Paul Foytack.

17. July 22, 1956 vs. Kansas City's Art Ditmar.

18. August 29, 1956 vs. Kansas City's Jack McMahon: a 410-foot drive.

19. October 7, 1956 vs. Brooklyn's Ed Roebuck.

20. April 24, 1957 vs. Baltimore's Connie Johnson: a game-winner.

21. June 22, 1957 vs. Chicago's Jack Harshman: an opposite-field four-master.

22. July 23, 1957 vs. Chicago's Bob Keegan: a 472-foot shot that bangs against the rear wall of the Stadium to the right of the scoreboard in right-center field.

23. July 6, 1958 vs. Boston's Ike Delock.

24. September 15, 1959 vs. Chicago's Bob Shaw: a 440-footer marks Mickey's 100th left-handed hitting homer in the Bronx ballyard.

25. May 28, 1960 vs. Washington's Jim Kaat: an opposite-field 400-footer.

26. July 31, 1960 vs. Kansas City's Johnny Kucks.

27. August 15, 1960 vs. Baltimore's Jerry Walker: 420-foot drive that ricochets against the back fence of the right-center bullpen.

28. August 26, 1960 vs. Cleveland's Jim Perry: 420-foot drive over the right-center field auxiliary scoreboard.

29. September 20, 1960 vs. Washington's Jack Kralick: over the 407-foot auxiliary scoreboard in right-center field.

30. June 5, 1961 vs. Minnesota's Don Lee: Mantle launches a 420-foot drive into the right-center field bleachers.

31. July 26, 1961 vs. Chicago's Ray Herbert.

32. September 3, 1961 vs. Jerry Staley: a titanic, 450-foot shot that marks his 50th home run of the year.

33. May 6, 1962 vs. Washington's Dave Stenhouse: the ball slams into the last row of the lower right field bleachers which separate the spectators from the back wall of the Stadium and the rest of the Bronx.

34. July 4, 1962 vs. Kansas City's Dan Pfister: a 410-foot drive into the right-center field bleachers.

35. June 28 or 29, 1962 vs. Minnesota's Jack Kralick: a 400-foot opposite field drive to right-center field drive.

36. July 4, 1962 vs. Kansas City's Dan Pfister.

37. July 25, 1962 vs. Boston's Earl Wilson.

38. August 28, 1962 vs. Cleveland's Jim "Mudcat" Grant.

39. May 23, 1964 vs. Los Angeles' Bo Belinsky: a 420-foot opposite-field shot.

40. August 18, 1965 vs. California's Dean Chance: a 425-foot drive over the right-center field auxiliary scoreboard.

41. September 4, 1965 vs. Boston's Dennis Bennett: a 420-foot drive into the right field bleachers.

42. April 29, 1967 vs. California's Jack Sanford.

43. May 17, 1967 vs. Cleveland's Steve Hargan.

44. June 24, 1967 vs. Detroit's Fred Gladding: a 420-foot drive into the right-center field bleachers.

45. July 22, 1967 vs. Detroit's Earl Wilson.

Among the rafters in the right-field upper deck is seen the filigree that Mickey Mantle would impact three times in his career, mere inches from clearing the roof of the vaunted Stadium—the longest home runs ever hit at the magnificent yard.

RIGHT-FIELD UPPER DECK (54)

1. September 13, 1951 vs. Detroit's Virgil Trucks.

2. May 25, 1953 vs. Boston's Mickey McDermott: a 400-foot drive to the opposite field.

3. July 7, 1954 vs. Boston's Tom Brewer.

4. September 2, 1954 vs. Cleveland's Bob Lemon: a tremendous shot that arches high into the third deck of the filigreed grandstand 100 above the 344-foot marker at the field level.

5. June 17, 1955 vs. Chicago's Dick Donovan: a towering drive that lands 10 rows deep into the third tier.

6. June 19, 1955 vs. Chicago's Sandy Consuegra: 20 rows deep into the third level of the grandstand.

7. July 28, 1955 vs. Chicago's Connie Johnson: a high blast that impacts against the front facing of the right-field deck's facade.

8. August 4, 1955 vs. Cleveland's Ray Narleski.

9. August 24, 1955 vs. Detroit's Steve Gromek: the tail-end roundtripper of back-to-back home runs with Yogi Berra.

10. April 21, 1956 vs. Boston's George Susce, Jr.: a 435-footer that lands 20 rows high into the uppermost tier of the ballyard.

11. May 5, 1956 vs. Kansas City's Moe Burtschy: six rows deep into the upper deck before crashing into the seats and rebounding another 100 feet to the left and over the right-center field bullpen gate.

12. May 30, 1956 vs. Washington's Pedro Ramos: a prodigious shot estimated to fly between 550 and 600 feet had its flight not been interrupted when this high, deep, and arching drive slams against the uppermost, right-field facade some 18" from clearing the Stadium's green-coppered roof.

13. May 30, 1956 vs. Washington's Camilo Pascual: halfway up to the top of the upper deck of the right-field grandstand.

14. June 14, 1956 vs Chicago's Jim Wilson: a prodigious belt that spans high over the field, landing 20 rows deep into the third tier of the right-field grandstand.

15. August 11, 1956 vs. Baltimore's Hal Brown.

16. May 19, 1957 vs. Cleveland's Bob Lemon.

17. May 26, 1957 vs. Washington's Camilo Pascual.

18. June 2, 1957 vs. Baltimore's Hal Brown: a back-to-back special with Yogi Berra.

19. June 23, 1957 vs. Chicago's Dick Donovan: Mantle's blast crashes against the right-field facade of the roof that, if uninterrupted in flight, may have traversed some 550 to 575 feet.

20. July 31, 1957 vs. Kansas City's Wally Burnette.

21. July 5, 1958 vs. Boston's Dave Sisler.

22. July 11, 1958 vs. Cleveland's Ray Narleski: the ball soars eight rows into the top deck of the right-field grandstand.

23. August 9, 1958 vs. Boston's Dave Sisler.

24. June 17, 1959 vs. Chicago's Ray Moore: a towering clout that sails 10 rows deep into the highest tier of the grandstand.

25. July 16, 1959 vs. Cleveland's Gary Bell: an upper-deck game-winner.

26. August 16, 1959 vs. Boston's Jerry Casale.

27. August 16, 1959 vs. Boston's Bill Monbouquette.

28. April 22, 1960 vs. Baltimore's Hoyt Wilhelm.

29. August 15, 1960 vs. Baltimore's Hoyt Wilhelm.

30. September 17, 1960 vs. Baltimore's Chuck Estrada.

31. April 17, 1961 vs. Kansas City's Jerry Walker: a towering shot that smashes against the second-deck facing of the right-field grandstand.

32. April 20, 1961 vs. Los Angeles' Eli Grba: 12 rows deep into the upper deck.

33. April 20, 1961 vs. Los Angeles' Eli Grba: the second upper-tiered lazer that lands 10 rows into the uppermost level.

34. June 11, 1961 vs. Los Angeles' Eli Grba.

35. July 2, 1961 vs. Washington's Johnny Klippstein.

36. July 8, 1961 vs. Boston's Tracy Stallard: a game-winner.

37. August 2, 1961 vs. Kansas City's Jim Archer.

38. September 5, 1961 vs. Washington's Joe McClain: six rows behind the upper-deck railing.

39. May 5, 1962 vs. Washington's Marty Kutyna: an arching drive that lands 14 rows deep into the uppermost tier.

40. July 2, 1962 vs. Kansas City's Ed Rakow: a prodigious belt that soars halfway to the top of the filigreed stadium.

41. July 3, 1962 vs. Kansas City's Jerry Walker.

42. July 4, 1962 vs. Kansas City's John Wyatt: a back-to-back blast with Roger Maris.

43. May 15, 1963 vs. Minnesota's Camilo Pascual: the high drive carries into the upper deck where it disappears through the third exit opening from the extreme-left edge of the right-field grandstand tier.

44. May 22, 1963 vs. Kansas City's Bill Fischer: a tremendous clout, projected at 650-to-700 feet away from the plate. Incredibly, the ball was still rising when it crashed six feet from the top edge of the Stadium roof.

45. May 23, 1964 vs. California's Bo Belinsky: an opposite-field, 420-foot belt into the third deck.

46. May 24, 1964 vs. California's Fred Newman.

47. July 4, 1964 vs. Minnesota's Al Worthington: a three-run, game-winner.

48. October 10, 1964 vs. St. Louis' Barney Schultz: the "called" Game Three game-winner, a prodigious belt a mere few feet from clearing the roof.

49. April 21, 1965 vs. Minnesota's Camilo Pascual.

50. June 23, 1966 vs. Baltimore's Jim Palmer: a first-row upper-decker.

51. July 23, 1966 vs. California's Marcelino Lopez: a high, opposite-field blast into the uppermost seats of the ballyard in right.

52. April 30, 1967 vs. California's George Brunet: an opposite-field drive into the upper deck.

53. July 22, 1967 vs. Detroit's Earl Wilson: the upper-decker ties Mantle with Hall-of-Famer Johnny Mize for career home runs among left-handed sluggers.

54. April 26, 1968 vs. Detroit's Earl Wilson: the upper-decker ties him on the all-time list with Hall-of-Famer Ted Williams.

APPENDIX XI. MICKEY MANTLE'S SIGNATURE "TAPE-MEASURE" SHOTS ON-THE-ROAD (83 HOME RUNS)

In the history of the ancient ballyard, only Mantle would clear the left-center field bleachers, ticking the Bohemian Beer sign before exiting the park. It is this 565-foot, "tape-measure" journey that no player would ever exceed. And in center field, only "Babe" Ruth would propel a ball that would fly into the tree beyond the 31-foot high center-field barrier—until Mickey would do it in the 1956 Season Opener. Unbelievably, in the same tilt, Mickey would also belt another "tape-measure" shot which would hit a roof of a building located across the street from the right field wall.

GRIFFITH STADIUM

(Home of the Washington Senators—9)

1. April 17, 1953 off Chuck Stobbs (LH)
    The original "tape-measure" shot: a monstrous 565-foot drive that nicks the right top edge of the scoreboard situated atop the left-center field bleachers, some 60-feet above the playing field. The ball then departs the ballyard, landing in the back-yard of a tenement house across the street and one block down.

2. July 10, 1955 off Dean Stone (LH)
    A 425-foot drive into the left-center field grand-stand. There will be in this most massive of ballyards only 28 home runs hit all year in the left-field and center-field sectors.

3. July 10, 1955 off Dean Stone (LH)
    A soaring, 450-foot power shot that falls into the left field bleachers halfway up the distant grand-stand.

4. April 17, 1956 off Camilo Pascual (RH)
    A 525-foot drive over the building-protection wall in center field, a remote section beyond the ballyard and into a clump of trees, reached previously only by two players: "Babe" Ruth and Larry Doby.

5. April 17, 1956 off Camilo Pascual (RH)
    A 500-foot drive that carries over the building-protection wall to the right of dead-center field, landing on the roof of a building located across the street from the massive ballpark.

6. May 29, 1957 off Pedro Ramos (RH)
    A 438-foot drive into the right-center field bullpen.

7. July 3, 1958 off Russ Kemmerer (RH)
    A 465-foot, opposite-field blast that carries high over that point in the ballyard situated to the right of left-center field at the bend in the bleachers while landing some two-thirds up the high-backed left-center field grandstand.

8. April 21, 1959 off Pedro Ramos (RH)
    A 400-foot blast into the center-field bleachers.

9. July 18, 1961 off Joe McClain (LH)
    A tremendous clout that soars high towards the light standard directly over the center-field Senators bullpen and the massive scoreboard in right-center field. The ball crashes against the tall light standard before caroming sharply down into the center-field bullpen.

Depicted in this panoramic shot of the vaunted ballyard of lore in Detroit are the right field auxiliary press boxes over which Mantlesque clouts would soar four times. And in the remote, center-field grandstand, some 440 feet away, Mantle's prodigious drives would pepper the second deck with a frequency known by no other player—and he would do it from both sides of the plate.

BRIGGS STADIUM/TIGER STADIUM

(Home of the Detroit Tigers—22)

1. June 17, 1952 off Billy Hoeft (LH)
   A 400-foot game-tying home run.

2. July 25, 1952 off Art Houtteman (RH)
   An upper deck shot into the right-field grandstand.

3. July 26, 1952 off Ted Gray (LH)
   An upper deck shot to left-field.

4. June 11, 1953 off Art Houtteman (RH)
   A long, soaring shot that lands on the right-field roof above the auxiliary press boxes 110 feet above the ground.

5. July 26, 1953 off Steve Gromek (RH)
   An upper deck shot to left field.

6. August 8, 1954 off Billy Hoeft (LH)
   A high, towering, opposite-field drive that hugs the right-field foul line before soaring over the

auxiliary press box and clearing the roof, soaring out of the ballpark—six feet foul.

7. June 6, 1955 off Bob Miller (LH)
    A 440-foot drive over the center-field bullpen screen.

8. June 18, 1956 off Paul Foytack (RH)
    A 525-foot drive that carries over the roof and out of the ballyard.

9. June 20, 1956 off Billy Hoeft (LH)
    An upper deck shot to left field that sails over the on-field 400-foot marker.

10. June 20, 1956 off Billy Hoeft (LH)
    A mammoth 510-foot smash that crashes into the seats of the second tier to the right of straightaway center-field and above the 370-foot marker.

11. August 5, 1956 off Jim Bunning (RH)
    An upper deck shot that hits the facing of the right-field grandstand.

12. June 7, 1957 off Jim Bunning (RH)
    A towering fly that lands on top of the 110-foot high roof of the right-field grandstand.

13. August 26, 1957 off Frank Lary (RH)
    A long, soaring shot that disappears into the center-field grandstand 440 feet away.

14. September 17, 1958 off Jim Bunning (RH)
    A 510-foot shot that sails over the right-field roof and out of the ballpark.

15. September 10, 1960 off Paul Foytack (RH)
    A 560-foot drive that carries cleanly through the light standard in right-center-field and over the roof and beyond the ballpark's structural confines.

16. April 26, 1961 off Jim Donohue (RH)
    An upper deck shot into the right-field grandstand.

17. April 26, 1961 off Hank Aguirre (LH)
    An upper deck shot into the left-field grandstand.

18. September 10, 1962 off Hank Aguirre (LH)
    A 450-foot drive into the lower center-field grand-stand.

19. May 6, 1963 off Hank Aguirre (LH)
    A high, towering poke that carries into the left-field upper deck.

20. May 20, 1967 off Denny McLain (RH)
    The drive carries 40 feet over the 370-foot marker on the right-center field wall.

21. July 22, 1967 off Earl Wilson (RH)
    An upper deck clout into the right-field grandstand..

22. September 19, 1968 off Denny McLain (RH)
    A clout that carries into the second tier of the right-field grandstand

Once in an exhibition game, Mantle's left-handed swing blasted a ball over the roof of the right-field grandstand, a feat accomplished by only two players before him. In center field, Mantle, playing in the 1960 World Series, would launch a titanic blow to center, becoming the first right-handed batter ever to conquer the distant green of Schenley Park located beyond the center field wall.

FORBES FIELD

(Home of the Pittsburgh Pirates—2)

1. April 9, 1953 off Bill MacDonald (RH)

   During an exhibition game played against the Pirates, Mantle slams the ball high and far off rookie righthanded hurler Bill MacDonald, becoming only the third batter ever, following "Babe" Ruth and Ted Beard who preceded Mickey, to clear the right-field grandstand on the fly and clear out of the ancient stadium.

2. October 6, 1960 off Freddie Green (LH)

   Mantle crushes an opposite-field home run over the 12-foot high, ivy-lined, brick, right-center field wall, over the 436-foot marker. Mickey is the only right-handed hitter ever to hit a ball out of that remotest of sectors in the massive ballyard. Only three left-handed batters have belted one as long, Duke Snider, Stan Musial, and Dale Long.

Between the left-field and left-center field light standards, Mantle's 500-foot shot would clear the roof and clinch the pennant in 1956 for the Bronx Bombers.

THE OLD COMISKEY PARK

(Home of the Chicago White Sox—15)

1. May 1, 1951 off Randy Gumpert (RH)
   A 440-foot home run to right-center field.

2. April 30, 1953 off Gene Bearden (LH)
   A 400-foot drive to left-center field.

3. June 4, 1953 off Billy Pierce (LH)
   A 435-foot home run into the right-center field grandstand.

4. June 3, 1955 off Jack Harshman (LH)
   A long drive that carries high over the 365-foot left-center fence where it impacts against the left-center field facing some 45 feet above the playing field.

5. June 5, 1955 off Billy Pierce (LH)
   A 500-foot shot that lands atop the 90-foot high roof of the left-field grandstand.

6. May 18, 1956 off Billy Pierce (LH)
   An upper deck shot into the second tier of the left-field pavilion.

7. May 18, 1956 off Dixie Howell (RH)

An upper deck into the right-field grandstand.

8. September 18, 1956 off Billy Pierce (LH)
   A 550-foot home run over the left-field roof.

9. May 5, 1957 off Billy Pierce (LH)
   A towering shot into the left-field grandstand.

10. June 11, 1957 off Jim Wilson (RH)
    A long drive into the second tier of the right-field grandstand.

11. June 13, 1957 off Bob Keegan (RH)
    A hot smash that carries into the center-field bullpen some 415 feet away.

12. June 24, 1958 off Early Wynn (RH)
    A 420-foot shot into the center-field bullpen.

13. June 18, 1960 off Bob Rush (RH)
    A 415-foot home run to the center field bullpen.

14. July 13, 1961 off Early Wynn (RH)
    A 500-foot home run that carries into the center-field upper deck above the bleachers.

15. June 21, 1964 off Juan Pizarro (LH)
    A shot into the left-field upper deck.

MUNICIPAL STADIUM

(Home of the Cleveland Indians—8)

1. August 5, 1954 off Ray Narleski (RH)
   Deep into the second deck of the right-center field grandstand.

2. May 16, 1956 off Bud Daley (LH)
   A clout high, deep and over the 410-foot center-field barrier that carries some 485 feet and into the center field bleachers. Mantle is only one of two players ever to reach the center field bleachers.

3. May 8, 1957 off Early Wynn (RH)
   Aa 440-foot drive into the center-field bleachers.

4. June 5, 1957 off Early Wynn (RH)
   A 450-foot clout over the right-field fence.

5. September 9, 1958 off Cal McLish (RH)
   A drive that clears the 410-foot fence.

6. June 16, 1962 off Gary Bell (RH)
   A 400-foot home run over the right-center field wall.

7. September 12, 1962 off Pedro Ramos (RH)
   A 400-foot clout to right-center field.

8. September 25, 1965 off Lee Stange (RH)
   A 415-foot drive over the center-field barrier.

MEMORIAL STADIUM

(Home of the Baltimore Orioles—5)

1. August 10, 1957 off Ray Moore (RH)

    Batting left-handed, Mantle pounds out a tremendous blast to dead center field that carries over the 425-foot center-field fence, flies over a 10-foot hedge located in front of the scoreboard, bounces on a cinder track, and slams against the center-field scorebard. It is the only time that a batter has ever powered a ball that hit the scoreboard 475 feet away.

2. July 1, 1958 off Jack Harshman (LH)

    A 425-foot shot that soars over the distant center-field fence.

3. May 24, 1959 off Billy O'Dell (LH)

    A poke that clears the 410-foot center-field fence.

4. April 21, 1961 off Steve Barber (LH)

    A booming, towering shot to straightaway center-field that carries over the 410-foot center-field fence and over a 10-foot-high hedge which is situated 30 feet beyond that before landing on a cinder track and bouncing against the scoreboard. The poke is esti-mated to have travelled 475 feet. Only one other ballplayer has ever touched the scoreboard with a batted ball—Mantle, four years before, batting lefthanded. This day's boomer came from the right side of the plate.

5. May 15, 1965 off Dick Hall (RH)

    A 400-foot shot into the left-field grandstand.

MUNICIPAL STADIUM

(Home of the Kansas City Athletics—3

1. May 21, 1956 off Moe Burtschy (RH)

    A tremendous shot to right field that carries over the right-field fence and flies over the second fence atop an incline at the back of the ballpark. The distant clout covers 450 feet in its rapid journey out of the old ballyard off the switch-hitter's bat.

2. June 21, 1961 off Bob Shaw (RH)

    Muscling up for the contest, Mantle powers one ball this day that speeds high and far until it bangs into the distant scoreboard 525 feet away in right-center field.

In the same game in Kansas City in 1961, Mantle would connect twice with tremendous belts covering 475 to 500-feet, the first of which actually bounded off the distant right-center field scoreboard.

3. June 21, 1961 off Bob Shaw (RH)
    For the second time in the same game, Mantle connects once more to the nether regions of right-center field where the ball has been propelled 475 feet, sailing over the the 387-foot fence, soaring past the old, 27-ton Boston Braves scoreboard that has been erected in right-center field, clearing the second fence as well, and landing on the traffic-congested Brooklyn Avenue outside the ballpark.

4. August 17, 1962 off Bill Fischer (RH)
    An opposite-field 400-foot blast to left-center field

5. August 18, 1962 off Diego Segui (RH)
    Another opposite-field tape measure-shot that car-ries 420 feet over the left-center field fence.

6. August 4, 1964 off John O'Donoghue (LH)
    A 400-foot, opposite-field blow over the left-center field fence.

In the only time of his career, Mickey Mantle would belt a prodigious pinch-hit grandslam home run, powering a gargantuan shot 530-feet away from home plate and out of the storied ballpark.

SHIBE PARK

(Home of the Philadelphia Athletics—2)

1. July 5, 1952 off Alex Kellner (LH)

   Supplying all of his power on a slow, change-up pitch, Mantle pounds out a prodigious home run that sails over the playing field, carries past the grand-stand spectators, and lands high and deep into the upper reaches of the upper deck grandstand in left field.

2. July 6, 1953 off Frank Fanovich (LH)

   The drive is rocketed some 530 feet in a high, towering trajectory that carries over the 12-foot high outfield wall in left-center, over the upper deck grandstand roof and, out of the storied confines of old Shibe Park.

Mantle's long-ball pyrotechnics would produce a mammoth shot which would fly past the prominent scoreboard in left field on the fly, a super-charged drive that would be jettisoned out of the historic ballyard.

SPORTSMAN'S PARK

(Home of the St. Louis Browns—2)

1. May 4, 1951 off Duane Pillette (LH)
    The ball rockets out of the ballyard landing over the roof some 450 feet away from home plate.

2. April 28, 1953 off Bob Cain (LH)
    Lefthander Cain's pitch never reaches his catcher's mitt, as Mantle unloads on the ball, connecting solidly to left field with a prodigious drive that carries past the light standard in left and over the giant Budweiser Beer scoreboard that is located behind the left-field grandstand. The mammoth shot is calculated to have carried between an estimated distance of 485 and 530 feet and one of the longest home runs ever hit at the old ballyard.

FENWAY PARK

(Home of the Boston Red Sox—6)

1. May 7, 1955 off Ike DeLock (RH)
   The blow is a rifle-shot off Mantle's bat that propels the ball 420 feet into the centerfield bleachers.

2. September 21, 1956 off Frank Sullivan (RH)
   Another prodigious drive that carries over the heads of every spectator in the centerfield grandstand, crashing against the second-to-last row of seats adjoining the back wall of the ballyard's concrete infrastructure. The ball is estimated to have bul-leted 480 feet away. Yankee teammate and pitcher Tom Sturdivant will later declare that he never saw a ball "move so fast."

3. May 30, 1961 off Mike Fornieles (RH)
   The ball is pounded to the deepest corner of the ballpark, just to the right of dead center where the bullpen begins and over the nine-foot wall marked by the 430-foot sign.

4. May 31, 1961 off Billy Muffett (RH)
   A 400-foot blow that carries into the right-center field bullpen.

5. July 18, 1962 off Galen Cisco (RH)
   A 410-foot shot into the right-field bleachers

6. May 11, 1965 off Arnold Earley (LH)
   A 400-foot plus blast into the center field bleachers

METROPOLITAN STADIUM

(Home of the Minnesota Twins—3)

1. May 2, 1961 off Camilo Pascual (RH)
   A 430-foot shot to straightaway center field.

2. May 4, 1963 off Jim Kaat (LH)
   An opposite-field, 407-foot shot to right-center field.

3. August 1, 1964 off Dick Stigman (LH)
   A 415-foot drive over the center-field screen.

WRIGLEY FIELD

(Home of the Los Angeles Angels—1)

1. June 26, 1961 off Ken McBride (RH)
   A drive over the center field barrier 412 feet away

DODGER STADIUM

(Temporary Home of the the California Angels—1)

1. September 2, 1965 off Marcelino Lopez (LH)
   A 400-foot drive over the left-center field wall.

ANAHEIM STADIUM

(Home of the California Angels—2)

1. April 18, 1968 off Jim McGlothlin (RH)
   A 406-foot over the sign in center field.

2. August 12, 1968 off George Brunet (LH)
   A 400-foot blast over the right-center field fence.

D.C. STADIUM

(later renamed Robert F. Kennedy Stadium; Home of the Washington Senators—2)

1. July 2, 1966 off Mike McCormick (LH)
   The ball is rocketed into the mezzanine area of the straightaway center-field some 450 feet away.

2. June 15, 1967 off Frank Bertaina (LH)
   A 462-foot drive that crashes into the second row of the upper deck of the left-center field bleachers.

APPENDIX XII.
SWITCH-HITTING RECORDS

MAJOR LEAGUE RECORDS

All-Time Record for Highest Batting Average in a Season by a switchhitter in the modern era—365 in 1957 (In 1889, Tommy Tucker batted .372 in the American Association)

All-Time Record for Most RBIs in a Season by a switchhitter—130

All-Time Record for Most Walks in a Season by a switchhitter—146

The Most Lifetime Walks by a switch-hitter in Major League Baseball History—1,734 (5th place-all time inclusive of all hitters)

The Most Lifetime Strikeouts by a switch-hitter in history with 1,710 (9th place all-time inclusive of all hitters)

The Most Seasons (Lifetime) Leading the League in Strikeouts by a Switch-hitter—5

Mantle also owns the highest marks for the most home runs in a single season by a switch-hitter—5, as well as seven of the first eight places for most switch-hitting roundtrippers

The Most Consecutive Years of Leading the League in Strikeouts by a Switch-hitter—3

The Most Home Run Titles by a Switch-hitter in the history of Major League Baseball—4

In modern Major League history, Mickey Mantle becomes, by hitting .353 in 1956, the most prolific switch-hitter in a single season, attaining the highest batting average in a single season by a switch-hitter that wins the league batting title.

In Major League history, Mickey Mantle becomes, in 1956, the most prolific switch-hitter ever in a single year, becoming the first and only switch-hitter in baseball history to win the Triple Crown.

In Major League history, Mickey Mantle produces the highest slugging average ever by a switch-hitter when he generates a .705 slugging average in 1956.

In Major League history, Mickey Mantle totals more home runs by a switch-hitter in a single season with 54 home runs in 1961.

In Major League history, Mickey Mantle totals more career home runs by a switch-hitter with 536 home runs.

In Major League history, Mickey Mantle becomes the only switch-hitter in major league history to hit 50 home runs in one season two different times, in 1956 and 1961.

In Major League history, Mickey Mantle becomes in 1956 the most prodigious switch-hitter of all-time by producing 376 total bases in a single season.

In Major League history, Mickey Mantle attains the highest career slugging average for a switch-hitter, .557, tying for tenth for all hitters with Willie Mays.

In Major League history, Mickey Mantle collects the second most career extra bases for a switch-hitter, second only to Pete Rose.

In Major League history, Mickey Mantle scores the second highest number of career runs for a switch-hitter, second only to Pete Rose.

In Major League history, Mickey Mantle earns the most walks ever attained by a switch-hitter.

In Major League history, Mickey Mantle attained the most strikeouts ever for a switch-hitter.

In Major League history, Mickey Mantle attains the third highest number of career total bases for a switch-hitter, third only to Pete Rose and Eddie Murray.

In Major League history, Mickey Mantle belts out the most home runs hit by a switch-hitter against one team, 11, against the Cleveland Indians in 1956 and the Washington Senators in 1961.

In Major League history, Mickey Mantle belted out the most home runs in a single season, 54 in 1961, without winning the home run title.

In Major League history, Mickey Mantle ties fellow record-holders for homering in every league ballpark in the same season.

In Major League history, the most home runs, 20, ever hit by any player through May 31st in a season.

AMERICAN LEAGUE RECORDS

In American League history, Mickey Mantle collects the most career runs batted in by a switch-hitter.

In American League history, Mickey Mantle establishes the highest number of bases on balls in a season ever issued to a switch-hitter, 146 in 1957.

In American League history, Mickey Mantle becomes the all-time season leader in 1961 for striking out with 126 Ks.

In American League history, Mickey Mantle becomes on May 23, 1957 the first American League switch-hitter ever to hit for the cycle.

In American League history, Mickey Mantle establishes record for leading the league in strikeouts for three consecutive seasons.

NEW YORK YANKEE RECORDS

As a member of the New York Yankees, Mickey Mantle becomes the all-time leader in games played on the greatest franchise in baseball history, 2,401.

As a member of the New York Yankees, Mickey Mantle becomes the all-time leader on the greatest franchise in baseball history coming to the plate to bat, 8,102 at-bats.

Mickey Mantle also holds the all-time Yankee record for career strikeouts with 1,710 whiffs.

In fielding, Mickey Mantle also holds the all-time fielding records for Yankee center fielders with 4,273 putouts.

In fielding, Mickey Mantle established a new career record for the fewest average number of errors per year by commiting a mere 6.5 errors per year, breaking Joe DiMaggio's Yankee record of an average of 8 errors per year.

In fielding, Mickey Mantle also accepted the most career total of fielding chances by a center fielder wioth 4,460 total chances.

Mickey Mantle would also establish a new record for center fielders with the highest career fielding percentage of .983 that would stand for 15 years, before it was broken by center fielder Bobby Murcer whose career ended in 1983.

As a member of the New York Yankees, Mickey Mantle becomes the third all-time leader on the greatest franchise in baseball history scoring 1,677 runs, exceeded only by Babe Ruth and Lou Gehrig.

As a member of the New York Yankees, Mickey Mantle becomes the third all-time leader on the greatest franchise in baseball history collecting 2,415 hits, exceeded only by Lou Gehrig and Babe Ruth.

As a member of the New York Yankees, Mickey Mantle becomes the fourth all-time leader on the greatest franchise in baseball history belting out 344 doubles, exceeded only by Lou Gehrig, Babe Ruth, and Joe DiMaggio.

As a member of the New York Yankees, Mickey Mantle becomes tied for ninth on the all-time list on the greatest franchise in baseball history smacking 72 triples.

As a member of the New York Yankees, Mickey Mantle becomes the second all-time leader on the greatest franchise in baseball history be connecting for 536 home runs, exceeded only by Babe Ruth.

As a member of the New York Yankees, Mickey Mantle becomes the third all-time leader on the greatest franchise in baseball history by driving in 1,509 runs, exceeded only Babe Ruth and Lou Gehrig.

As a member of the New York Yankees, Mickey Mantle becomes the third all-time leader on the greatest franchise in baseball history pounding out 952 extra base hits, exceeded only by Lou Gehrig and Babe Ruth.

As a member of the New York Yankees, Mickey Mantle becomes the eighth all-time leader on the greatest franchise in baseball history by hitting for a .298 batting average.

As a member of the New York Yankees, Mickey Mantle becomes the fourth all-time leader on the greatest franchise in baseball history generating a .557 slugging average, exceeded only by Babe Ruth, Lou Gehrig, and Joe DiMaggio.

As a member of the New York Yankees, Mickey Mantle possesses the record for the most home runs ever hit, 266, at Yankee Stadium.

In this 1963 shot of a pinch-hit home run by Mantle at Yankee Stadium, Mickey shows the form that made the slugger the force behind 118 game-winning home runs.

APPENDIX XIII.
GAME-WINNING HOME RUNS (118)

1951 (2)

1. September 8, 1951: With the score knotted at 0-0, Mantle poles a tremendous line-drive home run that keeps going until it carries into right-center field bleachers for a 3-0 lead in an eventual 4-0 victory.

2. September 19, 1951: Mickey's three-run shot off Lou Kretlow in a 5-3 contest proves to be the sealer of doom for the White Sox.

1952 (6)

3. June 27, 1952: In a 10-0 cakewalk, the young Mantle's roundtripper off Philadelphia's Bob Hooper produces the first runs in the contest against the Athletics.

4. July 29, 1952: Mickey's second career grand slam home run provides the game-winning margin in a 10-7 slugfest at Comiskey Park.

5. August 11, 1952: Mickey's solo home run in the first inning off Sid Hudson is the initial run batted in for the Yankees and cause enough for producing the winning margin. The Yankees win the contest, 7-0.

6. September 24, 1952: At Fenway Park, Mantle's fourth-inning, three-run home run off southpaw Mel Parnell provides the Yankees with the game-winning margin. The Yankees win the contest, 8-6.

7. October 6, 1952: At Ebbets Field during the 1952 World Series, Mantle pounds out a Game Six game-winning home run against Billy Loes. Yankees win 3-2.

8. October 7, 1952: In the seventh inning of the deciding Game Seven of the 1952 World Series, being played this day at Ebbets Field, Mantle connects off Joe Black. Yankees win, 4-2.

1953 (6)

9. April 17, 1953—Belting his first home run of the year, Mickey Mantle powers his first prodigious, "tape-measure" home run of his career, pounding out a 565-foot wallop, the longest officially documented blast in a wallop-filled career. The titanic blow drives in the fourth run in a 7-3 Yankee victory over the hometown Washington Senators.

10. April 23, 1953: At Yankee Stadium, Mantle slashes a game-winning home run off Ellis Kinder of the Boston Red Sox. Yankees win, 6-3.

11. June 11, 1953: At Briggs Stadium in Detroit, Mantle lights up Tiger righthander Art Houtteman when he explodes for a tremendous shot that clears the 110-foot rim of the Stadium roof of the auxiliary press box of the right-field grandstand. The blast accounts for the two runs that give the Yankees the lead for good. The Bombers win, 6-3.

12. August 7, 1953: Mickey's inside-the-park home run off Connie Johnson drives in three, all the runs required for a Yankee 6-1 victory.

13. September 1, 1953: At Comiskey Park, Mantle wins the game for the Yanks with a long home run off Virgil Trucks. Later in the game, the Yankees win, 3-2.

14. October 1, 1953: In Game Two of the World Series, played this day at Yankee Stadium, Mantle beats the Brooklyn Dodgers when he connects on a liner into the lower leftfield grandstand bleachers. The Yankees win, 4-2.

1954 (6)

15. May 7, 1954: In a Yankee Stadium game with the Phila- delphia Athletics, Mantle homers off Morrie Martin which beats the A's 2-0.

16. July 3, 1954: In a game against the Washington Senators, Mantle pounds out a home run against Bob Porterfield at Yankee Stadium. Yankees win, 3-2.

17. July 5, 1954: Mickey's titanic blast off righthander Arnie Portocarrera provides the go-ahead runs in the 7-4 competition against the visiting A's.

18. July 22, 1954: In a close 4-3 tilt, Mantle connects off Don Johnson for a 10th-inning triumph in the

curtain-raiser of the Stadium twinbill with the Chisox.

19. July 28, 1954: Facing Jack Harshman of the Chicago White Sox, Mantle scorches a ninth-inning, three-run shot that paces the Bombers to a 7-5 victory in the Bronx.

20. August 24, 1954: Playing at Briggs Stadium, Mantle connects off Tiger righthander Steve Gromek for a game-winner. The Yankees win, 3-2.

1955 (11)

21. April 28, 1955: Mantle's home run knocks in the fifth run against the Athletics' righthander Charlie Bishop that paces the 11-4 victory over Philadelphia.

22. May 6, 1955: Mickey pounds in the first runs scored in the game with his game-winning shot off Frank Sullivan in the Yankee 6-0 whitewash of the Boston Red Sox.

23. May 13, 1955: Mickey's performance at Yankee Stadium, including the belting of three "tape-measure" home runs, drives in all the runs in a winning Yankee effort as the Bombing "Switcher" himself paces the 5-2 triumph over the visiting Detroit Tigers.

24. June 22, 1955: Mantle poles an opposite-field home run that knocks in the go-ahead second run in a 6-1 triumph over Art Ditmar and the Kansas City A's.

25. July 10, 1955: In the second game of a twinbill with the Washington Senators, Mickey connects off Ted Abernathy for a home run that tallies the go-ahead and winning run in an 8-3 victory.

26. August 7, 1955: At Yankee Stadium in the Bronx, Mantle belts a long home run against "Babe" Birrer of the Detroit Tigers. The Yankees win, 3-2.

27. August 14, 1955: In the eventual 7-2 Yankee triumph, Mickey's long ball accounts for the winning runs when he pounds out a home run against former teammate and current Oriole southpaw Ed Lopat.

28. August 15, 1955: Mickey connects from both sides of the plate for the second time in his career which propels the Yankees ahead to stay in the 12-6 contest.

29. August 24, 1955: Facing righthander Steve Gromek, Mickey blasts the tail-end home run in a back-to-back sequence with Yogi Berra that gives the Yankees a 3-2 victory over the Detroit nine.

30. August 28, 1955: Mantle powers in the go-ahead run in a 6-1 triumph over the Chicago White Sox when he pounds out the key home run in the Yankee triumph.

31. September 2, 1955: Against the Washington Senators at Yankee Stadium, Mantle homers off Bob Porterfield for a game-winner. The Yankees win, 4-2.

1956 (12)

32. April 21, 1956: Mantle poles a 415-foot home run off Bosox righthander George Susce, Jr. that drives in the winning run against the Sox in a 14-10 slugfest.

33. May 5, 1956: Mickey pounds out two home runs against the visiting Athletics, his second being the game-winner off Moe Burtschy. The Yankees win, 5-2.

34. May 8, 1956: Mickey's seventh-inning roundtripper in a Yankee Stadium contest gives the pinstripers

a 4-3 victory over burly Indian righthander Early Wynn.

35. May 21, 1956: Poling his second home run of the game, Mantle's 450-foot clout off Moe Burtschy drives in the winning run as the Yanks beat the Athletics, 8-7.

36. June 16, 1956: At Cleveland's Municipal Stadium, Mantle connects off the fireballing lefthanded pitching sensation, Herb Score, for a game-winner. The Yankees win, 3-1.

37. June 18, 1956: Mantle's right-field roof shot at Briggs Stadium off Paul Foytack wins the game, 7-4, against the astonished hometown Tigers who marvel at the sheer prodigiousness of the drive.

38. July 1, 1956: Against the visiting Washington Senators, in the second game of an afternoon twinbill, Mantle connects off Bud Byerly for the Yankee Stadium victory. Yankees win, 8-6.

39. July 30, 1956: Mantle connects for a grand slam home run off Bob Lemon of the Cleveland Indians that pushes the Yankees past the Indians for good. The Yankees crush the Tribe, 13-6.

40. August 31, 1956: Off Camilo Pascual, Mickey Mantle pounds out the game-winning home run that gives the Yankees a 6-4 triumph over the Senators.

41. September 13, 1956: Mickey connects off Tom Gorman for the third and winning run against the A's.

42. September 18, 1956: Mickey Mantle's "tape-measure" shot carries high and far until it soars over the left-center field grandstand and out of the ballyard, beating the hometown White Sox, 3-2, and clinching the American League pennant.

43. October 8, 1956: In Game Five of the World Series, Don Larsen pitches a perfect game for the Yankees and Mantle belts in the first run of the game with a line-drive home run. Yankees beat the Dodgers, 2-0.

1957 (7)

44. April 24, 1957: Unleashing a powerful drive off Connie Johnson, the ball sails into the right-field bleachers for an eighth-inning decider.

45. May 12, 1957: Against the Orioles, Mantle homers off Baltimore righthander Hal "Skinny" Brown for a game-winner at Memorial Stadium. The Yankees win, 4-3.

46. May 16, 1957: At Yankee Stadium, Mantle belts out a long home run against Alex Kellner for the game-winner. The Yankees win, 3-2.

47. June 2, 1957: Mickey powers in the first three runs of a 13-0 shellacking of the White Sox for the victory.

48. July 1, 1957: At Memorial Stadium in Baltimore, Mantle homers off George Zuverink which allows the Yankees to taste the fruits of victory on the road. The Yankees win, 3-2.

49. July 11, 1957: At the Municipal Stadium in Kansas City, Mantle homers off A's righthander Tom Morgan for an extra-inning victory. Yankees win, 3-2, in the 11th.

50. August 13, 1957: At Fenway Park, Mantle's homer powers in all of the Yankee runs in a 3-2 victory over the Red Sox.

1958 (8)

51. April 17, 1958: Mantle pounds out a towering shot to the opposite field over the left-center field portion of the "Green Monster."

52. June 2, 1958: Mickey connects off Jim Wilson for the first runs in the game for the Bombers, all the runs that the Yankees will need for victory.

53. June 3, 1958: Mickey's blast off Dick Donovan into the right-field grandstand seats provides the first three tallies in a lopsided 13-0 shutout.

54. July 1, 1958: In the second game of a doubleheader, Mickey's eighth-inning blast provides the winning edge in the 2-1 tilt.

55. July 3, 1958: Mickey's prodigious blast gives the Yanks their go-ahead runs in an 11-3 rout.

56. July 24, 1958: Against Paul Foytack of the Detroit Tigers, Mantle connects for an eighth-inning game-winner against the Tigers.

57. August 5, 1958: At Memorial Stadium in Baltimore, Mantle homers off Connie Johnson for the three-run game-winner. The Yankees win, 4-1.

58. September 24, 1958: Mantle propels a long, towering drive over the left-center field portion of the "Green Monster" some 380 feet away from home plate at the base of the 37-foot high wall which gives the Yankees their go-ahead and winning run in the 7-5 contest.

1959 (6)

59. June 3, 1959: Mantle's blow carries the day for the Yankees which produces the game-winning margin for the Bombers. The Yankees win, 6-5.

60. June 17, 1959: At Yankee Stadium, Mantle homers against Ray Moore of the Chicago White Sox which helps beat the visiting Sox, 7-3.

61. June 18, 1959: At Yankee Stadium, Mantle connects off Jerry Staley of the Chicago White Sox for an extra-inning game-winning home run. Yankees win, 5-4, in the 10th.

62. July 16, 1959: Mantle powers a two-out, two-run home run off Gary Bell that wins the game for the Yankees, 7-5, in the 10th inning.

63. August 16, 1959: At Yankee Stadium, in the second game of a doubleheader, Mantle homers off Bill Monbouquette of the Boston Red Sox which gives the Yankees a 4-2 victory.

64. September 13, 1959: Facing Jack Harshman, Mantle hits a long home run that beats the Chicago White Sox in Yankee Stadium, 2-1.

1960 (9)

65. June 9, 1960: Pounding out a home run against the fireballing Dick Donovan, Mickey drives in two runs, including the game-winning scores.

66. June 10, 1960: At Yankee Stadium, Mantle homers off Dick Stigman which gives the Yankees a 4-3 Yankee victory over the Cleveland Indians.

67. June 18, 1960: At Comiskey Park, Mickey belts a long home run off Chisox righthander Bob Rush to

straight-away center field that soars over the center-field bullpen, the remotest point in the spacious ball yard. The timely blow drives in the fifth and sixth runs in the 12-5 Bomber victory.

68. July 3, 1960: Mickey's three-run home run off southpaw Pete Burnside is the game-winner over the Tigers in the 6-2 Yankee victory.

69. July 26, 1960: Mantle's home run off lefty Dick Stigman provides the Yankees with the winning margin against the Cleveland Indians.

70. August 15, 1960: In the Bronx, Mantle powers a Hoyt Wilhelm knuckleball into the grandstands for a game-winner over the Baltimore Orioles. Yankees win, 4-3.

71. September 10, 1960: At Briggs Stadium, Mickey launches a Herculean blast that sails out of the ballpark, clearing everything, while knocking in the three runs that win the contest for the Bombers, 4-1.

72. September 11, 1960: Batting against Carl Mathias with two outs in Cleveland's Municipal Stadium, Mantle homers in extra innings to win the game for the Yankees, 3-2, in the 11th.

73. September 24, 1960: Off Ted Wills, Mantle powers a home run out of Fenway Park for a game-winner against the Boston Red Sox. The Yankees win, 6-5.

1961 (11)

74. April 17, 1961: Against the Kansas City Athletics, Mantle belts out a home run against righthander Jerry Walker in the 3-0 Yankee triumph.

75. April 21, 1961: Playing at Memorial Stadium against the Baltimore Orioles Angeles Angels, Mantle connects off Steve Barber which gives the Yankees a 4-2 win over the hometown Orioles.

76. April 26, 1961: Facing Hank Aguirre in the 10th inning, Mantle crashes an extra-inning shot that wins it for the Yanks, 13-11, over the hometown Tigers.

77. May 2, 1961: Against Camilo Pascual in Bloomington's Metropolitan Stadium, Mantle powers a grand slam home run that proves to be the game-winner against the Minnesota Twins. The Yankees win, 6-4, in the 10th.

78. May 31, 1961: Mantle poles a long, 400-foot home run off Red Sox righthander Billy Muffett, that carries into the Red Sox bullpen in right-center field, and gives the Yankees a 7-6 victory.

79. June 11, 1961: Mantle's three-run shot in the first inning proves to be the decisive blow for the Yankees early in the affair. The Bombers win, 5-1.

80. June 21, 1961: Mickey lights up the Kansas City diamond with two prodigious drives which account for all of the Yankees' five runs in the 5-4 victory over the Athletics.

81. July 8, 1961: Mantle's upper deck shot into the right-field grandstand off Tracy Stallard provides the Bombers with the sixth and game-winning run. The Yankees beat the Red Sox, 8-5.

82. July 13, 1961: Connecting once more off his favorite "cousin," the burly righthander Early Wynn, Mickey drives in the third and winning run. The Bombers beat the Pale Hose, 6-2.

83. July 18, 1961: Mickey's two home runs off the Senators' Joe McClain prove to combine for the game-winner in the 5-3 Yankee victory.

84. August 20, 1961: Mickey's first-inning blow off righthander Jim Perry is the ultimate decider in the game as the Yankees whitewash the Indians, 6-0.

1962 (4)

85. July 3, 1962: Against the Kansas City Athletics, Mantle pounds out a home run against Gordon Jones which wins the game at Municipal Stadium for the Yankees, 8-7.

86. August 28, 1962: Playing against the Cleveland Indians, Mantle homers off Jim "Mudcat" Grant which beats the visiting Indians. Yankees win, 2-1.

87. September 11, 1962: Playing against the Cleveland Indians, Mantle connects off Pedro Ramos which proves a game-winner on the road in Municipal Stadium. Yankees win, 5-2.

88. September 18, 1962: Mickey powers a first-inning, three-run blast off Senator righthander Tom Cheney that gives the Yankees the winning margin in the 7-1 victory.

1963 (4)

89. May 21, 1963: Against the Kansas City A's, Mantle's roundtripper against Diego Segui provides the Yankees' winning margin in the 7-4 victory at the Stadium.

90. May 22, 1963: Against the Kansas City A's, Mantle connects for a prodigious home run against Athletic righthander Bill Fischer. The Yankees win, 8-7.

91. May 26, 1963: Mantle connects off Don Rudolph of the Washington Senators which gives the Yankees all the runs they need in the 7-1 triumph.

92. September 11, 1963: Facing Ed Rakow of the Kansas City A's, Mantle belts out a game-winning home run at Municipal Stadium against the hometown favorites. Yankees win, 8-2.

1964 (8)

93. May 16, 1964: Belting a 410-foot home run off Moe Drabowsky gives Mickey and the Bombers the winning margin against the A's when his two-run smash knocks in the seventh and eighth runs in the 10-6 victory.

94. June 11, 1964: Mickey's second clout in the game against Bill Monbouquette accounts for the game-winning run againmst the Red Sox. The Yankees beat the Sox, 8-4.

95. July 4, 1964: Squaring off against Al Worthington of the Minnesota Twins, Mickey propels a three-run shot into the upper deck of the right-field grandstand. The Yankees win, 7-5.

96. July 13, 1964: Mantle pounds out a line-drive home run off Gary Bell which drives in the fifth run, the decider, in the 10-4 contest.

97. August 1, 1964: Selecting a 3-and-0 pitch to hit, Mantle connects off southpaw Dick Stigman, rifling the horsehide over the center-field screen for the game-winning run.

98. August 22, 1964: Mantle's first-inning, two-run blast off Jack Lamabe accounts for all the runs that the Yankees need for their 5-1 victory over Boston.

99. September 22, 1964: Mickey connects for a first-inning, two-run blast off Dick Donovan which settles matters early for the Yankees in their 8-1 victory.

100. October 10, 1964: At Yankee Stadium in Game Three of the World Series, Mantle connects off Barney Schultz leading off the ninth inning which gives the Yankees a 2-1 triumph over the St. Louis Cardinals.

1965 (5)

101. April 17, 1965: In Mickey's final at-bat in the game, he powers the ball over the fence off John Wyatt which drives in the third and fourth runs of the game for the Yankees in the 5-2 triumph over the Athletics.

102. April 25, 1965: At Yankee Stadium, Mantle homers off Rudy May of the Los Angeles Angels which provides the the only run scored in the game. Yankees win, 1-0.

103. May 15, 1965: At Baltimore's Memorial Stadium, Mantle belts out a home run against Oriole hurler Dick Hall that proves to be the game-winner. Yankees win, 3-2.

104. June 18, 1965: Batting righthanded against the left-handed Mel Nelson, Mantle powers the ball into the opposite-field grandstand for a grand slam home run and the deciding runs in a 10-2 victory.

105. September 2, 1965: Mickey's first-inning, three-run belt off Marcelino Lopez accounts for all the runs required for the Yankee win. The Bombers beat the Angels, 8-1.

1966 (2)

106. July 7, 1966: With two outs in the ninth inning, Mantle pounds out a three-run home run which gives the Yankees a 5-2 victory over the Boston Red Sox.

107. August 26, 1966: At Yankee Stadium, Mantle beats the Tigers, 6-5, when he connects off southpaw Hank Aguirre for a game-winning home run.

1967 (8)

108. April 29, 1967: At Yankee Stadium, Mantle launches a prodigious clout into the distant right-center field bleachers which gives the Yankees a 4-3 triumph.

109. April 30, 1967: At Yankee Stadium, Mickey connects into the upper tier of the right-field grandstand for a one-out, 10th-inning, three-run wallop off Minnie Rojas. The Yankees win, 4-1.

110. May 14, 1967: At the Stadium, Mantle's milestone 500th roundtripper wins the game when he connects off Stu Miller deep into the lower right field grandstand. The Yankees win, 6-5.

111. May 24, 1967: At Memorial Stadium in Baltimore, Mantle belts out a game-winning home run against Steve Barber. Yankees win, 2-0.

112. June 5, 1967: Mickey belts a pinch-hit, opposite-field, home run at the Stadium off Darold Knowles which seals the Yankees' 4-2 victory.

113. June 15, 1967: At D.C. Stadium in the Nation's Capitol, Mantle homers off Senator hurler Frank Bertaina which provides the Yankees with the 2-0 winning margin.

114. June 24, 1967: At Yankee Stadium, the Yankees win the contest, 4-3, when Mantle belts out a game-winning home run against Fred Gladding of the Detroit Tigers.

115. September 2, 1967: Playing against the Washington Senators at Yankee Stadium, the pinch-hitting Mick connects off Bob Priddy which gives the Yankees a 2-1 triumph.

1968 (3)

116. April 18, 1968: Mantle drives in the Yankees' first two runs with a first-inning, two-run clout off Jim McGlothlin that fuels the 6-1 victory over the Angels.

117. May 30, 1968: Mickey's second home run of the game, coming off Bob Humphreys, gives the Yankees the winning margin they require for the 13-4 victory over the Washington Senators.

118. June 16, 1968: Mantle's poke to deep left off southpaw Clyde Wright gives Mickey and his teammates a 4-3 victory over the hometown California Angels.

In his career, Mickey Mantle slammed 536 home runs against American League opponents, 118 of which had been directly responsible for winning the game for the New York Yankees. By the time of his retirement, only two major league ballplayers, "Babe" Ruth and Willie Mays had hit more home runs. Showing phenomenal consistency, the clucth nature of his long-range production is simply mind-boggling. For every five home runs that Mickey clouted during his 18-year Hall-of-Fame career, one of them proved to be a game-winner for the New York Yankees. It is difficult to imagine a more dominating presence at the plate over so long a time than when Mickey Mantle, injured or not, came up to the dish to hit.

APPENDIX XIV.
MULTIPLE HOME RUNS IN THE SAME GAME
DURING MICKEY MANTLE'S CAREER
(REGULAR SEASON: 46 TIMES)

1. August 11, 1952 vs. Sid Hudson and Ralph Brickner of the Boston Red Sox in a 7-0 Yankee victory at the Stadium.

2. August 5, 1954 vs. Early Wynn and Ray Narleski of the Cleveland Indians in a 5-2 Yankee victory at the Stadium.

3. May 14, 1955 vs. Steve Gromek twice and Bob Miller once against the Detroit Tigers in a 5-2 Yankee victory at the Stadium.

4. Jly 10, 1955 vs. Dean Stone of the Washington Senators twice in a 6-4 Senator victory at Griffith Stadium.

5. August 7, 1955 vs. Frank Lary and "Babe" Birrer of the Detroit Tigers in a 3-2 Yankee victory at the Stadium.

In this 1961 image of Mantlesque determination and upper body strength, the photo records the moment of the 28th time that Mickey hit two or more home runs in the same game. In his career Mantle would blast multiple home runs on 46 different occasions.

6. August 15, 1955 vs. Ray Moore and Art Schallock of the Baltimore Orioles in a 12-6 Yankee victory at Memorial Stadium in Baltimore.

7. April 17, 1956 vs. Camilo Pascual of the Washington Senators twice in a 10-4 Yankee victory at Griffith Stadium.

8. May 5, 1956 vs. Lou Kretlow and Moe Burtschy of the Kansas City A's in a 5-2 Yankee victory at the Stadium.

9. May 18, 1956 vs. Billy Pierce and "Dixie" Howell of the Chicago White Sox in a 8-7 Yankee victory at Comiskey Park in Chicago.

10. June 20, 1956 vs. Billy Hoeft twice of the Detroit Tigers in a 4-1 Yankee victory at Briggs Stadium in Detroit.

11. July 1, 1956 vs. Dean Stone and Bud Byerly of the Washington Senators in an 8-6 Yankee victory at the Stadium.

12. July 30, 1956 vs. Bob Lemon and Bob Feller of the Cleveland Indians in a 13-6 Yankee victory at the Municipal Stadium in Cleveland.

13. August 4, 1956 vs. Virgil Trucks twice of the Detroit Tigers in a 5-4 Tiger victory at Briggs Stadium in Detroit.

14. June 13, 1957 vs. Jack Harshman and Bob Keegan of the Chicago White Sox in a 7-6 White Sox victory at Comiskey Park.

15. June 6, 1958 vs. Dick Tomanek twice of the Cleveland Indians in a 6-5 Yankee victory at the Stadium.

16. July 3, 1958 vs. Russ Kemmerer twice of the Washington Senators in an 11-3 Yankee victory at Griffith Stadium.

17. July 28, 1958 vs. Dick Tomanek and Ray Herbert of the Kansas City A's in a 14-7 Yankee victory at the Municipal Stadium in Kansas City.

** WORLD SERIES: October 2, 1958 in Game Three of the 1958 World Series vs. Lew Burdette in a 13-5 victory by the Milwaukee Braves at County Stadium.

18. June 22, 1959 vs. Ray Herbert and Bob Grim of the Kansas City A's in an 11-6 victory at the Municipal Stadium in Kansas City.

19. September 15, 1959 vs. Billy Pierce and Bob Shaw of the Chicago White Sox in a 4-3 Chicago victory at the Stadium.

20. June 8, 1960 vs. Bob Shaw and Ray Moore of the Chicago White Sox in a 6-0 Yankee victory at the Stadium.

21. June 21, 1960 vs. Frank Lary twice of the Detroit Tigers in a 6-0 Yankee victory at Briggs Stadium.

22. August 15, 1960 vs. Jerry Walker and Hoyt Wilhelm of the Baltimore Orioles in a 4-3 Yankee victory at the Stadium.

23. September 28, 1960 vs. Chuck Stobbs twice of the Washington Senators in a 6-3 Yankee victory at Griffith Stadium in the Nation's Capitol.

** WORLD SERIES: October 6, 1960 in Game Two of the 1960 World Series vs. Freddie Green and Joe Gibbon in a 16-3 bashing of the Pittsburgh Pirates at Forbes Field.

24. April 20, 1961 vs. Eli Grba twice of the Los Angeles Angels in a 7-5 Yankee victory at the Stadium.

25. April 26, 1961 vs. Jim Donahue and Hank Aguirre of the Detroit Tigers in a 13-11 Yankee victory at Briggs Stadium.
26. May 30, 1961 vs. Gene Conley and Mike Fornieles of the Boston Red Sox in a 12-3 Yankee victory at Fenway Park in Boston.

27. June 21, 1961 vs. Bob Shaw of the Kansas City A's twice in a 5-3 Yankee victory at the Municipal Stadium in Kansas City.

28. July 1, 1961 vs. Carl Mathias of the Washington Senators in a 7-6 Yankee victory at the Stadium.

29. July 18, 1961 vs Joe McClain of the Washington Senators twice in a 5-3 Yankee victory at Griffith Stadium in the Nation's Capitol.

30. August 6, 1961 vs. Pedro Ramos of the Minnesota Twins twice in a 7-6 Yankee victory at the Stadium.

31. September 3, 1961 vs. Jim Bunning and Jerry Staley of the Detroit Tigers in an 8-5 Yankee victory at the Stadium.

32. May 6, 1962 vs. Pete Burnside and Jim Hannan of the Washington Senators in an 8-0 Yankee triumph at the Stadium.

33. July 3, 1962 vs. Jerry Walker and Gordon Jones of the Kansas City A's in an 8-7 Yankee victory at the Stadium.

34. July 4, 1962 vs. Dan Pfister and John Wyatt of the Kansas City A's in a 7-3 Yankee victory at the Stadium.

35. July 6, 1962 vs. Camilo Pascual of the Washington Senators twice in a 7-5 Yankee win at the Stadium.

36. September 18, 1962 vs. Tom Cheney of the Washington Senators in a 7-1 Yankee victory at Griffith Stadium.

37. May 21, 1963 vs. Orlando Pena and Diego Segui of the Kansas City A's in a 7-4 Yankee triumph at the Stadium.

38. June 11, 1964 vs. Bill Monbouquette of the Boston Red Sox in an 8-4 Yankee victory at Fenway Park.

39. August 12, 1964 vs. Ray Herbert and Frank Baumann of the Chicago White Sox in a 7-3 Yankee victory at the Stadium.

40. May 25, 1966 vs. Dean Chance and Lew Burdette of the California Angels in an 11-6 Yankee victory at the Stadium.

41. June 28, 1966 vs. Jose Santiago of the Boston Red Sox twice in a 5-3 Red Sox victory at Fenway Park.

42. June 29, 1966 vs. Roland Sheldon and Lee Stange of the Boston Red Sox in a 6-5 Yankee victory at Fenway Park.

43. July 2, 1966 vs. Mike McCormick of the Washington Senators twice in a 10-4 Senator victory at Griffith Stadium.

44. July 4, 1967 vs. Jim "Mudcat" Grant of the Minnesota Twins in an 8-3 Twin victory at the Metropolitan Stadium in Bloomington, Minnesota.

45. May 30, 1968 vs. Joe Coleman and Bob Humphreys of the Washington Senators in a 13-4 Yankee victory at the Stadium.

46. August 10, 1968 vs. Jim Merritt of the Minnesota Twins in a 3-2 Twin victory at the Stadium.

APPENDIX XV.
BOTH SIDES OF THE PLATE IN THE SAME GAME
(10 TIMES)

Hitting Home Runs from Both Sides of the Plate in the Same Game was a major league record Mickey Mantle held for more than a quarter-century.

May 13, 1955: Batting lefthanded, Mantle propels two home runs against Steve Gromek in a game at the Stadium against the Detroit Tigers. Batting righthanded, Mantle belts a home run against southpaw Bob Miller. Yankees win, 5-2.

August 15, 1955: Batting lefthanded, Mickey Mantle pounds out a home run against Ray Moore of the Baltimore Orioles. Mantle later bats righthanded against southpaw Art Schallock when he poles another home run into the stands at Memorial Stadium in Baltimore. Yankees win, 12-6.

May 18, 1956: Playing at Comiskey Park, Mantle first blasts a home run hitting righthanded against Billy Pierce of the Chicago White Sox. Later, in the same game, Mantle launches another home run, this time batting leftthanded against "Dixie" Howell. Yankees win, 8-7.

July 1, 1956 (second game): Playing against the Washington Senators at the Stadium, Mantle propels one home run from the right side of the dish against southpaw Dean Stone, before turning around and hitting another home run batting lefthanded against Bud Byerly. Yankees win, 8-6.

June 13, 1957: At Comiskey Park, Mantle blasts one home run batting righthanded against lefty Jack Harshman. Later, in the same game, Mantle smashes a second home run, this time batting lefthanded against righthanded-throwing Bob Keegan. Chicago wins, 7-6.

July 28, 1958: Playing in Kansas City at Municipal Stadium, Mantle hits one home run batting right- handed against Dick Tomanek. Later, Mantle propels a long shot against Ray Herbert batting from the left side of the plate. Yankees win, 14-7.

September 15, 1959: At the Stadium in the Bronx, Mantle hits a home run batting righthanded against Billy Pierce of the Chicago White Sox. Mantle later turns around and connects off the righthanded Bob Shaw in the same game. Chicago wins, 4-3.

April 26, 1961: At Briggs Stadium, Mantle bats lefthanded against Jim Donohue when he homers into the grandstand. Batting righthanded against Hank Aguirre later in the same game, Mantle again propels a long blast into the stands for another home run. Yankees win, 13-11.

May 6, 1962: In a game against the Washington Senators at Yankee Stadium, Mantle first homers against Dave Stenhouse, before turning around to face lefty Pete Burnside and promptly homering again. Washington wins, 4-2.

August 12, 1964: Batting lefthanded against Ray Herbert, Mantle blasts a home run against the Chicago White Sox. Then, turning around to bat righthanded against southpaw Frank Baumann, Mantle unleashes another long shot for his second home run. Yankees win, 7-3.

APPENDIX XVI.
THE CUMULATIVE RECORD OF
AMERICAN LEAGUE HOME RUNS

Mickey Mantle's Record for Home Runs in American League Ballyards (15) and Yankee Stadium

ON-THE-ROAD   Total 270

Briggs Stadium/Tiger Stadium (Detroit)	41
Fenway Park (Boston)	38
Municipal Stadium (Cleveland)	36
Comiskey Park (Chicago)	31
Griffith Stadium (Washington D.C.)—(1953-1961)	28
Municipal Stadium (Kansas City)	26
Memorial Stadium (Baltimore)	26
Metropolitan Stadium (Bloomington, Minnesota)	14
D.C. Stadium (Washington D.C.)—(1962-1968)	10
Connie Mack Stadium/Shibe Park (Philadelphia)	6
Sportsman's Park (St. Louis) vs. the Browns	4
Anaheim Stadium in (Anaheim) vs. the Angels	4
Wrigley Field (Los Angeles) vs. the Angels	2
Dodger Stadium (Los Angeles) vs. the Angels	2
Oakland Coliseum (Oakland)	2

YANKEE STADIUM   Total 266

vs. the Chicago White Sox	42
vs. the Kansas City Athletics	35
vs. the Detroit Tigers	32
vs. the Boston Red Sox	31
vs. the Cleveland Indians	29
vs. the Washington Senators (1951-1961)	28
vs. the Washington Senators (1962-1968)	13
vs. the Baltimore Orioles (1954-1967)	19
vs. the Los Angeles Angels/California Angels	16
vs. the Minnesota Twins (1961-1968)	13
vs. the Philadelphia A's (1951-1954)	5
vs. the St. Louis Browns (1951-1953)	2
vs. the Oakland A's	1

CUMULATIVE AMERICAN LEAGUE OPPONENTS

The Washington Senators/The Minnesota Twins	83
The Philadelphia/Kansas City/Oakland A's	75
The Chicago White Sox	73
The Detroit Tigers	73
The Boston Red Sox	69
The Cleveland Indians	65
The St. Louis Browns/Baltimore Orioles	51
The Los Angeles/California Angels	24
The Washington Senators (1962-1968)	23

CUMULATIVE TOTALS   Total 536

In the 1954 season, Mickey Mantle hit home runs in every park in the American League, including Yankee Stadium, Shibe Park, Memorial Stadium in Baltimore, Municipal Stadium in Cleveland, Fenway Park in Boston, Griffith Stadium in Washington D.C., Comiskey Park in Chicago, and Briggs Stadium in Detroit. In the 1955 season, Mickey Mantle hit home runs in every park in the American League, including Yankee Stadium, Municipal Stadium in Kansas City, Memorial Stadium in Baltimore, Municipal Stadium in Cleveland, Fenway Park in Boston, Griffith Stadium in Washington D.C., Comiskey Park in Chicago, and Briggs Stadium in Detroit.

In the 1957 season, Mickey Mantle hit home runs in every park in the American League, including Yankee Stadium, Municipal Stadium in Kansas City, Memorial Stadium in Baltimore, Municipal Stadium in Cleveland, Fenway Park in Boston, Griffith Stadium in Washington D.C., Comiskey Park in Chicago, and

Briggs Stadium in Detroit.

In the 1958 season, Mickey Mantle hit home runs in every park in the American League, including Yankee Stadium, Municipal Stadium in Kansas City, Memorial Stadium in Baltimore, Municipal Stadium in Cleveland, Fenway Park in Boston, Griffith Stadium in Washington D.C., Comiskey Park in Chicago, and Briggs Stadium in Detroit.

In the 1959 season, Mickey Mantle hit home runs in every park in the American League, including Yankee Stadium, Municipal Stadium in Kansas City, Memorial Stadium in Baltimore, Municipal Stadium in Cleveland, Fenway Park in Boston, Griffith Stadium in Washington D.C., Comiskey Park in Chicago, and Briggs Stadium in Detroit.

In the 1961 season, Mickey Mantle hit home runs in every park in the American League, including Yankee Stadium, Municipal Stadium in Kansas City, Memorial Stadium in Baltimore, Municipal Stadium in Cleveland, Fenway Park in Boston, Griffith Stadium in Washington D.C., Comiskey Park in Chicago, Briggs Stadium in Detroit, Metropolitan Stadium in Bloomington, Minnesota, and Wrigley Field in Los Angeles, California.

In the 1964 season, Mickey Mantle hit home runs in every park in the American League, including Yankee Stadium, Municipal Stadium in Kansas City, Memorial Stadium in Baltimore, Municipal Stadium in Cleveland, Fenway Park in Boston, D.C. Stadium in Washington D.C., Comiskey Park in Chicago, Briggs Stadium in Detroit, and Metropolitan Stadium in Bloomington, Minnesota, and Dodger Stadium in Los Angeles, California.

Seven different times, Mickey Mantle belted home runs in each ballyard of the American League. Five of those seasons came in a time when the league was comprised of eight teams, before the league had expanded to 10 teams. Twice, Mantle belted home runs in each of the 10 ballparks in the league. Seven seasons of hitting home runs in every league park is a major league record for switch-hitters.

In his 18-year career, Mickey Mantle played in 2,401 games. In 488 of those games, Mantle homered. In those games when Mantle homered, the Yankees won 345 of those contests, lost 142, and tied their opponents twice. The record of Yankee triumphs when Mickey homered amounted to a .707 winning percentage.

APPENDIX XVII.
GRAND SLAM HOME RUNS
(REGULAR SEASON: 9 AND WORLD SERIES: 1)

DATE	SITE	PITCHER	TEAM
1. July 26, 1952	Briggs	Ted Gray (LH)	Detroit Stadium Tigers
2. July 29, 1952	Comiskey Park	Billy Pierce (LH)	Chicago White Sox
3. July 6, 1953	Shibe Park	Frank Fanovich (LH)	Philadelphia Athletics
4. Oct. 4, 1953	Ebbets Field	Russ Meyer	Brooklyn Dodgers (WORLD SERIES)
5. May 18, 1955	Yankee Stadium	Mike Fornieles	Chicago White Sox
6. July 30, 1956	Municipal Stadium	Bob Lemon	Cleveland Indians
7. Aug. 19, 1962	Municipal Stadium	Jerry Walker	Kansas City Athletics
8. June 23, 1964	Memorial Stadium	Chuck Estrada	Baltimore Orioles
9. June 18, 1965	Yankee Stadium	Mel Nelson (LH)	Minnesota Twins
10. July 23, 1966	Yankee Stadium	Marcelino Lopez (LH)	California Angels

APPENDIX XVIII.
ATTENDANCE

In 55 of the Yankees' biggest games, the most widely attended contests, defined as 40,000-plus spectators in the stands, but excluding the millions of television viewers watching the New York Yankees in their homes, over 3 million baseball fans personally watched Mickey Mantle belt out a home run. In these heavily attended contests, the New York Yankees win 39 games, while losing 15, and tying 1 game for a .722 winning percentage—all of which occur in a game in which Mantle homered at least once.

DATE	ATTENDANCE	SCORE	DATE	ATTENDANCE	SCORE
9/14/52	73,609	7-1,NY	6/20/56(2)	47,756	4-1,NY
6/15/52	69,468	8-2,NY	6/17/52	47,544	7-6,Det
8/9/58	67,916	9-6,Bos	6/23/53	46,756	11-3,Chi
8/25/51	66,110	7-3,NY	7/25/61	46,240	12-0,NY
6/23/57	64,936	4-3,Chi	6/26/54	46,192	11-9,NY
6/19/51	61,596	11-9,NY	8/16/59	46,041	6-5,Bos
8/25/56	60,683	4-2,Chi	6/10/60	46,030	4-3,NY
7/24/60	60,002	8-2,NY	7/15/60	45,714	8-4,Det
9/10/61	57,824	9-3,NY	7/1/57	45,276	3-2,NY
7/19/59	57,057	6-4,NY	9/1/52	45,003	3-2,NY
7/25/65	56,634	7-4,Cle	5/21/67	44,862	9-4,Det
8/26/60	56,508	7-6,NY	7/17/61	44,332	5-0,NY
8/20/61	56,307	6-0,NY	6/19/55	44,060	5-2,NY
9/3/61(2)	55,676	8-5,NY	7/13/61	43,960	6-2,NY
8/14/56	52,409	12-2,NY	7/5/58	43,821	3-3,tie
7/28/62	52,038	4-3,NY	7/15/52	43,673	7-3,NY
7/21/57	51,670	7-4,Cle	6/7/57	43,474	6-3,Det
6/17/61	51,509	12-10,Det	7/14/61	43,450	6-1,Chi
7/17/52	51,114	11-6,NY	6/17/60	43,320	4-2,NY
7/24/64	51,044	10-5,NY	6/3/59	43,146	6-3,NY
8/11/52	51,005	7-0,NY	7/23/57	42,422	10-6,NY
8/28/55	50,990	6-1,NY	7/25/52	41,538	2-1,Det
7/3/60	50,556	6-2,NY	8/30/61	41,357	4-0,NY
6/16/62	50,254	10-9,Cle	7/6/62	40,994	7-5,NY
7/26/52	49,717	5-3,Det	5/20/60	40,970	5-3,Chi
8/5/54	49,483	5-2,NY	6/16/56	40,964	3-1,NY
6/11/57	49,114	3-2,NY	6/8/58	40,903	5-4,Cle
4/30/67	47,980	4-1,NY	9/13/59	40,807	2-1,NY
8/28/60	47,971	8-5,NY	6/13/57	40,033	7-6,Chi
6/22/52	47,970	2-1,Chi	6/3/55	40,020	3-2,NY

APPENDIX XIX.
CAREER TOTALS WITH OPPOSING PITCHERS (220)

13 HOME RUNS: (1 pitcher)

Early Wynn

12 HOME RUNS: (1 pitcher)

Pedro Ramos

11 HOME RUNS: (1 pitcher)

Camilo Pascual

9 HOME RUNS: (2 pitchers)

Frank Lary and Billy Pierce

8 HOME RUNS: (3 pitchers)

Dick Donovan, Gary Bell and Chuck Stobbs

7 HOME RUNS: (4 pitchers)

Ray Herbert, Connie Johnson, Jim Kaat, and Frank Sullivan

6 HOME RUNS: (6 pitchers)

Jim Bunning, Steve Gromek, Billy Hoeft, Jack Harshman, Paul Foytack, and Bob Lemon

5 HOME RUNS: (11 pitchers)

Hank Aguirre, Earl Wilson, Virgil Trucks, Jim Perry, John O'Donoghue, Ray Narleski, Ray Moore, Alex Kellner, Jim "Mudcat" Grant, Ike Delock, and Hal "Skinny" Brown

4 HOME RUNS: (16 pitchers)

Jerry Walker, Jim Wilson, Dick Stigman, Bob Shaw, Mel Parnell, Juan Pizarro, Don Mossi, Jack Kralick, Russ Kemmerer, Lou Kretlow, Mike Garcia, Chuck Estrada, George Brunet, Tom Brewer, and Steve Barber

3 HOME RUNS: (29 pitchers)

Frank Baumann, Pete Burnside, Bob Cain, Dean Chance, Art Ditmar, Bennie Daniels, Moe Drabowsky, Bill Fischer, Mike Fornieles, Tom Gorman, Eli Grba, Sid Hudson, Mickey Lolich, Mike McCormick, Carl Mathias, Denny McLain, Joe McClain, Jim Merritt, Willard Nixon, John "Blue Moon" Odom, Bob Porterfield, Arnie Portocarrero, Milt Pappas, Bobby Shantz, Dean Stone, Dave Sisler, Diego Segui, Dick Tomanek, Hoyt Wilhelm, and Hal Woodeshick

2 HOME RUNS: (37 pitchers)

Ted Abernathy, Moe Burtschy, Dick Bosman, Harry Byrd, Tex Clevenger, Jerry Casale, Tom Cheney, Bud Daley, Randy Gumpert, Ted Gray, Hal Griggs, Fred Gladding, Bob Hooper, Art Houtteman, Jim Hannan, Ellis Kinder, Bob Keegan, Ed Lopat, Jim Lonborg, Marcelino Lopez, and Bob Miller, Cal McLish, Sam McDowell, Jim McGlothin, Mickey McDermott, Billy Muffett, Hal Newhouser, Phil Ortega, Gary Peters, Ed Rakow, Herb Score, Jerry Staley, Lee Stange, Jose Santiago, Ralph Terry, John Wyatt, and George Zuverink

1 HOME RUN: (109 pitchers)

Al Aber, Jim Archer, Ralph Brickner, Lou Brissie, Gene Bearden, Ralph Branca, Charlie Bishop, Babe Birrer, Bud Byerly, Wally Burnette, Charley Beamon, Ted Bowsfield, Bo Belinsky, Dennis Bennett, Lew Burdette, Dave Boswell, Frank Bertaina, Sandy Consuegra, Art Ceccarelli, Rip Coleman, Gene Conley, Galen Cisco, Pete Charton, Joe Coleman, Joe Dobson, Sonny Dixon, Murray Dickson, Jim Donohue, Ryne Duren, Bob Duliba, Bill Dillman, Arnold Earley, Frank Fanovich, Bob Feller, Don Ferrarese, Eddie Fisher, Marv Grissom, Ned Garver, Bob Grim, Bobo Holloman, Bill Henry, Gene Host, Dick Hyde, Steve Hamilton, Dick Hall, Bruce Howard, Steve Hargan, Bob Humphreys, Joel Horlen, Dixie Howell, Gordon Jones, Don Johnson, Leo Kiely, Johnny Kucks, Johnny Klippstein, Marty Kutyna, Darold Knowles, Bill Kunkel, Paul LaPalme, Ken Lehman, Turk Lown, Barry Latman, Jack Lamabe, Don Lee, Don Larsen, Morris Martin, Duke Maas, Jack McMahan, Tom Morgan, Bob Meyer, Rudy May, Don McMahon, Stu Miller, Ken McBride, Fred Newman, Mel Nelson, Jim Nash, Billy O'Dell, Duane Pillette, Satchel Paige, Dan Pfister, Orlando Pena, Jim Palmer, Bob Priddy, Dick Rozek, Bob Rush, Phil Regan, Don Rudolph, Dick Radatz, Pete Richert, Minnie Rojas, Dick Starr, Marlin Stuart, Art Schallock, George Susce, Jr., Bob Sadowski, Tracy Stallard, Don Schwall, Al Schroll, Dave Stenhouse, Roland Sheldon, Jack Sanford, Sonny Siebert, Bob Trowbridge, Fred Talbot, Bill Wight, Willie Werle, Ted Wills, Al Worthington, and Clyde Wright

APPENDIX XX.
HALL OF FAME PITCHERS OFF WHOM MANTLE HAS HOMERED: (10 PITCHERS, 35 HOME RUNS)

Early Wynn		13 home runs
Bob Lemon		6 home runs
Jim Bunning		6 home runs
Hoyt Wilhelm		3 home runs
Hal Newhouser		2 home runs
Satchel Paige		1 home run
Bob Feller		1 home run
Jim Palmer		1 home run
Bob Gibson	(World Series)	1 home run
Sandy Koufax	(World Series)	1 home run

APPENDIX XXI.
THE 1961 YANKEE SAGA OF "THE M & M BOYS"

Mickey Mantle (54)	vs.	Date	vs.	Roger Maris (61)
off Walker	K.C.	April 17		
off Grba (2)	L.A.	April 20		
off Barber	Balt.	April 21		
off Estrada	Balt.	April 23		
off Donohue	Det.	April 26	Det.	off Foytack
off Aguirre	Det.	" "		
off Pascual	Minn.	May 2		
		May 3	Minn.	off Ramos
off Sadowski	Minn.	May 4		
		May 6	L.A.	off Grba
off Woodeshick	Wash.	May 16		
		May 17	Wash.	off Burnside
		May 19	Clev.	off Perry
		May 20	Clev.	off Bell
		May 21	Balt.	off Estrada
		May 24	Bost.	off Conley
		May 28	Chi.	off McLish
off Delock	Bost.	May 29		
off Conley	Bost.	May 30	Bost.	off Conley
off Fornieles	Bost.	" "	Bost.	off Fornieles
off Muffett	Bost.	May 31	Bost.	off Muffett
		June 2	Chi.	off McLish
		June 3	Chi.	off Shaw
		June 4	Chi.	off Kemmerer
off Lee	Minn.	June 5		
		June 6	Minn.	off Palmquist
		June 7	Minn.	off Ramos
off Herbert	Chi.	June 9	Chi.	off Herbert
off Nuxhall	K.C.	June 10		
off Grba	L.A.	June 11	L.A.	off Grba
		" "	L.A.	off James
		June 13	Clev.	off Perry
		June 14	Clev.	off Bell
off Grant	Clev.	June 15		
off Foytack	Det.	June 17	Det.	off Mossi
		June 18	Bost.	off Casale
		June 19	K.C.	off Archer

		June 20	K.C.	off Nuxhall
off Shaw (2)	K.C.	June 21		
		June 22	K.C.	off Bass
off McBride	L.A.	June 26		
off Duren	L.A.	June 28		
off Donovan	Wash.	June 30		
off Mathias (2)	Wash.	July 1	Wash.	off Sisler
off Klippstein	Wash.	July 2	Wash.	off Burnside
		" "	Wash.	off Klippstein
		July 4	Det.	off Lary
		July 5	Clev.	off Funk
off Stallard	Bost.	July 8		
		July 9	Bost.	off Monbouquette
off Wynn	Chi.	July 13	Chi.	off Wynn
off Pizarro	Chi.	July 14		
		July 15	Chi.	off Herbert
off Barber	Balt.	July 16		
off Pappas	Balt.	July 17		
off McClain (2)	Wash.	July 18		
off Donovan	Wash.	July 19		
off Monbouquette	Bost.	July 21	Bost.	off Monbouquette
off Baumann	Chi.	July 25	Chi.	off Baumann
		" "	Chi.	off Larsen
		" "	Chi.	off Kemmerer
		" "	Chi.	off Hacker
off Herbert	Chi.	July 26		
off Archer	K.C.	August 2		
		August 4	Minn.	off Pascual
off Ramos (2)	Minn.	August 6		
off Schroll	Minn.	" "		
off Burnside	Wash.	August 11	Wash.	off Burnside
		August 12	Wash.	off Donovan
off Daniels	Wash.	August 13	Wash.	off Daniels
		" "	Wash.	off Kutyna
		August 15	Chi.	off Pizarro
		August 16	Chi.	off Pierce (2)
off Perry	Clev.	August 20	Clev.	off Perry
		August 22	L.A.	off McBride
		August 26	K.C.	off Walker
off Kaat	Minn.	August 30		
off Kralick	Minn.	August 31		
		September 2	Det.	off Lary
		" "	Det.	off Aguirre
off Bunning	Det.	September 3		
off Staley	Det.	" "		
off McClain	Wash.	September 5		

		September 6	Wash.	off Cheney
		September 7	Wash.	off Stigman
off Bell	Clev.	September 8		
		September 9	Clev.	off Grant
off Perry	Clev.	September 10		
		September 16	Det.	off Lary
		September 17	Det.	off Fox
		September 20	Balt.	off Pappas
off Schwall	Bost.	September 23		
		September 26	Balt.	off Fisher
		October 1	Bost.	off Stallard

OBSERVATIONS ON ONE SEASON'S GREATEST ONE-TWO PUNCH

In 1961, Yankee teammates Roger Maris and Mickey Mantle become the most terrifying tandem of power in the history of the game, combining for an unprecedented and to date unduplicated bashing of 115 home runs in one season. Never before have teammates wreaked such mutual havoc on opposing pitching with such long-ball ruthlessness. In a season of slugging sensations, "the M & M Boys" were the most sensational. In 1961, the inaugural year of the expanded schedule in modern baseball, a slate of 162 games, at least one home run would be hit by Mantle or Maris every other game in the Yankee schedule. On 14 separate instances, both men homered in the same game. Indeed, on four of those occasions, they homered back-to-back. Maris and Mantle connected off the same pitcher in the same contest 11 times. In addition, at least one of "the M & M Boys," homered at least twice in a game 14 times with each slugger accounting for multiple roundtrippers seven different times. No hurler in the league seemed to move through the season untouched by the twin models of long-ball power and run production. Indeed, without counting the Yankee pitching staff, there were 146 pitchers among all the rest of the American League staffs who had toiled on big league mounds all over Baseball America. Even though some of these pitchers would not face either man, Mantle and Maris still managed to touch 44 percent of all of the remaining American League staffs for at least one roundtripper during the year. In all, the "M & M Boys" had touched 64 different opposing pitchers throughout the league. On the other hand, the two pinstriped teammates punished 29 different American League pitchers, mostly mound mainstays who ended up surrendering home runs to both men at one time or another in this colossal year. In his Mantle biography, author David Falkner makes his own observation, pointing out, Maris had 115 at bats, had 7 home runs and 12 RBIs, and a .174 batting average with Mickey Mantle not on deck. And another enlightening statistic, not once in 1961 did Roger Maris ever get an intentional pass to get to Mickey Mantle who was to hit next.

APPENDIX XXII.
THE ALL-STAR GAME RECORD OF MICKEY MANTLE
(1952-1967)

	Date	Site/Score	AB	R	H	2B	3B	HR	RBI	SB	BB	SO	B.A.
1.	7/8/52	Shibe Park (in Philadelphia, 3-2,NL)	DID NOT PLAY										
2.	7/14/53	Crosley Field (in Cincinnati, 5-1,NL)	2	0	0	0	0	0	0	0	-	-	.000
3.	7/13/54	Municipal Std. (in Cleveland, 11 9,AL)	5	1	2	0	0	0	0	0	-	-	.400
4.	7/12/55	County Stadium (at Milwaukee, 6-5,NL)	6	1	2	0	0	1	3	0	-	-	.333
5.	7/10/56	Griffith Stadium (in Wash.DC, 7-3,NL)	4	1	1	0	0	1	1	0	0	3	.250
6.	7/9/57	Sportsman's Park (in St. Louis, 6-5,AL)	4	1	1	0	0	0	0	0	1	1	.250
7.	7/8/58	Memorial Stadium (in Baltimore, 4-3,AL)	2	0	1	0	0	0	0	0	0	0	.500
8.	7/7/59	Forbes Field (in Pittsburgh, 5-4,NL)	0	0	0	0	0	0	0	0	0	0	.000
9.	8/3/59	Memorial Coliseum (in Los Angeles, 5-3,AL)	3	0	1	0	0	0	0	0	1	1	.333
10.	7/11/60	Municipal Stadium (in Kansas City, 5-3,NL)	0	0	0	0	0	0	0	0	0	0	.000
11.	7/13/60	Yankee Stadium (in New York City, 6-0,NL)	4	0	1	0	0	0	0	0	0	1	.250
2.	7/11/61	Candlestick Park (in San Francisco, 5-4,NL, in 10)	3	0	0	0	0	0	0	0	0	2	.000
13.	7/31/61	Fenway Park (in Boston, 1-1,TIE)	3	0	0	0	0	0	0	0	1	2	.000

14.	7/10/62	Griffith Stadium (in Wash.DC, 3-1,NL)	1	0	0	0	0	0	0	0	1	1	.000		
15.	7/30/62	Wrigley Field (in Chicago, 9-4,AL)	DID NOT PLAY												
16.	7/9/63	Municipal Stadium (in Cleveland, 5-3,NL)	DID NOT PLAY												
17.	7/7/64	Shea Stadium (in New York City, 7-4,NL)	4	1	1	0	0	0	0	0	0	2	.250		
18.	7/13/65	Metropolitan Std. (in Bloomington, 6-5,NL)	DID NOT PLAY												
19.	7/12/66	Busch Stadium (at St. Louis, 2-1,NL)	DID NOT PLAY												
20.	7/11/67	Anaheim Stadium (in Anaheim, 2-1,NL)	1	0	0	0	0	0	0	0	0	1	.000		
21.	7/9/68	the Astrodome (in Houston, 1-0,NL)	1	0	0	0	0	0	0	0	0	1	.000		

TOTALS:	AB	R	H	2B	3B	HR	RBI	SB	BB	K	BA
	43	5	10	0	0	2	4	1	4	15	.233

Of those All-Star Games in which Mickey Mantle had been selected to participate, (17 games) the American League All-Star record was less than stellar in their endeavors against their National League counterparts, losing 12 of the 16 mid-summer classics, winning a mere four while tying once.

APPENDIX XXIII
INDIVIDUAL AWARDS

THE HICKOK AWARD FOR THE MOST OUTSTANDING PROFESSIONAL ATHLETE OF THE YEAR—1956

THE SPORTING NEWS' PLAYER OF THE YEAR AWARD—1956

AMERICAN LEAGUE MOST VALUABLE PLAYER—1956, 1957, 1962

BASEBALL WRITERS ASSOCIATION OF AMERICA MVP: 1956

THE SPORTING NEWS AMERICAN LEAGUE PLAYER OF THE YEAR: 1956

BASEBALL WRITERS ASSOCIATION OF AMERICA MVP: 1957

BASEBALL WRITERS ASSOCIATION OF AMERICA MVP: 1962

THE SPORTING NEWS AMERICAN LEAGUE PLAYER OF THE YEAR: 1962

APPENDIX XXIV.
MISCELLANEOUS KUDOS

The longest winning streak in Yankee history during the Mantle Years and the third best all-time in baseball history occured when the Yankees won 18 straight games, three at home and 15 on the road in 1953.

Multiple Home-Home Run Games Produced by Mickey Mantle during his career—46, ties the Oklahoman slugger with Harmon Killebrew for eighth place on the all-time list and the highest number ever for a switch-hitter in the history of major league baseball.

Career Grand Slam Home Runs—9 (not including one in the World Series).

The Most Lifetime Strikeouts in All-Star Competition—16.

During his career, from 1953 to 1968, Mickey Mantle was selected to play in 20 All-Star Games, 16 in which he participated, battling .233, with 5 runs scored, and 10 hits, that included no doubles, no triples, and two home runs. He drove in four runs, walked four times, and struck out 16 times. In these contests, the American League's record was 4-11-1.

In the exclusive club of the 17 major league baseball players in history to have won a Triple Crown in either league, that is, leading the league in batting, home runs and RBIs in the same season, Mickey Mantle is the only switch-hitter ever to accomplish this magnificent achievement.

Mickey Mantle hit the most home runs ever hit by a runner-up for the home run title in either league with 54 in 1961.

In his 18 years of major league service to the New York Yankee baseball club, Mickey Mantle produced 118 clutch, game-winning home runs, including three in the World Series.

On January 16, 1974, Mickey Mantle was inducted into Baseball's Hall of Fame in Cooperstown, New York, when he garnered 322 of 365 ballots cast by the Baseball Writer's Association of America. Mickey Mantle, Number Seven, is only the seventh player in history to be enshrined in the Hall in his first year of eligibility.

In a special process of selection, Mickey Mantle was voted the greatest switch-hitter in the history of baseball by the Society of American Baseball Researchers. In his career, Mickey Mantle pounded out 369 home runs from the left side of the plate, while belting out another 167 home runs batting righthanded.

In this photo, Mickey is shown hitting in the plate appearance immediately after having launched what is considered by many the longest home run that has ever been hit in major league history. Incredibly, Mantle would belt more than 235 home runs in his career that would exceed 400 feet. What follows is the litany of the longest 100.

APPENDIX XXV.
MICKEY'S 100 GREATEST HITS
("TAPE MEASURE" HOME RUNS EXCEEDING 420
FEET IN DISTANCE FROM HOME PLATE)

1951 (5)

1. March 28, 1951—At USC in Los Angeles: 580-610 feet (projected), over the 400-foot marker just to the right-of-center in center field and over the entire width of an adjoining practice football field.
2. May 1, 1951—At Comiskey Park in Chicago: Mickey's first major league home run: 440 feet, left corner of the center-field grandstand.
3. May 4, 1951—At Sportsman's Park in St. Louis: 450 feet over the right-field pavilion roof.
4. May 16, 1951—At Yankee Stadium: first home run at the Stadium: 420 feet into left-field lower grandstand.
5. September 8, 1951—At Yankee Stadium: 450 feet, right-center field bleachers.

1952 (5)

6. May 30, 1952—At Yankee Stadium: 420 feet, over auxiliary scoreboard in left field to the left of the visitors' bullpen.

7.   July 5, 1952—At Shibe Park in Philadelphia, 440 feet into the upper deck of the left-field grandstand.
8.   July 25, 1952—At Briggs Stadium in Detroit: 430 feet, into the right-field upper deck.
9.   July 26, 1952—At Briggs Stadium in Detroit: 425 feet, into upper deck of the left-field grandstand.
10. September 17, 1952—At Briggs Stadium in Detroit: 450 feet into the left-field upper deck.

1953 (8)

11. April 9, 1953—At Forbes Field in Pittsburgh: 500 feet, over right-field roof of the massive ballyard.
12. April 17, 1953—At Griffith Stadium in Washington D.C.: 565 feet, ticking the left-center field football scoreboard and landing in the back yard of a tenement house one block away.
13. April 28, 1953—At Sportsman's Park: estimated 485 to 530 feet, beyond the left field scoreboard and out of the ballyard.
14. June 4, 1953—At Comiskey Park in Chicago: 435 feet, into visitors' bullpen.
15. June 11, 1953—At Briggs Stadium in Detroit: 480 feet, on to right-center grandstand field roof.
16. June 21, 1953—At Yankee Stadium: 425 feet, Yankee bullpen.
17. July 6, 1953—At Shibe Park in Philadelphia: 530 feet, over the left-center field roof.
18. September 12, 1953—At Yankee Stadium: 620 feet (projected), after impacting 80 feet high, 425 feet away into upper deck of the left-field grandstand.

1954 (4)

19. May 7, 1954—At Yankee Stadium: 425 feet, six rows deep into the upper deck of the left-field grandstand.
20. August 5, 1954—At Municipal Stadium in Cleveland: 475 feet, into upper deck of the double decked right-field grandstand.
21. August 8, 1954—At Briggs Stadium in Detroit: 475 feet (six feet foul, opposite-field) which soars out of the stadium landing across the street.
22. September 2, 1954—At Yankee Stadium: 450 feet into upper deck of the right field grandstand.

1955 (8)

23. May 7, 1955—At Fenway Park in Boston: 420 feet, into center-field bleachers.
24. May 13, 1955—At Yankee Stadium: (1) 420 feet into right-center field bleachers; (2) 430 feet into right-center field bleachers; and (3) 455 feet into the right-center field bleachers.
25. June 5, 1955—At Comiskey Park in Chicago: 500 feet, atop the left-center field grandstand roof.
26. June 6, 1955—At Briggs Stadium in Detroit: 440 feet into elevated center field bleacher seats above the center-field background screen.
27. June 17, 1955—At Yankee Stadium, 430 feet, 10 rows into the upper deck of the right-field grandstand.
28. June 18, 1955—At Yankee Stadium: 455 feet, halfway up the upper deck of the right-field grandstand.
29. June 21, 1955—At Yankee Stadium: 486 feet, over the center-field wall.
30. July 10, 1955—At Griffith Stadium in Washington Stadium: (1) 425 feet, into left field bleachers; and (2) 450 feet, into left-center field bleachers.

1956 (17)

31. April 17, 1956—At Griffith Stadium in Washington D.C:
     (1) 525 feet, over the center-field wall, out of the ballyard, and into a clump of trees.

(2) 500 feet, to the right of straightaway center field, flying over the street and landing on a roof across the street.

32. May 3, 1956—At Yankee Stadium: 440 feet, deep into the lower left-field grandstand bleachers.

33. May 5, 1956—At Yankee Stadium: 510 feet, into the upper deck of the right-field grandstand before banging into the Yankee bullpen.

34. May 16, 1956—At Municipal Stadium in Cleveland: 485 feet, over the center field fence.

35. May 18, 1956—At Comiskey Park in Chicago: 460 feet, 15 rows deep into the upper deck of the left-field grandstand.

36. May 21, 1956—At Municipal Stadium in Kansas City: 450 feet, over both fences in right field, out of the yard and onto the street.

37. May 30, 1956—At Yankee Stadium:
    (1) 550 to 600 feet (projected), against the top rim of Yankee Stadium in right field, 18 inches from clearing the majestic ballyard.
    (2) 465 feet into right-center field bleachers where it flies to the base of the huge scoreboard behind the right-center bleacher section of the Stadium's "Death Valley."

38. June 14, 1956—At Yankee Stadium: 460 feet, 20 rows deep into the upper deck of the right-field grandstand.

39. June 18, 1956—At Briggs Stadium in Detroit: 525 feet, roof shot to the right of the 370-foot marker in right-center field.

40. June 20, 1956—At Briggs Stadium in Detroit:
    (1) 455 feet, over the dead center field grandstand bleachers as high as the fourth row from the top of the ballpark.
    (2) 510 feet, deep into the seats of the top levels of the right-center field bleachers just under the roof.

41. July 1, 1956—At Yankee Stadium: 525 feet, upper deck of the left-field grandstand.

42. July 10, 1956—At Griffith Stadium in Washington D.C.: 450 feet, into the left-center field bleachers in the All-Star Game.

43. July 14, 1956—At Yankee Stadium: 425 feet, next to the visitors' bullpen in left field.

44. August 23, 1956—At Yankee Stadium: 550 feet, into the upper deck of the left-field grandstand, missing the Stadium roof by 20 feet.

45. September 18, 1956—At Comiskey Park in Chicago: 550 feet, over the left-center field grandstand roof and out of the park.

46. September 21, 1956—At Fenway Park in Boston: 480 feet, against the back wall of the ballyard to the right of the scoreboard in center field.

47. October 7, 1956—At Yankee Stadium: 440 feet, World Series poke into the right-center field grandstand.

1957 (11)

48. May 8, 1957—At Municipal Stadium in Cleveland: 440 feet, over the center field fence.

49. May 29, 1957—At Griffth Stadium in Washington D.C.: 438 feet, off the light standard in right-center field before bounding into the center-field bullpen.

50. June 5, 1957—At Municipal Stadium in Cleveland: 450 feet, into right-field seats.

51. June 7, 1957—At Briggs Stadium in Detroit: 475 feet, roof shot onto the top of the 110-foot high auxiliary press box.

52. June 11, 1957—At Comiskey Park in Chicago: 450 feet, into the upper deck of the right-field grandstand.

53. June 13, 1957—At Comiskey Park in Chicago: 430 feet into the center-field bullpen.

54. June 23, 1957—At Yankee Stadium: 550 to 575 feet (projected), against the top filigree of the right- field rim of Yankee Stadium.
55. July 11, 1957—At Municipal Stadium: 465 feet over the left-field wall.
56. July 23, 1957—At Yankee Stadium: 472 feet, into right-center field bleachers.
57. August 10, 1957—At Memorial Stadium in Baltimore: 475 feet, bouncing against the right-center field scoreboard.
58. August 26, 1957—At Briggs Stadium in Detroit: 440 feet, upper deck of the center-field bleachers.

1958 (8)

59. May 9, 1958—At Yankee Stadium: 450 feet, off the center-field wall.
60. June 4, 1958—At Yankee Stadium: 450 feet, 20 rows deep into the left-field bleachers adjacent to the visitors' bullpen.
61. June 6, 1958—At Yankee Stadium: 430 feet (projected), against the upper deck facing of the left-field grandstand.
62. June 24, 1958—At Comiskey Park in Chicago: 420 feet, into the center-field bullpen.
63. July 1, 1958—At Comiskey Park: 425 feet, over the center-field wall.
64. July 3, 1958—At Griffith Stadium in Washington D.C.: 465 feet, two-thirds up the left-center field bleachers.
65. August 12, 1958—At Yankee Stadium: 430 feet, next to the remote section of the left-field lower bleachers to the left of the visitors' bullpen.
66. September 17, 1958—At Briggs Stadium at Detroit: 510 feet, over the right field grandstand roof before hitting a building across Trumbull Avenue.

1959 (3)

67. May 8, 1959—At Municipal Stadium in Cleveland: 440 feet, center-field bleachers.
68. June 17, 1959—At Yankee Stadium: 420 feet, 10 rows into the upper deck of the right-field grandstand.
69. August 16, 1959—At Yankee Stadium: 461 feet, against the center-field wall for a double.

1960 (5)

70. August 15, 1960—At Yankee Stadium: 420 feet, rear of the Yankee bullpen in right-center field.
71. August 26, 1960—At Yankee Stadium: 420 feet, ricocheting off the rear wall of the Yankee bullpen in right-center field.
72. September 10, 1960—At Briggs Stadium in Detroit: 560 to 643 feet (estimated), out of the ballpark, landing across Trumbull Avenue.
73. October 6, 1960—At Forbes Field in Pittsburgh: 500 feet, the longest home run in Mantle's World Series career, over the center-field wall, the furthest ever in Forbes by a righthanded hitter in this section of the ballyard.
74. October 8, 1960—At Yankee Stadium: 430 feet, into the left-field bullpen.

1961 (10)

75. April 21, 1961—At Memorial Stadium in Baltimore: 475 feet, bouncing against the right-center field scoreboard.
76. May 2, 1961—At Metropolitan Stadium in Bloomington, Minnesota: 430-feet, center-field bleachers.
77. May 30, 1961—At Fenway Park in Boston: 430 feet, into the center-field bleachers.

78. June 5, 1961—At Yankee Stadium: 420 feet, into right-center field bleachers.
79. June 21, 1961—At Municipal Stadium in Kansas City: (1) 525 feet, off the top of the right-center field scoreboard; and (2) 475 to 500 feet (projected), clears both fences in right field and into the street aligning the ballpark.
80. June 30, 1961—At Yankee Stadium: 461 feet, slams against the center field wall on the fly for an inside-the-park home run.
81. July 1, 1961—At Yankee Stadium: 485 feet, into the left-center field bleachers.
82. July 13, 1961—At Comiskey Park in Chicago: 500 feet, into the center-field upper deck bleachers.
83. July 26, 1961—At Yankee Stadium: 435 feet, into right-center field bleachers.
84. August 30, 1961—At Metropolitan Stadium in Bloomington, Minnesota: 425 feet, halfway up the left-field bleachers.

1962 (5)
85. May 5, 1962—At Yankee Stadium: 430 feet, 14 rows deep into the upper deck of the right-field grandstand.
86. May 6, 1962—At Yankee Stadium: 476 feet, against the 32nd row of the right-center field bleachers.
87. July 20, 1962—At Yankee Stadium: 530 feet, into the upper deck of the left-field grandstand.
88. August 18, 1962—At Municipal Stadium in Kansas City: 420-feet, over the left-center field wall.
89. September 10, 1962—At Briggs Stadium in Detroit: 450 feet, into lower center-field grandstand.

1963 (1)
90. May 22, 1963—At Yankee Stadium: 650 to 700 feet (projected), against the rim of the roof of Yankee Stadium while still rising.

1964 (2)
91. August 12, 1964—At Yankee Stadium: 500 feet, into the center field bleachers.
92. October 10, 1964—At Yankee Stadium: 470 feet, into the highest, deepest, upper deck reaches of the right-field grandstand.

1965 (3)
93. June 22, 1965—At Yankee Stadium: 460 feet, into left-center field bleachers
94. August 18, 1965—At Yankee Stadium: 425 feet, over the auxiliary scoreboard and into the right-center field grandstand.
95. September 4, 1965—At Yankee Stadium: 420 feet, into the right-center field bleachers.

1966 (2)
96. July 2, 1966—At D.C. Stadium in Washington D.C.: 450 feet into center-field mezzanine area.
97. July 8, 1966—At Yankee Stadium: 450 feet, to the right of dead center field.

1967 (3)
98. June 15, 1967—At D.C. Stadium: 462 feet, against the second row of the elevated left-center field bleachers.
99. June 24, 1967—At Yankee Stadium: 420 feet, into the right-center field bleachers
100. July 25, 1967—At Yankee Stadium, 450 feet, 12 rows deep into the left-center field bleachers.

APPENDIX XXVI. MICKEY MANTLE'S BACK-TO-BACK HOME RUNS

Date	With	Versus	Score
1. April 21, 1954	Yogi Berra	Boston	5-1,NY
2. May 7, 1954	Yogi Berra	Phila. A's	2-0,NY
3. June 10, 1954	Bobby Brown	Detroit	9-5,NY
4. July 5, 1954	Joe Collins	Phila. A's	7-4,NY
5. August 5, 1954	Joe Collins	Cleveland	5-2,NY
6. July 31, 1955	Yogi Berra	Kansas City	5-2,NY
7. August 24, 1955	Yogi Berra	Detroit	3-2,NY
8. May 5, 1956	Yogi Berra	Kansas City	5-2,NY
9. May 14, 1956	Gil McDougald	Cleveland	3-2,CL
10. May 24, 1956	Joe Collins	Detroit	11-4,NY
11. July 10, 1956	Ted Williams	All-Star Game	7-3,NL
12. June 2, 1957	Yogi Berra	Baltimore	4-0,NY
13. September 2, 1958	Yogi Berra	Boston	6-1,NY
14. June 8, 1960	Roger Maris	Chicago	6-0,NY
15. June 18, 1960	Roger Maris	Chicago	12-5,NY
16. August 28, 1960	Yogi Berra	Detroit	8-5,NY
17. April 26, 1961	Roger Maris	Detroit	13-11,NY
18. July 13, 1961	Roger Maris	Chicago	6-2,NY
19. July 21, 1961	Roger Maris	Boston	11-8,NY
20. July 25, 1961	Roger Maris	Chicago	12-0,NY
21. September 3, 1961	Yogi Berra	Detroit	8-5,NY
22. May 6, 1962	Roger Maris	Washington	8-0,NY
23. July 3, 1962	Roger Maris	Kansas City	8-7,NY
24. July 4, 1962	Roger Maris	Kansas City	7-3,NY
25. July 6, 1962	Roger Maris	Minnesota	7-5,NY
26. May 21, 1963	Roger Maris	Kansas City	7-4,NY
27. May 6, 1964	Hector Lopez	Washington	9-2,NY
28. September 4, 1964	Elston Howard	Kansas City	9-7,NY
29. October 14, 1964	Roger Maris (WS)	St. Louis	8-3,NY
30. June 29, 1966	Bobby Richardson & Joe Pepitone	Boston	6-0,NY

Yankees Record: 26 wins, 1 loss and one All-Star Game loss

Totals: 30 (Individually with Roger Maris: 12; with Yogi Berra: 9; with Joe Collins: 3; with Bobby Brown, Gil McDougald, Ted Williams (All-Star Game), Elston Howard, Hector Lopez, and with Bobby Richardson and Joe Pepitone: one each)

BIBLIOGRAPHY

Allen, Maury. *You Could Look It Up: The Life of Casey Stengel,* New York: Times Books, 1979.

_____. *Damn Yankee: The Billy Martin Story,* New York: Times Books, 1980.

_____. *Roger Maris: A Man for All Seasons,* New York: Donald L. Fine, Inc., 1986.

Alston, Walter and Si Burick. *Alston and the Dodgers,* New York: Doubleday, 1966.

Anderson, Dave. *Pennant Races: Baseball At Its Best,* New York: Doubleday, 1994.

Berra, Yogi and Ed Fitzgerald. Yogi: *The Autobiography of a Professional Baseball Player,* New York: Doubleday, 1961.

Berra, Yogi with Tom Horton. *Yogi: It Ain't Over...,* New York: McGraw-Hill, 1989.

Bouton, Jim. *Ball Four: My Life and Hard Times Throwing the Knuckleball in the Big Leagues,* edited by Leonard Shecter, New York: World Publishing, 1970.

Bunning, Jim, *Whitey Ford, Mickey Mantle, and Willie Mays—Grand Slam: The Secrets of Power Baseball,* New York: Viking, 1965.

Cobbledick, Gordon. *Don't Knock the Rock: The Rocky Colavito Story,* New York: World Publishing, 1966.

Cohen, Elliott, *As edited by. My Greatest Day in Baseball,* New York: Simon and Schuster, 1991.

Cosgrove, Benedict. *Covering the Bases: The Most Unforgettable Moments in Baseball in the Words of the Writers and Broadcasters Who Were There,* San Francisco: Chronicle Books, 1997.

Cramer, Richard Ben. *Ted Williams: The Seasons of the Kid,* New York: Prentice Hall, 1991.

_____. *Casey: The Life and Legend of Charles Dillon Stengel,* New York: Prentice Hall, 1967.

Falkner, David. *The Last Hero: The Life of Mickey Mantle,* New York: Simon and Schuster, 1995.

Falls, Joe. *The Detroit Tigers: An Illustrated History,* New York: Walker, 1989.

Feller, Bob with Bill Gilbert. *Now Pitching, Bob Feller: A Baseball Memoir,* New York: Birch Lane Press, 1990.

Ford, Whitey with Phil Pepe. *Slick,* New York: William Morrow, 1987.

Forker, Dom. *The Men of Autumn: An Oral History of the 1949-1953 World Champion New York Yankees,* Dallas, TX: Taylor, 1989.

_____. *New York City Baseball: The Last Golden Age: 1947-1957,* New York: Macmillan, 1980.

Gershman, Michael. Diamonds: *The Evolution of the Ballpark— from Elysian Fields to Camden Yards,* New York: Houghton Mifflin, 1993.

Gibson, Bob with Phil Pepe. *From Ghetto to Glory: The Bob Gibson Story,* New York: Prentice Hall, 1968.

Gluck, Herb. *Baseball's Great Moments,* New York: Random House, 1975.

Golenbock, Peter. *Fenway: An Unexpurgated History of the Boston Red Sox,* New York: Putnam, 1992.

Gordon, Lois and Alan Gordon. *American Chronicles: Six Decades in American Life,* 1920-1980, New York: Atheneum, 1987.

Gutman, Dan. *Baseball's Biggest Bloopers: The Games That Got Away,* New York: Viking, 1993.

_____. *Baseball's Greatest Games,* New York: Viking, 1994.

Halberstam, David. *October 1964,* New York: Villard Books, 1994.

Hano, Arnold. *Sandy Koufax: Strikeout King,* New York: Putnam, 1967.

Herskowitz, Mickey. *Mickey Mantle: An Appreciation,* New York: William Morrow, 1995.

Hollingsworth, Harry. *The Best and Worst Baseball Teams of All Time,* New York: SPI Books, 1994.

_____. *The New York Yankees: An Illustrated History,* revised edition, New York: Crown, 1987.

Houk, Ralph and Robert W. Creamer. *Season of Glory: The Amazing Saga of the 1961 New York Yankees,* New York: Putnam, 1988.

Johnson, Lloyd. *Baseball's Dream Teams: The Greatest Major League Players— Decade By Decade,* New York: Crescent Books, 1990.

Kahn, Roger. *The Boys of Summer,* New York: Harper and Row, 1972.

_____. *The Era 1947-1957: When the Yankees, the Giants, and the Dodgers Ruled the World,* New York: Ticknor and Fields, 1993.

Kaplan, Jim. *Golden Years of Baseball,* Greenwich, CT: Brompton Books, 1992.

Klein, Dave. *Great Moments in Baseball,* New York: Cowles, 1971.

Koppett, Leonard. *The Man In the Dugout: Baseball's Top Managers and How They Got That Way,* New York: Crown, 1993.

Koufax, Sandy and Ed Linn. *Koufax,* (second printing), New York: Viking, 1966.

LaMar, Steve. *The Book of Baseball Lists,* Jefferson, NC: McFarland, 1993.

Linn, Ed. The Great Rivalry: *The Yankees and the Red Sox 1901-1990,* New York: Ticknor and Fields, 1991.

_____. *Hitter: The Life and Turmoils of Ted Williams,* New York: Harcourt Brace, 1993.

Liss, Howard. *Triple Crown Winners,* New York: Julian Messner, 1969.

Lowry, Philip J. *Green Cathedrals: The Ultimate Celebration of All 271 Major League and Negro League Ballparks Past and Present,* Reading, MA: Addison-Wesley, 1992.

Mantle, Merlyn. and Mickey, Jr., David, and Dan Mantle with Mickey Herskowitz. *A Hero All His Life: A Memoir by the Mantle Family,* New York: Harper Collins, 1996.

Mantle, Mickey. *The Education of a Baseball Player,* New York: Simon and Schuster, 1967.

Mantle, Mickey with Herb Gluck. *The Mick,* New York: Doubleday, 1985.

Mantle, Mickey with Mickey Herskowitz. *All My Octobers: My Memories of 12 World Series When the Yankee Ruled Baseball,* first edition, New York: Harper Collins, 1994.

Mantle, Mickey and Phil Pepe. *Mickey Mantle: My Favorite Summer 1956,* New York: Island /Dell, 1991.

Mayer, Ronald A. *Perfect!....14 Pitchers of "Perfect Games:" Biographies and Lifetime Statistics of 14 Pitchers of "Perfect" Baseball Games with Summaries and Boxscores,* Jefferson, NC: McFarland, 1991.

Mays, Willie with Lou Sahadi. *Say Hey: The Autobiography of Willie Mays,* New York: Simon and Schuster, 1988.

McBride, Joseph. *High & Inside: The Complete Guide to Baseball Slang,* New York: Warner Books, 1981.

Menke, Frank G. *The Encyclopedia of Sports: New and Revised Edition,* New York: A.S. Barnes, 1953.

Mercurio, John. *Boston Red Sox Records: A Year-By-Year Collection of Baseball Stats and Stories,* New York: SPI Books, 1993.

_____. *Babe Ruth's Incredible Records and the 44 Players Who Broke Them,* New York: SPI Books, 1993.

Musick, Phil. *Who Was Roberto? A Biography of Roberto Clemente,* an Associated Features Book, New York: Doubleday, 1974.

Nemec, David. *Great Baseball Feats, Facts and Firsts,* New York: Signet/Penguin, 1989.

_____, Matthew D. Greenberger, Dan Schlossberg, Dick Johnson, and Mike Tully (Contributing Writers). *Players of Cooperstown: Baseball's Hall of Fame,* Lincolnwood, IL: Publications International, 1995.

The New York Times dailies, New York: The New York Times, 1951-1969.

Paige, Satchel, as told to David Lipman. *Maybe I'll Pitch Forever: A Great Baseball Player tells the Hilarious Story Behind the Legend,* New York: Doubleday, 1962.

Rains, Rob: *The St. Louis Cardinals: The 100th Anniversary History,* New York: St. Martin's Press, 1992.

Reidenbaugh, Lowell. *The Sporting News' Take Me Out to the Ball Park,* revised second edition, Illustrations by Amadee, St. Louis: The Sporting News, 1987.

_____. *Lost Ballparks: A Celebration of Baseball's Legendary Fields,* New York: Viking, 1992.

Robinson, Brooks and Jack Tobin. *Third Base is My Home,* Waco, TX: Word Books, 1974.

Scheinin, Richard. *Field of Screams: The Dark Underside of America's National Pastime,* New York: Norton, 1994.

Schoor, Gene. *Roy Campanella: Man of Courage,* New York: Putnam, 1959.

_____. *The Ted Williams Story,* (seventh printing), New York: Julian Messner, Inc., 1963.

_____. *Ted Williams: A Baseball Life,* Chicago: Contemporary Books, 1991.

Shannon, Bill and George Kalinsky. *The Ballparks,* New York: Hawthorn, 1975.

Shapiro, Milton J. *The Roy Campanella Story,* New York: Julian Messner, Inc., 1958.

_____. *The Sal Maglie Story,* New York: Julian Messner, Inc., 1957.

_____. *Mickey Mantle: Yankee Slugger,* (fourth printing), New York: Julian Messner, Inc., 1963.

Siner, Howard. *Sweet Seasons: Baseball's Top Teams Since 1920,* New York: Pharos Books, 1988.

Sliwoff, Seymour. *The Book of Baseball Records,* New York: Elias Sports Bureau, 1990.

Snider, Duke with Bill Gilbert. *The Duke of Flatbush,* New York: Zebra Books, 1988.

The Sporting News, the editors of. *Take Me Out to the Ball Park,* revised second edition, written by Lowell Reidenbaugh, Illustrations by Amadee, and Edited by Bill Perry, St. Louis, MO: The Sporting News, 1987.

Stengel, Casey as told to Harry T. Paxton. *Casey at the Bat: The Story of My Life in Baseball,* second printing, New York: Random House, 1962.

Veeck, Bill with Ed Linn. *Veeck— As in Wreck: The Autobiography of Bill Veeck,* New York: Putnam, 1962.

Wallace, Joseph (General Editor). *The Baseball Anthology: 125 Years of Stories, Poems, Articles, Photographs, Drawings, Interviews, Cartoons, and Other Memorabilia,* New York: Harry N. Abrams, 1995.

Winehouse, Irwin. *The Duke Snider Story,* (third printing), New York: Julian Messner, Inc., 1965.

Williams, Ted as told to John Underwood. *My Turn at Bat: The Story of My Life,* New York: Pocket Books, 1970.

Wolff, Rick (Editorial Director). *The Baseball Encyclopedia: The Complete and Official Record of Major League Baseball,* (eighth edition, revised, updated, and expanded), New York: Macmillan, 1990.

WORLD OF BASEBALL SERIES, The Explosive Sixties: Baseball's Decade of Expansion, by James A. Cox, Alexandria, VA: Redefinition, 1989.

WORLD OF BASEBALL SERIES, The Hurlers: Pitching Power and Precision, by Kevin Kerrane, Alexandria, VA: Redefinition, 1989.

WORLD OF BASEBALL SERIES, October's Game: The World Series, by Paul Adomites, Alexandria, VA: Redefinition, 1990.

WORLD OF BASEBALL SERIES, The Sluggers: Those Fabulous Long Ball Hitters, by John Holway, Alexandria, VA: Redefinition, 1989.

MAGAZINES

Baseball Digest: 50 Years of Baseball: 1942-1992— 50th Anniversary Special Edition— 1992; Evanston, IL: Century Publishing, 1991.

The Daily News, The Editors of, *The Daily News. The 1955 Brooklyn Dodgers: 40th Anniversary Collector's Edition,* New York, 1995.

VIDEOS, SPECIAL PROGRAMMING, AND OTHER DOCUMENTARY SOURCES

The Brooklyn Dodgers: The Original America's Team, hosted by Roger Kahn.

The Golden Age of Baseball

Boys of Summer with Roger Kahn

10 Greatest Moments in Yankee History, Major League Baseball, narrated by Mel Allen

Mickey Mantle: The American Dream Comes to Life

Baseball's Greatest Pennant Races, Major League Baseball

ESPN's 500-Home Run Club, a seminar with Ted Williams, Ernie Banks, Eddie Mathews, Frank Robinson, Harmon Killebrew, Mike Schmidt, Reggie Jackson and emceed by Ray Firestone

PHOTO CREDITS

CHAPTER HEADER PHOTOS

1. Joe DiMaggio and Mickey Mantle in 1951—Header Photo for CHAPTER TWO "All Rolled into One" PHOTO CREDIT: (AP)

2. Whitey Ford, Mickey Mantle, and Billy Martin—Header Photo for CHAPTER THREE "Night Riders in Pinstripes" PHOTO CREDIT: (unknown)

3. Swinging left-handed in Stadium game against the Detroit Tigers—Header Photo for CHAPTER FOUR "Coming of Age" PHOTO CREDIT: (AP)

4. '62 Opening Game HR against the Baltimore Orioles—Header Photo for CHAPTER FIVE "Breakout" PHOTO CREDIT: (Wide World/AP)

5. Mantle on a Stretcher—Header Photo for CHAPTER SIX "Harbingers of Pain" PHOTO CREDIT: (NATIONAL BASEBALL HALL OF FAME LIBRARY, COOPERSTOWN, NY)

6. "The M & M Boys"—Header Photo for CHAPTER SEVEN "The Summit Seasons" PHOTO CREDIT: (AP)

7. 1956 Series catch in Larsen's "Perfect Game"—Header Photo for CHAPTER EIGHT "The Lengthening Shadows of October" PHOTO CREDIT: (Bettman Archive)

8. Mantle Among the Monuments—Header Photo for CHAPTER NINE "Twilight" PHOTO CREDIT: (unknown)

III. APPENDIX SECTION PHOTOS

9. Mantle swinging left-handed generic—Major League Record of Mickey Mantle PHOTO CREDIT: (Carl Kidwiler/SNF Weidemann)

10. Home Plate Reception at Stadium—Game Between Home Run Profile and Mickey Mantle's winning HR Profile PHOTO CREDIT: (Bettman Archive)

11. Ebbets Field—Between World Series Hitting and World Series Records PHOTO CREDIT: (Donald Papp/CSU)

12. Dugout Reception after '53 Series Grand Slam HR—Series Home Run Record of Mickey Mantle PHOTO CREDIT: (AP)

13. Whitey on Mound in '62 Opener Yankee Stadium, LF Upper Deck PHOTO CREDIT: (UPI/Bettmann)

14. Aerial of Left-Field "Death Valley" Yankee Stadium, LC Bleachers PHOTO CREDIT: (NATIONAL BASEBALL HALL OF FAME LIBRARY, COOPERSTOWN, NY)

15. Home Run over Gene Stephens' head in CF Yankee Stadium, CF Bleachers PHOTO CREDIT: (NATIONAL BASEBALL HALL OF FAME LIBRARY, COOPERSTOWN, NY)

16. Mantle Shift vs. KC Yankee Stadium, RC Bleachers PHOTO CREDIT: (UPI/SNF)

17. Right field rafters shot of Yankee Stadium, RF Upper Deck PHOTO CREDIT: (AP)

18. Griffith Stadium: Tape Measures on-the-road PHOTO CREDIT: (Martin Luther King Library/Washington Star/ Paul Schnick)

19. Tiger Stadium: Tape Measures on-the-road PHOTO CREDIT: (Creative Vision/Jonathan Busser)

20. Forbes Field: Tape Measures on-the-road PHOTO CREDIT: (NATIONAL BASEBALL HALL OF FAME LIBRARY, COOPERSTOWN, NY)

21. Comiskey Park: Tape Measures on-the-road PHOTO CREDIT: (unknown)

21a. Connie Mack Stadium PHOTO CREDIT: (NATIONAL BASEBALL HALL OF FAME LIBRARY, COOPERSTOWN, NY)

21b. Municipal Stadium, Kansas City: PHOTO CREDIT: (unknown)

22. Sportsman's Park: Tape Measures on-the-road PHOTO CREDIT: (unknown)

23. Mantle home run off George Brunet—Game-winning Home Runs PHOTO CREDIT: (unknown)

24. Mantle home run off Marcelino Lopez—Career Grand Slam Home Runs PHOTO CREDIT: (*N.Y. Times*)

25. 565-foot home run photo diagram Mickey's—100 Greatest Hits PHOTO CREDIT: (Bettman Archive)